Carl Ellison
5 Dec 2000

W9-CGX-920

Rethinking Public Key Infrastructures and Digital Certificates

Rethinking Public Key Infrastructures and Digital Certificates

Building in Privacy

Stefan A. Brands

The MIT Press

Cambridge, Massachusetts

London, England

Library of Congress Cataloging-in-Publication Data
Brands, Stefan A.
   Rethinking public key infrastructures and digital certificates : building in privacy /
   Stefan A. Brands.
      p. cm.
   Includes bibliographical references and index.
   ISBN 0-262-02491-8 (alk. hc)
   1. Computer networks—Security measures. 2. Computer network protocols. 3.
   Data encryption (Computer science). 4. Computer security. I. Title.
TK5105.59 B73 2000
005.8—dc21   00-032866

Dedicated to the memory of Petr Švestka

Contents

Foreword

Stefan Brands' Ph.D. thesis, updated and published here in book form, makes major contributions to the state of the art of achieving privacy in an electronic world.

Whit Diffie and Susan Landau, in their excellent book *Privacy on the Line*, proclaim:

> "Privacy encompasses the right to control information about ourselves, including the right to limit access to that information. ...The right to privacy means the right to enjoy solitude, intimacy and anonymity."

Yet today, the identity and on-line behavior of individuals is routinely recorded; users often have little knowledge of or control over such surveillance.

While encryption may protect your credit card number from a wiretapper, it does not prevent the merchant who receives and legitimately decrypts your credit card number from selling it, misusing it, or using it to link the current transaction to a dossier of your previous transactions.

Similarly, conventional public-key digital signatures and certificates can provide reliable identification over a network, so that users can authenticate a merchant's web site and vice versa. An adversary can not impersonate a user, or set up a fraudulent web site, without defeating the digital signature scheme or stealing a secret key. But once you have been reliably identified by your digital signature and corresponding certificate you have lost any hope of remaining anonymous or preventing merchants from cross-linking their records about you.

In cyberspace, the most dangerous threat to your privacy is not a wiretapper, but the other party to your transaction.

While privacy can be enhanced by appropriate legislation and regulation, workable technical approaches, when they can be found, are often more effective. Compare laws against "peeping toms" to window shades!

This book provides new cryptographic communication and transaction techniques so that users can limit the information provided to another party to a bare minimum. For example, a user can remain anonymous while still reliably convincing an information provider that he is a paid subscriber. Moreover, the user's sessions are "unlinkable"—the information provider cannot even tell if the (anonymous) user currently logged in is the same as the user who logged into some previous session.

Brands' techniques allow an organization or service to issue "credentials" to a user that the user may show anonymously in later sessions. To protect his anonymity maximally, the user may choose to show only a selected portion of any credential he has been issued. To achieve such anonymity, the issuing process is cleverly "blinded" so that the issuer can not identify the user in the later sessions. The issuer may, if he wishes, issue a modified "limited-use" credential that the user can use at most a given number of times. Many extensions and variations are described and discussed.

The cryptographic techniques presented are novel and powerful. They are based on familiar cryptographic foundations such as RSA and the discrete logarithm problem. Brands has invented fascinating new ways of representing certificates and credentials, and proves the security of his techniques using standard cryptographic assumptions.

Brands explains clearly how his new privacy-protecting techniques relate to electronic cash, public-key infrastructures, and smart cards. He also speaks eloquently about the importance of privacy from a larger perspective, and argues against privacy-defeating techniques such as "key escrow."

This book, for both its conceptual framework and technical elaboration, is an important landmark in the evolution of privacy-enhancing technology.

Ronald L. Rivest
Webster Professor of Electrical Engineering and Computer Science
MIT EECS Department
April 30, 2000

Preface

> *The real danger is the gradual erosion of individual liberties through the automation, integration, and interconnection of many small, separate recordkeeping systems, each of which alone may seem innocuous, even benevolent, and wholly justifiable.*
>
> — Privacy Protection Study Commission, *Personal Privacy in an information Society*, July 1977

Paper-based communication and transaction mechanisms are being replaced by electronic mechanisms at a breath-taking pace. On the one hand, this transition improves security and efficiency, and opens up a mind-boggling range of new opportunities. On the other, it greatly increases the scope for identity fraud and erodes privacy in a manner unimaginable just a couple of decades ago. If the prevailing ideas about how to secure the global information highway are left unchallenged, then it will not take long before everyone is forced to communicate and transact in what will be the most pervasive electronic surveillance tool ever built.

What this book is about

This book proposes highly practical cryptographic building blocks that can be used to design privacy-protecting electronic communication and transaction systems. The new techniques allow individuals, groups, and organizations to communicate and transact securely, in such a way that at all times they can determine for themselves when, how, and to what extent information about them is revealed to others, and to what extent others can link or trace this information. At the same time, the new techniques minimize the risk of identity fraud, overcome many of the efficiency and security shortcomings of the currently available mechanisms, and offer a myriad of benefits to organizations. They can be implemented in low-cost smartcards without cryptographic coprocessors, admit elliptic curve implementations with short keys, and encompass today's views about digital certificates and public key infrastructures as a special case. ·

The new techniques are beneficial in any authentication-based communication or transaction environment in which there is no strict need to identify certificate holders at each and every occasion. The only acceptable role, if any, for identity certificates in such environments is to facilitate registration in case certificate applicants must be identified; this is similar to the way in which drivers' licenses and passports are traditionally used to acquire a permit or some other kind of authentication proof.

Any subset of the presented techniques (with the exception of those with conflicting objectives) can be applied in combination. This facilitates a cookbook approach towards designing electronic communication and transaction systems. Applications of special interest include, but are not limited to: electronic cash; digital pseudonyms for public forums and virtual communities (such as Internet news groups and chat rooms); access control (to Virtual Private Networks, subscription-based services, Web sites, databases, buildings, and so on); digital copyright protection (anonymous certificates permitting use of works); electronic voting; electronic patient files; electronic postage; automated data bartering (integration with standardization efforts such as P3P is easy); online auctions; financial securities trading; pay-per-view tickets; public transport ticketing; electronic food stamps; road-toll pricing; national ID cards (but with privacy); permission-based marketing; Web site personalization; multi-agent systems; collaborative filtering (i.e., making recommendations to one person based on the opinions of like-minded persons); medical prescriptions; gift certificates; loyalty schemes; and, electronic gambling. The design of specific applications is outside the scope of this book, though.

How the book is organized

Chapter 1 examines the role and the importance of digital certificates in communication and transaction mechanisms. It evaluates the major trends, and points out their security, efficiency, and privacy shortcomings. It also contains an outline of the techniques in the remainder of the book. While it is not necessary to read this chapter to understand the remainder of the book, much of the motivation would be missed.

Chapter 2 gives an overview of preliminary cryptographic notions and techniques, and introduces several new cryptographic primitives that are central to the constructions in the remaining chapters.

Chapter 3 presents certificate showing protocol techniques that enable the selective disclosure of personal (and other) data, and analyzes their privacy and security properties. This chapter should not be read without first reading at least parts of Chapter 2.

Chapter 4 presents certificate issuing protocol techniques that enable an issuer to encode attributes into certified key pairs that are unlinkable and untraceable in all other respects, and analyzes their security. This chapter builds on Chapter 2, but may be read independently of Chapter 3.

Chapter 5 describes how to combine the showing protocol techniques of Chapter 3 with the issuing protocol techniques of Chapter 4, and introduces a variety of additional techniques to improve privacy and security. For instance, software-only techniques are described for implementing limited-show certificates and for discouraging certificate holders from lending their certificates. This chapter builds on Chapters 2, 3, and 4.

Chapter 6 shows how to lift the techniques of the preceding three chapters to a setting in which certificate holders use smartcards or other tamper-resistant devices. Many security, efficiency, and functionality benefits are realized in this setting without adding complexity and without downgrading privacy. We also show how to tune our smartcard-enhanced protocols to accommodate any degree of privacy desired. The material in this chapter draws on all four preceding chapters.

The Epilogue argues that privacy is best protected by supplementing privacy-enhancing techniques (such as those developed in this book) with legislative measures. To support this claim it is shown how non-technical approaches toward privacy fail. The popular approach of "key escrow" is examined as well, and it is argued that this approach does nothing but mislead individuals into believing that they have privacy.

Acknowledgments

This book is an updated version of my self-published dissertation of September 1999. The unconventional history of how that dissertation came about can be found in the acknowledgments section of the dissertation, and is not repeated here.

My thanks go to my parents Jan and Bea, and to Vera and her parents Wil and Wim, for their support and encouragement throughout the years.

I am indebted to Professor Richard Gill, who in 1991 brought me in contact with the subject of cryptography and through his enthusiasm and encouragement got me hooked.

My gratitude also goes to Professors Ron Rivest, Claus Schnorr, and Adi Shamir, for taking place in my thesis reading committee and providing helpful suggestions and comments. Dr. Berry Schoenmakers of Eindhoven University of Technology also provided insightful comments on the draft dissertation.

Finally, I thank all those individuals and organizations around the world who are contributing in a positive manner to protect privacy. Your efforts, ranging from Internet discussions and press clippings to extensive resource archives and in-depth studies, have been an important source of inspiration to my work.

Stefan Brands
Montreal
April 30, 2000

Summary

Introduction

Paper-based communication and transaction mechanisms are being replaced by automated transaction mechanisms at a breath-taking pace. Traditional security mechanisms such as photographs, paper-based certificates, and handwritten signatures are rapidly becoming outdated: they require physical transport or proximity, are increasingly vulnerable to counterfeiting and unauthorized duplication, and can be stolen, extorted, or irreversibly destroyed. The enormous potential of communicating and transacting in cyberspace (including the Internet, e-mail, cable TV, and mobile phone networks such as GSM) and in the physical world (by means of smartcards and hand-held computers) can only be unlocked if the new communication and transaction mechanisms are adequately safeguarded.

Digital certificates are by far the most promising technique for safeguarding electronic communications and transactions. Just like passports, diplomas, drivers' licenses, and other traditional certificates, they can specify any kind of data. Digital certificates are no more than cryptographically protected sequences of zeros and ones, and so they can be transferred electronically to any place on earth (and in space) without noticeable loss in time or costly human intervention. Digital certificates offer unprecedented security: even if all the computing power on earth could be tapped, it would take millions of years to forge a digital certificate.

Digital certificates are already widely used on the Internet, to authenticate e-mail, Web servers, and software. The most popular Web browsers have built-in capabilities for storing, sending, and verifying digital certificates. Digital certificates are also playing an increasingly important role in electronic payments, access control (to Web sites, databases, etcetera), digital copyright protection, electronic voting, electronic patient files, and so on. Around the world, transport organizations, municipalities, health care providers, financial institutions, and other influential organizations are planning to provide their customers with digital certificates that will be the sole means of participating in their systems. In the near future, digital certificates may be built into any device or piece of software that must be able to communicate securely with other devices or with individuals. This includes mobile phones, watches, televisions, cars, and conceivably even computerized household appliances.

The problem

While their prospects look bright and shiny, digital certificates have a dark side that has received surprisingly little attention thus far. Unless drastic measures are taken, it will not take long before everyone is forced to communicate and transact in what will be the most pervasive electronic surveillance tool ever built. Each digital certificate can be traced uniquely to the person to whom it has been issued (or to the device in which it has been incorporated) and can be followed around instantaneously and automatically as it moves through the system. Even digital certificates that do not explicitly specify the identity of their holder can be traced in a trivial manner, because the string of zeros and ones that makes up a digital certificate for security reasons must be unique; digital certificates in this respect offer no more privacy than Social Security numbers, credit card numbers, and health registration numbers. On the basis of these unique serial numbers, which will travel along whenever an individual engages in a communication or a transaction, organizations and individuals can compile extremely detailed personal dossiers. The dossiers can be compiled and linked without human intervention, can be dynamically updated in near real time, and will contain minute information about a person's financial situation, medical history and constitution, lifestyle, habits, preferences, movements, and so on. Any digital signatures made by certificate holders can be added to their dossiers; they form self-signed statements that cannot be repudiated. With the cost of digital storage space dropping all the time, all dossiers will be stored potentially forever.

Furthermore, digital certificates can be misused to deny a certificate holder access to services, and to block his or her communication attempts in real time. For example, certificate blacklists can be built into Internet routers. Also, transaction-generated data conducted with target certificates can be filtered out by surveillance tools, and delivered electronically to law enforcement and other third parties for examination or immediate action. Online certificate validation services even enable central authorities to learn in real time who communicates with whom and to falsely deny access.

These exceptional surveillance powers will be enjoyed not only by all the organizations that a person directly communicates or transacts with, but also by a myriad of private and public organizations that routinely acquire dossiers, by unscrupulous employees, by hackers, by law enforcement and intelligence agencies, and by all organizations that issue digital certificates. Typical representatives of the latter group will be financial institutions, governments (local, state, and federal), insurance companies, health care providers, post offices, public transport organizations, and consumer credit bureaus.

Smartcards exacerbate the privacy problems. As Moreno, the inventor of the first generation of smartcards, remarked, smartcards have the potential to become "Big Brother's little helper." It is almost impossible to verify that a smartcard does not leak personal data stored inside the card, and different applications can all share the same card data without the consent of the cardholder.

The solution

This book analyzes and documents the privacy dangers of digital certificates. On the basis of the findings, practical digital certificates are constructed that preserve privacy without sacrificing security. The new certificates function in much the same way as cash, stamps, cinema tickets, subway tokens, and so on: anyone can establish the validity of these certificates and the data they overtly specify, but no more than just that. A "demographic" certificate, for instance, can specify its holder's age, income, marital status, and residence, all digitally tied together in an unforgeable manner.

The new certificates are not only much more secure and efficient than their non-electronic counterparts, but also much more powerful. For instance, each certificate holder can decide for him or herself, depending on the circumstances, which property to disclose of the data encoded into a digital certificate. This goes beyond the analogy of using a marking pen to cross out data fields on a paper-based certificate; a certificate holder can prove that he or she is either over 65 or under 18, for instance, without revealing which is the case. More generally, certificate holders can demonstrate any satisfiable proposition from proposition logic, where the atomic propositions are linear relations in the encoded data; any other information remains unconditionally hidden.

Also, a certificate can be presented in such a manner that no evidence is left at all of the transaction; this is much like waving a passport when passing customs. Alternatively, it can be presented in such a manner that the only information left is self-authenticating evidence of a message or a part of the disclosed property; this is much like presenting a paper-based certificate with crossed-out data fields so that a photocopy can be made. Furthermore, the self-authenticating evidence can be limited to designated parties.

The new techniques enable certificate issuers to discourage lending of personal certificates. An issuer of gender certificates (needed to gain access to gender-specific online forums, say) could encode into each certificate not only a bit indicating the gender of the designated receiver, but also the credit card number or some other secret of the receiver. While certificate holders can hide their built-in secrets when they show their certificates, it is not possible to show a certificate without knowing the built-in secret. Therefore, certificate holders cannot lend their certificates without revealing their secrets.

Another useful technique makes it possible for a central authority to compute all the data that have been encoded into a certificate once that certificate is shown more than a predetermined number of times. In particular, a built-in identifier can be computed even if the certificate holder never discloses any of the built-in data when showing his or her certificates. This magical security property holds even when the certificate holder is free at each occasion to choose the property that he or she demonstrates when presenting the certificate. It allows the certificate issuer to trace and contain fraud with limited-show certificates (such as subway tokens and electronic coins), to (further) discourage unauthorized lending and copying of personal certificates, and to discourage the destruction of unfavorable certificates (such as a mark for drunk driving or late payment).

Yet another technique enables a certificate issuer to refresh a previously issued certificate without knowing the encoded data. The unknown encoded data can even be updated before it is recertified. By way of example, a doctor could issue a prescription to a patient for 20 doses of a penicillin cure. Each time the patient visits a drugstore to collect some of the doses, the drugstore can verify that the patient is still eligible and can decrement the number of remaining penicillin doses. On the other hand, no drugstore can determine the total number of doses prescribed or the number remaining at the time of a visit, nor can different visits by the same patient be linked. Using our certification techniques, the patient could even pay for each dose in untraceable electronic cash and receive a digital receipt that could be used to get reimbursed by his or her health insurance company.

We also describe techniques to improve the privacy of organizations. In particular, we show how an organization can verify a certificate in such a manner that it receives self-authenticating evidence that proves that the certificate has been shown but unconditionally hides all or an arbitrary part of the property that has been demonstrated. In applications where organizations submit the certificates they receive to a central authority, to enable the latter to compute statistics or to combat fraud, this property prevents the central authority from learning which information an organization's customers disclosed. Organizations cannot provide false information to the central authority, but in the case of disputes they can always reveal additional information about the demonstrated properties.

All these and other software-only techniques can be implemented in tamper-resistant smartcards. The smartcard offers strong protection against loss, theft, extortion, lending, copying, and discarding of certificates, and can restrain its holder from other undesired behavior. More generally, the smartcard can be used either to strengthen our software-only security provisions or to add security features that software-only techniques cannot enable at all. Also, the presence of the smartcard removes the need for online authorization or frequent distribution of certificate revocation lists. At the same time, the smartcard can be prevented from learning the certificates of its holder, the information encoded into the certificates, and even the properties that are demonstrated when showing digital certificates. In addition, any data leakage by or to the smartcard can be blocked. The cardholder can even prevent his or her smartcard from developing information that would help the card issuer to retroactively trace the cardholder's transactions should the card's contents become available to the card issuer. Transactions can be completed within as little as $1/20$-th of a second by a standard 8-bit smartcard processor, so that road-toll pricing and other demanding applications are entirely feasible.

Our techniques protect privacy in the strongest possible sense: even if all organizations (including those that issue certificates and those that verify them) conspire and have infinite computing resources, and issue smartcards that are programmed in adverse manners, they cannot learn more about (honest) certificate holders than the assertions they voluntarily demonstrate. Different actions by the same certificate holder cannot be linked, unless the certificate holder consents and cooperates.

Our certification techniques are advantageous not only to individuals, but also to organizations: they prevent certificate issuers and other central parties from competing unfairly; they minimize the need to consult certificate revocation lists or online certificate validation services; they minimize the scope for law enforcement intrusions on databases; they minimize the need to protect online databases against intrusions by hackers and insiders; they reduce the scope for discrimination and identity fraud; they foster fair competition with respect to the collection and use of personal data; they are the cheapest and most effective way to comply with most of the fair information principles of privacy legislation and codes of conduct; they improve transaction finality; and, they cultivate goodwill among customers.

The presented techniques could help stimulate the public acceptance of smartcards, because low-cost smartcards without cryptographic coprocessors can be used and smartcards cannot be misused for the purpose of surveillance. They could even stimulate the growth of electronic commerce by providing a firm grounding for upcoming digital signature legislation. Namely, secret keys protected by smartcards (or other tamper-resistant devices) with biometric protection are not vulnerable to theft, extortion in cyberspace, and unauthorized use, and can therefore be reliably associated with a particular individual.

List of Figures

Chapter 1

Introduction

In this chapter we examine the role and the importance of digital certificates in communication and transaction mechanisms. We discuss the main developments and point out their security, efficiency, and privacy shortcomings. Next we examine the meager previous efforts to protect privacy in public key infrastructures. Amongst others, we show that the popular suggestion to offer privacy by issuing pseudonymous certificates is not only insecure in almost all situations, but also ineffective to protect privacy. On the basis of the previous findings we list basic desirable privacy properties. Finally, we outline how the techniques that will be developed in later chapters meet these and other privacy properties and at the same time help overcome the security and efficiency problems.

1.1 Digital certificates and PKIs

1.1.1 From paper-based to digital certificates

Individuals and organizations often have a legitimate need to verify the identity or other attributes of the individuals they communicate or transact with. The traditional method for demonstrating that one meets certain qualifications is to disclose one or more paper-based certificates. As defined in the third edition of the American Heritage Dictionary of the English Language, a certificate is "a document testifying to the truth of something." Photographs, handwritten signatures, and physical cues help the verifier to establish the identity of the holder of a certificate. Embedded security features (such as special paper, watermarks, ink that appears different when viewed from different angles, and microprinted words and other detail that is hard to replicate) serve to protect against counterfeiting and unauthorized duplication.

Since the advent of computers and telecommunication networks, paper-based transaction mechanisms are being replaced by electronic transaction mechanisms at a breath-taking pace. Many forces drive this unstoppable transition:

- The theft, loss, or destruction of a paper-based certificate coincides with the theft, loss, or destruction of at least part of its value. It may be expensive, difficult, or impossible to obtain a new copy from the issuer.

- Paper-based certificates are subject to wear and tear, add to the depletion of forests, are costly to handle, and in many situations are inefficient. Electronic certificates can be manufactured, distributed, copied, verified, and processed much more efficiently and at lesser cost.

- Paper-based certificates are not suitable to convey negative qualifications of their holders. An individual carrying a certificate attesting to the fact that he or she has been in prison, say, can simply discard the certificate. Sometimes negative qualifications can be tied in with positive ones (e.g., a mark for drunk driving on a driver's license), but this measure is not always an option.

- Cyberspace (the conglomeration of networks that enable remote communication, including the Internet, e-mail, cable TV, and mobile phone networks such as GSM) offers huge benefits over face-to-face communications and transactions in the physical world. Many of the benefits cannot be realized using paper-based certificates, however, since these require physical transport.

- The public at large can avail itself at modest cost of ever-advancing desktop reprographic equipment. A nationwide study conducted in 1998 by U.S. corporate investigation firm Kessler & Associates found resume and credential fraud to be of "almost epidemic proportions." Counterfeiting rarely requires perfection; it usually suffices to produce something that will pass casual human inspection. Ultimately, the counterfeiting threat can be overcome only by moving to certificates that are cryptographically secured and that can be verified with 100 percent accuracy by computers.

In many applications, symmetric cryptographic techniques are inappropriate: they require a trusted third party to set up a secret key for any two parties that have not communicated previously, and cannot offer non-repudiation. Thus, there is a fundamental need for public key cryptography. Public key cryptography enables the parties in a system to digitally sign and encrypt their messages. When two parties that have not communicated before want to establish an authenticated session, they need merely fetch the public key of the other; there is no need for a trusted third party to mediate every transaction.

In their seminal paper [136] on public key cryptography, Diffie and Hellman pointed out the problem of authenticating that a public key belongs to an entity. They suggested using secure online repositories with entries that specify name–key bindings. In 1978, Kohnfelder [238] proposed to avoid this potential bottleneck by having

a trusted entity, called the Certificate Authority[1] (CA), vouch for the binding
a public key and its holder. A *digital certificate* is a signed assertion about a
key. More specifically, it is a digital signature of the CA that binds a public key
to some other piece of information, in Kohnfelder's case the name of the legitimate
holder of the public key. This enables all system participants to verify the name–key
binding of any presented certificate by applying the public key of the CA. There is
no need to involve the CA in the verification process; verification can be off-line.

A *public key infrastructure* (PKI), also called key management infrastructure, is
an infrastructure for a distributed environment that centers around the distribution and
management of public keys and digital certificates. It is widely recognized that PKIs
are an essential ingredient for secure electronic communications and transactions in
open environments. See, for instance, Feghhi, Williams, and Feghhi [167], Ford and
Baum [172], Froomkin [177], Lewis [251], and Zimits and Montano [395].

The CA can be made responsible not only for certifying public keys and authenticating certificate applicants, but also for notarizing electronic documents, resolving
disputes, and keeping track of revoked keys. Some or all of these functions may be
managed by separate trusted parties. For instance, the registration and approval of
certificate applicants may be done by a separate Registration Authority.

In practice, a PKI can have multiple CAs, so that certificate applicants and verifiers need not trust a single CA. CAs can certify the public keys of other CAs, and
in this manner arbitrary CA structures can be formed. This gives rise to such notions
as certificate chains, bridge CA's, and cross certification; see Burr [68]. Our techniques enable anyone to be the issuer of their own digital certificates, and all issuers
can coexist in a single PKI. We will not address multi-CA PKIs, though, because the
techniques for these are straightforward and largely orthogonal to the techniques that
we will develop in this book. For simplicity, we will always assume that each PKI
has only a single CA, unless explicitly stated otherwise.

Also for simplicity, we will often equate certificate holders with individuals, and
certificate verifiers with organizations. More generally, the entities that retrieve, hold,
show, verify, or otherwise operate on certificates may be software programs, hardware devices, or anything else that can perform the required logical steps.

1.1.2 Identity certificates

An object *identifier* is any data string that can readily and uniquely be associated
with the object. What Kohnfelder called a digital certificate is better referred to as
an *identity certificate*, because it binds a public key to a person identifier, such as a
credit card number, a "true name," a fingerprint, a Social Security number, or a health
registration number.

The X.509 certificate framework [216] is the best known example of identity
certificates. In 1988, the International Telecommunications Union (formerly the In-

---

[1]In recent years the term Trusted Third Party (TTP) has gained in popularity.

ternational Consultative Committee on Telephone and Telegraphy) started working on X.509. X.509v1 was designed to certify the public keys of principals that are uniquely named in X.500 [80, 195, 385], an online database listing globally unique names; an entry in an X.500 directory can be a person, a device, or anything else that can be assigned a "Distinguished Name." X.509v2, released in 1993, provided for a more flexible choice of identifiers. X.509v3, announced in June 1997 (see [218] for amendments), greatly improved the flexibility of X.509 certificates, by providing for a generic mechanism to extend certificates. Also, X.509v3 allows the use of local names in certificates, acknowledging that a global naming scheme is unworkable.

Numerous (draft) standards and CA products have been developed based on the X.509 framework. X9.55 [8, 11], for example, is an ANSI-adopted standard developed by the American Bankers Association that is similar to X.509 but targeted at the financial services industry. Another effort is PKIX [4, 114], a draft standard by the Internet Engineering Task Force (IETF) to make X.509v3 certificates suitable for the Internet.[2] Other implementations of X.509 certificates include Privacy Enhanced Mail [86, 230] (PEM, an IETF e-mail standard proposal), Fortezza (the standard for secure e-mail and file encryption in the U.S. defense system), Secure/Multipurpose Internet Mail Extensions [140, 141] (S/MIME, an e-mail standard proposed by RSA Security), Secure Socket Layer version 3.0 [174] (SSL, developed by Netscape to support server and client authentication and session encryption), and Secure Electronic Transactions [257] (SET, proposed by MasterCard and Visa for securing card-not-present credit card transactions).

Also, virtually all the pilot PKI projects conducted by 24 U.S. federal agencies (including the NSA, the IRS, the FBI, the U.S. Department of Defense, and the Social Security Administration) as part of the Federal Public Key Infrastructure [163] (FPKI) use X.509v3 certificates, with application-dependent extensions. For instance, the U.S. Department of Defense is building a PKI "to ensure the authenticity of digital signatures on contracting documents, travel vouchers, and other forms that obligate taxpayer funds, to authenticate users of information systems, and protect the privacy of transactions over networks;" see the DoD Public Key Infrastructure Program Management Office [138, 139] for details.

Another U.S. federal PKI plan based on X.509v3 certificates is Access Certificates for Electronic Services [377, 378] (ACES), which will provide for public electronic access to government services and information. Furthermore, the Department of Justice, the Department of Defense, the NSA, and NASA formed a government-industry consortium called Security Proof Of Concept Keystone (SPOCK); its goal is to demonstrate commercial and federal PKI solutions in cooperation with security technology providers. According to the National Institute of Standards and Technology (NIST), which is responsible for U.S. federal computer security, the FPKI will be knit together from these and other PKI efforts.

---

[2]IBM and its Lotus Development subsidiary in July 1998 started making the source code for their PKIX implementation Jonah available to the public, to promote applications based on PKIX.

Other jurisdictions that are in advanced stages of planning federal PKIs include the United Kingdom (its CLOUD COVER initiative is aimed to stimulate the growth of a government-wide PKI), Australia (the Australian Public Key Authentication Framework, PKAF for short, will result from the Gatekeeper federal infrastructure program and efforts by the Certification Forum of Australia), Canada (in 1995, the Treasury Board endorsed a project called GOC PKI, for Government of Canada Public Key Infrastructure), and Hong Kong (in November 1999, the Hong Kong postal service started issuing identity certificates to most of the 6.5 million residents). All these efforts are compatible with the X.509v3 standard. For a snap-shot overview as of July 1999 of the PKI initiatives in 26 member countries of the Organisation for Economic Co-operation and Development (OECD, an international organization consisting of 29 primarily industrialized countries), see the Working Party on Information Security and Privacy [296] of the OECD.

Dozens of developers around the world specialize in CA products involving identity certificates, most of them based on X.509. Among the major players are VeriSign, Baltimore Technologies, Entrust Technologies, and Thawte Consulting (acquired in February 2000 by VeriSign). In recent years a host of companies joined them in their race to capture the identity certificate market (either products or services), including ABAecom, ActivCard, BelSign, Brokat, Celo Communications, Certco, CertiSign, Chrysalis-ITS, Cryptomathic, GTE CyberTrust, Cylink, Digital Signature Trust Company, Entegrity Solutions, EuroSign, EuroTrust, Frontier Technologies, Gemplus, GlobalSign, Internet Dynamics, Identrus, InterClear, KeyPOST, KeyWitness, Litronic, RSA Security, Sonera SmartTrust, Spyrus, Sun Certificate Authorities, Utimaco, ValiCert, Xcert International, and Zergo. Also, major corporations including American Express, AT&T, Canada Post, CompuSource, Equifax, Hewlett-Packard, IBM, Lotus Development, Microsoft, Motorola, Netscape, and Novell all support the X.509 digital certificate standard.[3] To accelerate the adoption of identity certificates, Baltimore Technologies, Entrust Technologies, IBM, Microsoft, and RSA Security in December 1999 founded an alliance that has since been joined by over 40 other companies.

Another well-known scheme based on identity certificates is Pretty Good Privacy [69, 396] (PGP). PGP certificates bind a public key to a common name and an e-mail address. PGP is based on a different *metric of authentication* (see Levien and Aiken [250] and Reiter and Stubblebine [321]) than X.509: anyone in the PGP "Web of Trust" can certify keys.

As these developments show, identity certificates are widely perceived as a fundamental technology for secure electronic communications and transactions. Market surveys confirm this. A study released in March 2000 by the Radicati Group, for instance, estimates that the market for CA software for identity certificates will grow from over 368 million U.S. dollar in revenues by year end 2000 to over 1.5 billion U.S. dollar by 2004. Another survey by IDC expects the market to grow to 1.3 billion

---

[3]Most companies offer services and products based on the CA toolkits of a select few.

U.S. dollar in 2003.

Identity certificates will also play a major role in the many plans outside cyberspace to migrate to chipcards. A *chipcard* is a plastic card that has the shape and thickness of a conventional credit card, and that contains one or more embedded integrated circuits. Around the world, public transport organizations, municipalities, health care providers, ministry departments, financial institutions, and other influential organizations are planning to provide all their customers with a chipcard that will be the sole means of participating in their systems. Due to the storage and computation limitations of current chipcard technologies, identity certificates do not yet have a prominent place in many of these plans. However, over time the move towards digital certificates is inevitable, for security reasons; see Section 1.1.6 for details.

1.1.3 Central database paradigm

In many applications with a need for authentication, organizations are not (primarily) interested in the identity of a key holder, but in the confirmation of previous contacts, the affiliation of the key holder to a group, the authenticity of personal data of the key holder, the eligibility or capability of the key holder to perform certain actions, and so on. Identity certificates can be used by organizations as authenticated pointers into central database entries that contain the relevant data, and thus support any such authentication needs. This central database paradigm allows organizations to consult any databases they are interested in, to update database entries as they see fit, and to securely maintain negative data about system participants. It also enables organizations to build profiles of individuals for the purpose of inventory management, direct marketing, and so on.

It is easy to see why the use of identity certificates in conjunction with central database look-up has become the model of choice: until recently, it was expensive or impractical to resort to decentralized computing and distributed databases. The centralized model, however, has many drawbacks for organizations and other certificate verifiers:

- The transaction process requires a sufficient delay to identify and correct frauds and other undesirable conditions. This may result in organizations being unable to serve as many customers as they could otherwise.

- Because certificate holders are not ensured that their transactions will be authorized, significant uncertainty is introduced in the transaction process. Requests may be rejected on the basis of erroneous or irrelevant data, or simply because the online connection fails due to peak load, a natural disaster, or otherwise. (The chances of an off-line terminal failing are much slimmer, and moreover the certificate verifier may take immediate action to overcome the problem.)

- In case the verifying agents of an organization are geographically distributed, central database verification may be expensive (because of telecommunications cost or the difficulty of dealing with peak load) or simply not an option because of the absence of network connections.

- Requests for central database look-up may be dishonored for any reason and may be expensive (especially if databases are operated by commercial organizations such as consumer reporting bureaus).

- It is increasingly difficult for organizations to protect their online databases against intrusions by hackers and insiders. This exposes organizations to incidents that might incur legal liability or hurt their reputation.

- The trend is for governments to require organizations that handle personal data[4] to adhere to (legal or self-enforced) privacy standards. Significant compliance costs are involved with personnel training, making databases accessible to external auditors, and so on.

- The possession of data about the personal preferences and lifestyle of individuals enables organizations to discriminate against their customers in all kinds of ways. This increases the scope for false complaints and legislative actions.

It is ironic that digital certificates today are considered by many to be a secure way to provide access to personal data stored in central databases. The practice of looking up data in real time in a central database goes against the philosophy behind digital certificates, which is to allow off-line verification of digital signatures. In many PKIs it is a waste of efficiency to use digital certificates in combination with central database look-up; one might as well do away with digital certificates altogether and simply check the validity of public keys in a central database. Indeed, Wheeler and Wheeler [388] and the Accredited Standards Committee X9 [3] for this reason propose a return to the online key repository model of Diffie and Hellman. (This model cannot protect the privacy of certificate holders, though, as we will see later on.)

The central database paradigm is even less desirable from the perspective of individuals:

- Individuals can be discriminated against on the basis of data that is not relevant for the situation at hand. Such discrimination could go about without the individual being aware of the source of the discrimination, the nature of the data used against him or her, or even the mere fact of the discrimination. A qualified job applicant may be rejected just because some manager who bothered to consult a few databases (such as Internet newsgroup archives) cannot relate to his or her lifestyle. Likewise, individuals soliciting a loan or anyone of a myriad of other services may find their applications turned down because somewhere in the process someone discriminated against them, or in favor of others, on the grounds of irrelevant data.

---

[4]The OECD defines [294] personal information as "any information relating to an identified or identifiable individual (data subject)."

Material damage may result when personal data is accessed with malicious intent. Stalkers, murderers, and extortioners use address information from credit reports and other sources that reveal consumer data to track down their victims. Blackmailers persuade their victims by threatening to reveal sensitive personal data, and kidnappers and robbers plan when to strike by following the whereabouts of their victims. Many criminals are not concerned about targeting a particular individual, but instead select their victims on the basis of their profile; robbers and blackmailers mainly target wealthy singles, and political aggressors are often interested in individuals with particular political or religious convictions.

- When data records do not reflect an individual's true situation, perfectly eligible individuals may end up losing their insurances, loans, housing, jobs, reputations, and so on. Errors are far from uncommon. For instance, the sixth study of the U.S. Public Interest Research Group [314] on credit report accuracy and privacy issues found that 29% of U.S. credit reports contain serious errors that could result in the denial of credit, loans, or jobs, and that altogether 70% of credit reports contain mistakes. Data in central databases may not reflect an individual's true situation for a number of reasons:

    – A substantial portion of all captured data is outdated. One cannot reasonably expect individuals to inform all database operators each time their personal circumstances change; individuals in developed countries are stored on average in roughly a 1000 databases, most of which are unknown to them.

    – Another portion contains information that was composed by drawing incorrect inferences from other sources of data.

    – Whenever data is conveyed orally or in writing, errors are bound to be made when the data is translated into machine-readable form.

    – Data stored in databases may be modified or destroyed by hackers and other outsiders. With the rise of the Internet, the risks are increasing dramatically. Hackers almost routinely gain access to databases, both commercial and governmental, and are rarely prevented from erasing or modifying data records without leaving a trace. In an infamous hack in the mid 1980s, a hacker broke into the databases of Experian (one of the three largest U.S. credit bureaus) to peak into the credit records of Ronald Reagan, and discovered 63 other requests for Reagan's records, all logged on the same day.

    – Data stored in databases may be modified or destroyed by authorized database users and other insiders. Any organization of substantial size is bound to have employees who are willing to accept bribes or have malicious intentions of their own. A 1998 survey [215] by the Computer Security Institute found that the attack that was by far the most reported by its respondents (520 security practitioners in U.S. corporations, government agencies, financial institutions, and universities) was unauthorized access by employees.

- Misbehavior by identity thieves often ends up registered in the database entries of their victims. The incidence of *identity fraud* has been rising dramatically since the mid eighties. Since 1996, calls on identity theft have been the number one topic on the hotline of the U.S. Privacy Rights Clearinghouse. For details on identity fraud, see Cavoukian [78], the Federal Trade Commission [164], the General Accounting Office [183], Givens [186], and the U.S. National Fraud Center [392].

Since errors spread throughout the system and accumulate as data is disseminated and merged, victims may find themselves affected by the same errors over and over again.

- Individuals have lost all control over how personal data in databases is becoming available to others. Collectors of personal data are always tempted to sell the data or to provide access to it in other ways (thousands of information resellers already offer their services over the Internet to anyone willing to pay), information brokers and private investigators resort to trickery ("pretexting") to obtain all kinds of personal data, and most countries around the world have laws that require database maintainers to provide access to law enforcement when presented with a court order or a warrant. Also, personal data increasingly becomes available to others by error. In recent years the popular press has reported on numerous cases whereby commercial organizations (such as providers of free e-mail services, credit bureaus, and Internet merchants) as well as government organizations (including social security administrations, law enforcement, and taxation authorities) inadvertently released sensitive personal data to the wrong parties or to the public at large.

In many cases it is virtually impossible for victims to seek and obtain redress. The basis or source of discrimination, misuse, or other harmful actions may never become known in the first place, and even if it does, it may be very hard to repudiate the action.

1.1.4 Attribute certificates

In the early 1990s, the idea of *attribute certificates* gained interest. An attribute certificate binds a public key to one or more *attributes*, which X.501 [81] (also known as ISO/IEC 9594-2) defines as "information of any type."[5]

---

[5]This terminology makes sense when considering the dictionary meaning of "attribute." The third edition of the American Heritage Dictionary of the English Language defines an attribute as "a quality or characteristic inherent in or ascribed to someone or something."

Attribute certificates are a generalization of identity certificates (an identifier is just one of infinitely many attributes), and have naturally evolved from them. Indeed, identity certificates typically specify other data than just a person identifier and a public key. For instance, an X.509v3 certificate also specifies a version number, a serial number (for revocation purposes), a signature algorithm identifier, a CA name, a validity period, a subject name, a CA signature algorithm identifier, a subject public key algorithm identifier, and (optional) CA and subject identifiers and extensions. However, identity certificates typically contain no other personal data than a person identifier.

From now on we reserve the term attribute certificates to refer to digital certificates that serve primarily to enable verifiers to establish attributes other than the identity of the key holder (such as access rights, authorities, adherence to standards or legal requirements, privileges, permissions, capabilities, preferences, assets, demographic information, and policy specifications).

Attribute certificates have important advantages over identity certificates:

- It is inconvenient for millions of individuals to make a physical appearance before CAs. In November 1998, market researcher INTECO Corp. found that only 64% of Internet users would be willing to appear in person to have their identity verified for a digital certificate. For many types of attribute certificates, there is no need to show up in person at a CA.

- It is typically much harder, more error-prone, and more costly for a CA to establish a person's identity than to establish authorities and other personal attributes. In PKIs where organizations are interested only in non-identity attributes, not including identities can therefore bring substantial savings in cost and time, and can reduce the risk of identity fraud.

- Identity certification may expose a CA to much greater liability. Typically, only government agencies and major organizations such as credit bureaus and financial institutions are in a good position to take on the role of establishers of identity.[6] Indeed, Kaufman Winn and Ellison [228] argue that the CA cannot legally make users liable for actions for which they cannot reasonably be expected to control the risks and losses, because PKIs cannot subsume risk at the technical level. (The latter observation is also at the heart of critiques against

---

[6]Recent market developments are in line with this. In December 1998, for instance, the government of Ontario, representing over a third of Canada's citizens, announced that it will issue identity certificates to its 11 million residents. Identrus [376], a joint venture set up in October 1998 by eight international banks, issues identity certificates for business-to-business electronic commerce. Equifax Secure, a division of Equifax (one of the three major U.S. consumer credit bureaus), in May 1999 announced an identity certificate service that matches information provided by individuals against data from Equifax Credit Information Services and other consumer and business information sources, to establish identity in real time. Strassman and Atkinson [363] propose that the U.S. Department of Motor Vehicles issue identity certificates.

identity-based PKIs by Geer [182], Kaufman Winn [227], Gladman, Ellison, and Bohm [187], Guida [200], and Ellison and Schneier [148].[7])

- As Garfinkel [181, Chapter 4] explains, the approach of creating a society in which every person can be held accountable for his or her own actions by replacing *anonymity* (i.e., the privacy of identity) with absolute identity is fundamentally flawed. Identity will have to be established on the basis of legacy paper-based systems, and thus will inherit their insecurity. Also, identities may erroneously or maliciously be swapped or forged. Criminals who manage to steal identity certificates or to assume the identities of unwitting people will be able to misuse certificates in cyberspace on a global scale, while their victims take the blame. Punishment of the wrong individuals will make others reluctant to participate.

- In PKIs in which communicating or transacting parties have not established a prior relation, certificate verifiers will primarily be interested in the privileges and other non-identity attributes of certificate holders. If an individual's certificate includes all the attributes that a verifier needs to know in order to locally decide what action to take, many of the drawbacks of central database look-up are overcome.

Placing the data that would otherwise be listed in central database entries into attribute certificates is most natural in closed PKIs. A closed PKI is a PKI which has one issuer and clear contractual relationships between the issuer, certificate applicants, and verifiers. Closed PKIs are much more viable than open PKIs, where each certificate serves to establish authenticity in a potentially unbounded number of applications, since it is much easier to determine the risks and liabilities in a closed PKI. Moreover, organizations typically are not willing to let others issue certificates on their behalf, for commercial and liability reasons.

An early proposal for attribute certificates is due to Brands [54], in 1993. This proposal aims to protect the privacy of certificate holders, and forms the basis for many of the techniques that will be developed in this book. Conceptually, it builds on paradigms developed by Chaum [87, 88, 93, 107] in the period 1985–1992. Chaum advocated the use of credentials, which he defined [93] as "statements concerning an individual that are issued by organizations, and are in general shown to other organizations." Chaum's credentials are not attribute certificates, though; they are digitally signed random messages that do not include a public key. For a discussion of the drawbacks of Chaum's approach, see Section 1.2.2.

In 1996, Blaze, Feigenbaum, and Lacy [33] also argued in favor of attribute certificates that do not reveal identity. Their focus is not on digital certificates, though, but on the design of a trust management system (called PolicyMaker) that enables

---

[7]Be warned that several of the fears and doubts that Ellison and Schneier [148] raise are in no way specific to PKIs.

verifiers to make decisions when presented with attributes and a request for access to a service. (See Blaze, Feigenbaum, Ioannidis, and Keromytis [32] for details of PolicyMaker and KeyNote, a related trust management system designed specifically for making Boolean decisions based on attribute certificates.) A similar trust management system is REFEREE [116], which forms the basis of the DSig [115] initiative of the World Wide Web Consortium; DSig is a proposed standard format for making digitally-signed, machine-readable assertions about a particular information resource. All these developments are orthogonal to, and can be used in conjunction with, the techniques that we will develop in this book.

A standardization effort for attribute certificates is the Simple Public Key Infrastructure [151] (SPKI). SPKI rejects not only the identity focus of the X.509 framework, but also its use of global names and its hierarchic certification structure; see Ellison [147, 149] for details on the SPKI design philosophy. In April 1997, SPKI merged with the Simple Distributed Security Infrastructure [324] (SDSI). SDSI is a PKI proposal by Rivest and Lampson; it is based on local names spaces, and centers around public keys rather than individuals. SPKI/SDSI 2.0 [152] combines the SDSI local names spaces and the SPKI focus on attribute certificates.

Tokeneer [319, 320], a PKI proposal by the NSA, heavily relies on attribute certificates as well, mainly because in federal agency applications immediate connectivity to a trusted authentication server is not always possible.

In 1997, VeriSign announced that it would personalize its digital ID's with a zip code, age, gender, and personal preferences, to facilitate integration with the Open Profiling Standard [209] (OPS). OPS was announced in November 1997 by Netscape, Firefly Network, and VeriSign as a framework for the automated transport of personal data of individuals to Web sites. The idea of OPS is that an individual enters his or her personal data once, after which it is stored in the form of a Personal Profile in encrypted form on his or her personal computer. Some or all of the personal data in a Profile may be digitally certified. A set of rules is then used to determine how and when the data can be disclosed to online services. In 1998, the Platform for Privacy Preferences [393] (P3P) of the World Wide Web Consortium subsumed OPS. P3P allows Web sites and visitors to automatically negotiate a degree of privacy, based on the privacy practices of the Web site and privacy preferences specified by the individual in his or her browser.

Several PKI proposals use signed attribute objects that are in fact not true attribute certificates, because they do not bind attributes to a public key. This approach is followed in X.509v3 extensions, and has been adopted amongst others by Netscape's Transport Layer Security (TLS) 3.1 and X9.57 of the American Bankers Association. An X.509v3 "attribute certificate" has the same syntax as an X.509v3 certificate, but has a null public key; to prevent replay, it has an embedded link to a standard X.509 identity certificate, the public key of which is used for authentication. A key holder may have multiple of these signed attribute objects associated with the same identity certificate. Advantages of this approach are that the attributes do not increase the size of the identity certificate, and attributes can be refreshed independently of the identity certificate. RSA's PKCS #6 [330] embeds X.509 certificates into a structure that adds additional attributes before the whole package is signed, to provide backward compatibility with X.509 certificates; the resulting structure is a genuine attribute certificate.

Note that the validity period of an attribute certificate may not exceed that of the attribute with the shortest validity period. For instance, if an attribute specifies the age of a person, then any certificate in which that attribute is specified should not have an expiry date that extends beyond the person's next birthday. In this particular example, the problem can be removed by encoding the date of birth instead of age, but this is not always possible. In other words, there is an incentive to use *short-lived* certificates (i.e., certificates with short validity periods).

1.1.5 Certificate revocation and validation

Certificates are valid until they expire, unless they are revoked beforehand. Many things can happen that require the revocation of a certificate. For example, the secret key may be lost or irreversibly destroyed, the certificate holder may cease operation, the certificate holder's identifier may need to be updated due to a name change, one of the (other) attributes in the certificate may have become invalid, or the secret key may have been compromised. It is not necessarily the certificate holder who desires to revoke a certificate. For example, when a company fires an employee, it is often necessary to revoke all his or her access privileges. Also, a certificate holder who uses a *limited-show certificate* (e.g., a discount coupon or a public transit ticket) more times than allowed must be stopped from continuing the fraud.

While revocation is an exceptional circumstance, the task of verifiers to check the revocation status of unexpired certificates unfortunately is not. They must either have the certificate status validated online (at the time of the communication or transaction) or regularly download a digitally signed update of a blacklist called the Certificate Revocation List (CRL). In both cases the status of certificates must be maintained by the CA (or by a special Revocation Authority). Note that the certificate revocation or validation data must itself be authenticated.

X.509v1 and PEM rely on the distribution of full CRLs. X.509v2 introduced the notion of delta-CRLs, which are in essence CRL updates. In X.509v3, the set of all issued certificates is subdivided into fragments that each have their own CRL; each X.509v3 certificate has a pointer to the CRL fragment that indicates its revocation status ("CRL Distribution Points"). See Perlman and Kaufman [300], van Oorschot, Ford, Hillier, and Otway [292], and Adams and Zuccherato [5] for related proposals.

As an alternative to the CRL approach of X.509v3, the PKIX working group is standardizing an online validation method, called the Online Certificate Status Protocol [270] (OCSP), for time-critical applications. ACES rejects the CRL approach altogether in favor of an online validation check, to facilitate a "pay as you go" business model; the idea is that federal agencies pay a certificate validation fee each time they rely on certificates issued by commercial CAs for authentication.

Online certificate validation avoids the need for verifiers to manage their own versions of a CRL and to deal with certificates they are not interested in, but suffers from all the problems of the central database paradigm. One of the primary problems is scalability to large communities, not in the least because responses to queries must be authenticated by the trusted central database. In fact, in many PKIs (especially those with just one CA) it makes little sense to use digital certificates in combination with online certificate validation; organizations or the CA might as well keep copies of public keys on file. Improvements of the basic mechanism for online certificate validation have been proposed (see Kocher [235], Micali [268], Aiello, Lodha, and Ostrovsky [7], and Naor and Nissim [273]), but these do not remove the main problems.

Distribution of CRLs (or their updates), is more attractive in many respects, but creates a lag between the time a certificate becomes invalid and when it appears on the next CRL update. If validity periods are long, CRLs will grow and additional computing resources are needed for searching and storing them.

Either way, certificate revocation seriously reduces the finality of secure communications and transactions. In 1994, the MITRE Corporation [27] estimated that the yearly running expenses of an authentication infrastructure derive almost entirely from administrating revocation. Its cost estimates are based on the distribution of full CRLs, but would be similar for CRL updates, and probably worse for online certificate validation. Another serious problem is that revocation requires secure time stamping, because otherwise one can simply backdate signatures. (Likewise, verifiers need a secure clock to verify the expiry dates or validity windows of certificates.)

PGP leaves it to key holders themselves to notify their correspondents in case their keys are to be revoked, and relies on the revocation information to propagate. This approach works well in small communities, but is not workable in large-scale PKIs where key holders have transient relations.

In the currently prevailing certificate paradigm, certificates are *long-lived*; validity periods are typically in the order of many months or even years. The use of long-lived certificates is often taken for granted, presumably for historical reasons: getting multiple copies of a paper-based certificate whenever desired is not a feasible option. However, with today's computers and electronic networks, getting 100 certificates is hardly less efficient than getting a single one, and one can always reconnect with the issuer to download a new batch of certificates. In many cases, issuing certificates with short validity periods is sufficient to deal with the revocation problem, as Kaufman [226] and others observed. Elaborating on this observation, Stubblebine [365] proposed to include recency information (validity windows) and freshness policies within certificates, to reduce the importance of timely revocation information. (See McDaniel and Jamin [260] for a related proposal.) Rivest [323] proposed to abolish certificate revocation altogether, by having the certificate holder supply all the evidence needed by the verifier to check the validity of a certificate; freshness is achieved by showing a more recently issued certificate.[8] SDSI 2.0 for this reason uses no revocation mechanism at all. Diversinet, which provides what it calls digital permits (similar to the X.509v3 construct for "attribute" certificates), also follows this approach.[9] Clearly, the model of short-lived certificates fits well with many types of limited-show certificates. In Chapters 5 and 6 we will see that the paradigm of short-lived limited-show certificates has many other benefits over that of long-lived unlimited-show certificates.

Note that revocation is not needed when a secret key has been destroyed or its holder voluntarily ceases operation, assuming the certificate served only for authentication purposes and certificate holders act only on their own behalf.[10]

1.1.6 Smartcard integration

Everything discussed thus far applies to certificates implemented in *software-only computing devices*. These devices may be obtained on the open market and may be modified freely by their holders; they do not contain any tamper-resistant components that serve to protect the security interests of their issuer. Examples are desktop computers, notebooks, palmtop computers, cellular telephones, and smart watches. Software-only implementations have many advantages: mass-scale software is cheap (software needs to be written only once), can be manufactured in-house by any software producer, and is easy to distribute over the Internet and other networks (no need for physical transportation); any individual can issue his or her own certificates (low start-up cost); and, it is relatively easy to verify claims about the operation of the software.

Nevertheless, software-only implementations are not preferable in most PKIs. A distinct problem is theft. If the secret key of a certificate is generated and stored on a personal computer or the like, it is virtually impossible to prevent its compromise, loss, disclosure, modification, or unauthorized use. Gutmann [204], for instance, in 1997 found that "no Microsoft Internet product is capable of protecting a user's keys from hostile attack," due to design and implementation flaws. Shamir and van Someren [348] note that software run by an attacker (in the form of a virus or a Trojan horse, or simply from a floppy during lunch-time) may be able to rapidly detect cryptographic keys stored on a PC by scanning for data sections with unusually high entropy. Encrypting the secret key does not overcome the problem: encrypting it using a password is vulnerable to a brute force attack, and in any case the secret key must at some stage be in the clear to be usable.

---

[8]McDaniel and Rubin [261] argue that this approach is not preferable over CRLs in all circumstances.

[9]A Diversinet certificate attests to the binding between a public key and an anonymous identifier that can be uniquely linked to centrally maintained identity information and other attributes; see Brown [64].

[10]In contrast, a public key used for encryption should be revoked when the secret key is lost, but there is no satisfactory way to do this securely. Another secret key must be established to enable authenticated communication with the CA; this shifts the problem but does not overcome it.

Also, in many PKIs participants are not allowed to lend, share, or give away their certificates. Software-only devices cannot protect against this. Examples of *personal certificates* are driver's licenses, diplomas, subscriptions, electronic passports, and employee badges. To limit transferability, Lessig and Resnick [249] suggest to include location data (such as an IP address) in certificates or to make certificates traceable (so that abusers can be punished); both methods offer inadequate security, though, and destroy privacy. For some odd reason, the lending problem is not widely acknowledged, as witnessed by the limited amount of work done to protect against it.

A convenient way to protect against these and other risks is to store secret keys on a *smartcard*. This is a chipcard that contains a microprocessor that is capable of making arithmetic decisions.[11] Smartcards can process data in intelligent manners, by taking actions based on secret data that never needs to leave the card. Memory access and input/output are guarded against unauthorized access, and the card can disable itself after a false PIN has been entered several times. (Alternatively, the card can store an electronic representation of its holder's fingerprint, and match this against a fingerprint entered on a trusted card reader or directly on the card.) Tampering with a smartcard in order to get to its contents can set off an alarm in the card that blocks it or overwrites the memory contents with all zeros (a process known as zeroization).

Implementations based on tamper-resistant smartcards offer a multitude of benefits, many of which have systematically been overlooked by PKI researchers and developers:

- It is easy to protect smartcards against viruses and Trojan horses aimed at capturing their secret keys.

- If the smartcard has an access control mechanism (PIN, password, or otherwise), certificates cannot be shown by smartcard thieves and other parties not authorized by the card's legitimate holder.

- If the smartcard has an access control mechanism that scans a biometric of the card holder (e.g., his or her fingerprint), certificate holders can be prevented from lending their personal certificates.

- The tamper-resistance can prevent certificate holders from making copies of limited-show certificates. In software-only implementations, the only way to protect against fraud with limited-show certificates is to require online clearing with a central party for all transactions.

---

[11] The term smartcard is used differently by different organizations. The definition of smartcards used by ISO 7816-1 of the International Organization for Standardization, and applied by the Smart Card Forum, includes memory cards. It stands to reason that organizations aiming to promote and commercialize a new technology prefer to use a single term as broadly as possible. However, a memory card can hardly be said to be "smart," even if it has hardwired logic.

- If the smartcard has a tamper-resistant internal clock, the burden of checking the expiry date of a certificate can be moved from the certificate verifier to the smartcard, with the latter refusing to (help) show a certificate if the date is outside of its validity period. This avoids the need for certificate verifiers to run a secure clock that cannot be reset by an attacker to a time within the validity period.

- If the smartcard has a tamper-resistant internal clock, it can add a timestamp to any digital signatures made when showing certificates.

- If the smartcard has a tamper-resistant internal clock, it can limit the number of certificate showings within a given time period; this may be desirable for certain types of certificates or CA liability arrangements.

- Certificates that specify negative qualifications can be discarded only by muzzling the smartcard. The smartcard can then enter into suspension mode, so that its holder can no longer show any certificates.

- More generally, the smartcard can locally decide whether its holder may engage in certain transactions, and can prevent undesired behavior.

- Certificate holders cannot fall victim to extortioners in cyberspace who (possibly anonymously) extort them into transmitting their certified key pairs to them; an extortioner cannot reasonably expect his or her victim to be able to break the tamper-resistance of the smartcard.

- The smartcard can prevent its holder from helping remote parties (over a radio link or the like) to gain access to services for which they do not have the proper certificates themselves. (Details will be provided in Section 6.5.3.)

- The smartcard can do internal book-keeping in the interest of its issuer, such as keep track of an electronic cash balance. It could even keep a log of all transactions, which could be inspected by law enforcement agents that have a court order. Of course, any reliance on smartcard book-keeping is acceptable only when the damage that can result from tampering with a card's contents is outweighed by the cost of breaking the card's tamper-resistance.

- The vulnerability of secret keys stored in software-only devices makes it difficult to reliably associate a digital signature with a particular individual. This makes the legal status of digital signatures doubtful, which in turn hampers the progress of electronic commerce. Tamper-resistant devices for certificate holders help give digital signatures a firm legal grounding.

- The need to rely on revocation mechanisms greatly reduces. The latency and scalability problems of software-only CRL distribution are largely overcome:

the risk of theft is minimized (assuming the presence of an access control mechanism), it takes significant time to physically extract keys from stolen smartcards, and a card holder's capabilities can be revoked by taking back the smartcard. Consequently, there should rarely be a need for online certificate validation and the expected size of CRLs (assuming certificates are used only for authentication) is zero. In many closed smartcard-based PKIs, the validity of certificates can even be made the liability of the CA.

• Smartcards offer portability.

• Smartcards have a clear psychological advantage over software-only implementations.

In sum, there are many reasons to prefer smartcard-based implementations over software-only implementations. Of course, any other tamper-resistant hardware devices may be used instead. Although smartcards are a natural choice in many situations, other embodiments may be more appropriate for securely implementing an internal battery, a clock, a live access control mechanism, or other desirable features. One interesting alternative is the iButton[12] produced by Dallas Semiconductor. For concreteness, however, throughout this book we will always refer to smartcards whenever there is a need for tamper-resistant devices for certificate holders.

One of the most successful smartcard-based PKI implementations is Fortezza. Other smartcard-based PKIs relying on identity certificates are Chip-Secure Electronic Transactions [20] (C-SET) and version 2.0 of SET. Pretty Good Privacy and Schlumberger Electronic Transactions in April 1997 announced a strategic alliance for the development and marketing of PGP-enhanced smartcards. VeriSign in November 1999 announced to bundle its Class 1 Digital IDs with Litronic's NetSign, a technology that integrates Netscape Communicator with smartcards for increased portability. Identrus and GTE CyberTrust have announced similar plans. In June 1999, Gemplus Software (a division Gemplus) announced GemSAFE Enterprise, a smartcard solution intended to integrate seamlessly with X.509 and other popular certificate standards and products. In the same month, eFed, Entrust Technologies, and NDS Americas demonstrated a smartcard-based PKI procurement solution for the federal marketplace, based on X.509 certificates. More recently, in November 1999, the U.S. Department of Defense announced that it will use smartcards in its PKI plans, in order to securely identify military, civilian and contractor employees when they gain access to its buildings, computers, Internet and private networks, and so on; by the end of 2000 a roll-out of some 4 million smardcards will begin.

---

[12]The iButton is a 16mm computer chip housed in a stainless steel can, which can be affixed to a ring, key fob, wallet, watch, or badge. The cryptographic iButton version contains a microprocessor and high-speed 1024-bit coprocessor for public-key cryptographic operations, runs a Java virtual machine, has 6 kilobytes of SRAM that will zeroize its contents in case of an attempted physical compromise, and transfers data at up to 142 kilobits per second.

ACES also foresees an important role for identity certificates stored on smartcards. According to the U.S. Federal Card Services Task Force [161], the goal of the U.S. government is "to adopt an interoperable multi-application smart card that will support a wide range of governmentwide and agency-specific services. This goal sets the target for every federal employee to carry a smart card that can be used for multiple purposes – travel, small purchases, identification, network and building access, and other financial and administrative purposes– by the year 2001. [...] This plan calls for a smart card based extended ID authentication function to support multiple applications based on public key technology using the standard X.509v.3 digital certificate and authentication framework as an operating model."

One of the few smartcard-based PKI proposals specifically designed for attribute certificates is NSA's Tokeneer [320]. As its authors [319] note, there is an urgent need to minimize the amount of data transferred both to and from the smartcard:

"In the case where the certificate is stored in a token (such as a smartcard), storage area may be a critical factor. Each certificate requires at least one signature. The size of the signature depends on the exact signature algorithm being used (128 bytes in the case of a 1024 bit RSA signature). Adding other data fields and ASN.1 encoding overhead, each certificate can be on the order of several hundred bytes. [...] In systems where I/O throughput is a factor (especially in smartcard based systems where I/O may be limited to 9600 baud/second) the data size of the certificate may be a concern. Separating the certificate into several certificates will be beneficial only if transfer is limited to one certificate per service request. Separating attributes into several different certificates may also be detrimental to overall system performance if multiple certificates are required."

The computation, communication, and storage burden is frequently cited as one of the main reasons why smartcard implementations of certificate mechanisms are stalling. Indeed, current proposals all require sophisticated smartcards with large EEPROM[13] and cryptographic coprocessors. Efficiency considerations are of prime importance in smartcard implementations, especially for short-lived and limited-show certificates. The addition of complex circuitry and software is expensive and can easily lead to new weaknesses in the internal defense mechanisms. Also, with smartcard components already cramming for space, adding circuitry adversely affects reliability. A "dead" card inconveniences and frustrates its holder, and can have dramatic consequences in medical and other applications.

The techniques that we will develop in this book overcome all these problems.

---

[13]EEPROM, or Electrically Erasable Programmable Read Only Memory, is non-volatile memory that enables data to be erased by discharging gates electrically.

1.2   Privacy issues

The efficiency and security problems of certificate revocation and smartcards are not the only shortcomings of the current proposals for PKIs and certification mechanisms. In this section we examine the privacy dangers, and discuss the meager efforts that have been undertaken to protect privacy. On the basis of this analysis we then list desirable privacy properties for digital certificates and PKIs.

1.2.1   Privacy dangers

As defined by Westin [387], (information) *privacy* is the claim of individuals, groups, or institutions to determine for themselves when, how, and to what extent information about them is communicated to others.[14] It is a fundamental postulate of this book that if the current visions about the global PKI (i.e., the collection of all regional, national, and international PKIs) turn into reality, then everyone will be forced to transact and communicate in what will be the most pervasive electronic surveillance tool ever built. (*Surveillance* is the act of systematically monitoring, tracking, or assessing the actions of individuals.)

To apprehend the magnitude of the privacy problem, consider the following aspects:

- All the communications and transactions of an individual in a PKI can be linked on the basis of his or her identity certificates. In this manner, dossiers can automatically be compiled for each individual about his or her habits, behavior, movements, preferences, characteristics, and so on. Many parties enjoy this dossier forming capability:

  - The CA sees the certificates it issues, and typically sees them again once they are shown or at a later moment. This enables the CA to trace and link all communications and transactions of each key holder. Reasons why the CA may get to see the certificates that are shown to verifiers include: the verifiers in the PKI may belong to the same entity as the CA (closed system); verifiers may be incited to deposit a copy of the transcript of each transaction they engage in (e.g., to enable detection of certificate forgery or fraud with limited-show certificates, or to support commercial goals); and, verifiers may resort by default to online certificate validation with the CA.[15]

---

[14]Westin's definition is frequently cited in the academic literature and in court decisions, and forms the basis for the U.S. Privacy Act of 1974 (for an overview, see, e.g., the Office of Technology [285, Chapter 1]) and similar legislation in many other developed countries around the world (see the Global Internet Liberty Campaign [153] and Rotenberg [329]).

[15]Today's PKIs seldomly require certificate verifiers to deposit their transcripts to the CA, but this can be expected to change as the awareness of the security benefits grows.

- Each verifier can store all the certificates that are presented to it, and can link them on the basis of their key holder identifiers, public keys, or CA signatures. Different verifiers can exchange and link their data on the same basis. Developments are underway to streamline the latter process. For instance, the Information Content & Exchange protocol (ICE), announced by the ICE working group in June 1998, provides organizations with a standardized automated method for exchanging personal data obtained through P3P and other mechanisms. Another planned standard, the Customer Profile Exchange (CPEX), announced in November 1999, is intended to take automated exchange and integration of personal data to an even further level. The eXtensible Markup Language (XML), designed by the World Wide Web Consortium, will play an important role in these initiatives.

- In case the communications or transactions of key holders are not securely encrypted, wiretappers see the same information as verifiers. If they can wiretap the certificate issuing process as well, they can learn everything the CA knows. One particularly nasty aspect is that the certified public key of at least one of the two parties in a transaction or communication is always sent in the clear to bootstrap a secure session.

  Parties that actively monitor the Internet and other telecommunication infrastructures, or at least have the capability to do so, include government agencies (international wiretapping efforts include Echelon[16] and Enfopol[17]), non-profit organizations (such as the Internet Archive, which stores over 14 terrabytes of information gathered from news groups, Web pages, and other publicly accessible Internet sites), and commercial enterprises (e.g., Internet routers, Internet service providers, and the commercial offshoot of the Internet Archive). The U.S. Communications Assistance for Law Enforcement Act [145, 159, 160, 286] and similar legislation [359] in other countries require the telecommunications industry to build wiretapping capabilities into their infrastructures.

- The CA can trivially link each dossier to the identity of each individual. For verifiers and wiretappers, linking dossiers to identities typically is straightforward as well: either separate entries or the aggregated contents of a dossier reveal the identity, or the match can be made in another way (e.g., on the basis

---

[16]Echelon is an international surveillance system that taps into most of the world's non-military satellite, radio, and land-based communications systems. It is operated by the United States in cooperation with Great Britain, Canada, New Zealand, and Australia. Echelon systematically scans e-mail, fax, cellular, telex, and telephone communications for keywords, to identify and extract messages deemed of interest. See [75, 206, 207, 308] for details.

[17]The Council of the European Union and the FBI have been cooperating since 1992 on a plan for intercepting all mobile phone calls, Internet communications, and fax and pager messages in Europe. See [129, 262, 344, 362] for details.

of voice or facial recognition or by tracing the source of an Internet connection). Sending your digital certificate offers no more privacy than sending your Social Security number or credit card number.

Worse, all the dossiers that are compiled by linking and tracing the actions of participants in one PKI can be tied to the dossiers compiled in other PKIs. In the original X.509 proposal, each key holder would be assigned a globally unique identifier, providing a highly convenient method to link the actions of key holders across different PKIs. The SPKI authors [151] rightfully note that this "would constitute a massive privacy violation and would probably be rejected as politically impossible." The use of local names, as in SDSI, makes it more difficult to link transactions across different PKIs, but clearly with today's network resources and linking power the barrier that is raised is low; after all, local names and other kinds of identifiers are strongly correlated to true names. In any case, different local names of the same individual can all be linked when CAs cooperate.

- Attribute certificates worsen the problem, since the dossiers that CAs, verifiers, and wiretappers can compile are often even more intrusive. Attribute certificates that do not specify explicit identifiers can be linked and traced as easily as identity certificates, on the basis of their public key or the signature of the CA. (The same holds for X.509v3 "attribute" certificates and Diversinet's digital permits, in spite of the latter's claim[18] that its digital certificates assure "total anonymity and privacy by separating authorization credentials into permits;" protection against unsophisticated wiretappers is a far cry from privacy, and can simply be achieved by line encryption.) Also, each CA gets to learn all the attributes of each certificate applicant, because otherwise it cannot or will not issue a certificate. Some CA service providers, such as Thawte Certification, are promoting PKI models whereby a single CA validates all the attributes of a certificate applicant, to avoid cumbersome verification procedures; this further increases the power of the CA.

Ellison [150] states: "Because SPKI certificates will carry information that, taken together over all certificates, might constitute a dossier and therefore a privacy violation, each SPKI certificate should carry the minimum information necessary to get a job done." Indeed, SPKI certificates are not programmable; they have 5 exactly fields (Issuer, Subject, Delegation, Authorization, Validity Dates). A noble sacrifice, but one that one would prefer to avoid; in many PKIs, everyone benefits when more attributes can be encoded.

- Any digital signatures that are made by certificate holders can be added to their dossiers. They form self-signed statements that cannot be repudiated,

---

[18] At www.dvnet.com/about_us/what_we_do.htm, last checked March 30, 2000.

proving to the whole world who is the originator of a message. As Directorate-General XIII of the European Commission [137] notes, "Digital signatures could even bring significant law enforcement benefits as they allow for example messages to be attributed to a particular reader and/or sender." In the words of Walsh [386], a former deputy director-general of the Australian equivalent of the NSA, "If you ever allow people to get near authentication keys you'll corrupt the administration of justice."

In a similar manner, anyone who gets to see a digital certificate, either by wiretapping a communication or by consulting online certificate repositories or CRLs, has convincing evidence that the identity and any other attributes signed by the CA belong together. Obtaining this information is often perfectly legitimate even for outsiders; many schemes (e.g., X.509 and PGP) store certificates in mail servers or other public depositories. The American Bar Association [9] states: "Publication of a certificate which has not been accepted by the subscriber may disclose an identification, business relationship, or other fact which the purported subscriber wishes to keep confidential, and may have a right to keep confidential under applicable privacy law." Clearly, accepting subscribers have similar concerns.

- Any uniquely identifying data in a certificate (such as a key holder identifier, the public key, or the CA's signature) can be misused to deny a key holder access to PKI services, and to block his or her communication attempts in real time. For example, blacklists can be built into Internet routers. Similarly, transaction-generated data conducted with target public keys can be filtered out by surveillance tools, and electronically delivered to third parties for examination or immediate action. More generally, entire groups can be discriminated against on the basis of attributes encoded into their certificates.

- Revocation mechanisms cause additional privacy problems. CRLs (or their updates) are distributed to all verifiers, and potentially to anyone who requests them. In this manner, entities can collect data about key holders they have never communicated or transacted with. Furthermore, the CA can falsely add public keys to its CRL, to block the communications and transactions of targeted certificate holders. (The methods of Kocher [235], Micali [268], Aiello, Lodha, and Ostrovsky [7], and Naor and Nissim [273] do not protect against false claims of the CA that a certificate has been revoked; they protect merely against a misbehaving Revocation Authority that gets authenticated revocation information from an honest CA.[19])

---

[19] An improvement would be for blacklists to list the (serial numbers of) certified public keys together with a "suicide note," a revocation message signed using the secret key. This approach, which is applied in PGP, cannot be used when the secret key is lost, while preparing a suicide note in advance is not an adequate solution.

Online certificate validation services are even worse: they allow anyone to verify not only negative data but also positive data, and enable the Revocation Authority to falsely deny access to certificate holders and to learn in real time who communicates with whom. This cripples the privacy of certificate verifiers as well.

- The integration of smartcards exacerbates the privacy problem. Moreno, the inventor of the first generation of smartcards in the early seventies, warned that smartcards have the potential to become "Big Brother's little helper." The tamper-resistance of a smartcard shields its internal operations from its holder. It is difficult or even impossible to verify that a card does not leak personal data and other attributes that may be stored inside the card. Leakage may take place by exploiting the van Eck effect,[20] by sending out or receiving radio signals, by sending along additional data when engaging in a protocol, by encoding information in message fields or random numbers specified in the protocol, by timing the delay before transmitting a message, or by halting at a specific step of a protocol. Also, the smartcard issuer (typically the CA from which the holder obtains certificates) can program the card in such a manner that it will lock its holder out of services upon receiving a signal from (the terminal of) a certificate verifier or another party. See Section 6.1.1 for details.

  As more and more personal data is stored inside smartcards, individuals will be mislead into believing that they have control over their own data. Consumer protection agencies such as the Privacy Commissioner of Canada [287] and the Privacy Commissioner of the Commonwealth of Australia [311] have already expressed great concern. See also Cavoukian, Johnston, and Duncan [79], Clarke [117], Connolly [120], Fancher [158], Schwartz [343], and Wright [394].

Since the surveillance of automated transaction systems is more surreptitious than wiretapping, it has even greater potential to law enforcement and intelligence agencies. Transaction-generated data trails can readily be picked up by computers, stored in databases, searched for patterns of activity, processed to distill profiles, and merged and matched with census data, credit report data, postal codes, car registrations, birth certificates, and so on. Moreover, transactions need not be monitored in real time; once stored, data trails are permanent for the record and can be examined at any time. Indeed, as NIST's FPKI chairman Burr [68] notes: "Archives provide a long term storage of CA files and records. The life time of CAs may be relatively short. But it may be important to verify the validity of signatures on very old documents. CAs must make provisions to store the information needed to verify the signatures of

---

[20]Microprocessors, keyboards, computer monitors, serial cables, printers, and other peripheral devices all emit electromagnetic radiation that passes over large distances and through solid walls, and that can be remotely captured and viewed; see van Eck [379] for the (purposely incomplete) paper that brought this phenomenon to the attention of the public.

its users, in archives that will be able to make the data available at a much later date, perhaps several decades later."

Hardly surprising, individuals are feeling increasingly threatened. A survey conducted in April 1998 by Louis Harris & Associates and Westin for Privacy & American Business and Price Waterhouse found that 87% of American computer users are concerned about threats to their personal privacy. The threats do not merely pertain to abuse by the private sector. Indeed, as Singleton [356] points out, "Although both private and government databases can be abused, the abuse of government databases poses a more serious threat for one reason: government controls the courts, the police, and the army." Commercial organizations have a commercial self-interest in protecting the privacy of individuals, and often are less interested in the behavior of identified persons than government agencies. Moreover, the surveillance technologies used by governments are typically more advanced and covert than those used by the private sector. In an influential study conducted in 1996, the U.S. National Research Council [278] "acknowledges the concerns of many law-abiding individuals about government surveillance. It believes that such concerns and the questions they raise about individual rights and government responsibilities must be taken seriously. It would be inappropriate to dismiss such individuals as paranoid or overly suspicious."

ACES and other government PKIs without privacy-protection measures intrude even more on privacy than the national ID cards that many developed countries are considering in order to combat tax evasion, social security fraud, illegal immigration, insurance fraud, fraudulent work authorization documents, and so on. These plans have already lead to public outcry in the United States, Great Britain, Canada, New Zealand, Australia, and other countries. See Privacy International [312] for an overview of (proposed) national ID cards around the world.

1.2.2 Previous privacy-protection efforts and their shortcomings

Surprisingly, the issue of privacy in PKIs has received virtually no attention. Most certification technologies and standardization efforts do not deal with the issue at all, or only allow users to encrypt their communications and transactions at the transport layer. Confidentiality is a weak privacy measure, though. As Baker [18], then chief council for the NSA, remarked: "The biggest threats to our privacy in a digital world come not from what we keep secret but from what we reveal willingly. [...] Restricting these invasions of privacy is a challenge, but it isn't a job for encryption. Encryption can't protect you from the misuse of data you surrendered willingly."

The European Commission [137] recommends that individuals be allowed to obtain digital certificates that specify a pseudonym, unless the law specifies that true names must be used. This approach is supported by the OECD Cryptographic Policy Guidelines [295] and by the European Privacy Directive [157].[21] *Pseudonymous cer-*

---

[21] The European Privacy Directive is an extensive set of privacy guidelines established in 1995 by the

tificates are recommended also by, amongst others, Birch [31], Gladman, Ellison, and Bohm [187], Hill and Hosein [211], and Standards Australia [361]. PKI efforts that provide for pseudonymous certificates include X.509v3 (certain agents may protect their identity through the use of role-titles; "residential persons" do not enjoy this capability, though), PEM (pseudonymous certificates can be retrieved through so-called Persona CAs), SDSI (its free-form identity certificate syntax allows the specification of pseudonyms), VeriSign's Digital IDs (VeriSign issues identity certificates with anonymous identifiers), and PGP (users can specify false email addresses). Clearly, pseudonymous certificates that can only be obtained by certificate applicants who identify themselves to the CA offer no better privacy than Social Security numbers and credit card numbers; at least their issuer can readily follow them around and trace them to the identity of their holder. The alternative of anonymous registration of certificate applicants offers better privacy, but unfortunately suffers from serious drawbacks:

- It may be very difficult to register without being identified by cameras or personnel, or via one's IP address. Typically it is easier to realize an anonymous channel when showing a certificate than when retrieving the certificate, especially in the physical world. Identification in any one interaction with the CA results in one's communications and actions becoming traceable.

- Anonymous registration does nothing to prevent linkability of all the communications and transactions of certificate holders. To overcome this problem, each certificate must be retrieved anonymously on a separate occasion, with a significant random delay between each retrieval to prevent linkability by the CA. Not only is this impractical, it also prevents certificate applicants from building a reputation with the CA. In particular, the CA cannot distinguish frequent from infrequent certificate applicants and cannot lock out fraudulent users.

- Many types of certificates, in particular personal certificates, are issued only to identified applicants. Even if the CA certifies only personal attributes that do not identify the certificate holder, such as age and marital status, often the only way for the CA to verify the attributes is by establishing the applicant's identity and using this to look up the attributes in a trusted database.

- Non-repudiation and recovery of lost or stolen certificates are hard to implement.

- It is hard or even impossible to protect against basic forms of fraud, including unauthorized lending, copying, and discarding of certificates. Many applica-

European Union, requiring the 15 member states to harmonize their national laws to protect personal information. It has taken effect in October 1998, and applies to commercial as well as governmental information processing. Numerous non-EU countries have adopted privacy policies that are in alignment with the European approach; see Davies [130].

tions require mechanisms through which misbehaving key holders can be identified, so that they can be locked out from further participation and possibly be sued for damages. Traceability also serves to discourage those contemplating fraud. Anonymously issued certificates do not offer these security measures, in fact the CA cannot even contain the damages due to fraud.

- It is impossible to purchase certificates from the CA while remaining anonymous, unless one can pay using hard cash or a privacy-protecting electronic cash system.

These drawbacks make anonymous registration of certificate applicants a highly undesirable course of action in the vast majority of PKIs (unless one resorts to the cryptographic techniques that will be developed Section 5.5.1).

OPS and P3P are erroneously hailed as technical solutions to the privacy problem. They make it much easier to obtain personal data from individuals, and can be abused by service providers to turn away or discriminate against persons who do not want to disclose their identity and other personal data; in this manner they compel people to give up their privacy. The Data Protection Working Party of the European Union [214] criticized P3P on the grounds that it seeks to "formalise lower common standards," and that it "could mislead EU-based operators into believing that they can be discharged of certain of their legal obligations (e.g. granting individual users a right of access to their data) if the individual user consents to this as part of the on-line negotiation."

VeriSign issues certificates that contain encrypted attributes that can be unlocked only by verifiers that meet the qualifications necessary to receive the required decryption key from a trusted third party. This encryption measure does not reduce the surveillance capabilities of the most powerful parties in any way, nor does it prevent anyone from linking and tracing all the actions of each certificate holder.

Another attempt to protect privacy is for the CA to digitally sign (salted) one-way hashes of attributes, instead of (the concatenation of) the attributes themselves. When transacting or communicating with a verifier, the certificate holder can selectively disclose only those attributes needed.[22] This generalizes the dual signature technique applied in SET [257]. Although certificate holders now have some control over which attributes they reveal to verifiers, they are forced to leave behind digital signatures. Furthermore, they are seriously restricted in the properties they can demonstrate about their attributes; Boolean formulae, for instance, are out of the question. Worse, nothing prevents the CA and others from tracing and linking all the communications and transactions of each certificate holder.

Ellison [150] states: "Because one use of SPKI certificates is in secret balloting and similar applications, an SPKI certificate must be able to assign an attribute to a blinded signature key." *Blind signatures* are a concept introduced by Chaum for the

---

[22]Lamport [244] proposed this hashing construct in the context of one-time signatures. When there are many attributes, they can be organized in a hash tree to improve efficiency, following Merkle [267].

purpose of anonymous electronic cash [91, 92, 96] and credential mechanisms [87, 93, 107].[23] While they can be used to overcome several of the drawbacks associated with anonymous registration of certificate applicants, they are not suitable to design attribute certificates:

- Because users can fully blind all the certificate data they obtain from the CA, it is not possible for the CA to encode person identifiers that must be disclosed in certain circumstances but may remain hidden in others.

- For the same reason, the CA cannot encode expiry dates into certificates. At best it can use a different signing key for different certificate issuances, and declare in advance when each issuance will become invalid.

- More generally, the blinding prevents the CA from encoding attributes into a certificate. It is possible to represent each combination of attribute values by a different signing key of the CA, but this seriously limits the number of attributes that can be encoded and their value ranges, and moreover an exhaustive list of the meanings associated with all possible signature types must be published in advance.[24]

- Certificate holders cannot selectively disclose their attributes, since verifiers need to know which public key of the CA to apply to verify a certificate. A blind signature guarantees absolute anonymity and untraceability; it does not enable one to negotiate a degree of privacy.

- Chaum's credentials must all be created by the same party; different organizations who wish to issue credentials must all rely on this central party to do the factual issuance.

- Chaum's cash and credential mechanisms rely heavily on a real-time connection with a central party during each transaction. The requirement of online clearing and central database look-up during each transaction strikes against the philosophy behind digital certificates.

---

[23] A blind signature scheme enables a receiver to obtain a signed message from a signature issuer in such a manner that the signed message is statistically independent from the issuer's view in the protocol execution.

[24] In Chaum's proposal for RSA signatures, the signer uses the same RSA modulus but a different public exponent v_i (specifically, the i-th odd prime in sequence) to issue blind signatures that represent the i-th message in a public list. A variation would be for the CA to declare merely that the signing of a particular message requires as the public signature exponent the nearest prime exceeding the message (when viewing its binary representation as an integer), but this is impractical as well: a coding scheme must be applied to ensure that messages have sufficiently large Hamming distance, and generating and verifying a (new) signature type in addition to the normal workload requires (possibly a great many) applications of a primality test.

- Chaum's credentials do not have a built-in secret key to authenticate actions performed with them, and so the problem of replay arises. To prevent replay, the credential holder must authenticate the showing of a credential to an organization by applying the secret key of a digital pseudonym established (previously or at the same time) with that organization.

- Certificates that contain unfavorable attributes (i.e., attributes that the holder would prefer to hide, such as a mark for drunk driving) can simply be discarded by their holder. In many cases it is impractical to require all certificate holders to obtain and show attributes that indicate the absence of unfavorable attributes.

- Blind signatures cannot prevent or discourage the unauthorized lending of certificates. This drawback by itself renders the blinding technique useless for the majority of certificate applications.

- An extortioner can digitally extort certificates by forcing the victim to retrieve certificates for which the extortioner instead of the victim supplies the blinded messages. The victim merely signs the certificate request and passes the responses of the issuer on to the extortioner. The extortioner can subsequently at his or her leisure show the certificate. At no stage is there a need for physical proximity or a physical communication or delivery channel,[25] and so the extortioner can remain untraceable throughout.

- Chaum's smartcard techniques require smartcards with cryptographic coprocessors and plenty of memory, to guarantee that the required operations can be performed in reasonable time.

- More seriously, Chaum's smartcard techniques are not secure. Since attributes are encoded by the smartcard rather than by the CA, physical compromise of a smartcard enables its holder to forge attributes, and to lend, give away, or distribute copies of new certificates. The CA cannot trace fraud, and containment can only be accomplished by suspending the entire system. See Section 6.2.2 for details.

- Chaum's technique [90, 98] for one-show certificates makes high computation and communication demands on both the issuer and the receiver. Furthermore, it does not extend to limited-show certificates, does not admit zero-knowledge proofs, and cannot be migrated to a setting with smartcards without further

---

[25] The extortioner can transmit from behind a computer that is part of a network located behind a firewall, use some a computer at an Internet cafe or a public library, deploy anonymous remailers, pseudonymous remailers, or Mixmaster remailers (see Goldberg, Wagner, and Brewer [190] for an overview), or use anonymity or pseudonymous services like Janus [35], Babel [203], Crowds [322], Freedom [189], and Onion Routing [368]. Also, most Internet access providers dynamically assign IP addresses to each client session; these identify only the host name of the computer used by the access provider to establish the session.

degrading efficiency. Also, it does not give certificate holders the ability to selectively disclose information about attributes.

In spite of their unsuitability for digital certificates and PKIs, Chaum's paradigms and methodologies provide valuable insight in how the privacy problems of PKIs may be overcome.

The certification mechanisms that will be presented in this book overcome all the problems mentioned in this section.

1.2.3   Desirable privacy properties

In many situations there is no need to disclose one's identity. For example, when a police agent stops an individual for speeding, all that the officer normally needs to know is whether the individual has a valid driver's license. When requesting entry to a gaming parlor it suffices to demonstrate one's age or year of birth. Likewise, a county database service may merely need to know that someone requesting a file is a resident. More generally, in many PKIs the use of identity is no more than a way of adding a level of indirection to the verifier's authentication algorithm; recall Section 1.1.3.

Even in PKIs where one would expect only identified actions, there may be a need for the ability to hide identity; the MITRE Corporation [27, page D-14], for instance, points out an application where an undercover FBI agent must file a report from a remote computer.

In today's computerized world we cannot expect others to protect our privacy. In order to protect privacy, we must operate under the following assumptions:

- (Persistence) Whenever data about certificate holders can be collected, it will be collected and stored indefinitely (if only because not collecting data that can so easily be collected must be considered a waste of resources). Every piece of information that is electronically submitted is there for the public record, even though the sender rarely intends the data to endure forever.

- (Loss of Control) Once made available, disclosed data will inevitably be used for purposes (not necessarily known at the time of the collection) beyond the purpose for which it was disclosed. Underlying this assumption is the premise that the mere existence of something is sufficient to tempt people to use it in whatever way they see fit to suit their needs and desires. The public and private sector will inevitably find new uses to improve the efficiency, security, or reach of their operations; foregoing opportunities can easily result in a loss of competitive edge. Law enforcement agencies will inevitably seek access to the data in the belief that it will help their investigative practices.

- (Linkability) Data disclosed in one transaction will inevitably be linked to data disclosed in other transactions (if not for reasons related to security then for marketing, inventory management, or efficiency purposes), unless the cost of linking outweighs the benefits. With the trend or at least the capability of organizations to merge their databases at ever decreasing cost, it is naive to believe that linkable data that is submitted to different locations will remain unlinked.

To empower individuals to control their own data, PKIs must meet a number of basic privacy goals:

- Without the ability to remain anonymous, individuals have no control over their own privacy. Anonymity serves as the base case for privacy. In many situations, anonymity does more than serve privacy. If there is one thing that can be learned from the dramatic rise in identity fraud, it is that the use of person identifiers more often enables than prevents fraud. Disciplines such as treatments for medical conditions have long acknowledged that misuse can only be prevented through patient anonymity. The explosive rise of identity fraud in recent years illustrates that the same should hold true for most transaction mechanisms.

- Forcing individuals to use fully anonymous communication and transaction methods is almost as much an invasion on privacy as the other way around. Different individuals have disparate privacy preferences; surveys by Equifax and Louis Harris & Associates indicate that about 55% of people are privacy "pragmatists," who are willing to trade personal data depending on a number of factors, including the benefits they will receive in return. Another important reason not to hardwire absolute anonymity into communication and transaction systems is that in many situations anonymity does not benefit anyone. In recognition of these facts, privacy-enhancing digital certification mechanisms should not make the property of anonymity invariant, but should enable each individual to decide for him or herself how much data to disclose in each transaction; this is called the *selective disclosure* paradigm.

- Anonymity of each transaction by itself is a necessary but insufficient condition to prevent linking of different transactions; any correlation that exists in the transcripts of any two protocol executions, for instance in the form of a public key, may be used to link them. Without unlinkability individuals cannot control how much data they actually disclose, since the aggregate information learned by linking different transactions will typically reveal much more than the data items that were willingly disclosed on each separate occasion. Without control over the degree of linkability, the paradigm of selective disclosure loses its power with each new disclosure. In particular, if a person is identified in a single transaction, then all his or her past and future transactions become traceable. *Unlinkability* is essential to prevent gradual erosion of privacy.

- In case a certificate holder authenticates his or her certificate showings by means of a digital signature, he or she leaves a permanent self-authenticating record that can be verified by anyone. This gives coercive powers to the receiver and anyone else who sees the signed statement. If transactions are untraceable, little harm may come from this, but there is always the possibility that signed data disclosed in one anonymous transaction can be linked to later transactions in which an identifier is revealed. For this reason, it is desirable that individuals can authenticate messages and attribute data in a manner that does not leave a self-authenticating record.

- Given the enormous security benefits offered by smartcard-based implementations, there is an urgent need to preserve all these privacy properties in this setting. In particular, smartcards should be unable to leak personal data and other attributes stored inside, and should be unable to learn any information from the outside world other than what their holders consent to. These properties should hold in the strongest possible sense, namely in the presence of CAs that have access to cryptographic backdoors and conspire with certificate verifiers.

In Chapters 2 to 6 we will develop cryptographic techniques that meet these privacy objectives and overcome the security and efficiency problems in Section 1.1. In the next section we give an overview of these techniques.

1.3 Outlook

1.3.1 Basic building blocks

Throughout the rest of the book the term "digital certificate" will always refer to the CA's signature only; it does not include the public key or any information associated with it by the CA's signature. This convention is not mainstream[26] but makes it easier to distinguish between various cryptographic objects.

We start in Chapter 2 with an overview of the cryptographic preliminaries needed to understand the material in the other chapters. Several new primitives will be introduced that play a fundamental role in the other chapters. In particular, we introduce two functions that are one-way and collision-intractable, and for both we design practical techniques for proving knowledge of an inverse and for constructing digital signatures. We also introduce a new kind of digital certificates.

In Chapters 3 and 4 we develop two basic building blocks:

- A certificate *issuing protocol* with the following properties:

---

[26]Many publications consider a certificate to be the data structure comprised of the CA's signature, the public key it certifies, and any information assigned to that public key.

- The receiver receives an unforgeable triple of the form (secret key, public key, certificate). The (secret key, public key) of the triple is a key pair for use by the receiver, while the certificate is digital signature of the issuer, made using its own secret key.

- The receiver can ensure that the (public key, certificate) pair of the triple is fully blinded. (Consequently, at least part of the secret key is blinded as well, since the public key corresponds uniquely to the secret key.)

- The receiver cannot blind a non-trivial blinding-invariant part of the secret key of the triple. In this blinding-invariant part, the issuer can encode an arbitrary number of attributes.

- A certificate *showing protocol* with the following properties:

  - To show a retrieved triple, the receiver discloses the (public key, certificate) pair and uses the secret key of the triple to authenticate a message. (This authentication serves at the very least to prevent replay.) The authentication mechanism allows the receiver to avoid leaving behind a self-authenticating record.

  - The authentication mechanism is such that the receiver not only authenticates the message, but also demonstrates a property of the attributes encoded into its certified key pair. The receiver has full control over which property is demonstrated: it can be any satisfiable proposition from proposition logic, where the atomic propositions are relations that are linear in the encoded attributes. Any other information about the attributes remains unconditionally hidden.

An automated negotiation mechanism such as that of OPS/P3P could be used to implement the negotiation process in the showing protocol.

The certificate showing protocol techniques will be developed in Chapter 3 and the issuing protocol techniques in Chapter 4. In Section 5.1 we will show how to seamlessly combine the issuing and showing protocol techniques, without adding complexity and without compromising security or privacy.

The new certificates function in much the same way as do cash, stamps, cinema tickets, subway tokens, and so on: anyone can establish the validity of certificates and the non-identity data they certify, but no more than just that. A "demographic" certificate, for instance, can certify its holder's age, income, marital status, and residence, all neatly tied to one public key by means of a single digital signature of the certificate issuer. Because the attributes are encoded into the certificate applicant's secret key, certificate holders can decide for themselves, depending on the circumstances, which attributes to disclose. This goes beyond the analogy of using a marking pen to cross out data fields on a paper-based certificate; for instance, the holder of a demographic certificate can prove that he or she is either over 65 or under 18, without revealing which is the case or anything else. Furthermore, actions involving different certificates cannot be linked on any other basis than by what is explicitly disclosed.

The basic building blocks are highly practical. They can be based on the RSA assumption as well as on the Discrete Logarithm assumption, and admit elliptic curve implementations with short public keys. The communication and computation complexity of the issuing protocol are virtually independent of the number of attributes encoded into a certified key pair, and the showing protocol is almost as efficient as protocols that cannot provide selective disclosure.

1.3.2   Additional privacy techniques

Section 5.2 is devoted to additional techniques to improve privacy for certificate holders:

- (Anonymous updating) In many cases one's right to access a service comes from a pre-existing relationship in which identity has already been established. We provide a technique that enables an individual to anonymously present a certified public key for updating to the CA. The CA can recertify the attributes, or updated versions of them, without needing to know their current values. A special application is to prevent the CA from learning the entire set of attributes of a certificate applicant. Different CAs can even certify different attributes for the same certified key pair.

- (Simulatable certificate information) To prevent online certificate repositories from serving as data warehouses containing indisputable information about certificate holders, so-called secret-key certificates (developed in Section 2.6) may be used. These certificates allow anyone to generate directory entries that are indistinguishable from the entries that list certificates issued by the CA, yet offer the same basic security. Secret-key certificates also have the advantage that a showing protocol execution is entirely zero-knowledge when the attribute property is demonstrated in zero-knowledge.

- (Hiding participation in a PKI) Using secret-key certificates, users can simulate certified public keys for PKIs in which they do not or may not participate. They can prove to be a participant of (at least) one out of many PKIs or to have attributes certified by a subset of several CAs, without revealing more. This reduces the scope for discrimination on the basis of one's (lack of) PKI access rights.

- (Selective disclosure for multiple attribute certificates) Rather than encoding many attributes into a single certified key pair, it may be preferable to distribute them across multiple certified key pairs. This helps avoid the aggregation of an individual's attributes by a single CA, improves efficiency, and removes the need to update certificates more frequently than otherwise needed. Our selective disclosure techniques can be applied not only to attributes encoded into a single certified key pair, but also to attributes in different key pairs (possibly certified by different CAs). Likewise, different certificate holders can jointly demonstrate that their combined attributes meet certain properties.

- (Self-linkability) Certificate holders can anonymously prove in a simple variation of the showing protocol to be the originator of a plurality of showing protocol executions. As a special application, we show how to enable certificate holders in the showing protocol to build up reputations with organizations.

In Section 5.3 we will describe techniques to improve the privacy of certificate verifiers. Specifically, we will show how to perform the showing protocol in such a manner that the verifier receives a signed statement that proves that a certificate has been shown but unconditionally hides all or part of the attribute property that has been demonstrated. In applications where verifiers submit their showing protocol transcripts to the CA, for instance to enable the CA to detect and combat fraud, this property prevents the CA from learning which formulae the verifiers require their customers to demonstrate. At the same time, verifiers are unable to provide false information to the CA.

Our use of certified public keys has two side benefits: a secure session can be established without enabling wiretappers to identify the session initiator from its certified public key, and fraudulent CAs cannot falsely revoke certified public keys that are used only once.

1.3.3 Security techniques

In Section 5.4 we will show how to combine our issuing and showing protocols in such a manner that either one of the following two properties is achieved:

- (Unlimited-show certificates) Even if a certificate is shown an arbitrary number of times, the information that is revealed is no more than the aggregate information that is willingly disclosed in each of the individual showing protocol executions. (Multiple showings of the same certificate are all linkable, though; a certified public key in effect is a digital pseudonym.)

- (Limited-show certificates) If and only if a certificate is shown more than a predetermined number of times, the aggregate information that is revealed allows the computation of the entire secret key of the certificate holder (and in particular all the encoded attributes). The threshold can be arbitrarily set.

The limited-show property holds even if the certificate holder is free to choose the attribute property that it demonstrates in each showing protocol execution, and can be combined with the verifier privacy technique described in Section 5.3. (That is, the CA will be able to trace perpetrators regardless of whether certificate verifiers hide a part of the formulae demonstrated.) Even conspiring certificate holders and verifiers cannot defeat the limited-show property.

The limited-show technique is highly practical: to compute one of the hidden attributes (for instance an identity attribute) in case of fraud, even in a military-strength implementation a "footprint" of a mere 60 bytes must be stored per showing protocol transcript, regardless of the complexity of the formula demonstrated and the number of encoded attributes.

In Section 5.5 we will show how to apply the limited-show techniques to discourage unauthorized lending and copying of certificates, and the deliberate discarding of certificates that contain attributes that the certificate holder does not want to show. These security techniques do not require tamper-resistant devices for certificate holders, nor do they require online certificate validation. When issuing gender or age certificates for gaining access to Internet discussion groups or Web sites, for instance, the issuer can encode into each certified key pair not only the designated receiver's gender or age, but also some information that the receiver would like to keep secret (such as his or her credit card information, redeemable electronic coins, or an account access key). While the certificate holder can hide this secret when showing the certificate (by using our selective disclosure techniques), the certificate cannot be shown without actually knowing the encoded secret; lending therefore requires the certificate holder to give away the secret.

Furthermore, we show in Section 5.5 how to achieve non-repudiation for limited-show certificates, to prevent the CA from framing certificate holders by falsely claiming that limited-show certificates have been shown too many times. The evidence of fraud can be obtained in the form of a self-signed confession, and can be made unconditionally convincing. A particularly surprising feat is that the non-repudiation techniques can be made to work even when certificate applicants are anonymous to the certificate issuer.

We also describe in Section 5.5 measures to protect against leakage and misuse of the CA's secret key, including measures to cope with attackers with infinite computing power (to prevent PKI meltdown). Another technique described in Section 5.5 concerns digital bearer certificates; these hide or do not contain any attributes that can be uniquely traced or linked to one person or to a select group.

Our techniques are not complementary to the currently prevailing ideas about digital certificates and PKIs, but encompass them as a special case. By way of example we will show in Section 5.5.1 how to encapsulate X.509v3 certificates. The new techniques are beneficial in any authentication-based communication or transaction environment in which there is no strict need to identify certificate holders at each and every occasion. The only acceptable role for X.509 and other identity certificates in such environments is to facilitate registration in case certificate applicants must be identified to the CA, similar to the way in which drivers' licenses and passports are traditionally used to acquire a permit or some other kind of authentication proof; even for this purpose, however, our certificates can be used.

In none of the techniques in this book do certificate verifiers need tamper-resistant devices.

1.3.4   Smartcard integration

All our techniques can be applied not only in the setting of software-only devices, but also in a setting where certificate holders in addition to a software-only device hold a smartcard. In Chapter 6 we first describe the many shortcomings of smartcard-only implementations, and list the advantages of combining smartcards with user-controlled software-only computers. We then show how to securely lift the software-only techniques of the preceding chapters to the smartcard setting in such a manner that the following privacy properties are guaranteed:

- The smartcard cannot learn the (public key, certificate) pair of its holder's certified key pairs, and cannot learn any encoded attributes its holder desires to keep secret.

- The smartcard cannot learn the property that is demonstrated in the showing protocol. In particular, regardless of the complexity of the formula demonstrated and the number of attributes encoded into a certified key pair, the smartcard performs exactly the same protocol. The smartcard cannot even decide whether multiple invocations of its assistance are for the purpose of showing the same certificate or different certificates, and can be prevented from learning any information on the number of certificates issued to its holder.

- All possible data leakages by and to the smartcard are prevented. This includes not only leakages that can be detected, but also subliminal channels. Consequently, the verifier learns nothing beyond the status of the formula(e) demonstrated; it cannot even distinguish whether the certificate holder is assisted by a smartcard or uses merely a software-only device.

- The smartcard can be prevented from developing any data that is statistically correlated to data known to the outside world (in particular, to the CA and certificate verifiers), so that even the contents of a returned smartcard that has been adversely programmed cannot reveal any information about the communications and transactions conducted by its holder (other than an upper bound on the number of showing protocol executions).

In this manner, the task of each smartcard is reduced to the absolute minimum, namely to protect the most basic security interests of the certificate issuer and its holder. This is desirable not only in light of privacy, but also for efficiency and security.

Our techniques accommodate situations in which the smartcard's task is deliberately broadened, for the purpose of controlling to which parties a certificate can be shown, which properties may be demonstrated, and so on. For instance, it may be desirable for individuals that their smartcard can assist in the showing protocol only when the designated verifier provides an identifier; as will be shown in Section 6.4.4, this suffices to protect against extortion attacks conducted over networks. Also, in some high-risk PKIs law enforcement may need the ability to trace the past actions of a designated certificate holder (but only with that person's awareness). In general, the smartcard can be prevented from learning anything beyond what it is expressly supposed to learn in order to perform a well-defined task known to its holder. This suffices to accommodate any legitimate needs to reduce the attainable privacy level.

The certificate issuing and showing protocols for software-only devices in Chapters 3 to 5 are a self-contained subset of the smartcard-enhanced protocols. An important advantage of this architecture is that all the security protections of the software-only system apply in the (presumably hypothetical) case that the tamper-resistance of a large number of smartcards is compromised overnight. It also enables PKI implementations in which some certificate holders hold software-only devices and others use smartcards. In particular, a PKI can be introduced as a software-only system and migrate gradually to a smartcard-enhanced system as the demand rises for greater efficiency, functionality, and security.

The computation and storage requirements for the smartcard do not depend on the number of encoded attributes or the complexity of the demonstrated formulae. Our smartcard techniques can even be implemented using low-cost 8-bit smartcards with limited memory and no cryptographic coprocessor, as will be shown in Section 6.5.1. This minimizes the cost for all parties, and allows manufacturers to devote the bulk of smartcard logic to improved tamper-resistance measures.

Different PKIs can make use of the same smartcard without being able to interchange personal data (unless the card holder consents). Certificate applications can be built on top of widely available smartcards that provide only basic identification or signature functionality.

When limited-show short-lived certificates are issued, the need to rely on (timely) revocation greatly reduces, and so our smartcard techniques also help overcome the cost, efficiency, and privacy problems of off-line and online certificate revocation and validation mechanisms. (Revocation of encryption keys can be avoided by randomly generating one-time encryption keys afresh at the start of each authenticated session.)

In Section 6.5 we show how certificate holders can securely return to the CA any retrieved certificates that have not yet been shown, how to discourage certificate holders from using their certificates to help remote parties gain access to services for which they do not hold the proper certificates themselves, how to design secure bearer certificates with optimal privacy, and how to prevent organizations and other verifiers from discriminating against certificate holders who do not disclose their built-in identifiers.

1.3.5   Security and privacy guarantees

All the techniques can be based on the RSA assumption as well as on the Discrete Logarithm assumption, and admit elliptic curve implementations with short public keys. Many of the security aspects can rigorously be proved equivalent to the security of either one of these assumptions in the so-called random oracle model.

All the privacy properties are guaranteed in the strongest possible sense: even if all the verifiers, smartcards, and CAs conspire in an active attack, are given infinite computing power, and jointly establish secret information in an preparatory phase, they cannot learn more than what can be inferred from the assertions that are voluntarily demonstrated in executions of the showing protocol. Consequently, individuals can prevent secondary use of their attribute data and can at all times ensure the correctness, timeliness, and relevance of their own data. At the same time, the risk of identity fraud is minimized.

While this information-theoretical privacy guarantee is very strong, it is important to realize that computational privacy would be unsatisfactory:

- The infeasibility assumption at the heart of breaking computational privacy is based on a specific distribution of the system parameters and key material generated by the CA. It may be hard or even impossible to verify that these are indeed generated in accordance with the proper probability distribution. A clever method of generating the system parameters or the key material may enable the CA to trace communications and transactions with modest computational effort.

- Another danger of computational privacy is that one or two decades from now it may be entirely practical for CAs to retroactively trace any or all of today's communications and transactions. The expected advances in algorithmics and progression in sheer computing power[27] will make it possible then to break implementations based on key sizes deemed sufficiently strong today, without needing a polynomial-time attacking algorithm. Indeed, virtually all the cryptographic systems in use today employ keys that for efficiency reasons are as small as possible; these key sizes do not guarantee invulnerability for more than a decade.

In either of these two cases, the resulting level of privacy-intrusion may be much more damaging than that of PKIs without any form of privacy to begin with, because certificate holders will be less inhibited in their actions.

The difference between computational and information-theoretical privacy can be viewed as follows. With computational privacy all the secrets of individuals end up

---

[27]In 1965, Moore predicted that the number of components on integrated circuits would double every year for ten years. In 1975 he predicted a doubling every two years instead of every year. Thus far, Moore's prediction has been remarkably accurate. It is anticipated that by the year 2010 we will be down to atomic dimensions.

in the outside world, encrypted under a public key. Information-theoretical privacy guarantees that the secrets do not get out there in the first place.

In a practical implementation of a design that offers information-theoretical privacy, certificate holders should be given the freedom to select their own method of generating the random numbers needed to protect their own privacy. Those who desire the strongest privacy level should use random bits produced by a noise generator (post-processed by arithmetical methods to remove correlations), while others may be comfortable using pseudorandom bit generators or other methods that offer at most computational privacy. The fundamental difference with a system that has computational privacy hardwired into its design is that each certificate holder is free to choose or produce his or her own source of randomness, including the security parameters and seed values for pseudorandom generators.

For a general discussion of the difference between privacy-protecting methods and methods that merely create the illusion of privacy, see the Epilogue.

Our techniques do not protect against wiretapping and traffic analysis, but allow the modular adoption of session encryption, anonymous remailers, and other measures as an additional layer. Techniques to prevent wiretapping and traffic analysis are largely platform dependent and not necessarily based on cryptography. Note also that confidentiality can be trivially achieved once the authenticity problem is solved; the authenticity proof can include a public key to be used for encryption. The independence of encryption is good design practice in any case, and avoids regulatory issues such as export controls.

1.3.6   Applicability

Our techniques facilitate a cookbook approach towards designing electronic communication and transaction systems. Applications of special interest include, but are not limited to: electronic cash; digital pseudonyms for public forums and virtual communities (such as Internet news groups and chat rooms); access control (to Virtual Private Networks, subscription-based services, Web sites, databases, buildings, and so on); digital copyright protection (anonymous certificates permitting use of works); electronic voting; electronic patient files; electronic postage; automated data bartering (integration with standardization efforts such as P3P is easy); online auctions; financial securities trading; pay-per-view tickets; public transport ticketing; electronic food stamps; road-toll pricing; national ID cards (but with privacy); permission-based marketing; Web site personalization; multi-agent systems; collaborative filtering (i.e., making recommendations to one person based on the opinions of like-minded persons); medical prescriptions; gift certificates; loyalty schemes; and, electronic gambling. The design of specific applications is outside the scope of this book, but is relatively straightforward in many cases.

Chapter 2

Cryptographic Preliminaries

In this chapter we review all the basic cryptographic primitives needed in the rest of the book: one-way and collision-intractable functions, proofs of knowledge, digital signatures, and public-key certificates. We introduce two new functions that are one-way and collision-intractable, and for both design practical techniques for proving knowledge of an inverse and for constructing digital signatures. These functions are central to our constructions of issuing and showing protocols in the next two chapters. We also introduce a new kind of digital certificates, called secret-key certificates; the benefits of these will become clear in Chapters 4 and 5.

2.1 Notation, terminology, and conventions

2.1.1 Basic notation

The notation "$x := y$" means that the value of y is assigned to x. Typically, y is an arithmetic expression. The "$=$" symbol denotes equality; upon $x := y$ we have $x = y$.

Whenever we say that a number is chosen "at random" from a set V, we imply a uniform distribution over the set V, independent of the probability distributions of any other variables explicitly considered in the same context. Within a figure, the notation $x \in_{\mathcal{R}} V$ is used to denote the same.

All the constructions in this book are based on elementary algebra. The notation $\mathbb{Z}_t$ denotes the ring of integers modulo t and $\mathbb{Z}_t^*$ its multiplicative group, and GF_t denotes the finite field with t elements. Computations involving numbers in a finite ring or in a multiplicative group must always be interpreted as computations in these structures. For example, if $x, y \in \mathbb{Z}_t^*$, then "xy" stands for $xy \bmod t$. In cases where we consider arithmetic involving exponents, the modulo operator is often made explicit for greater certainty. In mathematical proofs, an element in $\mathbb{Z}_t$ or in $\mathbb{Z}_t^*$ may be interpreted in the algebraic sense of denoting a congruence class, but in constructions of algorithms and protocols it always represents a unique number between 0 and $t-1$, usually encoded in binary. In particular, if $x, y \in \mathbb{Z}_t$, then "$x = y$" means that x and y are the same number, not merely that they are congruent modulo t.

For any $x \in \mathbb{Z}$ and any $y \in \mathbb{N}$, $x \bmod y$ denotes the number $x^* \in \{0, \ldots, y-1\}$ such that $x^* - x$ is an integer multiple of y. In keeping with mathematical tradition, the mod operator acts on the entire arithmetic expression preceding it, unless parentheses specify otherwise. For instance, $a + b \bmod y$ stands for $(a + b) \bmod y$.

The notation div is defined by $x = x \bmod y + y (x \text{ div } y)$, for any $x \in \mathbb{Z}$ and any $y \in \mathbb{N}$. Parentheses indicate the arithmetic expression on which div operates.

The notation "$|X|$" can have three different meanings. If X is a set, then $|X|$ denotes the size of X, i.e., the number of elements in X; if X is a number in $\mathbb{R}$, then $|X|$ denotes its absolute value; and if X is by definition a positive integer then $|X|$ denotes its binary size (length). The appropriate meaning will always be clear from the context.

2.1.2 Algorithms, security parameters, and probability

An *algorithm* is a procedure that, on given some input, always halts after a finite number of steps. For concreteness, intractability assumptions are always stated in the uniform complexity model, and we construct algorithms that can be formalized by Turing machines.[1] Thus, all algorithms have a read-only *input tape*, a *work tape*, and a write-only *output tape*. Probabilistic algorithms in addition have a *random tape* containing their coin flips. Once the computation of an algorithm comes to a halt, its finite-state control enters into either an **accept** or **reject** state; correspondingly, the algorithm is said to accept or reject. In addition, it may have written an output onto the cells of its output tape; $A(x)$ denotes the output of algorithm A on input x. If A is probabilistic, then $A(x)$ is a random variable whose probability distribution is taken over the coin flips of A; that is, $A(x)$ defines a probability space of output strings. We write $x := A(y)$ or $A(y) = x$ to specify that x is generated by running algorithm A on input y.

A *security parameter* is a number that is taken from an infinite subset of the set of positive integers. Security parameters are used to measure the time and space complexity of an algorithm, the binary sizes of algorithm inputs and outputs, success probabilities, and security levels. Although multiple security parameters may be specified for any one protocol or system, for simplicity all the protocols and systems in this book make reference to only a single security parameter, denoted by k. The notation 1^k denotes k encoded in unary.

For inputs of the same binary size, the possible outputs of an algorithm are all

---

[1]It would be easy to rephrase our constructions and security reductions in the non-uniform complexity model of Boolean circuits, since they do not hinge on the use of polynomial-size advice strings that cannot be computed in polynomial time.

assumed to be of the same binary size; this can be achieved by the standard practice of padding.

As is common in the cryptographic literature, we measure the *running time* of an algorithm in terms of elementary algebraic operations, typically modular multiplications, instead of in terms of the number of transitions of the Turing machine's read-write head. The terms *feasible* and *infeasible* have the standard complexity-theoretical meaning: feasible computations are those that can be performed in time polynomial[2] in k, while infeasibility corresponds to *superpolynomial* running time[3] (which includes *subexponential* and *exponential* running time). Whenever we speak of a polynomial-time algorithm, it may be either deterministic or probabilistic.

A function $f : \mathbb{N} \mapsto [0, 1]$ is *negligible* in k if $f(k)$ is smaller than the inverse of any polynomial in k, for all sufficiently large k; it is *non-negligible* if there exists a positive integer c such that $f(k)$ is greater than $1/k^c$, for all sufficiently large k; and, it is *overwhelming* if $1 - f(\cdot)$ is negligible. (Note that a function can be neither negligible nor non-negligible.) An *intractable* problem is one that cannot be solved in polynomial time with non-negligible probability of success.

The notation $\mathsf{P}_k(E_k)$ denotes the probability of event E_k. For probability spaces $S_1, S_2, \ldots$, the notation

$$\mathsf{P}_k(E_k(x_1, x_2, \ldots) \mid x_1 := S_1; x_2 := S_2; \ldots)$$

denotes the probability that the event $E_k(x_1, x_2, \ldots)$ holds when each x_i is chosen, in the given order, from the corresponding probability space S_i.

An *expected* polynomial-time algorithm is a probabilistic algorithm whose expected running time (over its coin flips) is polynomial for any input. By running a probabilistic polynomial-time algorithm that has non-negligible success probability $\epsilon(k)$ an expected number of $k/\epsilon(k)$ times, one can construct an expected polynomial-time algorithm that has overwhelming success probability.

A *language* over an alphabet is a subset of the set of all finite strings of symbols from that alphabet. If A is a probabilistic algorithm and L a language, then the collection $\{A(x)\}_{x \in L}$ is an *ensemble* of random variables. Two ensembles $\{A(x)\}_{x \in L}$ and $\{B(x)\}_{x \in L}$ are *perfectly indistinguishable* if, for all $x \in L$, the random variables $A(x)$ and $B(x)$ have the same distribution. They are *statistically indistinguishable* (or almost-perfectly indistinguishable) on L if for all $x \in L$ of binary size k their statistical difference

$$\sum_{\alpha} \left| \mathsf{P}_k(A(x) = \alpha) - \mathsf{P}_k(B(x) = \alpha) \right|$$

---

[2]A function $f(\cdot)$ is polynomial in k if there exists a positive integer c such that $f(k) \leq k^c$ for all sufficiently large k.

[3]A function $f(\cdot)$ is superpolynomial in k if for all positive integers c, $f(k) \geq k^c$ for all sufficiently large k.

is negligible in k.[4] Finally, they are *computationally indistinguishable* on L if, for all polynomial-time algorithms D with Boolean output (representing accept or reject), and for all $x \in L$ of binary size k,

$$\left| \mathsf{P}_k(D(y) = 1 \mid y := A(x)) - \mathsf{P}_k(D(y) = 1 \mid y := B(x)) \right|$$

is negligible in k.

2.1.3   Interactive algorithms and protocols

An algorithm may consist of two or more *interactive algorithms* that communicate according to one or more stepwise descriptions called *protocols*. Interacting parties in this book are always modeled as interactive algorithms. Formally, an interactive algorithm is a Turing machine enhanced with a *communication tape* and a read-only *common input tape*. A pair of interactive algorithms share their communication tapes, for exchanging messages, and their common input tapes. The work tape and random tape of each algorithm are private to the algorithm, and their private input tapes enable each to make use of *auxiliary input*, also known as private input; this may be present initially, or computed as protocol executions are taking place.

More generally, there can be any number of interactive algorithms communicating with each other in an arbitrary fashion. This can easily be formalized by endowing each interactive algorithm with a set of communication and common input tapes for any other algorithm it needs to be able to communicate with. Correspondingly, protocols may be defined among more than two parties. In general, any collection of interactive algorithms can be viewed as a single (interactive or non-interactive) algorithm.

With $\mathcal{P}$ and $\mathcal{V}$ denoting two interactive algorithms, $(\mathcal{P}, \mathcal{V})$ denotes the protocol performed by them, and $<\mathcal{P}, \mathcal{V}>$ denotes the two algorithms viewed as a single (interactive or non-interactive) algorithm. The input of $<\mathcal{P}, \mathcal{V}>$ is the initial contents of their common input tape, and the output of $<\mathcal{P}, \mathcal{V}>$ is the concatenation of the contents on the output tapes of $\mathcal{P}$ and $\mathcal{V}$. Usually at most one of $\mathcal{P}$ and $\mathcal{V}$ is defined to produce an output.

A *move* in a protocol is a message transfer from one interactive algorithm to another; a *round* is two consecutive moves. After the last move in a protocol, the receiving algorithm checks a (protocol) *verification relation* in order to decide whether to accept or reject. Additional verifications may be applied in intermediate stages. A protocol is said to be *non-interactive* if it consists of a single move, and interactive if it has more. None of the protocols in this book have more than two rounds.

---

[4]The practical interpretation of this is that an infinitely powerful algorithm that is restricted to taking polynomially many samples cannot distinguish between the two distributions; such an algorithm can infer the same information from either distribution. Note that perfect indistinguishability corresponds to zero statistical difference.

Protocols are sometimes depicted in figures, together with a description of the preliminary stage for setting up keys and other prerequisite information. Within a figure, the actions performed by an interactive algorithm are all displayed in the same column, with a label on top indicating the algorithm that performs the actions. A move is shown in the form of an arrow from the transmitter to the receiver, with the message that is transferred displayed on top of the arrow. Protocol figures should be read from top to bottom. Any additional data that is displayed in a column that contains one or more message transmittals, such as a public key, is also considered known to both communicating parties.

The *transcript* of a protocol executed by two interactive algorithms is the entire ordered sequence of messages exchanged between them until one of them halts.

The *view* of an interactive algorithm in a protocol execution is an ordered set consisting of all the information that the algorithm has "seen" in the protocol execution. This comprises the protocol transcript, as well as the common input, any private input, and its own coin flips (if any). An *accepting view* of an interactive algorithm is the view of that algorithm in a protocol execution in which it accepts. Usually at least one of the algorithms in a protocol will be probabilistic, in which case the view is a random variable defined by the coin flips in the protocol. By parameterizing over all possible protocol executions an ensemble of random variables is obtained, and so we can consider indistinguishability of protocol views.

With $\mathcal{P}$ and $\mathcal{V}$ denoting two interactive algorithms, $\mathcal{V}_{\mathcal{P}_{(\mathsf{aux1})}}(x; \mathsf{aux2})$ denotes $\mathcal{V}$'s output when interacting with $\mathcal{P}$ on common input x, auxiliary input aux1 to $\mathcal{P}$ and auxiliary input aux2 to $\mathcal{V}$. When there is no auxiliary input to $\mathcal{V}$, we simply write $\mathcal{V}_{\mathcal{P}_{(\mathsf{aux})}}(x)$. In either case, for fixed inputs this is a random variable, whose probability distribution is taken over the coin flips (if any) of $\mathcal{P}$ and $\mathcal{V}$.

The notation $\mathcal{K}(x; A)$ denotes the output of algorithm $\mathcal{K}$ on input x, when having write access to the random tape and the private input tape of algorithm A that in all other respects behaves as a *black box* to $\mathcal{K}$. The standard method for extracting knowledge from an algorithm A is to rewind A for the same tape configurations but different queries. By means of oracle replay in the so-called random oracle model, which we discuss shortly, it may be possible to extract secrets even if rewinding is not an option, even though it is unclear in this case how to properly define knowledge outside the random oracle model. (See Assumption 4.3.9 for an example.)

2.1.4   Attack models

An *honest* interactive algorithm does not deviate from its behavior specified in the protocol description, and does not engage in any other actions. In particular, it follows the protocol description in all protocol executions in which it engages.

An *attacker* is an interactive algorithm that may deviate from its prescribed actions, for instance by deviating from its actions in the specified protocols or by wiretapping the protocol executions of others. When assessing the security of a new cryptographic construction, we typically view the subset of all parties that deviate from the prescribed protocol(s) (either cooperative or non-cooperative) as a single algorithm, which we then use as a subroutine for an algorithm to solve a supposedly intractable problem. A collection of attackers that may but need not share all their tapes is referred to as an *adversary*.[5]

In assessing whether a protocol satisfies a property of interest, one must consider not only the computing power of the attackers, but also the flexibility they have in engaging in executions of the protocol. Among the factors contributing to whether an adversary can break a presumed property of a protocol are the following:

- The extent to which multiple executions of the same protocol, or of different protocols, can be interleaved. Parallel executions of a protocol are more efficient than sequential executions, not only in the number of moves but also in that some additional operations (such as line encryption) may be applied once on all the moves that occur concurrently. On the other hand, parallelization may enable an adversary to compute information that it could not compute otherwise.

  The most powerful attack model is that of *arbitrary composition* of protocols or protocol executions; here, the adversary can adaptively (depending on its protocol views in the past) decide at each stage which moves of one protocol execution to interleave with which moves of another protocol execution (not necessarily of the same protocol), and in what manner.

- The number of protocol executions attackers are able to engage in.[6] A *passive* attacker is not allowed to interact at all, but can wiretap protocol executions that take place by honest parties; an *active attacker* is allowed to engage in protocol executions. In all our protocol descriptions in this book honest parties are assumed to be polynomial-time, and so even an infinitely powerful adversary can never engage in more than polynomially many protocol executions.

- The computing power given to the adversary. All the privacy results in this book are proved under the assumption that attackers have infinite computing power. Digital signatures, on the other hand, can be proved unforgeable only against attackers that are polynomially bounded.

---

[5]The protocol executions of an attacker that operates in isolation may be wiretapped by other attackers and in this manner add to their power; for this reason isolated attackers must be considered part of the adversary. The attempt to circumvent this by encrypting all message transfers is not satisfactory. First, it is unreasonable to characterize parties that do not properly encrypt their own messages as attackers of the system. Second, it would be poor design practice to let the requirement for session encryption interfere with the design of the system core and the analysis of systemic security.

[6]For example, in Section 5.4 we will construct proofs of knowledge in which the prover does not leak any information about its secret key when performing the protocol once, but multiple protocol executions using the same public key leak the entire secret key.

The power of an adversary with unlimited resources is not restricted to computations before or after a protocol execution; at each step, it may use infinite computing time to compute its next message. While this model may seem unrealistic, in the Turing machine model it makes perfect sense: the running time of an interactive algorithm is determined by the number of state transitions defined by the transition function, and so the time taken by one machine does not affect the running time of the other. Moreover, the model of infinite computing power serves as a useful abstraction to model the complete absence of one-way functions (see Section 2.2) and other intractable computational tasks. When a construction is proved invulnerable against an infinitely powerful adversary, there is no need to worry about attackers that have embedded cryptographic trapdoors or have come up with a cryptographic breakthrough.

The first two of these factors are under the control of the honest party that is being attacked. It can determine which protocol executions to perform sequentially and how many executions it engages in.

The *aggregate view* of an interactive algorithm in multiple executions of the same or of different protocols is the collection of its views in the individual protocol executions. The ordering of the components of the aggregate view is naturally defined by the fashion in which the protocol executions are interleaved.

Following Feige, Fiat, and Shamir [168], $\overline{\mathcal{A}}$ denotes an honest interactive algorithm, $\widehat{\mathcal{A}}$ denotes an attacker with polynomially bounded resources, and $\widetilde{\mathcal{A}}$ denotes an attacker with unbounded computing resources. Attack algorithms $\widehat{\mathcal{A}}$ and $\widetilde{\mathcal{A}}$ may but need not deviate from the protocol description, and can engage in as many protocol executions as they desire, confined only by the limitations imposed by the other parties in the protocols they engage in. For instance,

$$\widehat{\mathcal{V}}_{\overline{\mathcal{P}}_{(\text{aux1})}}(x; \text{aux2})$$

denotes $\widehat{\mathcal{V}}$'s output after interacting with $\overline{\mathcal{P}}$, whereby $\widehat{\mathcal{V}}$ can query $\overline{\mathcal{P}}$ as if it were an oracle; in particular, $\widehat{\mathcal{V}}$'s output may be the result of a phase in which $\widehat{\mathcal{V}}$ engages in a plurality of protocol executions. In contrast,

$$\overline{\mathcal{V}}_{\overline{\mathcal{P}}_{(\text{aux1})}}(x; \text{aux2})$$

always refers to a single execution of the protocol.

In analyzing whether a certain property holds for an honest party in a protocol, it is always assumed that the party aborts an execution of the protocol as soon as the other party (parties) deviates from the description of the protocol in a manner that is detectable with certainty by the honest party. The interpretation of "detectable" depends on the verification relations and other actions specified in the description of the protocol, as well as on actions that we always assume implicitly. Specifically, it is implicit in protocol descriptions that the parties to a protocol always apply range-checking to numbers supposed to be in an algebraic structure. For examples of attacks that become possible when a party inadvertently does not apply range checking, see Bleichenbacher [34] and Anderson and Vaudenay [14]. Arithmetic relations that must apply to these numbers (i.e., verification relations) are always mentioned explicitly. In some case it is necessary to perform group membership tests; see Section 2.4.3 for an example. Deviation by the other party from a specified probability distribution, though, does not constitute a reason to abort a protocol execution.

2.1.5 Security reductions and the random oracle model

Since the emphasis in this book is on practicality, *exact security* is of importance. Suppose that a problem P is conjectured to be intractable: problem instances of size k cannot be solved with non-negligible success probability $\epsilon(k)$ in fewer than $r_P(k)$ steps, for some superpolynomial running-time function $r_P(\cdot)$. To prove the infeasibility of a cryptanalytic attack on a new protocol construction, we construct an algorithm A that can solve problem instances of size k of problem P in polynomial time, with success probability negligibly close to $\epsilon(k)$, by making no more than polynomially many subroutine calls to a black-box algorithm B that can feasibly solve instances of the new construction. Suppose that, for inputs of size k, B runs in time $f_B(k)$, and A makes $f_A(k)$ calls to B, using $g_A(k)$ additional processing steps for each call and $h_A(k)$ additional one-time processing steps. The functions $g_A(\cdot)$ and $h_A(\cdot)$ are polynomials, typically of low degree. The total running time $r_{AB}(k)$ of A and B is equal to

$$f_A(k)\Big(f_B(k) + g_A(k)\Big) + h_A(k).$$

If $f_B(\cdot)$ is polynomially bounded there exists a positive integer k_0 such that

$$r_{AB}(k) < r_P(k) \quad \forall k \geq k_0,$$

contradicting the presumed intractability of problem P. But what practical assurances on the parameter sizes for the new construction can we infer from the proof reduction? We obtain a contradiction only for security parameter sizes that exceed k_0, and so it is desirable that k_0 be as small as possible. Hereto the functions $f_A(\cdot)$, $g_A(\cdot)$ and $h_A(\cdot)$ should all be as small as possible. In situations of practical interest $f_B(k)$ typically exceeds $h_A(k)$ by far, and so $f_A(\cdot)$ is the dominating contribution to the total running time. We therefore equate the *overhead factor* of a security reduction with the (expected) number of calls to algorithm B. A security reduction is *tight* if the overhead factor is a (small) constant, and *optimal* tightness is achieved when the overhead factor is negligibly close 1. For any given security level, a tight reduction allows one to implement the new construction using smaller parameter sizes than would be allowed by a non-tight reduction. Because practicality is an important objective of this book, we strive for tight security reductions throughout. In practice it is recommended to choose k in such a manner that an adversary needs an expected number of at least 2^{80} elementary operations to break the construction at hand. (Imagine a supercomputer that can do 1 elementary operation each picosecond, and that 300 of these are running in parallel; it would take over 128 years to cycle through all 2^{80} operations.)

Sometimes the security of a new construction can be proved only in the *random oracle model*. In this model, a function that is believed hard to invert may be *idealized* by substituting applications of the function by calls to a random oracle. The oracle, on input an element in the domain of the function, produces a random output in the range of the function, to be interpreted as the outcome of the function. Of course, multiple oracle queries with the same input produce the same output. The success probability of the resulting security reduction is taken over the space of all random functions. Cannetti, Goldreich, and Halevi [76] concocted example constructions that are provably secure in the random oracle model but provably insecure when the oracle is instantiated using any function. Therefore, the ability to give a security reduction in the random oracle model in general does not imply that a successful attack requires the exploitation of a weakness in the function that is being idealized. Nevertheless, in the "natural" cryptographic constructions that arise in practice, and in particular in this book, provable security in the random oracle model is believed to be a relevant measure of security. Most of the constructions in this book are amenable to security proofs in the random oracle model.

2.2 One-way functions

2.2.1 Definition

From now on we are mainly interested in functions $f(\cdot)$ that can be expressed as an infinite collection of functions, $\{f_i(\cdot)\}_{i\in V}$. Each $f_i(\cdot)$ operates on a finite domain, D_i, and V is an enumerable infinite *index set*, with i uniquely specifying D_i. A description of $f(\cdot)$ entails specifying V and the mapping $f_i(\cdot)$. Any collection of functions $\{f_i(\cdot)\}_{i\in V}$ can be represented by a single function $f(\cdot)$ that operates on an infinite domain, by defining

$$f(i, x) := (i, f_i(x)),$$

and so the two notions can be used interchangeably.

Informally, a one-way function is a function that is easy to compute, but computing inverses is difficult on average. To formalize this notion, we require an *instance generator* for the function. An instance generator for a collection of functions, $\{f_i(\cdot)\}_{i\in V}$, is a pair (I, D) of probabilistic polynomial-time algorithms, operating as follows:

- I takes as input 1^k, and outputs an index $i \in V$ of binary size $l(k)$, where $l(\cdot)$ is a fixed polynomial; and

- D takes as input the output i of I, and outputs an element x in the domain D_i of $f_i(\cdot)$. (Elements in D_i may occur with zero probability as an output of $D(i)$.)

The output of (I, D) is (i, x). We will simply write $(i, x) \in V \times D_i$ to denote that first i is taken from V and then x is taken from D_i. (Although this is not the standard Cartesian product, no confusion can arise.)

Definition 2.2.1. *A collection of functions,* $\{f_i(\cdot)\}_{i \in V}$, *is (strongly) one-way over an instance generator* (I, D) *if and only if the following two properties hold:*

1. *(Computable in one direction) There exists a deterministic polynomial-time algorithm that, on input any* $(i, x) \in V \times D_i$, *outputs* $f_i(x)$; *and*

2. *(Uninvertable in the other direction) For any polynomial-time algorithm A, the probability function defined by*

$$\mathsf{P}_k\Big(f_i(A(i, f_i(x))) = f_i(x) \mid i := I(1^k); x := D(i)\Big)$$

is negligible in k.

Whenever we say that a function $f(\cdot)$ is one-way, we mean that the collection of functions that it represents is one-way, in the above sense. In case the instance generator is clear from the context, we will not mention it explicitly.

Note that functions with superpolynomial range are always one-way when idealized in the random oracle model.

If $\{f_i(\cdot)\}_{i \in V}$ is one-way over (I, D), then (I, D) is said to be an *invulnerable* instance generator for $\{f_i(\cdot)\}_{i \in V}$. The usefulness of the notion of invulnerability (originating from Abadi, Allender, Broder, Feigenbaum, and Hemachandra [1]) becomes apparent when reducing the problem of inverting a function that is conjectured to be one-way to the problem of breaking a new construction, to prove the security of the latter. Instead of specifying a particular instance generator for the conjectured one-way function, it is sometimes possible to make the same security reduction work for all invulnerable instance generators; this makes the resulting security statement much stronger. All the security reductions in this book are of this form. Note that if an instance generator is invulnerable for a function, then so are all instance generators with a computationally indistinguishable output distribution.

A *commitment function* enables a sender to commit to a secret, in such a manner that the receiver cannot determine the secret until the sender *opens* the commitment, while the sender cannot open the commitment to reveal a different secret than that originally committed to. A one-way permutation can serve as a commitment function that is unconditionally secure for the receiver and computationally secure for the sender. Hereto the sender embeds its secret into the hard-core bits[7] of an otherwise randomly chosen argument x to a one-way permutation $f(\cdot)$.

We now discuss two well-known functions that are widely believed to be one-way. Their one-wayness is crucial to the security of all the constructions in this book.

2.2.2 The DL function

The output of an instance generator (I, D) for a *DL function*, defined below, satisfies the following format:

- On input 1^k, with $k \geq 2$, I generates a pair (q, g), satisfying the following properties:

    - q is a prime number of binary size k that uniquely specifies a group of order q, from now on denoted by G_q. Without loss of generality, the group operation is assumed to be multiplication.

    - g is a generator of G_q.

- On input (q, g), D generates an element x in $\mathbb{Z}_q$.

A DL function is a collection of functions, $\{f_i(\cdot)\}_{i \in \{(q,g)\}}$, defined as follows:

$$f_{q,g} : x \mapsto g^x.$$

The number x is called the *discrete logarithm* of g^x with respect to g. Note that different algebraic constructions for G_q give rise to different DL functions.

Under what conditions is a DL function one-way? If the construction of G_q is such that multiplication in G_q is feasible, then $f_{q,g}(x)$ can be feasibly computed by means of repeated squaring (see Menezes, van Oorschot, and Vanstone [266, Section 14.6]), possibly in combination with additional preprocessing.[8] The hardness of inverting a DL function depends on the construction of G_q and on the instance generator (I, D). The following two constructions are widely believed to give rise to a one-way DL function.

(**Subgroup construction**) G_q is a subgroup of $\mathbb{Z}_p^*$, where p is a prime such that $q \mid (p - 1)$ and $|p|$ is polynomial in k. The following instance generator is believed to be invulnerable:

---

[7]If $f(\cdot)$ is one-way, then there must exist a Boolean predicate of the bits of the argument of $f(\cdot)$ that is at least somewhat hard to compute when given $f(x)$. A Boolean predicate $b(\cdot)$ is said to be hard-core for $f(\cdot)$ if $b(\cdot)$ can be computed in polynomial time, but no probabilistic polynomial-time algorithm can compute $b_i(x)$ from $f_i(x)$ with success probability non-negligibly greater than $1/2$. More generally, several bits are said to be (simultaneously) hard-core for $f(\cdot)$ if no polynomial-time algorithm can extract any information about these bits of x when given $f_i(x)$.

[8]Alternatively, addition chains or other techniques may be used. For overviews and comparisons of exponentiation methods, see Knuth [232, Subsection 4.6.3], Menezes, van Oorschot, and Vanstone [266, Chapter 14.6], von zur Gathen and Nöcker [383], Gordon [196], and O'Connor [280].

- q is generated at random from the set of all primes of binary size k, using a primality test. The number p is the first prime in the sequence $aq + 1$, for successive (even) integer values a, starting from a fixed positive integer a_0 that is "hard-wired" into I; heuristic evidence suggests that only polynomially many values of a need to be tested (see Wagstaff [384]). It is not known how to test primality in deterministic polynomial time. A polynomial-time primality test with negligible error probability may be used instead, though, because its outputs are computationally indistinguishable.

- g is generated at random from $G_q \setminus \{1\}$. This can be accomplished by taking $g := f^{(p-1)/q}$, for a random $f \in \mathbb{Z}_p^*$, and testing that $g \neq 1$. (There is only one subgroup with order q.) Other distributions are not necessarily improper, but results of Bleichenbacher [34] and Anderson and Vaudenay [14] for groups of non-prime order suggest that a random selection is preferred.

- x is best chosen at random from $\mathbb{Z}_q$. This maximizes its entropy, and allows one to prove the hardness of inverting assuming the seemingly weaker assumption that any polynomial-time algorithm for inverting the DL function has non-negligible error probability. In particular, either this choice is successful or the DL-function cannot be one-way at all.

Alternatively, one first generates a random prime p and checks whether $q = (p - 1)/a_0$ is a prime, repeating this process until a prime q is found. Another variation is to generate a random composite with known prime factorization (see Bach [16]), and to test whether its increment by one is a prime, p; if this is the case, then with high probability the binary size of the largest prime factor of $p - 1$ is proportional to $|p|$. (In this case $|q|$ should be allowed to be linear in k.)

Primes p of a special form may provide even better protection against attacks. For instance, it is believed preferable to generate p subject to the restriction that $(p - 1)/2q$ contains only prime factors greater than q. Other reasons for generating p of a special form are related to security issues of protocols that operate in G_q; see Section 2.4.3.

In practical applications it is often important that the pair (p, q) do not contain a trapdoor that enables the rapid computation of discrete logarithms. Although no trapdoor constructions are known in the public literature that cannot be feasibly detected (and, therefore, tested for), confidence can be increased by using an instance generator that generates q and p in a pseudorandom manner, starting from a seed value that must be output as well by the instance generator; see Federal Information Processing Standards no. 186 [277, Appendix 2]. In addition, a succinct proof may be output for proving that g has been generated using a pseudorandom process.

(Elliptic curve construction) G_q is an elliptic curve of order q over a finite field. (See Menezes [263] for an introduction to elliptic curves as applied in cryptography.) It is common to take $\mathbb{Z}_p$ as the underlying field, for a prime p such that $|p|$ is polynomial in k. The following three instance generators are believed to be invulnerable:

- Select a (probable) prime p, and randomly try elliptic curve coefficients until a curve of prime order is found. (The process could be sped up by allowing $|q|$ to be linear in k.) The elliptic curve coefficients must be specified as part of the output of the instance generator. Generate g and x at random from $G_q \setminus \{1\}$ and $\mathbb{Z}_q$, respectively.

- Alternatively, the coefficients determining the elliptic curve are hardwired into the instance generator, and p and q of the appropriate form are sought by trial and error. The numbers g and x are generated at random from $G_q \setminus \{1\}$ and $\mathbb{Z}_q$, respectively.

- Another possibility is to generate an elliptic curve of prime order together with a generator g, using an algorithm of Koblitz [234]. As before, x is best chosen at random from $\mathbb{Z}_q$.

Alternatively, one can generate elliptic curves over a field of the form GF_{2^m} instead of over $\mathbb{Z}_p$; as we will see shortly, this offers practical advantages.

Any uncertainty about the presence of a trapdoor can be removed in the manner described for the subgroup construction.

Other constructions have been proposed, but these are considerably more difficult to understand and have not been scrutinized by more than a few experts. See Biehl, Meyer, and Thiel [28] and the references therein for constructions in real-quadratic number fields, and Koblitz [233] for a construction in groups obtained from Jacobians of hyperelliptic curves.

The prime q need not be generated at random, if only the underlying field is chosen in a substantially random manner. A smart choice for q enables one to speed up the reduction modulo q. Example choices for q are $2^{127} - 1$ (a Mersenne prime) or, more generally, $2^a \pm b$, for small b. Furthermore, in some applications it may be useful to use the same q in combination with multiple primes p_i, all chosen at random subject to the condition $q \mid (p_i - 1)$.

With the exception of the technique described in Section 4.4.1, none of the constructions in this book depend on the manner in which G_q is constructed. In general, we merely need the following assumption to be true.

Assumption 2.2.2. *There exists a DL function that has an invulnerable instance generator.*

From now on we will use the notation $(I_{\mathrm{DL}}, D_{\mathrm{DL}})$ to denote an invulnerable instance generator for "the" DL function. Although specific embodiments may have additional outputs, such as p, elliptic curve coefficients, a compact proof that g has been generated at random, and information evidencing that no trapdoor has been built in, for concreteness we will always assume that the output of $(I_{\text{DL}}, D_{\text{DL}})$ is (q, g, x). We will also assume that (q, g) is always *properly formed*, meaning that q is a prime and g a generator of G_q, but will never make any assumptions about the probability distribution of the outputs of $(I_{\text{DL}}, D_{\text{DL}})$.

The one-wayness of a function is an asymptotic property. For overviews of algorithms to compute discrete logarithms, see Odlyzko [281] and McCurley [259]. In practice, the binary size of the parameters must be selected such that adequate security for the application at hand is offered. For instance, the parameter sizes for a digital signature that is to have legal meaning several decades from now must be much greater than for an identification protocol that only seeks to withstand replay attacks. Currently recommended parameter sizes for the DL function are as follows:

(Subgroup construction) To compute discrete logarithms in G_q, one can either work in G_q or proceed indirectly[9] by computing discrete logarithms with respect to generators of $\mathbb{Z}_p^*$.

The best known algorithms for computing discrete logarithms in $\mathbb{Z}_p^*$ all have subexponential running time. In May 1998, Joux and Lercier computed a discrete logarithm modulo a 299-bit prime using a network of Pentium PRO 180 MHz personal computers and a total of 4 months of CPU time. Odlyzko [282] states that primes p should be at least 1024 bits even for moderate security, and at least 2048 bits for anything that should remain secure for a decade.[10] This recommendation is based on the presumption that future progress in algorithmic and hardware capabilities will be along the lines witnessed in the past. According to Silverman [353], it has been estimated that for large k, breaking a discrete logarithm of $k - 30$ bits takes about the same time as factoring a k-bit composite that is the product of two random primes of approximately equal binary size, but Odlyzko [283] recommends to ignore this difference when choosing parameter sizes.

In G_q itself, only exponential-time algorithms are known, with running time $O(\sqrt{q})$. Shoup [352] proved in his so-called generic string encoding model that algorithms with a better performance than $O(\sqrt{q})$ operations must make use of the structure of G_q, suggesting that a universal subexponential-time inverting algorithm that works for any construction of G_q cannot exist. Assuming that the best algorithms for computing discrete logarithms in G_q have running time $O(\sqrt{q})$, a 160-bit prime q offers the same security level as a 1024-bit p; see Menezes [264]. Odlyzko [282] recommends primes q of 200 bits for

---

[9]With $(p - 1)/q$ polynomial in k, the infeasibility of computing discrete logarithms in G_q follows from that in $\mathbb{Z}_p^*$.

[10]This overturns an earlier recommendation of Odlyzko [283] to use 1024-bit primes for long-term security (i.e., at least the next two decades) and 768-bit primes for medium-term security.

long-term security. Lenstra and Verheul [247] are more optimistic; for security until the year 2020 they recommend using primes p of at least 1881 bits and primes q of at least 151 bits.

(Elliptic curve construction) As with the subgroup construction, the fastest methods known for computing discrete logarithms in G_q require $O(\sqrt{q})$ steps. When so-called supersingular curves are used, one can invert the DL function indirectly (by computing discrete logarithms in the underlying field $\mathbb{Z}_p$ or an extension of it) in subexponential time, and the binary size of p must be comparable to that in the subgroup construction; see Menezes, Vanstone, and Okamoto [265]. A linear-time algorithm for so-called trace-1 elliptic curves was announced in September 1997 independently by Smart [357] and by Satoh and Araki [335]. Both cases occur with negligible probability for randomly chosen curves, and can easily be detected. For randomly generated curves only exponential-time algorithms are known, taking $O(\sqrt{p})$ steps. Barring algorithmic breakthroughs, numbers in the base and numbers in the ring of exponents can therefore be taken of the same binary size; this is a huge efficiency improvement over the subgroup construction.

In May 1998, a Certicom elliptic curve challenge over a field $\mathbb{Z}_p$ with a 97-bit prime p was solved after 53 days of distributed computation using more than 1200 computers from at least 16 countries. In a whitepaper [85], Certicom estimates that a 160-bit prime p offers the same security as factoring a 1024-bit composite, and that a 210-bit prime p compares with factoring a 2048-bit composite. More recently, Lenstra and Verheul [247] estimated that a 139-bit p and a 1024-bit composite or a 160-bit p and a 1375-bit composite offer computationally equivalent security. They estimate that, for security until the year 2020, key sizes of at least 161 bits should be used if no cryptanalytic progress is expected, and at least 188 bits to "obviate any eventualities."

Assuming again that subexponential-time inverting algorithms do not exist, working over a field of the form GF_{2^m} offers significant advantages. VLSI circuits have been designed that can rapidly perform operations in these fields; see Agnew, Mullin, and Vanstone [6] for a VLSI implementation of $GF_{2^{155}}$. Even in general software environments, the use of GF_{2^m} offers performance advantages over $\mathbb{Z}_p$. Wiener [390] estimates that m should be in the range 171–180 to make computing discrete logarithms as hard as factoring 1024-bit composites. In his analysis, Wiener assumes the strongest attack known: a parallel collision search attack using a fully pipelined chip for elliptic curve additions over GF_{2^m}. In April 2000, a team led by Harley, Doligez, de Rauglaudre, and Leroy broke an elliptic curve challenge for $m = 108$ after four months of distributed computation using 9500 computers; the estimated workload for solving a 163-bit challenge is about 100 million times larger.

The belief in the strength of short moduli for the elliptic curve construction is not ubiquitous. Odlyzko [282] warns that "it might be prudent to build in a considerable safety margin against unexpected attacks, and use key sizes of at least 300 bits, even for moderate security needs." Several renowned cryptographers have even expressed disbelief that the complexity of the discrete logarithm problem for elliptic curves is more than subexponential.

2.2.3   The RSA function

The output of an instance generator (I, D) for the *RSA function*, defined below, satisfies the following format:

- On input 1^k, with $k \geq 4$ and k even, algorithm I generates a pair (n, v), satisfying the following properties:

  - n is the product of binary size k of two primes, p and q.
  - v is a number smaller than n that is co-prime to $\varphi(n)$, where $\varphi(\cdot)$ is Euler's phi-function.

- On input (n, v), algorithm D generates an element x in $\mathbb{Z}_n^*$.

The *RSA function* is a collection of functions, $\{f_i(\cdot)\}_{i \in \{n,v\}}$, defined as follows:

$$f_{n,v} : x \mapsto x^v.$$

Under what conditions is the RSA function one-way? Clearly, the RSA function can be evaluated efficiently, using repeated squaring or addition chain techniques. Note that the exponent is fixed instead of the base number; this makes repeated squaring less and addition chains more attractive than in the case of the DL function. The following instance generator is believed to be invulnerable:

- p and q are chosen at random[11] from the set of primes of binary size $k/2$, using a (probabilistic) primality test. In case p and q are generated after v has been determined, a test for $\gcd(\varphi(n), v) = 1$ can be used to decide whether to keep (p, q) or to repeat the experiment.

- v can be chosen in an almost arbitrary fashion, including an invariant choice hard-wired into I. Certain choices must be avoided, such as (n, v) such that $v^{-1} \bmod \varphi(n) < n^{0.292}$ (see Wiener [389] and Boneh and Durfee [36]), but bad choices are believed to be detectable and so they can be easily avoided. In fact, they should occur with negligible probability if v and n are generated independently at random.

---

[11]Rivest and Silverman [326] argue that for practical purposes using random primes is as secure as using primes of a special form.

- x is best chosen at random from $\mathbb{Z}_n^*$, for the same reasons as with the DL function. In particular, either this choice is successful or the RSA function cannot be one-way at all.

Other methods for generating (n, v) have been proposed, all differing in the distribution according to which p and q are generated; see, for example, Boneh [37] and Kaliski and Robshaw [225].

Although v may be an arbitrary small constant or a composite, in the rest of this book we are interested only in primes v that are superpolynomial in k. The reasons for this will become apparent in Section 2.4.4 and in the next two chapters.

Assumption 2.2.3. *There exists an invulnerable instance generator for the RSA function that outputs primes v that are superpolynomial in k.*

Boneh and Venkatesan [40] proved that breaking RSA with small v cannot be equivalent to factoring n under algebraic reductions unless factoring is easy, but their result does not apply to superpolynomial v. Consequently, it may well be the case that there exists an invulnerable instance generator such that inverting the RSA function is as hard as factoring.

From now on we use the notation $(I_{\text{RSA}}, D_{\text{RSA}})$ to denote an invulnerable instance generator for the RSA function that outputs primes v superpolynomial in k. Its output is (n, v, x), and we will always assume that (n, v) is always *properly formed*, meaning that v is a prime that is co-prime to $\varphi(n)$. In practice, additional outputs may be specified, such as a succinct proof demonstrating that (n, v) is properly formed. (In the applications in this book, the proof that v is co-prime to $\varphi(n)$ will always be implicitly given by the party that generates v, as a side consequence of its protocol executions; see Section 4.2.3.) Moreover, in Sections 4.2.2 and 4.4.2 we will construct protocols on the basis of an invulnerable instance generator that provides the prime factorization of n as "side information." We will never make any assumptions about the probability distribution of the outputs of $(I_{\text{RSA}}, D_{\text{RSA}})$.

The fastest known algorithms for inverting the RSA function all proceed by factoring n; for an overview, see Bressoud [61]. They have subexponential running time and have been used successfully to factor composites of up to 512 bits.[12] Shamir's TWINKLE device [345] brings 512-bit moduli within reach of a single device. According to Odlyzko [282], "even with current algorithms, within a few years it will be possible for covert efforts (involving just a few people at a single institution, and thus not easily monitored) to crack 768 bit RSA moduli in a year or so." Lenstra and Shamir [246] estimate that it would take 5000 TWINKLE devices connected by a fast network to 80 000 standard Pentium II computers in order to factorize a 768 bit composite within 6 months. Odlyzko [282] projects that "even 1024 bit RSA moduli

---

[12]RSA-155, which has 512 bits and is the product of two 78-digit primes, was factored in August 1999 using the Number Field Sieve algorithm. The effort used the equivalent of roughly 8000 mips years, and involved 292 desktop computers and a Cray C916 supercomputer. See Cavallar et al. [77] for details.

might be insecure for anything but short-term protection." Lenstra and Verheul [247] recommend using RSA moduli of at least 1881 bits for security until the year 2020, and Odlyzko [282] recommends to use at least 2048-bit moduli. Silverman [353], however, argues that these estimates are highly unrealistic on the grounds that taking the total number of computing cycles on the Internet as a model of available computing power ignores memory and accessibility problems. In particular, he strongly disagrees with the conclusion of Lenstra and Verheul [247] that 1024 bit moduli are insecure after 2002, and estimates that 1024 bit moduli will remain secure for at least 20 years and 768 bit moduli for perhaps another 10 years.

The requirement that v be superpolynomial can be met in practice by taking the binary size of v similar to that of q in the DL function; at least 160 bits is recommended, and 200 bits is preferable. As in the case of q, v need not be chosen at random. In particular, a smart choice for v enables a faster reduction modulo v.

2.3   Collision-intractable functions

2.3.1   Definition

In practical applications, it is often required of a function that it be infeasible to compute two arguments that are mapped to the same outcome. Formally:

Definition 2.3.1. *A collection of functions, $\{f_i(\cdot)\}_{i \in V}$, is collision-intractable over an instance generator (I, D) if and only if the following two properties hold:*

1. *(Computable in one direction) There exists a deterministic polynomial-time algorithm that, on input any $(i, x) \in V \times D_i$, outputs $f_i(x)$; and*

2. *(Collision-intractable in the other direction) For any polynomial-time algorithm A, the probability function defined by*

   $$\mathsf{P}_k\Big(A(i) = (x, y) \text{ such that } x, y \in D_i, \ x \neq y, \ f_i(x) = f_i(y) \mid i := I(1^k) \Big)$$

   is negligible in k.

Note that the coin flips of algorithm D are irrelevant. We may therefore say that the function is collision-intractable over I.

For many-to-one functions, collision-intractability is *non-trivial* and is a stronger property than one-wayness. Note that functions with superpolynomial range are always collision-intractable when idealized in the random oracle model.

A non-trivial collision-intractable function $f(\cdot)$ can serve as a commitment function that is unconditionally secure for the sender and computationally secure for the receiver. The straightforward implementation whereby the sender commits to x by sending $f_i(x)$ is unsatisfactory, though: the distribution of x in general will differ from the distribution for which one-wayness is guaranteed, and even if it is the same there is no guarantee that no partial information leaks. This problem can be fixed by using a function $f(\cdot)$ with special uniformity properties. (We omit a formal definition, because it is irrelevant for the purposes of this book.) The candidate collision-intractable functions that will be introduced in the next two sections meet these properties and are at the heart of all the constructions in the remainder of this book.

2.3.2 The DLREP function

We refer to the collection of functions considered in this section as the *DLREP function*. The output of an instance generator (I, D) for the DLREP function satisfies the following format:

- On input 1^k, with $k \geq 2$, algorithm I generates a tuple

$$(q, g_1, \ldots, g_l)$$

satisfying the following properties:

- q is a prime number of binary size k that uniquely specifies a group G_q of order q.

- $g_1, \ldots, g_l$ are elements of G_q, for an integer $l \geq 1$, and $g_l \neq 1$. The integer l can be hard-wired into I, but may also be determined by I itself, depending on its input; in the latter case l may be polynomial in k. (Since l can be inferred from the output of (I, D), it is not made explicit in I's output.)

- On input $(q, g_1, \ldots, g_l)$, algorithm D generates a tuple

$$(x_1, \ldots, x_l),$$

with $x_1, \ldots, x_l \in \mathbb{Z}_q$.

A DLREP function is a collection of functions, $\{f_i(\cdot)\}_{i \in \{q, g_1, \ldots, g_l\}}$, defined as follows:

$$f_{q, g_1, \ldots, g_l} : (x_1, \ldots, x_l) \mapsto \prod_{i=1}^{l} g_i^{x_i},$$

with domain $(\mathbb{Z}_q)^l$. The tuple $(x_1, \ldots, x_l)$ is called a *DL-representation* of $h :=$ $\prod_{i=1}^{l} g_i^{x_i}$ *with respect to* $(g_1, \ldots, g_l)$. The tuple $(0, \ldots, 0)$ is a DL-representation of 1 with respect to any tuple $(g_1, \ldots, g_l)$; we call this the *trivial* DL-representation. We simply call $(x_1, \ldots, x_l)$ a DL-representation of h in case $(g_1, \ldots, g_l)$ is clear from the context. Note that we do not require the g_i's to be generators, in contrast to g in the DL function, nor do we require the g_i's to be different from one another.

The DLREP function is a generalization of the DL function. As with the DL function, different constructions for G_q give rise to different DLREP functions. The following construction is of special importance to our later constructions in this book.

Construction 2.3.2. *Given an invulnerable instance generator* $(I_{\mathrm{DL}}, D_{\mathrm{DL}})$ *for the DL function, construct an instance generator* $(I_{\mathrm{DLREP}}, D_{\mathrm{DLREP}})$ *for the DLREP function as follows:*

- *On input* 1^k, *with* $k \geq 2$, I_{DLREP} *calls* I_{DL}, *on input* 1^k, *to obtain a pair* (q, g). I_{DLREP} *generates* $l - 1$ *exponents,* $y_1, \ldots, y_{l-1}$, *at random from* $\mathbb{Z}_q$, *and computes* $g_i = g^{y_i}$, *for all* $i \in \{1, \ldots, l - 1\}$. I_{DLREP} *sets* $g_l := g$, *and outputs* $q, (g_1, \ldots, g_l)$. *(Alternatively, if the construction of* G_q *is such that it is easy to generate random elements from* G_q *without knowing an element in* G_q, I_{DLREP} *may generate random* $g_1, \ldots, g_{l-1}$ *directly.)*

- D_{DLREP} *generates* x_l *at random from* $\mathbb{Z}_q$. *The other elements,* $x_1, \ldots, x_{l-1}$, *may all be generated in an arbitrary manner.*

Proposition 2.3.3. *If* $(I_{\mathrm{DL}}, D_{\mathrm{DL}})$ *is invulnerable, then the DLREP function is one-way and collision-intractable over* $(I_{\mathrm{DLREP}}, D_{\mathrm{DLREP}})$.

Proof. The DLREP function is easy to compute, using l exponentiations and $l - 1$ multiplications. (More efficient methods are discussed shortly.)

The DLREP function is trivially one-way if $l = 1$. For the case $l \geq 2$, note that if $(x_1, \ldots, x_l)$ is a DL-representation of $h \in G_q$ with respect to $(g_1, \ldots, g_l)$, then $x := \sum_{i=1}^{l-1} x_i y_i + x_l \bmod q$ is the discrete logarithm of h with respect to g; therefore, an efficient algorithm for inverting the DL function can be constructed from one for inverting the DLREP function.

Collision-intractability is vacuously true for the case $l = 1$. Consider now the case $l \geq 2$. If $(x_1, \ldots, x_l)$ and $(y_1, \ldots, y_l)$ are any two different DL-representations of the same number, then $(x_1 - y_1 \bmod q, \ldots, x_l - y_l \bmod q)$ is a non-trivial DL-representation of 1. Consequently, if we can find collisions then we can find a non-trivial DL-representation of 1, at virtually no overhead. We may therefore assume that we are given an algorithm B that, on input $(q, (g_1, \ldots, g_l))$ generated by I_{DLREP}, outputs a non-trivial DL-representation of 1 in at most t steps, with success probability ϵ. We construct an algorithm A that, on input $((q, g), h)$, computes $\log_g h \bmod q$, as follows:

Step 1. A generates $2l - 2$ random numbers, $r_1, \ldots, r_{l-1}, s_1, \ldots, s_{l-1} \in \mathbb{Z}_q$. A sets
$$g_i := h^{r_i} g^{s_i} \quad \forall i \in \{1, \ldots, l - 1\},$$
and $g_l := g$. A then feeds $(q, (g_1, \ldots, g_l))$ to B.

Step 2. A receives $(x_1, \ldots, x_l)$ from B, and checks whether or not it is a non-trivial DL-representation of 1. If it is not, then A halts.

Step 3. If $\sum_{i=1}^{l-1} r_i x_i = 0 \bmod q$, then A halts.

Step 4. A computes

$$-(\sum_{i=1}^{l-1} s_i x_i + x_l)(\sum_{i=1}^{l-1} r_i x_i)^{-1} \bmod q,$$

and outputs the result.

It is easy to verify that the output in Step 4 is equal to $\log_g h \bmod q$, and that the total running time is $O(l\,k)$ plus the running time of B. We now determine the success probability of A.

Because the joint distribution of $(g_1, \ldots, g_l)$, generated in Step 1, is the same as that induced by the output of I_{DLREP}, the transition from Step 2 to Step 3 occurs with probability ϵ. To determine the probability that the transition from Step 3 to Step 4 takes place, we observe that there exists an integer $j \in \{1, \ldots, l-1\}$ such that $x_j \neq 0 \bmod q$ (because B's output is non-trivial). Therefore, there are exactly q^{l-2} "bad" tuples $(r_1, \ldots, r_{l-1}) \in (\mathbb{Z}_q)^{l-1}$, for which $\sum_{i=1}^{l-1} r_i x_i = 0 \bmod q$: for any choice of $(r_1, \ldots, r_{j-1}, r_{j+1}, \ldots, r_{l-1})$, the remaining number, r_j, exists and is uniquely determined because q is a prime. The tuple $(r_1, \ldots, r_{l-1})$ is unconditionally hidden from B, owing to the randomness of the s_i's and the fact that g is a generator of G_q, and it is therefore independent of B's output. Any choice of $(r_1, \ldots, r_{l-1})$ is equally likely to have been made by A, and so the probability of having chosen a bad tuple is $q^{l-2}/q^{l-1} = 1/q$.

Because Step 4 takes place only if Step 3 is successful, and Step 3 takes place only if Step 2 is successful, the overall success probability of A is $\epsilon(1 - 1/q)$. $\square$

The proof reduction is optimally tight. Because the influence of l on the running time overhead is merely linear in the security parameter, using the parameter sizes recommended for the DL function to implement the DLREP function results in roughly the same security level. In particular, a prime q of 200 bits should offer long-term protection against collision-finding attempts.

Note that Proposition 2.3.3 also applies if g_l is generated at random; Construction 2.3.2 is simply more general.

The number x_l need not be generated at random. Construction 2.3.2, however, is all we need for our purposes in this book. From now on, $(I_{\text{DLREP}}, D_{\text{DLREP}})$ always denotes an invulnerable instance generator that has been constructed from an invulnerable instance generator $(I_{\text{DL}}, D_{\text{DL}})$ for the DL function in the manner of Construction 2.3.2. Of course, it is permitted to use any instance generator with a distribution that is indistinguishable from that generated by $(I_{\text{DLREP}}, D_{\text{DLREP}})$.

The constructed DLREP function can be used by a sender to commit to $l-1$ attributes, $(x_1, \ldots, x_{l-1})$. As we will show in Chapter 3, this commitment function has a special property: the sender can *gradually open* its commitment to an infinitely powerful receiver, and in intermediate stages demonstrate all sorts of properties about the attributes without leaking additional information about them.

The method described in the proof of Proposition 2.3.3 for computing the DLREP function is polynomial-time, but is not very practical for large l in case (some of) the x_i's are large or randomly chosen. For $l \geq 2$, one can evaluate $\prod_{i=1}^{l} g_i^{x_i}$ much more efficiently by using simultaneous repeated squaring with a single precomputed table whose $2^l - 1$ entries consist of the products of the numbers in the non-empty subsets of $\{g_1, \ldots, g_l\}$. See Knuth [232, Exercises 27 and 39 of Section 4.6.3].

Several variations and optimizations of this basic technique exist. For example, one can process $t > 1$ exponent bits at once; the size of the precomputed table then increases by a factor close to $2^{(t-1)l}$, while the number of multiplications decreases by a factor of t and the number of squarings remains unaffected. For large l one can break up the computation into a number of blocks: with $1 < j \leq l$, the product $\prod_{i=1}^{l} g_i^{x_i}$ can be computed using $d = \lceil l/j \rceil$ precomputed tables, using simultaneous repeated squaring for each of the d subproducts and multiplying the subproduct results.

Alternatively, one can apply vector addition chain techniques; see, for instance, Coster [121].

2.3.3 The RSAREP function

We refer to the collection of functions considered in this section as the *RSAREP function*. The output of an instance generator (I, D) for the RSAREP function satisfies the following format:

- On input 1^k, with $k \geq 4$ and k even, algorithm I generates a tuple

$$(n, v, g_1, \ldots, g_l)$$

  satisfying the following properties:

  - n is the product of binary size k of two primes, p and q.
  - v is a prime smaller than n that is co-prime to $\varphi(n)$.
  - $g_1, \ldots, g_l$ are elements of $\mathbb{Z}_n^*$, for an integer $l \geq 0$. The integer l can be hard-wired into I but may also be determined by I itself, depending on its inputs; in the latter case l may be polynomial in k.

- On input $(n, v, g_1, \ldots, g_l)$, algorithm D generates a tuple

$$(x_1, \ldots, x_{l+1}),$$

  with $x_1, \ldots, x_l \in \mathbb{Z}_v$ and $x_{l+1} \in \mathbb{Z}_n^*$.

The RSAREP function is a collection of functions, $\{f_i(\cdot)\}_{i \in \{n,v,g_1,\ldots,g_l\}}$, defined as follows:

$$f_{n,v,g_1,\ldots,g_l} : (x_1,\ldots,x_l,x_{l+1}) \mapsto \prod_{i=1}^{l} g_i^{x_i} x_{l+1}^{v},$$

with domain $(\mathbb{Z}_v)^l \times \mathbb{Z}_n^*$. The tuple $(x_1,\ldots,x_l,x_{l+1})$ is an *RSA-representation* of $h := \prod_{i=1}^{l} g_i^{x_i} x_{l+1}^v$ *with respect to* $(g_1,\ldots,g_l,v)$. The tuple $(0,\ldots,0,1)$ is an RSA-representation of 1 with respect to any tuple $(g_1,\ldots,g_l,v)$; we call this the *trivial* RSA-representation. We simply call $(x_1,\ldots,x_l,x_{l+1})$ an RSA-representation of h in case $(g_1,\ldots,g_l,v)$ is clear from the context. Note that we do not require the g_i's to be different or to have large order.

While a tuple $(y_1,\ldots,y_l,y_{l+1}) \in \mathbb{Z}^l \times \mathbb{Z}_n^*$ satisfying

$$h = \prod_{i=1}^{l} g_i^{y_i} y_{l+1}^v$$

is not an RSA-representation in case one of $y_1,\ldots,y_l$ is not in $\mathbb{Z}_v$, it is easy to check that the *normalized* form

$$(y_1 \bmod v,\ldots,y_l \bmod v, \prod_{i=1}^{l} g_i^{y_i \operatorname{div} v} y_{l+1})$$

is an RSA-representation of h. In practice, it may sometimes be more efficient to use $(y_1,\ldots,y_l,y_{l+1})$ directly in a computation, instead of first normalizing it; this avoids one multi-exponentiation. On the other hand, normalization is desirable for the purpose of implementing simultaneous repeated squaring or related techniques.

The following construction is of special importance to our later constructions in this book.

Construction 2.3.4. *Given an invulnerable instance generator* $(I_{\text{RSA}}, D_{\text{RSA}})$ *for the RSA function, construct an instance generator* $(I_{\text{RSAREP}}, D_{\text{RSAREP}})$ *for the RSAREP function as follows:*

- *On input* 1^k, *with* $k \geq 4$ *and* k *even,* I_{RSAREP} *calls* I_{RSA}, *on input* 1^k, *to obtain a pair* (n,v). I_{RSAREP} *generates* l *random numbers,* $g_1,\ldots,g_l$, *from* $\mathbb{Z}_n^*$, *and outputs* $n,v,(g_1,\ldots,g_l)$.

- D_{RSAREP} *generates* x_{l+1} *at random from* $\mathbb{Z}_n^*$. *The other elements,* $x_1,\ldots,x_l$, *may all be generated from* $\mathbb{Z}_v$ *in an arbitrary manner.*

Proposition 2.3.5. *If* $(I_{\text{RSA}}, D_{\text{RSA}})$ *is invulnerable, then the RSAREP function is one-way and collision-intractable over* $(I_{\text{RSAREP}}, D_{\text{RSAREP}})$.

Proof. The RSAREP function is easy to compute, using $l + 1$ exponentiations and l multiplications. (For practicality, one can apply the techniques mentioned in Section 2.3.2 to $\prod_{i=1}^{l} g_i^{x_i}$, and multiply x_{l+1}^v into the result.)

The RSAREP function is trivially one-way if $l = 0$. For the case $l \geq 1$, note that from an RSA-representation of $h \in \mathbb{Z}_n^*$ with respect to $(g_1, \ldots, g_l, v)$ it is easy to compute the v-th root of h, assuming one knows the v-th root of each g_i; from this observation it is easy to see how an efficient inverting algorithm for the RSA function can be constructed from one from the RSAREP function.

Collision-intractability is vacuously true for the case $l = 0$. Consider now the case $l \geq 1$. If $(x_1, \ldots, x_l, x_{l+1})$ and $(y_1, \ldots, y_l, y_{l+1})$ are any two different RSA-representations of the same number, then

$$(x_1 - y_1 \bmod v, \ldots, x_l - y_l \bmod v, \prod_{i=1}^{l} g_i^{(x_i - y_i) \operatorname{div} v} x_{l+1} y_{l+1}^{-1})$$

is a non-trivial RSA-representation of 1. Consequently, if we can find collisions then we can find a non-trivial RSA-representation of 1, at modest cost. We may therefore assume that we are given an algorithm B that, on input $(n, v, (g_1, \ldots, g_l))$ generated by I_{RSAREP}, outputs a non-trivial RSA-representation of 1 in at most t steps, with success probability ϵ. We construct an algorithm A that, on input $((n, v), h)$, computes $h^{1/v}$, as follows:

Step 1. A generates l random numbers, $r_1, \ldots, r_l \in \mathbb{Z}_v$, and l random numbers, $s_1, \ldots, s_l \in \mathbb{Z}_n^*$. A sets

$$g_i := h^{r_i} s_i^v \quad \forall i \in \{1, \ldots, l\},$$

and feeds $(n, v, (g_1, \ldots, g_l))$ to B.

Step 2. A receives $(x_1, \ldots, x_l, x_{l+1})$ from B, and checks whether or not it is a non-trivial RSA-representation of 1. If it is not, then A halts.

Step 3. If $\sum_{i=1}^{l} r_i x_i = 0 \bmod v$, then A halts.

Step 4. Using the extended Euclidean algorithm, A computes integers $e, f \in \mathbb{Z}$ satisfying

$$e \left(\sum_{i=1}^{l} r_i x_i \right) + fv = 1.$$

A then computes

$$h^f (x_{l+1} \prod_{i=1}^{l} s_i^{x_i})^{-e},$$

and outputs the result.

It is easy to verify that the output in Step 4 is equal to $h^{1/v}$, and that the total running time is $O(l|v|)$ plus the running time of B. We now determine the success probability of A.

Because the joint distribution of $(g_1, \ldots, g_l)$, generated in Step 1, is the same as that of the output of I_{RSAREP}, the transition from Step 2 to Step 3 occurs with probability ϵ. To determine the probability that the transition from Step 3 to Step 4 takes place, we observe that there exists an integer $j \leq l$ such that $x_j \neq 0 \bmod v$ (because B's output is non-trivial). Therefore, there are exactly v^{l-1} "bad" tuples $(r_1, \ldots, r_l) \in (\mathbb{Z}_v)^l$, for which $\sum_{i=1}^{l} r_i x_i = 0 \bmod v$: for any choice of $(r_1, \ldots, r_{j-1}, r_{j+1}, \ldots, r_l)$, the remaining number, r_j, exists and is uniquely determined because v is a prime. The tuple $(r_1, \ldots, r_l)$ is unconditionally hidden from B, owing to the randomness of the s_i's and the fact that v is co-prime to $\varphi(n)$, and it is therefore independent of B's output. Any choice of $(r_1, \ldots, r_l)$ is equally likely to have been made by A, and so the probability of having chosen a bad tuple is $v^{l-1}/v^l = 1/v$.

Because Step 4 takes place only if Step 3 is successful, and Step 3 takes place only if Step 2 is successful, the overall success probability of A is $\epsilon(1 - 1/v)$. □

The proof reduction is optimally tight, and so using the parameter sizes recommended for the RSA function to implement the RSAREP function results in roughly the same security level. In particular, taking a 2048-bit n and 200-bit v should suffice for long-term security.

As in the case of the DLREP function, Construction 2.3.4 is not the only one for which Proposition 2.3.5 can be proved, but it suffices for our purposes in this book. From now on, $(I_{\text{RSAREP}}, D_{\text{RSAREP}})$ always denotes an invulnerable instance generator constructed from an invulnerable instance generator $(I_{\text{RSA}}, D_{\text{RSA}})$ for the RSA function in the manner of Construction 2.3.4. Of course, it is permitted to use any instance generator with a distribution that is indistinguishable from that generated by $(I_{\text{RSAREP}}, D_{\text{RSAREP}})$.

The constructed RSAREP function can be used by a sender to commit to l attributes, $(x_1, \ldots, x_l)$. We will show in Chapter 3 how the sender can gradually and selectively open its commitment to an infinitely powerful receiver, and more generally can demonstrate all sorts of properties about its attributes without leaking additional information about them.

2.3.4   Comparison

It is clear that the DLREP function and the RSAREP function have much in common, and indeed most constructions in this book can be based on either function. There are some notable differences, though:

- In the RSAREP function the factorization of n can serve as a trapdoor, enabling the computation of arbitrary RSA-representations for any number in $\mathbb{Z}_n^*$. The

DLREP function is not known to have a trapdoor.

- In the RSAREP function, v can be arbitrarily small or be a fixed constant (hard-wired into the instance generator). It is easy to see that Proposition 2.3.5 remains valid for these choices (but the reduction is no longer optimally tight). Similar choices do not exist for the DLREP function, because the infeasibility of collision-finding is directly related to the binary size of q.

As a result, the RSAREP function offers greater flexibility. As we will see in the next section, though, a large v is desirable to construct highly practical showing protocols, and so the second advantage of the RSAREP function is not of interest to us.

For our purposes in this book the DLREP function is usually preferable, for reasons related to practicality:

- The DLREP function can be evaluated faster than the RSAREP function.

- The DL-representation takes less storage space than the RSA-representation for the same security level, assuming that exponents are smaller than numbers in the base.

- Assuming the elliptic curve construction for G_q resists subexponential-time inverting algorithms, storage of numbers in G_q requires significantly less space than storage of numbers in $\mathbb{Z}_n^*$ for the same security level, and computations involving base numbers are much faster.

Moreover, as we will see in the next section, the real-time operations needed to prove knowledge of a DL-representation are much fewer than in the case of an RSA-representation, because all exponentiations can be precomputed.

2.4 Proofs of knowledge

2.4.1 Definition

With (i, x) denoting the output of an instance generator for a function $\{f_i(\cdot)\}_{i \in V}$, and with i understood, $f_i(x)$ may be called a *public key* and x a *secret key* (or *witness*) corresponding to the public key. A *key pair* consists of a secret key and a public key. The outputs of algorithm I form the *system parameters*, and the process of running D and forming the public key is referred to as the *key set-up*.[13]

The public key uniquely corresponds to the secret key, but unless $f_i(\cdot)$ is a permutation there may be many secret keys corresponding to each public key. On input i and the public key, it is infeasible to compute a corresponding secret key if and

---

[13]This definition in terms of collections of one-way functions is not standard, but makes sense in our situation as well as in most other cases that consider only polynomially bounded key holders.

only if the function is one-way over (I, D). Moreover, if the function is collision-intractable over (I, D), no party that is given i can feasibly generate a public key for which it knows two corresponding secret keys.

We now come to the notion of a proof of knowledge, originating from Goldwasser, Micali, and Rackoff [193]. Informally, this is a protocol by means of which one party can convince another that it "knows" a secret key corresponding to its public key.

Definition 2.4.1. *A proof of knowledge* $(\mathcal{P}, \mathcal{V})$ *for a function* $\{f_i(\cdot)\}_{i \in V}$ *is a protocol performed by a pair of interactive polynomial-time algorithms.* $\mathcal{P}$ *is called the* prover *and* $\mathcal{V}$ *is called the* verifier. *The protocol* $(\mathcal{P}, \mathcal{V})$ *must satisfy the following two properties:*

- *(Completeness) For all k, for all* $(i, x) \in V \times D_i$,

$$\mathsf{P}_k\left(\overline{\mathcal{V}}_{\overline{\mathcal{P}}_{(x)}}(i, f_i(x)) \; accepts\right) = 1.$$

The probability is taken over the coin flips (if any) of $\overline{\mathcal{V}}$ *and* $\overline{\mathcal{P}}$.

- *(Soundness) There exists an expected polynomial-time algorithm* $\mathcal{K}$, *called a* knowledge extractor, *such that for all* $\widehat{\mathcal{P}}$, *for all constants $c > 0$, for all* $(i, x) \in V \times D_i$ *with* $|i|$ *sufficiently large, and for all auxiliary inputs* aux,

$$\left| \mathsf{P}_k\left(\overline{\mathcal{V}}_{\widehat{\mathcal{P}}_{(\mathsf{aux})}}(i, f_i(x)) \; accepts\right) - \mathsf{P}_k\left(f_i(\mathcal{K}((i, f_i(x)), \mathsf{aux}; \widehat{\mathcal{P}})) = f_i(x)\right) \right|$$

is smaller than $1/k^c$.

Loosely speaking, the two properties state that the prover can convince the verifier if and only if the prover knows a secret key corresponding to its public key.[14]

The simplest proof of knowledge is one in which $\mathcal{P}$ sends x to $\mathcal{V}$, whereupon $\mathcal{V}$ checks its correspondence to the public key by applying $f_i(\cdot)$. For our purposes in this book, however, $\mathcal{P}$ should not reveal its secret key. protocol.

2.4.2 Security for the prover

Soundness is a formalization of security for $\overline{\mathcal{V}}$. Many flavors of security for $\overline{\mathcal{P}}$ have been studied in the literature. We now examine the four most useful ones.

---

[14]Definition 2.4.1 originates from Feige and Shamir [169]. Bellare and Goldreich [22] provided a more general definition of proof of knowledge that takes into account provers that have superpolynomial computing power. We do not consider this alternative definition here, since it is considerably more complex and the presented one is adequate for our purposes.

Definition 2.4.2. *A proof of knowledge* $(\mathcal{P}, \mathcal{V})$ *for* $f(\cdot)$ *is computationally zero-knowledge if there exists an expected polynomial-time algorithm* S*, called a sim-ulator, such that for all* $\widehat{\mathcal{V}}$ *and for all auxiliary inputs* aux*, the two ensembles*

$$\left\{ \widehat{\mathcal{V}}_{\overline{\mathcal{P}}_{(x)}}((i, f_i(x)); \mathsf{aux}) \right\}_{(i,x) \in V \times D_i} \quad and \quad \left\{ S((i, f_i(x)), \mathsf{aux}; \widehat{\mathcal{V}}) \right\}_{(i,x) \in V \times D_i}$$

are computationally indistinguishable.

Equivalently, the views of $\widehat{\mathcal{V}}$ in protocol executions with $\overline{\mathcal{P}}$ can be simulated with indistinguishable probability distribution.

In a similar manner one can define statistical and perfect zero-knowledge; in these cases the simulator must be able to output protocol transcripts that are statistically indistinguishable from, or identically distributed to, the protocol transcripts that a verifier with unlimited computing power sees when interacting with $\overline{\mathcal{P}}$. Statistical and perfect zero-knowledge are meaningful notions in case $f_i(\cdot)$ is not a permutation; even though $\widehat{\mathcal{V}}$ can compute all secret keys corresponding to $\mathcal{P}$'s public key, it cannot find out more about which one is known to $\mathcal{P}$ than what is known in advance.

It is possible to construct protocols that are zero-knowledge when protocol executions are performed sequentially, but that leak the secret key of the prover in case attackers are able to engage in parallel executions of the protocol; see Feige and Shamir [169] for an example.

The zero-knowledge property states that a misbehaving $\mathcal{V}$ (with either polynomial or unlimited computing power, depending on the flavor) cannot learn any information beyond what it can infer from merely the system parameters and $\mathcal{P}$'s public key. A weaker notion, which will be very useful in Chapter 3 to prove the unforgeability of digital signature schemes in the random oracle model, is the following.

Definition 2.4.3. *A proof of knowledge* $(\mathcal{P}, \mathcal{V})$ *for a function* $f(\cdot)$ *is (computation-ally, statistically, perfectly) honest-verifier zero-knowledge if there exists an expected polynomial-time simulator* S *such that the two ensembles*

$$\left\{ \overline{\mathcal{V}}_{\overline{\mathcal{P}}_{(x)}}((i, f_i(x))) \right\}_{(i,x) \in V \times D_i} \quad and \quad \left\{ S((i, f_i(x)); \overline{\mathcal{V}}) \right\}_{(i,x) \in V \times D_i}$$

are (computationally, statistically, perfectly) indistinguishable.

The following notion (due to Feige and Shamir [169]) is also weaker than zero-knowledge, but in many applications it is at least as useful.

Definition 2.4.4. *A proof of knowledge* $(\mathcal{P}, \mathcal{V})$ *for a function* $f(\cdot)$ *is statistically witness-indistinguishable if, for any* $x_1, x_2 \in D_i$ *such that* $f_i(x_1) = f_i(x_2)$*, and for any auxiliary input* aux *to* $\widetilde{\mathcal{V}}$*, the two ensembles defined by*

$$\widetilde{\mathcal{V}}_{\overline{\mathcal{P}}_{(x_1)}}((i, f_i(x_1)); \mathsf{aux}) \quad and \quad \widetilde{\mathcal{V}}_{\overline{\mathcal{P}}_{(x_2)}}((i, f_i(x_2)); \mathsf{aux}),$$

respectively, are statistically indistinguishable.

In other words, $\tilde{\mathcal{V}}$ cannot learn any information about which particular secret key is applied by $\overline{\mathcal{P}}$. In a similar manner one can define computational and perfect witness-indistinguishable proofs of knowledge. More generally, one can define witness-indistinguishability for protocols that are not proofs of knowledge.

A proof of knowledge for a permutation is trivially witness-indistinguishable; this is an uninteresting property because it holds even for protocols in which $\mathcal{P}$ transmits its secret key to $\mathcal{V}$. Later in this section, and more importantly in Chapter 3, we will introduce witness-indistinguishable proofs of knowledge for many-to-one functions. The following proposition is due to Feige and Shamir [169].

Proposition 2.4.5. *Witness-indistinguishability is preserved under arbitrary composition of protocols.*

This property, which does not hold for zero-knowledge, applies not only to different executions of the same protocol but also to executions of different witness-indistinguishable protocols.

In contrast to the properties of completeness, soundness, (general and honest-verifier) zero-knowledge, and witness-indistinguishability, the last notion of security for $\overline{\mathcal{P}}$ discussed here is defined only over the output distribution of a specific instance generator.

Definition 2.4.6. *A proof of knowledge $(\mathcal{P}, \mathcal{V})$ for a function $f(\cdot)$ is* witness-hiding *over the instance generator (I, D) for $f(\cdot)$ if there exists an expected polynomial-time algorithm W, called a* witness extractor, *such that for all verifiers $\widehat{\mathcal{V}}$, for all constants $c > 0$, for all sufficiently large k, and for all auxiliary inputs* aux,

$$\left| \mathsf{P}_k \left(f_i(\widehat{\mathcal{V}}_{\overline{\mathcal{P}}_{(x)}}(i, f_i(x); \mathsf{aux})) = f_i(x) \mid i := I(1^k); x := D(i) \right) \right.$$
$$\left. - \mathsf{P}_k \left(f_i(W((i, f_i(x), \mathsf{aux}); \widehat{\mathcal{V}})) = f_i(x) \right) \right| < 1/k^c.$$

The witness-hiding property states that $\widehat{\mathcal{V}}$, after having engaged in (at most) polynomially many protocol executions with $\overline{\mathcal{P}}$, cannot compute an entire secret key that corresponds to $\overline{\mathcal{P}}$'s public key, unless it already knew or could compute such a secret key before any protocol executions with $\mathcal{P}$ were performed. The latter case is not interesting, and so we will refer to proofs of knowledge over vulnerable instance generators as being *trivial witness-hiding*. Note that non-trivial witness-hiding does not exclude the possibility that $\widehat{\mathcal{V}}$ can uniquely determine half of the bits of $\mathcal{P}$'s secret key, say, once it has engaged in sufficiently many protocol executions. Due to the soundness property, however, non-trivial witness-hiding offers adequate security in most applications of proofs of knowledge.

The following proposition also originates from Feige and Shamir [169].

Proposition 2.4.7. *Let (I, D) be an instance generator for a function $f(\cdot)$ such that the following two properties hold for each y in the range of $f_i(\cdot)$:*

- y has at least two preimages in the domain D_i of $f_i(\cdot)$; and

- conditional on the event that $D(i)$ outputs an element in the preimage set of y, none of the preimages of y has overwhelming probability of being output by $D(i)$.

Then the following holds: if $(\mathcal{P}, \mathcal{V})$ is a computationally witness-indistinguishable proof of knowledge for $f(\cdot)$, and $f(\cdot)$ is collision-intractable over (I, D), then $(\mathcal{P}, \mathcal{V})$ is non-trivially witness-hiding over (I, D).

To prove this result, suppose that $\widehat{\mathcal{V}}$ outputs a secret key corresponding to $\overline{\mathcal{P}}$'s public key, after having engaged in polynomially many protocol executions. Owing to the witness-indistinguishability property this key differs with non-negligible probability from the secret key used by $\overline{\mathcal{P}}$. Therefore, the algorithm $<\overline{\mathcal{P}}, \widehat{\mathcal{V}}>$ finds collisions for the function with non-negligible success probability.

Note that the key set-up and the process of generating the system parameters do not enter the definition of proofs of knowledge. Definition 2.4.1 simply assumes correct formation. When designing a system, care must be exercised as to which party controls algorithms I and D:

- The process of generating the system parameters must be controlled by the party or parties to whom improperly formed system parameters pose a security threat. For example, if $\mathcal{V}$ runs I then it may be able to embed trapdoor information so that it can feasibly compute a secret key corresponding to the public key of $\mathcal{P}$; whether this is a threat to the security of $\mathcal{P}$ depends on the application at hand. On the other hand, if $\mathcal{P}$ runs I, $\mathcal{P}$ may be able to determine system parameters for which it can find collisions. Again, whether or not this is a problem depends on the application at hand; for a situation in which $\mathcal{P}$ should not run I by itself, see Chapter 3.

  Any interests of $\mathcal{V}$ and $\mathcal{P}$ can be met by letting a trusted party run I. Using cryptographic multi-party computation techniques (see, for instance, Chaum, Crepeau, and Damgård [89] and Chaum, Damgård, and van de Graaf [106]), it is possible for $\mathcal{V}$ and $\mathcal{P}$ to create a "virtual" trusted party to run I. Although multi-party computation techniques are not practical in general, in all the constructions in this book they can be implemented in a practical manner. For instance, with the RSA-based constructions that we will present there is no need for the prover to prove that n is the product of two primes of equal size, and the proof that v is co-prime to $\varphi(n)$ is a by-product of the certificate issuing protocol. More generally, correct formation by one of $\mathcal{V}$ and $\mathcal{P}$ in our constructions can always be proved by providing an additional output evidencing that the process has taken as input a source of randomness substantially outside of its control.

- Normally the key set-up is performed by $\mathcal{P}$, to make sure that its secret key does not become known to $\mathcal{V}$. In some applications, $\mathcal{V}$ and $\mathcal{P}$ should jointly perform this process, by means of an interactive protocol. For example, Chapter 4 addresses the situation where the CA ensures that a part of the secret key generated for a receiver contains pre-approved attributes, while the receiver ensures that the CA cannot learn its entire secret key.

We now introduce practical proofs of knowledge for both the DLREP function and the RSAREP function. These will be central to our constructions of issuing and showing protocols in the next two chapters.

2.4.3 Proving knowledge of a DL-representation

Consider any instance generator for the DLREP function. $\mathcal{P}$'s public key is $h := \prod_{i=1}^{l} g_i^{x_i}$. In order to prove knowledge of a DL-representation of h with respect to $(g_1, \ldots, g_l)$, $\mathcal{P}$ and $\mathcal{V}$ perform the following protocol steps:

Step 1. $\mathcal{P}$ generates at random l numbers $w_1, \ldots, w_l \in \mathbb{Z}_q$. It then sends $a := \prod_{i=1}^{l} g_i^{w_i}$ to $\mathcal{V}$. The number a is called the *initial witness*.

Step 2. $\mathcal{P}$ computes l *responses*, responsive to a *challenge* $c \in \mathbb{Z}_s$ of $\mathcal{V}$, where $1 < s \leq q$, according to $r_i := cx_i + w_i \bmod q$, for $i = 1, \ldots, l$, and sends them to $\mathcal{V}$. (The role of s and the process of forming c will be discussed shortly.)

$\mathcal{V}$ accepts if and only if the verification relation $\prod_{i=1}^{l} g_i^{r_i} h^{-c} = a$ holds.

Note that both a and the left-hand side of the verification relation can be rapidly computed using simultaneous repeated squaring.

A variation is for $\mathcal{P}$ in Step 1 to send a one-way hash of a; $\mathcal{V}$ must then check whether this number is equal to the hash of $\prod_{i=1}^{l} g_i^{r_i} h^{-c}$. Also, if $\mathcal{V}$ knows $y_i := \log_g g_i$, for some generator g and all $i \in \{1, \ldots, l\}$, then the verification relation can be collapsed to

$$g^{\sum_{i=1}^{l} y_i r_i} h^{-c} = a.$$

We will not consider these variations any further.

The integer s in Step 2 must be known to both $\mathcal{P}$ and $\mathcal{V}$. It may be deterministically related to the system parameters (e.g., a predetermined rounded fraction of q, or q itself). Alternatively, it may be specified as part of the process of generating the system parameters or $\mathcal{P}$ may specify it when informing $\mathcal{V}$ of its public key.

The challenge c need not be generated at random, nor need it be generated by $\mathcal{V}$. Nevertheless, we will always refer to it as $\mathcal{V}$'s *challenge*, because it determines the security for $\mathcal{V}$.

The protocol description is *generic* in the sense that the binary size of s and the process of generating c have yet to be specified. Also, we have not yet stated any requirements for the instance generator.

Proposition 2.4.8. *($\mathcal{P}$, $\mathcal{V}$) is complete and perfectly witness-indistinguishable, regardless of the binary size of s and the process of generating $\mathcal{V}$'s challenge.*

Proof. Completeness follows from

$$
\prod_{i=1}^{l} g_i^{r_i} h^{-c} = \prod_{i=1}^{l} g_i^{cx_i + w_i} h^{-c}
$$
$$
= (\prod_{i=1}^{l} g_i^{x_i})^c (\prod_{i=1}^{l} g_i^{w_i}) h^{-c}
$$
$$
= h^c a h^{-c}
$$
$$
= a.
$$

To prove witness-indistinguishability, we will show that any view of $\widetilde{\mathcal{V}}$ could have resulted from any secret key of $\overline{\mathcal{P}}$, with equal probability. Suppose $\overline{\mathcal{P}}$ used secret key $(x_1^*, \ldots, x_l^*)$. In Step 1 it would have sent

$$
a^* := \prod_{i=1}^{l} g_i^{w_i^*}
$$

to $\mathcal{V}$, and in Step 3 it would have sent responses $r_i^* := cx_i^* + w_i^* \bmod q$, for $i \in \{1, \ldots, l\}$. From $r_i = r_i^* \bmod q$ it follows that $w_i^* = r_i - cx_i^* \bmod q$, for $i = 1, \ldots, l$, and since $\mathcal{P}$'s responses make $\widetilde{\mathcal{V}}$ accept it follows that

$$
a^* = \prod_{i=1}^{l} g_i^{w_i^*}
$$
$$
= \prod_{i=1}^{l} g_i^{r_i - cx_i^*}
$$
$$
= \prod_{i=1}^{l} g_i^{r_i} (\prod_{i=1}^{l} g_i^{x_i^*})^{-c}
$$
$$
= (h^c a) h^{-c}
$$
$$
= a.
$$

Since the w_i's are chosen at random from $\mathbb{Z}_q$, the view perfectly hides which secret key has been used, and the claimed result follows. □

Soundness and security for $\overline{\mathcal{P}}$ depend on the binary size of s and the process of generating c. Furthermore, for the property of witness-hiding we need to specify an instance generator. Assuming that c is chosen at random by $\mathcal{V}$, and becomes known to $\mathcal{P}$ only after $\mathcal{P}$ has chosen its initial witness a, the following security implications hold:

(**Large** s) If s is superpolynomial in k, then the protocol is a proof of knowledge as is; no repetitions are needed to achieve soundness. It is easy to prove that it is honest-verifier zero-knowledge: the simulator generates $r_1, \ldots, r_l$ and c at random, and computes $a := \prod_{i=1}^{l} g_i^{r_i} h^{-c}$. The following two cases describe conditions under which $(\mathcal{P}, \mathcal{V})$ is witness-hiding over $(I_{\text{DLREP}}, D_{\text{DLREP}})$:

- In case $\mathcal{V}$ in advance knows $(x_1, \ldots, x_{l-1})$ with overwhelming probability, but has no a priori information about x_l, the protocol is believed to be witness-hiding over $(I_{\text{DLREP}}, D_{\text{DLREP}})$. It is easy to prove that the case of arbitrary l is as secure as the special case $l = 1$, which is the Schnorr proof of knowledge [337]. In his generic string encoding model, Shoup [352] proved that an active attacker in the Schnorr proof of knowledge cannot learn enough information to be able to subsequently prove knowledge of $\mathcal{P}$'s secret key by itself. In other words, the Schnorr proof of knowledge is witness-hiding in the generic string encoding model, a result that can easily be adapted to the case of arbitrary l.

- In case $l \geq 2$ and $\mathcal{V}$ cannot identify $(x_1, \ldots, x_{l-1})$ in advance with overwhelming probability (i.e., $\mathcal{V}$ has *non-negligible uncertainty* about the tuple), it follows from Propositions 2.3.3, 2.4.7, and 2.4.8 that the protocol is provably (non-trivially) witness-hiding over $(I_{\text{DLREP}}, D_{\text{DLREP}})$.

In either case, the protocol can be made zero-knowledge by prepending a fourth move in which $\mathcal{V}$ commits to its challenge; the required strength of the commitment depends on whether or not $\mathcal{V}$ is polynomially bounded.[15] Alternatively, $\mathcal{P}$ and $\mathcal{V}$ determine $\mathcal{V}$'s challenge in a mutually random fashion.

(**Small** s) If s is polynomial in k, then the protocol steps must be repeated polynomially many times in order to result in a sound protocol. ($\mathcal{V}$ accepts if and only if it accepts in each iteration.) Two cases can be discerned:

- Sequential repetitions result in a zero-knowledge proof of knowledge.

- Parallel repetitions do not result in a zero-knowledge proof of knowledge. They are believed, however, to result in a proof of knowledge that is witness-hiding over $(I_{\text{DLREP}}, D_{\text{DLREP}})$. (This can be proved in case $l \geq 2$ and $\mathcal{V}$ initially has non-negligible uncertainty about $(x_1, \ldots, x_{l-1})$.) A zero-knowledge protocol can be obtained by prepending a fourth move in the manner described for the case of large s.

We will not consider the case of small s any further in this book, because the resulting protocols are significantly less efficient. In later chapters, we will often take $s := q$.

---

[15] As noted by Bellare (personal communication, January 8, 1999), the commitment may not be of the form $g_i^\alpha h^c$, for some $i \in \{1, \ldots, l\}$ and random $\alpha \in \mathbb{Z}_q$, since this would allow an attacker to always convince $\mathcal{V}$ without knowing a DL-representation of h. A commitment of the form $g_i^c h^\alpha$ should be fine, although it is unclear how to prove the soundness property.

The most practical way to obtain a protocol that is provably witness-hiding is to set $l = 2$, to generate x_2 at random from $\mathbb{Z}_q$, and to set x_1 equal to the outcome of a coin flip (not necessarily unbiased); the resulting three-move protocol (with large s) is an optimization of Okamoto's extension [288, page 36] of the Schnorr proof of knowledge. Taking $l > 2$ does not improve the provability of the witness-hiding property and only makes the protocol less efficient; for this reason the situation $l > 2$ has never been considered in the literature. In Chapter 3, however, we will see that there are legitimate reasons for resorting to $l > 2$.

The security results for $\overline{\mathcal{P}}$ hold only assuming that the system parameters are formed by running I_{DLREP}. Depending on the application at hand, both $\mathcal{P}$ and $\mathcal{V}$ may have security interests in seeing to it that the system parameters are formed in this manner. For example, if $\mathcal{P}$ is allowed to generate at least one g_i by itself, after $\mathcal{V}$ has formed the remaining ones, $\mathcal{P}$ can easily construct colliding secret keys. For our purposes in Chapter 3 it suffices that $\mathcal{V}$, or a party trusted by $\mathcal{V}$, runs I_{DLREP}. Additional outputs may be sent to $\mathcal{P}$ to prove that random or pseudorandom bits have been used in the process, and a proof of primality of q may be included.

Furthermore, depending on the application, it may be necessary for $\mathcal{P}$ and $\mathcal{V}$ to check membership in G_q of certain numbers:

- If $\mathcal{P}$ can get way with a public key h that is not a member of G_q, then a corresponding secret key does not exist, yet $\widehat{\mathcal{P}}$ may be able to make $\mathcal{V}$ accept with non-negligible probability. Burmester [67] pointed out for the Schnorr proof of knowledge that $\widehat{\mathcal{P}}$ can convince $\mathcal{V}$ with probability $1/2$ by multiplying in a non-trivial square root of unity; the same attack applies in the general case. This issue, which applies not only to the subgroup construction but also to the elliptic curve construction, will also play a role in Chapter 3.

  To circumvent the problem, $\mathcal{V}$ should check that $\mathcal{P}$'s public key h is a member of G_q. This one-time check can take place off-line, before the protocol takes place, and is especially practical in applications in which the same public key is used in many protocol executions. If G_q is a subgroup of a commutative group of order o, and q divides o but q^2 does not divide o, then the check $h^q = 1$ suffices to verify membership in G_q; see Herstein [210, Corollary on page 62]. It can also be shown that the check $h^q = 1$ suffices to prove membership in case G_q is not a subgroup of a cyclic group, provided the verifier accepts the protocol execution; cf. Verheul and Hoyle [382].

  In the digital certificate constructions in Chapters 4, 5, and 6, the problem does not play a role.

- Lim and Lee [252] showed that, in the subgroup construction for G_q, it may in general be dangerous for the prover to apply its secret key to base numbers supplied by the verifier without first checking that these are indeed members of G_q. Two ways around this are the following:

- The prover can check membership in G_q of each supplied base number a to which it is to apply its secret exponent.

- One can use a prime p such that $(p - 1)/2q$ contains only prime factors greater than q. This circumvents the need to perform real-time membership verifications.

In this book the issue is avoided altogether, because in our protocol constructions the prover never applies its secret key to base numbers supplied by the other party.

2.4.4 Proving knowledge of an RSA-representation

Consider any instance generator for the RSA function. $\mathcal{P}$'s public key is $h :=$ $\prod_{i=1}^{l} g_i^{x_i} x_{l+1}^{v}$. In order to prove knowledge of an RSA-representation of h with respect to $(g_1, \ldots, g_l, v)$, $\mathcal{P}$ and $\mathcal{V}$ perform the following protocol steps:

Step 1. $\mathcal{P}$ generates at random l numbers $w_1, \ldots, w_l \in \mathbb{Z}_v$ and a random number $w_{l+1} \in \mathbb{Z}_n^*$, and sends the initial witness $a := \prod_{i=1}^{l} g_i^{w_i} w_{l+1}^{v}$ to $\mathcal{V}$.

Step 2. $\mathcal{P}$ computes $l + 1$ responses, responsive to a challenge $c \in \mathbb{Z}_s$, where $1 < s \leq v$, as follows:

$$r_i := cx_i + w_i \bmod v \quad \forall i \in \{1, \ldots, l\},$$

$$r_{l+1} := \prod_{i=1}^{l} g_i^{(cx_i + w_i) \operatorname{div} v} x_{l+1}^{c} w_{l+1}$$

$\mathcal{P}$ then sends $r_1, \ldots, r_l, r_{l+1}$ to $\mathcal{V}$. (The role of s and the process of forming c will be discussed shortly.)

$\mathcal{V}$ accepts if and only if the verification relation

$$\prod_{i=1}^{l} g_i^{r_i} r_{l+1}^{v} h^{-c} = a$$

holds.

Note that a, r_{l+1} and the left-hand side of the verification relation can all be computed almost completely using simultaneous repeated squaring with a single precomputed table, since $(g_1, \ldots, g_l, h)$ are all fixed; only the v-th powers occurring in these expressions have to be multiplied separately into the products.

Proposition 2.4.9. *($\mathcal{P}$, $\mathcal{V}$) is complete and perfectly witness-indistinguishable, regardless of the binary size of s and the process of generating $\mathcal{V}$'s challenge.*

Soundness and security for $\overline{\mathcal{P}}$ depend on the binary size of s and the process of generating c. Furthermore, for the property of witness-hiding we need to specify an instance generator. In case c is chosen at random by $\mathcal{V}$, and becomes known to $\mathcal{P}$ only after it has chosen its initial witness a, we have similar security implications as described for the case of the DLREP function. We mention only the following two cases, both for s superpolynomial in k:

- In case $\mathcal{V}$ knows $(x_1, \ldots, x_l)$ with overwhelming probability, but does not know x_{l+1}, the protocol is believed to be witness-hiding over $(I_{\text{RSAREP}}, D_{\text{RSAREP}})$, even though this has yet to be proved. The special case $l = 0$ is the Guillou-Quisquater proof of knowledge [201, 202]. (Recall that v is a prime that is superpolynomial in k.)

- In case $l \geq 1$ and $\mathcal{V}$ initially has non-negligible uncertainty about $(x_1, \ldots, x_l)$, it follows from Propositions 2.3.5, 2.4.7, and 2.4.9 that the protocol is provably (non-trivially) witness-hiding over $(I_{\text{RSAREP}}, D_{\text{RSAREP}})$.

There is no point in using $s > v$: if $\widehat{\mathcal{P}}$ can respond to c then it can also respond to $c + jv$, for any integer j. In later chapters, we will frequently take $s := v$.

The most practical way to obtain a protocol that is provably witness-hiding is to set $l = 1$, to generate x_2 at random from $\mathbb{Z}_n^*$, and to set x_1 equal to the outcome of a coin flip (not necessarily unbiased); the resulting three-move protocol (with large s) is an optimization of Okamoto's extension [288, page 39] of the Guillou-Quisquater proof of knowledge. As in the case of the DLREP function, we will show in Chapter 3 that there are legitimate reasons for resorting to $l > 1$.

A four-move zero-knowledge proof of knowledge can be obtained by prepending a move in which $\mathcal{V}$ commits to c. One way to form the commitment is by encoding c into the hard-core bits of the commitment function of Håstad, Schrift, and Shamir [208]; another is to use the RSAREP function.

As in the case of the proof of knowledge for the DLREP function, the above security results hold only assuming that the system parameters are indeed formed by running I_{RSAREP}. Note that v need not be a prime or be co-prime to $\varphi(n)$ to make the protocol secure, assuming one is willing to restrict the set from which the g_i's and x_{l+1} and w_{l+1} are chosen.[16] In light of the goal that will be pursued in Chapter 3, though, we will only consider the choices for v and n made here.

---

[16]For example, the protocol is a witness-hiding proof of knowledge if n is a Blum integer, $v = 2$, the g_i's, x_{l+1}, and w_{l+1} are all quadratic residues, and the protocol moves are repeated polynomially many times. One can also consider a modification similar to that of Feige, Fiat, and Shamir [168], in which n is a Blum integer and $\mathcal{P}$ randomly multiplies ± 1 into r_{l+1} and a. Yet another choice is $v = 2^t$, for t such that v is superpolynomial in k; although the prover can convince the verifier with success probability $1/2^j$ if it knows an RSA-representation of the 2^j-th power of h for some j, the protocol can be proved secure against an active impersonator, relative to the factoring assumption (cf. Shoup [351] and Schnorr [338]).

2.5 Digital signatures

2.5.1 Definition

Informally, a digital signature is the electronic analogue of a handwritten signature. A digital signature on a message can be verified by anyone without the help of the signer, by applying the public key of the signer, but only the signer can compute signatures on valid messages, by applying its secret key. The following definition formalizes this.

Definition 2.5.1. *A digital signature scheme* consists of a function $\{f_i(\cdot)\}_{i \in V}$, an *invulnerable instance generator* (I, D), *two* message sets $\mathcal{M} = \{\mathcal{M}_i\}_{i \in V}$ and $\mathcal{M}^* = \{\mathcal{M}_i^*\}_{i \in V}$, a Boolean predicate $\text{pred}(\cdot)$ *that can be evaluated in polynomial time, and a protocol* $(\mathcal{P}, \mathcal{V})$ *performed by a pair of interactive polynomial-time algorithms.* $\mathcal{P}$ *is called the* signer, $\mathcal{V}$ *the* receiver, *and* $(\mathcal{P}, \mathcal{V})$ *the* (signature) *issuing protocol.* $(\mathcal{P}, \mathcal{V})$ *must satisfy the following two properties:*

- *(Signature generation) For all* $(i, x) \in V \times D_i$ *and for all* $m^* \in \mathcal{M}_i^*$, *if*

$$(m, \sigma) := \overline{\mathcal{V}}_{\overline{\mathcal{P}}_{(x)}}((i, f_i(x)), m^*)$$

  then $m \in \mathcal{M}_i$ *and* m *is a superstring[17] of* m^*, *and the probability function defined by*

$$\mathsf{P}_k\Big(\text{pred}(i, f_i(x), m, \sigma) = 1\Big)$$

  is overwhelming in k.

  The pair (m, σ) *is called a* signed message, *and* σ *is* $\mathcal{P}$*'s* digital signature *on* m.

- *(Unforgeability) For any* $t \geq 0$, *the following holds. The probability (taken over* (I, D) *and the coin flips of* $\widehat{\mathcal{V}}$ *and* $\overline{\mathcal{P}}$*) that* $\widehat{\mathcal{V}}$, *after having engaged in up to* t *protocol executions with* $\overline{\mathcal{P}}$, *outputs at least* $t + 1$ *distinct signed messages (with messages in* $\mathcal{M}$*) is negligible in* k.

  The digital signature scheme is said to be unforgeable *over* (I, D).

Whenever the instance generator is clear from the description of the signature scheme, we will simply say that the signature scheme is unforgeable.

Note that the capability to obtain two different signatures on the same message by engaging in a single execution of the protocol with the signer is not considered to

---

[17]That is, the binary string m^* can be obtained by pruning bits from the binary string m. For instance, any m is a superstring of the null string. Further examples are described shortly. Definition 2.5.1 could be generalized by considering messages m that have other relations to m^* (e.g., m is a preimage under a one-way function of m^*), but this is outside of the scope of the book.

fall under the scope of forgery. This convention is arbitrary, and adopted here merely for concreteness.

Definition 2.5.1 is based on the standard definition of Goldwasser, Micali, and Rivest [194], but differs in a few respects. The standard definition is not suitable to describe blind signature schemes and other schemes with interactive issuing protocols, including those that we will design in Chapter 4. Also, it includes the processes of generating the system parameters and the key set-up, but not a notion of security for the signer; this is opposite to the way the definition of proofs of knowledge is structured, and does not reflect the common basis of both notions. The definition given here is adequate for our purposes.[18]

The role of the auxiliary common input m^* in Definition 2.5.1 differs depending on the type of signature scheme:

- In the most widely considered digital signatures in the cryptographic literature, the signature issuing protocol is non-interactive, $\mathcal{M}$ equals $\mathcal{M}^*$, and m^* is equal to the message m. In this case, the unforgeability property implies that the receiver cannot obtain a signature on a message that the signer has not seen and knowingly signed.

- In the case of blind signatures (see Chaum [91, 92, 93, 94, 95, 96, 99, 100]), m^* is always the empty string and m is generated at random by $\mathcal{V}$. Specifically, a blind digital signature scheme is a digital signature scheme with the additional property that the signed message (m, σ) obtained by $\overline{\mathcal{V}}$ by interacting with $\widehat{\mathcal{P}}$ is statistically independent of $\widehat{\mathcal{P}}$'s view in the protocol execution. (Weaker flavors are possible. The weakest flavor is that in which $\widehat{\mathcal{P}}$ cannot correlate signed messages to its views of protocol executions.)

- In Section 4.2 we will construct issuing protocols in which the message m is chopped up into polynomially many message blocks, $x_1, \ldots, x_l, \alpha$. In this case, m^* equals the concatenation of $x_1, \ldots, x_l$; the remaining message block, α, is generated secretly at random by $\mathcal{V}$.

As with the witness-hiding and zero-knowledge properties for proofs of knowledge, the unforgeability property for digital signatures depends on a number of factors that have been described in Section 2.1.4. Specifically, the resistance of a digital signature scheme to forgery is influenced by the maximum number of protocol executions in which $\widehat{\mathcal{V}}$ can engage and by the degree to which the protocol executions can be interleaved. In addition, unforgeability depends on how, when, and by which party the message m^* is formed.

---

[18] A variation of Definition 2.5.1 is to move the unforgeability property outside of the definition (just like witness-hiding is not a part of the definition of a proof of knowledge), and instead to complement the "completeness" property (signature generation) by a "weak soundness" property that states that $(\mathcal{P}, \overline{\mathcal{V}})$ results in a signed message with probability 1 only if $\mathcal{P}$ knows a secret key corresponding to its public key $f_i(x)$. This introduces the problem of defining what it means for a non-interactive algorithm to "know" information.

An attack can proceed in several manners. In a successful *key-only attack* or *forgery from scratch*, $\widehat{\mathcal{V}}$ is able to forge signed messages without being given the opportunity to interact with $\overline{\mathcal{P}}$. At the other end of the spectrum is the *adaptively chosen message attack*, in which $\widehat{\mathcal{V}}$ has the freedom to choose all its contributions (e.g., messages, blinding factors, challenges) to each execution of the issuing protocol with $\overline{\mathcal{P}}$ in a manner that may depend on its aggregate view in all the protocol executions up to that point; $\widehat{\mathcal{V}}$ can use $\overline{\mathcal{P}}$ as an oracle, and is limited only by the level of interleaving of protocol executions that $\mathcal{P}$ allows.

A successful forgery may be due to a leakage of $\mathcal{P}$'s secret key x; in this case $\widehat{\mathcal{V}}$ is able to forge $\mathcal{P}$'s signature on any message. Such a *total break* can be prevented by using a signature issuing protocol that is non-trivially witness-hiding. $\widehat{\mathcal{V}}$ need not necessarily know $\mathcal{P}$'s secret key, however, to be able to forge a signed message. For instance, once $\widehat{\mathcal{V}}$ has obtained a number of signed messages it may be able to algebraically combine these in such a manner that an additional signed message results. In general, we will need to protect against *existential forgery*; in this case $\widehat{\mathcal{V}}$ is able to forge one signed message, for a message not necessarily of its own choice or under its control. The unforgeability property of digital signatures states that existential forgery is infeasible, even under an adaptively chosen message attack.

2.5.2 From proofs of knowledge to digital signature schemes

We now describe a general construction for converting a proof of knowledge into a digital signature scheme. Consider hereto a proof of knowledge for a one-way function $f(\cdot)$ that has the following structure:

Step 1. $\mathcal{P}$ generates a randomly distributed initial witness a. It sends a, which may in general be a vector of numbers, to $\mathcal{V}$.

Step 2. $\mathcal{V}$ generates a substantially random challenge, $c \in \mathbb{Z}_s$, with s superpolynomial in the security parameter k. It sends the challenge, which may represent a concatenation of several challenge numbers, to $\mathcal{P}$.

Step 3. $\mathcal{P}$ computes a response, r, as the outcome of a function of its secret key, the challenge and the coin flips used to construct a. It sends the response, which may in general be a vector of numbers, to $\mathcal{V}$.

$\mathcal{V}$ applies a Boolean polynomial-time computable predicate $\mathrm{pred}(\cdot)$ to the system parameters, $\mathcal{P}$'s public key, $\mathcal{P}$'s initial witness, its own challenge, and $\mathcal{P}$'s response, and accepts if and only if the outcome of the predicate is 1.

We refer to proofs of knowledge of this structure as *Fiat-Shamir type* proofs of knowledge, because the following technique for converting them into digital signature schemes was first proposed (for a particular instance) by Fiat and Shamir [171]. Note that the proofs of knowledge described in Section 2.4 are of this type.

The conversion into a digital signature scheme is brought about by replacing the role of $\mathcal{V}$ by a "virtual" verifier. This is accomplished by computing $\mathcal{V}$'s challenge according to $c := \mathcal{H}_i(m, a)$, where $m \in \mathcal{M}_i$ is any message and $\mathcal{H}(\cdot)$ is a sufficiently strong (see page 84 for details) one-way hash function that must be specified together with the system parameters or the public key of $\mathcal{P}$. The signature on m is defined to be $\sigma := (a, r)$, and anyone can verify it by computing c and applying $\text{pred}(\cdot)$. Because the digital signature on m is obtained by means of an issuing protocol that is derived from a proof of knowledge, it is also called a *signed proof*.

As a general rule, from a security perspective it is recommended to hash along all the information that $\mathcal{V}$ needs to check anyway to verify the signed proof, including the public key, algorithm identifiers, and purpose specifiers. (They may all be assumed to be part of the message, m.)

Note that the properties of witness-indistinguishable and witness-hiding are preserved under the conversion.

In case m is known to $\mathcal{P}$ at the start of the protocol, for instance because $\mathcal{M}$ is the empty set or $\mathcal{V}$ provides m before learning a, $\mathcal{P}$ can compute $c := \mathcal{H}_i(m, a)$ by itself, and the issuing protocol can be non-interactive; $\mathcal{P}$ simply sends (a, r) to $\mathcal{V}$. It is conjectured that the non-interactive signature scheme is unforgeable if the signature issuing protocol is witness-hiding. Modeling $\mathcal{H}(\cdot)$ as a random oracle, Pointcheval and Stern [307] proved the following unforgeability result.

Proposition 2.5.2. *Suppose that the binary sizes of the outputs of $f_i(\cdot)$ and $\mathcal{H}_i(\cdot)$ are linear[19] in k and let (I, D) be an invulnerable instance generator for $f(\cdot)$. If a Fiat-Shamir type proof of knowledge for $f(\cdot)$ is honest-verifier zero-knowledge, then its conversion to a non-interactive signature scheme is unforgeable over (I, D) in the random oracle model.*

This result holds even under an adaptively chosen message attack whereby the signer engages in polynomially many protocol executions that are arbitrarily interleaved.

In case $\mathcal{V}$ wants to hide (at least) the message m from $\mathcal{P}$, it must supply c itself. In this case the protocol remains interactive and the conditions of Proposition 2.5.2 are insufficient to prove unforgeability in the random oracle model. By generalizing a result due to Pointcheval [305], which is an optimization of a result of Pointcheval and Stern [306], it is possible to prove the following result.

Proposition 2.5.3. *Suppose that the binary sizes of the outputs of $f_i(\cdot)$ and $\mathcal{H}_i(\cdot)$ are linear in k. Let (I, D) be such that the condition in Proposition 2.4.7 holds, and suppose that $f(\cdot)$ is collision-intractable over (I, D). If a Fiat-Shamir type proof of knowledge for $f(\cdot)$ is computationally witness-indistinguishable and the prover performs no more than polylogarithmically[20] many protocol executions, then its con-*

---

[19]In fact, we merely need that $2^{-|\mathcal{H}_i(\cdot)|}$ is negligible in k.

[20]A function $f(\cdot)$ is polylogarithmic in k if there exists a positive integer c such that $f(k) \leq (\log k)^c$ for all sufficiently large k.

version to an interactive signature scheme is unforgeable over (I, D) in the random oracle model.

This result holds under an adaptively chosen message attack, and the protocol executions may be arbitrarily interleaved.

If it were only for the ability of $\mathcal{V}$ to hide m from $\mathcal{P}$, the interactive variant of the signature scheme would hardly be interesting. Okamoto and Ohta [289] showed that it is possible for $\mathcal{V}$, in interactive signature schemes derived from witness-hiding Fiat-Shamir type proofs of knowledge, to perfectly blind the issuing protocol, provided that certain properties hold. These properties, collectively referred to as *commutative random self-reducibility*, apply to virtually all practical Fiat-Shamir type proofs of knowledge proposed to date, including those described in Section 2.4. In case the condition in Proposition 2.5.3 holds, we obtain blind signature schemes that are provably secure in the random oracle model. However, as explained in Section 1.2.2, Chaum's blinding techniques are unsuitable for our purposes.

We now show how to construct practical digital signature schemes from our proofs of knowledge for the DLREP function and the RSAREP function.

2.5.3 Digital signatures based on the DLREP function

In Section 2.4.3 we investigated two variations for proving knowledge of a DL-representation: one in which s is small and the protocol steps are repeated in parallel polynomially many times, and the other in which no repetitions are needed because s is superpolynomial in k. Both protocols are readily seen to be Fiat-Shamir type proofs of knowledge, and can be converted into a digital signature scheme by applying the described technique. As mentioned in Section 2.4.3 we will not consider the case of small s, for reason of practicality. Consider now the case of large s. Let $\mathcal{H}(\cdot)$ be a one-way hash function, defined by

$$\mathcal{H}_{q,g_l}(\cdot) : \mathcal{M}_{q,g_l} \times G_q \mapsto \mathbb{Z}_s.$$

A description of $\mathcal{H}_{q,g_l}(\cdot)$ must be specified together with the system parameters or $\mathcal{P}$'s public key. The definition of $\mathcal{H}_i(\cdot)$ and $\mathcal{M}_i$ may also depend on $(g_1, \ldots, g_{l-1})$, $\mathcal{P}$'s public key, and any other information that is specified before protocol executions take place; for notational reasons we do not make this explicit in the notation. In practice the outputs of $\mathcal{H}_{q,g_l}(\cdot)$ will usually be t-bit strings, for some t with 2^t (possibly much) smaller than s.

$\mathcal{P}$'s digital signature on a message m is a vector $(a, r_1, \ldots, r_l)$ such that the relation

$$\prod_{i=1}^{l} g_i^{r_i} h^{-\mathcal{H}_{q,g_l}(m,a)} = a$$

holds. Alternatively, one can define the signature to be $(c, r_1, \ldots, r_l)$, and the signature verification relation is

$$c = \mathcal{H}_{q,g_l}\left(m, \prod_{i=1}^{l} g_i^{r_i} h^{-c}\right).$$

Since a signature of either one type is readily computed from one of the other type, the security for $\overline{\mathcal{P}}$ is not affected. Differences exist in terms of efficiency, though:

- Using $(c, r_1, \ldots, r_l)$ is favorable in case the subgroup construction is used to construct G_q, because the storage complexity of c is smaller than that of a. In particular, using the parameter sizes recommended in Section 2.2.2, many hundreds of bits are saved.

- Using $(a, r_1, \ldots, r_l)$ may be preferable when $t > 1$ digital signatures need to be verified. With $(a_i, r_{1i}, \ldots, r_{li})$ denoting $\mathcal{P}$'s digital signature on message m_i, for all $i \in \{1, \ldots, t\}$, $\mathcal{V}$ sets $\alpha_1 := 1$ and generates $\alpha_2, \ldots, \alpha_t$ at random from a set $V \subseteq \mathbb{Z}_q$. $\mathcal{V}$ then computes

$$c_i := \mathcal{H}_{q,g_l}(m_i, a_i) \quad \forall i \in \{1, \ldots, t\},$$

and verifies the compound verification relation

$$\prod_{i=1}^{l} g_i^{\sum_{j=1}^{t} \alpha_j r_{ij}} h^{-\sum_{i=1}^{t} \alpha_i c_i} = \prod_{i=1}^{t} a_i^{\alpha_i}.$$

It is easy to prove that if the compound verification relation holds, then the probability that all t signatures are valid is at least $1 - 1/|V|$. Since the left-hand side of the compound verification relation can be rapidly computed using simultaneous repeated squaring with a single precomputed table, this *batch-verification technique* is a substantial improvement over verifying all t digital signatures separately.[21]

The security of the digital signature scheme depends on which party specifies c:

(**Non-interactive issuing protocol**) Proposition 2.5.2 can be applied, since the proof of knowledge is honest-verifier zero-knowledge.

Proposition 2.5.4. *If (I_{DL}, D_{DL}) is invulnerable, and the binary size of outputs of $\mathcal{H}_i(\cdot)$ is linear in k, then non-interactively issued signed proofs are provably unforgeable over (I_{DLREP}, D_{DLREP}) in the random oracle model, for any distribution of $(x_1, \ldots, x_{l-1})$.*

---

[21] For large t it is more efficient to randomly partition the t verification relations into a suitable number of "buckets," and apply batch-verification to each bucket. Cf. Bellare, Garay, and Rabin [21].

We stress that this result holds even in case $(x_1, \ldots, x_{l-1})$ is known in advance to $\mathcal{V}$ with overwhelming probability, if only x_l is a random secret.

The special case $l = 1$ is the Schnorr signature scheme [337]. Note that $\mathcal{P}$ in the non-interactive issuing protocol need not transmit a to $\mathcal{V}$; it can be recovered from c and $\mathcal{P}$'s responses.

(Interactive issuing protocol) By applying Proposition 2.5.3 we obtain the following result.

Proposition 2.5.5. *Let $l \geq 2$ and suppose that $\mathcal{V}$ initially has non-negligible uncertainty about $(x_1, \ldots, x_{l-1})$. If the DL function used to implement the DLREP function is one-way, the binary size of outputs of $\mathcal{H}_i(\cdot)$ is linear in k, and $\mathcal{P}$ does not perform more than polylogarithmically many executions of the issuing protocol, then interactively issued signed proofs are provably unforgeable over $(I_{\mathrm{DLREP}}, D_{\mathrm{DLREP}})$ in the random oracle model, for any distribution of $(x_1, \ldots, x_{l-1})$.*

On the basis of this result[22] We make the following assumption, which will be needed in Chapter 4.

Assumption 2.5.6. *There exists a hash function $\mathcal{H}^*(\cdot)$ and a message set $\mathcal{M} = \{\mathcal{M}_i\}_{i \in \{q, g_l\}}$ with $\mathcal{M}_{q, g_l} \supseteq G_q$ such that interactively issued signed proofs are unforgeable over $(I_{\mathrm{DLREP}}, D_{\mathrm{DLREP}})$.*

It is easy to prove that this assumption holds for all $l \geq 1$ if it holds for $l = 1$, for the same choice of hash function.

In accordance with the blinding technique of Okamoto and Ohta [289], $\mathcal{V}$ can blind the issuing protocol by performing the following action after Step 1 of the proof of knowledge. It generates $l + 1$ random numbers, $\alpha_0, \ldots, \alpha_l \in \mathbb{Z}_q$, and computes $a' := ah^{\alpha_0} \prod_{i=1}^l g_i^{\alpha_i}$, $c' := \mathcal{H}_{q, g_l}(m, a')$, and $c := c' + \alpha_0 \bmod q$. It then sends its challenge c to $\mathcal{P}$. Upon receiving $\mathcal{P}$'s responses, $r_1, \ldots, r_l$, $\mathcal{V}$ computes $r_i' := r_i + \alpha_i \bmod q$, for all $i \in \{1, \ldots, l\}$. It is easy to verify that $(a', r_1', \ldots, r_l')$, or $(c', r_1', \ldots, r_l')$ for that matter, is $\overline{\mathcal{P}}$'s digital signature on m. Moreover, if $\mathcal{V}$ chooses m at random and accepts then the signed message is statistically independent of $\widetilde{\mathcal{P}}$'s view in the protocol execution. However, there are no practical advantages in using this scheme over Chaum's RSA-based blind signature scheme [91, 92] (with small v), unless one trusts an elliptic curve implementation with short system parameters. Furthermore, as

---

[22]In their "random oracle + generic" security model, Schnorr and Jakobsson [339] prove a sharp security bound for the unforgeability of interactively issued Schnorr signatures, assuming sequential protocol executions. They also showed that parallel attacks that beat the success rate of sequential attacks must solve the problem of finding an intersection point of a subset of randomized hyperplanes. Proposition 2.5.5 can be proved for all $l \geq 1$ under the same assumption in a similar manner.

explained in Section 1.2.2, Chaum's blinding paradigm is unsuitable for our purposes. In Chapter 3 we will introduce more intricate blinding techniques that result in all sorts of previously unattainable results.

In practice, one-wayness of $\mathcal{H}(\cdot)$ is not enough for unforgeability over $(I_{\mathrm{DLREP}}, D_{\mathrm{DLREP}})$. Existential forgery of non-interactively issued Schnorr signatures, for instance, is feasible in case two messages m_1, m_2 exist such that, for random $(a_1, a_2) \in G_q \times G_q$, it is feasible to compute with non-negligible success probability a third message m and two integers α, β such that the following correlation holds:

$$\alpha \mathcal{H}_{q,g_l}(m_1, a_1) + \beta \mathcal{H}_{q,g_l}(m_2, a_2) = \mathcal{H}_{q,g_l}(m, a_1^\alpha a_2^\beta) \bmod q.$$

In the interactive case, $\mathcal{H}(\cdot)$ must be even stronger. To guarantee unforgeability in practice, $\mathcal{H}(\cdot)$ must be *correlation-intractable*, meaning that it is infeasible to compute correlations like the one displayed. (Note that functions with superpolynomial range are always correlation-intractable when idealized in the random oracle model.) Because it is unclear how to formalize the notion of correlation-intractability in a useful way, we will from now on always speak of a *sufficiently strong* one-way function whenever we need a correlation-intractable function. In practice, hash functions such as SHA-I or RIPEMD-160 should suffice.[23]

Schnorr [337] suggests for his signature scheme that a one-way hash function with 10-byte outputs should suffice for long-term practical security. There seems to be no reason not to allow this choice for arbitrary l in the non-interactive case. In the interactive case this should hold as well, assuming that $\mathcal{P}$ does not respond to $\mathcal{V}$'s challenge in case the delay between sending the initial witness and receiving the challenge exceeds a short time bound. To be on the safe side, it is strongly recommended to always use a sufficiently strong collision-intractable hash function with at least 20-byte outputs. This choice is also preferred in light of the more intricate signed proofs that will be described in Chapter 3.

2.5.4 Digital signatures based on the RSAREP function

Consider the case of s superpolynomial in k in the proof of knowledge in Section 2.4.4, for a prime v superpolynomial in k and co-prime to $\varphi(n)$. Let $\mathcal{H}(\cdot)$ be a one-way hash function, defined by

$$\mathcal{H}_{n,v}(\cdot) : \mathcal{M}_{n,v} \times \mathbb{Z}_n^* \mapsto \mathbb{Z}_s.$$

The definition of $\mathcal{H}_i(\cdot)$ and $\mathcal{M}_i$ may also depend on $(g_1, \ldots, g_l)$, $\mathcal{P}$'s public key, and any other information that is specified before protocol executions take place.

---

[23]Note that these are not infinite collections of functions: they act on messages of any size, but their outputs are of fixed size.

$\mathcal{P}$'s digital signature on a message m is a vector $(a, r_1, \ldots, r_{l+1})$ such that the verification relation

$$\prod_{i=1}^{l} g_i^{r_i} r_{l+1}^v h^{-\mathcal{H}_{n,v}(m,a)} = a$$

holds. This form lends itself to batch-verification. Alternatively, and more compactly, one can define the signature to be $(c, r_1, \ldots, r_{l+1})$, and the corresponding signature verification relation is

$$c = \mathcal{H}_{n,v}(m, \prod_{i=1}^{l} g_i^{r_i} r_{l+1}^v h^{-c}).$$

Again, this does not affect the security for $\overline{\mathcal{P}}$.

As with the DLREP function, we distinguish two cases:

(Non-interactive issuing protocol) Proposition 2.5.2 can be applied, since the proof of knowledge is honest-verifier zero-knowledge.

Proposition 2.5.7. *If $(I_{\text{RSA}}, D_{\text{RSA}})$ is invulnerable, and the binary size of outputs of $\mathcal{H}_i(\cdot)$ is linear in k, then non-interactively issued signed proofs are provably unforgeable over $(I_{\text{RSAREP}}, D_{\text{RSAREP}})$ in the random oracle model, for any distribution of $(x_1, \ldots, x_l)$.*

The special case $l = 1$ is the Guillou-Quisquater signature scheme [201, 202].[24]

(Interactive issuing protocol) Proposition 2.5.3 can be invoked to prove the following result.

Proposition 2.5.8. *Let $l \geq 1$ and suppose that $\mathcal{V}$ initially has non-negligible uncertainty about $(x_1, \ldots, x_l)$. If the RSA function used to implement the RSAREP function is one-way, the binary size of outputs of $\mathcal{H}_i(\cdot)$ is linear in k, and $\mathcal{P}$ does not perform more than polylogarithmically many executions of the issuing protocol, then interactively issued signed proofs are provably unforgeable over $(I_{\text{RSAREP}}, D_{\text{RSAREP}})$ in the random oracle model, for any distribution of $(x_1, \ldots, x_l)$.*

Based on this result, we make the following assumption.

Assumption 2.5.9. *There exists a hash function $\mathcal{H}^*(\cdot)$ and a message set $\mathcal{M} = \{\mathcal{M}_i\}_{i \in \{n,v\}}$ with $\mathcal{M}_{n,v} \supseteq \mathbb{Z}_n^*$ such that interactively issued signed proofs are unforgeable over $(I_{\text{RSAREP}}, D_{\text{RSAREP}})$.*

---

[24]Four years earlier, Shamir [346] described essentially the same signature scheme, with the irrelevant difference that $\mathcal{V}$'s hashed challenge appears as the exponent of a instead of h. This scheme also pre-dates the paper of Fiat and Shamir [171] to which the conversion technique in Section 2.5.2 is generally attributed.

It is easy to prove that the assumption holds for all $l \geq 0$ if it holds for $l = 0$, for the same choice of hash function.

$\mathcal{V}$ can blind the issuing protocol, in accordance with the technique of Okamoto and Ohta [289], by performing the following action after Step 1 of the proof of knowledge. It generates $l + 1$ random numbers, $\alpha_0, \ldots, \alpha_l \in \mathbb{Z}_v$ and a random number $\alpha_{l+1} \in \mathbb{Z}_n^*$, and computes $a' := ah^{\alpha_0} \prod_{i=1}^{l} g_i^{\alpha_i} \alpha_{l+1}^v$, $c' := \mathcal{H}_{n,v}(m, a')$, and $c := c' + \alpha_0 \bmod v$. It then sends its challenge, c, to $\mathcal{P}$. Upon receiving $\mathcal{P}$'s responses, $r_1, \ldots, r_{l+1}$, $\mathcal{V}$ computes $r_i' := r_i + \alpha_i \bmod v$, for all $i \in \{1, \ldots, l\}$, and $r_{l+1}' := r_{l+1} \prod_{i=1}^{l} g_i^{(r_i + \alpha_i) \operatorname{div} v} \alpha_{l+1}$. It is easy to verify that $(a', r_1', \ldots, r_{l+1}')$, or $(c', r_1', \ldots, r_{l+1}')$ for that matter, is $\widetilde{\mathcal{P}}$'s digital signature on m. Moreover, if $\widetilde{\mathcal{V}}$ generates m at random and accepts then the signed message is statistically independent of $\widetilde{\mathcal{P}}$'s view in the protocol execution. However, there is no practical advantage over Chaum's blind signature scheme [91, 92], which is much more efficient because small v may be taken. Furthermore, as explained in Section 1.2.2, Chaum's blinding paradigm is unsuitable for our purposes. In Chapter 3 we will introduce more intricate blinding techniques that offer all sorts of benefits.

In practice, $\mathcal{H}(\cdot)$ must be a sufficiently strong one-way hash function. Similar considerations as in the case of the DLREP function apply to the binary size of the outputs of $\mathcal{H}(\cdot)$. Although in the interactive issuing protocol 10-byte outputs should be sufficiently secure when used in combination with a time-out, it is recommended to always use a sufficiently strong collision-intractable hash function with at least 20-byte outputs. In particular, this will be necessary in Chapter 3.

2.6   Digital certificates

2.6.1   Definition of public-key certificates

Finally, we get to a formal definition of digital certificates. We start with the traditional definition, which is a special case of the definition of digital signatures.

Definition 2.6.1. *A* public-key certificate scheme *is a digital signature scheme with the extra property that the message m specifies at least a public key p of $\overline{\mathcal{V}}$, for which $\overline{\mathcal{V}}$ knows a corresponding secret key, s.*

The pair (p, σ) is called a certified public key, *σ is $\mathcal{P}$'s digital certificate on m, and the triple (s, p, σ) is called a* certified key pair. *$\mathcal{P}$ is also referred to as the* Certificate Authority *(CA).*

$\overline{\mathcal{V}}$'s key pair may be generated either before or during the protocol execution.

In the case of conventional identity certificates (see Section 1.1.2), the message m is the concatenation of p and at least a key holder identifier. In the case of attribute certificates other attributes are concatenated, either along with the identifier or instead of the identifier.

As mentioned already in Section 1.3.1, our use of the term "digital certificate" differs from the mainstream use of the term, which considers a certificate to be the data structure comprised of the CA's signature, the public key it certifies, and any information assigned to that public key. Our convention makes it easier to distinguish between various cryptographic objects.

The definition of the key pair (s, p) for $\mathcal{V}$ may be the same as that of the key pair $(x, f_i(x))$ for $\mathcal{P}$, but need not; it may even be completely unrelated. Likewise, completely different instance generators may be used.

2.6.2 Definition of secret-key certificates

We now introduce a new kind of certificates that differ from public-key certificates in that anyone can generate certified public keys without the assistance of $\mathcal{P}$, but certified key pairs remain unforgeable. The formal definition is as follows.

Definition 2.6.2. *A* secret-key certificate scheme *is a digital signature scheme with the additional property that there exists another Boolean predicate,* $\mathsf{pred}^*(\cdot)$, *that can also be evaluated in polynomial time, such that:*

- *The message* m, *on which* $\overline{\mathcal{V}}$ *obtains a signature* σ *in an execution of the issuing protocol with* $\overline{\mathcal{P}}$, *is a secret key of* $\mathcal{V}$. *This secret key corresponds to a public key* p *of* $\mathcal{V}$ *such that*
$$\mathsf{pred}^*(i, f_i(x), p, \sigma) = 1.$$

- *There exists an expected polynomial-time algorithm* S, *called a* certificate simulator, *that, on input* $(i, f_i(x))$, *outputs a pair* (p^*, σ^*) *with a probability distribution that is indistinguishable from the probability distribution of* (p, σ).

As in the definition of a public-key certificate, σ *is called* $\mathcal{P}$'s digital certificate *on* $\mathcal{V}$'s public key, *the pair* (p, σ) *is called a* certified public key, *and the triple* (m, p, σ) *is called a* certified key pair.

The output distribution of the certificate simulator may be computationally, statistically, or perfectly indistinguishable.

Example 2.6.3. $\mathcal{P}$ *runs* I_{RSA} *to obtain a pair* (n, v) *together with the factorization of* n, *which serves as its secret key. This enables* $\mathcal{P}$ *to compute RSA digital signatures [325]. Its RSA signature on a message* m *is* $\sigma := f_{n,v}(m)^{1/v} \bmod n$, *where* $f(\cdot)$ *is a sufficiently strong one-way function.*

This signature scheme can be converted into a secret-key certificate scheme by viewing the pair $(m, f_{n,v}(m))$ *as a key pair for* $\mathcal{V}$. *If we take* $f(\cdot)$ *to be the DL function implemented using the subgroup construction (i.e.,* $f_{n,v}(m) = g^m \bmod p$, *for some prime p that is not much smaller than n), then it is easy to build a certificate simulator with indistinguishable outputs. The simulator picks a random $b \in \mathbb{Z}_n^*$ and checks whether $b^v \bmod n$ is an element of G_q; it repeats this experiment until successful, and then outputs the pair $(b^v \bmod n, b)$.*

How can a secret-key certificate be verified? In applications of practical interest, $\mathcal{V}$ will use its public key p in a subsequent showing protocol without disclosing the secret key m, and so certified public keys cannot be verified by applying $\mathsf{pred}(\cdot)$. Also, applying $\mathsf{pred}^*(\cdot)$ to (p, σ) does not prove that the certified public key has been issued by $\mathcal{P}$, in view of the simulation property. Instead, verification of $\mathcal{V}$'s certified public key takes place indirectly. Namely, the ability of $\mathcal{V}$ to perform a "cryptographic action" with respect to its public key attests to the fact that $\mathcal{V}$ knows a secret key corresponding to its public key, and this in turn convinces that the certificate has been issued by $\mathcal{P}$. Since there is no point in using public-key certificates without performing some cryptographic action that attests to the possession of a corresponding secret key, secret-key certificates offer the same basic functionality as do public-key certificates.[25] The following two cryptographic actions in the showing protocol will be of particular interest to us:

1. $\mathcal{V}$ performs a zero-knowledge proof of knowledge of a secret key corresponding to its public key. If $\mathcal{V}$ can successfully perform the proof, then the verifier is convinced not only that $\mathcal{V}$ knows a secret key corresponding to the public key, by virtue of the soundness property, but also that the certificate has been issued by $\mathcal{P}$. However, the transcript of the protocol execution does not convince anyone else of either one of these facts; the entire protocol execution is zero-knowledge. (This is an advantage over public-key certificates, for which the showing protocol is zero-knowledge in its entirety only when $\mathcal{V}$ proves possession of a certificate by means of a zero-knowledge proof as well.)

   In Example 2.6.3, $\mathcal{V}$ can prove knowledge of the secret key corresponding to its public key g^m by using the Schnorr proof of knowledge or its 4-move zero-knowledge variant.

2. $\mathcal{V}$ digitally signs a message. Given the message, the digital signature of $\mathcal{V}$, and the certified public key of $\mathcal{V}$, anyone is able to verify not only that the digital signature is genuine, but also that it was indeed made with respect to a public key certified by $\mathcal{P}$.

   In Example 2.6.3, $\mathcal{V}$ can sign a message using the Schnorr signature scheme; in the random oracle model, these signatures can be issued only by a party that knows the secret key.

---

[25]This idea is reminiscent of Shamir's [346] *self-certified* public keys, the goal of which is to avoid the need for an explicit certificate. Hereto the CA forms the public key of each applicant as a redundant message that encodes the applicant's identity, and issues a corresponding secret key to the applicant; key pairs should be unforgeable.

Note that a third cryptographic action can be performed: decrypting a message that has been encrypted with $\mathcal{V}$'s public key. In Example 2.6.3, $\mathcal{V}$ can decrypt messages that have been encrypted under its public key g^m by means of, for instance, the ElGamal encryption scheme [146] in G_q. Since decryption requires knowledge of the secret key, the party that encrypted the message is ensured that either $\mathcal{V}$'s public key has been certified by $\mathcal{P}$ or $\widetilde{\mathcal{V}}$ cannot decrypt. In the remainder of this book we will not be interested in the case of encryption; public keys for (hybrid) session encryption can always be formed at random at the start of an authenticated session.

2.6.3 Comparison

Secret-key certificates have several advantages over public-key certificates:

- They appear to be much better suited to design certificate issuing protocols with the following property: $\mathcal{V}$ is able to blind the certified public key but not a non-trivial part of its secret key. See Chapter 4 for details.

- A certified public key does not serve as signed evidence that its holder has been issued a certificate by the CA. This property is preserved if certified key pairs are used only to perform zero-knowledge proofs.

- The ability to simulate certified public keys enables individuals to hide in which of several PKIs they are participating. See Section 5.2 for details.

- Knowledge of certified public keys (obtained from repositories or otherwise) cannot help in attacking the certificate scheme of the CA.

On the other hand, care has to be taken when combining an interactive secret-key certificate issuing protocol with a showing protocol. Suppose a certificate simulation algorithm exists that outputs certified public keys for which the certificate simulation algorithm and $\mathcal{P}$ together know a corresponding secret key. Then an attacker may be able in the showing protocol to perform a cryptographic action with respect to a simulated public key by *delegating* part of the action to $\overline{\mathcal{P}}$; see Section 5.1.2 for an example.

Successful delegation to executions of protocols other than the certificate issuing protocol can simply be prevented by having $\mathcal{P}$ use independently generated keys for different tasks. Key separation is recommended practice anyway; see, e.g., Kelsey, Schneier, and Wagner [229]. To assess for a given application whether a cryptographic action can be delegated to an execution of the issuing protocol, it must be investigated whether certified public keys can be simulated in such a way that the cryptographic action in the showing protocol can be performed by using $\overline{\mathcal{P}}$ as an oracle. In the certificate schemes that will be developed in this book, delegation is never a problem; see Section 5.1.2 for details.

2.7   Bibliographic notes

The historical background of the DLREP function in Section 2.3.2 is quite diverse. In 1987, Chaum, Evertse, and van de Graaf [108] considered the case where all g_i's are random elements from $\mathbb{Z}_p^*$, and claimed that inverting is infeasible when elements from the domain are generated at random (hardly a useful instance generator). Chaum and Crepeau [60], Chaum and van Antwerpen [110], Chaum [101], Boyar, Kurtz, and Krentel [44], Pedersen [298], van Heijst and Pedersen [380], and Okamoto [288] all designed schemes based on the special case $l = 2$. Chaum, van Heijst, and Pfitzmann [111, 112] studied collision-intractability for the special case of fixed l, with g_i's in a group of prime order; their reduction is not tight, though, and takes exponential time for l polynomial in k. In 1993, Brands [46] examined the one-wayness and the collision-intractability of the DLREP function for arbitrary l polynomial in k, and provided a tight reduction to prove its collision-intractability; the overhead factor is approximately 2. Bellare, Goldreich, and Goldwasser [23] modified the reduction to simplify its analysis, but the overhead is slightly larger. Pfitzmann [301], elaborating on the reduction of Chaum, van Heijst, and Pfitzmann [111, 112], gave the first (fairly intricate) optimally tight reduction. The proof of Proposition 2.3.3 is similar to a simpler reduction by Schoenmakers [342], but differs in the assumption on the distribution of the g_i's (for reasons that will become clear in Chapter 3). Construction 2.3.2 is new.

The RSAREP function in Section 2.3.3 was introduced by Brands [54]. Previously only the case $l = 1$ appeared, in proofs of knowledge (see Okamoto [288]) and implicitly in some proofs of security (see, e.g., Guillou and Quisquater [201]). Construction 2.3.4 and Proposition 2.3.5 appear here for the first time.

The notion of secret-key certificates is due to Brands [56]; see also Brands [52, 53]. Definition 2.6.2 has not appeared previously. The possibility of delegation was first noted by Schoenmakers (personal communication, May 1995), in the context of the electronic coin system of Brands [49].

Chapter 3

Showing Protocols with Selective Disclosure

In this chapter we present highly flexible and practical showing protocol techniques that enable the holder of an arbitrary number of attributes to selectively disclose properties about them; any other information remains unconditionally hidden. All the techniques can be based on the DLREP function as well as on the RSAREP function. The demonstrations can take several forms, including zero-knowledge proofs and signed proofs. Signed proofs are provably unforgeable in the random oracle model under the mere assumption that there exists an invulnerable instance generator for the DL function or the RSA function. We do not yet make the connection with digital certificate issuing protocols; this will be the topic of Chapters 4 and 5.

3.1 Introduction

Consider a polynomial-time prover $\mathcal{P}$ that has committed, by means of a commitment function, to one or more attributes that are (represented by) elements of a finite ring. $\mathcal{P}$ is to demonstrate to a verifier $\mathcal{V}$ that its attributes satisfy a satisfiable formula from proposition logic, where the atomic propositions are relations that are linear in the attributes. By way of example, let x_1, x_2, x_3 denote $\mathcal{P}$'s attributes, and consider the formula

$$\Big((F_1 \ \text{AND} \ F_2) \ \text{OR} \ (\text{NOT} F_3 \ \text{AND} \ F_4)\Big) \ \text{AND} \ \text{NOT} F_5 \qquad (3.1)$$

where

$$
\begin{aligned}
F_1 &= (x_1 + 2x_2 - 10x_3 = 13) \\
F_2 &= (x_2 - 4x_3 = 5)
\end{aligned}
$$

$$F_3 = (x_1 + 3x_2 + 5x_3 = 7)$$
$$F_4 = (3x_1 + 10x_2 + 18x_3 = 23)$$
$$F_5 = (x_1 - 8x_2 + 11x_3 = 5)$$

We require that the computations of $\overline{\mathcal{V}}$ when interacting with $\mathcal{P}$ can be performed in polynomial time, but $\mathcal{V}$ is given infinite computing power in its attempts to learn additional information about $\mathcal{P}$'s attributes. The goal is to ensure that $\mathcal{P}$ does not reveal to $\widetilde{\mathcal{V}}$ any information about its attributes beyond the validity of the formula.

Regardless of the commitment function used, a constant-round zero-knowledge argument for this task can be constructed by reducing the formula to an instance of the NP-complete language Directed Hamiltonian Cycle and applying a protocol due to Feige and Shamir [170]. Alternatively, the formula can be reduced to an instance of the NP-complete language SAT and then subjected to a slightly more efficient protocol due to Bellare, Jakobsson, and Yung [24]. The resulting protocols are highly impractical, though, because statements must be encoded into Boolean circuits and auxiliary commitments must be used for each gate.

In the remainder of this chapter we show that truly practical techniques exist when $\mathcal{P}$ commits to its attributes in a special manner. Assuming parameter sizes sufficient to guarantee long-term security, the new techniques allow $\mathcal{P}$ to non-interactively demonstrate example formula (3.1) by sending a mere 275 bytes to $\mathcal{V}$. Forming and verifying the proof both require fewer than 940 modular multiplications of numbers in G_q or $\mathbb{Z}_n^*$.

In the next section we describe how $\mathcal{P}$ should commit. We then introduce techniques for demonstrating formulae of special forms. Finally, in Section 3.6 we show how to combine these techniques to demonstrate arbitrary Boolean formulae.

3.2   How to commit

Our proof techniques require $\mathcal{P}$ to commit to its attributes by means of either the DLREP function or the RSAREP function:

- To base the security on the hardness of inverting the DL function, the attributes must all be (represented by) numbers in $\mathbb{Z}_q$, and $\mathcal{P}$ computes $h := \prod_{i=1}^{l} g_i^{x_i}$. The system parameters and $\mathcal{P}$'s secret key must be generated in accordance with Construction 2.3.2, based on any invulnerable instance generator for the DL function. Recall from Construction 2.3.2 that $(x_l, \ldots, x_{l-1})$ may have an arbitrary distribution, but $\mathcal{P}$ must generate x_l at random from $\mathbb{Z}_q$.

- To base the security on the hardness of inverting the RSA function, the attributes must all be (represented by) numbers in $\mathbb{Z}_v$, and $\mathcal{P}$ computes $h := \prod_{i=1}^{l} g_i^{x_i} x_{l+1}^v$, where $x_{l+1} \in \mathbb{Z}_n^*$. The system parameters and $\mathcal{P}$'s secret key must be generated in accordance with Construction 2.3.4, based on any invulnerable instance generator for the RSA function. Recall from Construction 2.3.4 that $(x_1, \ldots, x_l)$ may have an arbitrary distribution, but $\mathcal{P}$ must generate x_{l+1} at random from $\mathbb{Z}_n^*$.

In either case, h is referred to as the public key of $\mathcal{P}$. Recall that l may be polynomial in the security parameter.

In case the security is based on the RSA function, there is a clean separation between the role of the attributes and that of x_{l+1}. This is not the case when the DL function is used, because one of the attributes must be chosen at random, and it will rarely make sense in practice to demonstrate a property about a random number. Nevertheless, the distinction is merely a notational one. If one insists on allowing $(x_1, \ldots, x_l)$ to have an arbitrary distribution, then $\mathcal{P}$ should form $h := \prod_{i=1}^{l+1} g_i^{x_i}$, where g_{l+1} is a generator of G_q and $\mathcal{P}$ generates x_{l+1} at random from $\mathbb{Z}_q$. We stick to the former notation, because it sometimes makes sense to demonstrate that the random x_l is unequal to zero; see Section 5.1.1.

As explained in Section 2.4, algorithms I_{DLREP} and I_{RSAREP} must be run by $\mathcal{V}$, by a party trusted by $\mathcal{V}$ and $\mathcal{P}$, or by means of a secure multi-party protocol between $\mathcal{V}$ and $\mathcal{P}$. In any case, it must be ensured that $\widehat{\mathcal{P}}$ cannot know more than one representation of h. On the basis of Propositions 2.3.3 and 2.3.5 it is easily seen how to accomplish this.

To avoid unduly repetition, throughout this chapter we detail our techniques for the case where the DLREP function is used to commit to $\mathcal{P}$'s attributes; for the RSAREP function we clarify only the differences. We also assume from now on that $l \geq 2$ when the DLREP function is used, for obvious reasons.

3.3 Formulae with zero or more "AND" connectives

We first consider the situation in which $\mathcal{P}$ is to demonstrate a satisfiable formula with zero or more "AND" connectives and no other logical connectives.

3.3.1 Technique based on the DLREP function

Without loss of generality, assume that $\mathcal{P}$ is to demonstrate that the DL-representation it knows of h with respect to $(g_1, \ldots, g_l)$ satisfies the following system of $t \geq 0$ independent linear relations:

$$\begin{pmatrix} \alpha_{11} & \cdots & \alpha_{1,l-t} & 1 & 0 & \cdots & 0 \\ \alpha_{21} & \cdots & \alpha_{2,l-t} & 0 & 1 & \cdots & 0 \\ \vdots & \vdots & \vdots & \vdots & \vdots & \ddots & \vdots \\ \alpha_{t1} & \cdots & \alpha_{t,l-t} & 0 & 0 & \cdots & 1 \end{pmatrix} \begin{pmatrix} x_{\pi(1)} \\ x_{\pi(2)} \\ \vdots \\ x_{\pi(l)} \end{pmatrix} = \begin{pmatrix} b_1 \\ b_2 \\ \vdots \\ b_t \end{pmatrix} \bmod q. \quad (3.2)$$

The coefficients α_{ij} are elements of $\mathbb{Z}_q$, and $\pi(\cdot)$ is a permutation of $\{1, \ldots, l\}$. Clearly, any satisfiable system of linear relations in $x_1, \ldots, x_l$ can be described in this form: if a system of linear relations contains dependent relations, it can be reduced to a system of independent linear relations, denoted in number by t here; then the matrix of coefficients can be brought into row canonical form, using Gaussian elimination; and, finally, by applying a suitable permutation $\pi(\cdot)$, the columns of the matrix of coefficients can be interchanged, arriving at the system displayed above. (In a practical implementation the latter step may be omitted, but here we need $\pi(\cdot)$ also to enable a generic description and analysis of the technique.)

If $t = l$ then $\mathcal{V}$ can verify the applicability of the formula without communicating with $\mathcal{P}$, by solving for the x_i's and checking that they form a preimage to h. Therefore we may assume that $t < l$.

Representing atomic propositions by linear relations over $\mathbb{Z}_q$, system (3.2) corresponds to the following Boolean formula:

$$(b_1 = \alpha_{11}x_{\pi(1)} + \cdots + \alpha_{1,l-t}x_{\pi(l-t)} + x_{\pi(l-t+1)} \bmod q) \; \mathsf{AND} \; \ldots$$

$$\ldots \; \mathsf{AND} \; (b_t = \alpha_{t1}x_{\pi(1)} + \cdots + \alpha_{t,l-t}x_{\pi(l-t)} + x_{\pi(l)} \bmod q). \tag{3.3}$$

The special case $t = 0$ corresponds to the "empty" formula, TRUE. Although $\mathcal{P}$'s attributes obviously satisfy this formula, it may certainly make sense to demonstrate it, as will become clear in the next three chapters.

Our technique for demonstrating formula (3.3) is based on the following result.

Proposition 3.3.1. *$\mathcal{P}$ can prove knowledge of a DL-representation of*

$$\left(\prod_{i=1}^{t} g_{\pi(l-t+i)}^{b_i}\right)^{-1} h$$

with respect to

$$\left(g_{\pi(1)} \prod_{i=1}^{t} g_{\pi(l-t+i)}^{-\alpha_{i1}}, \; \ldots, \; g_{\pi(l-t)} \prod_{i=1}^{t} g_{\pi(l-t+i)}^{-\alpha_{i,l-t}}\right)$$

if and only if it knows a set of attributes that satisfies the formula (3.3).

Proof. If $(x_1, \ldots, x_l)$ satisfies the formula (3.3), then

$$h \;=\; \prod_{i=1}^{l} g_{\pi(i)}^{x_{\pi(i)}}$$

$$\overset{(*)}{=}\; \left(\prod_{i=1}^{l-t} g_{\pi(i)}^{x_{\pi(i)}}\right)\left(\prod_{i=1}^{t} g_{\pi(l-t+i)}^{b_i - \sum_{j=1}^{l-t}\alpha_{ij}x_{\pi(j)}}\right)$$

$$\overset{(**)}{=}\; \left(\prod_{i=1}^{t} g_{\pi(l-t+i)}^{b_i}\right)\left(g_{\pi(1)}\prod_{i=1}^{t} g_{\pi(l-t+i)}^{-\alpha_{i1}}\right)^{x_{\pi(1)}} \cdots \left(g_{\pi(l-t)}\prod_{i=1}^{t} g_{\pi(l-t+i)}^{-\alpha_{i,l-t}}\right)^{x_{\pi(l-t)}},$$

and so the DL-representation that $\overline{\mathcal{P}}$ can prove knowledge of is $(x_{\pi(1)}, \ldots, x_{\pi(l-t)})$. (We will refer to the marked derivation steps later on.)

To prove the converse, suppose that $\widehat{\mathcal{P}}$ convinces $\mathcal{V}$ with non-negligible success probability. According to Definition 2.4.1, there exists a polynomial-time knowledge extractor $\mathcal{K}$ that outputs with non-negligible success probability a DL-representation $(y_1, \ldots, y_{l-t})$. By expanding the relation

$$(\prod_{i=1}^{t} g_{\pi(l-t+i)}^{b_i})^{-1} h = \prod_{i=1}^{l-t} (g_{\pi(i)} \prod_{j=1}^{t} g_{\pi(l-t+j)}^{-\alpha_{ji}})^{y_i},$$

it is seen that

$$(y_1, \ldots, y_{l-t}, b_1 - \sum_{j=1}^{l-t} \alpha_{1j} y_j \bmod q, \ldots, b_t - \sum_{j=1}^{l-t} \alpha_{tj} y_j \bmod q)$$

is a DL-representation of h with respect to $(g_{\pi(1)}, \ldots, g_{\pi(l)})$. This must be the DL-representation $(x_{\pi(1)}, \ldots, x_{\pi(l)})$ known to $\mathcal{P}$, because $\mathcal{P}$ must know at least one such DL-representation to perform the proof of knowledge (otherwise $\mathcal{K}$ can be used directly to compute DL-representations), and if this were different then $<\widehat{\mathcal{P}}, \mathcal{K}>$ could be used to invert the DL function (see Proposition 2.3.3).

It remains to check that the DL-representation satisfies the formula (3.3). From the left-hand side of the matrix equation (3.2) it follows, for all $i \in \{1, \ldots, t\}$, that

$$
\begin{aligned}
\sum_{j=1}^{l-t} \alpha_{ij} x_{\pi(j)} + x_{\pi(l-t+i)} &= \sum_{j=1}^{l-t} \alpha_{ij} y_j + (b_i - \sum_{j=1}^{l-t} \alpha_{ij} y_j) \\
&= b_i \bmod q.
\end{aligned}
$$

This completes the proof. $\square$

While the expressions appearing in this proposition are somewhat intimidating, the process of deriving them is simple and can easily be performed by pencil and paper using the following three steps:

1. As can be seen in the first part of the proof of Proposition 3.3.1 and in particular in the derivation step marked by $(*)$, we first substitute into $\mathcal{P}$'s commitment $h := \prod_{i=1}^{l} g_i^{x_i}$ the t expressions for $x_{\pi(l-t+1)}, \ldots, x_{\pi(l)}$ that must hold if the formula (3.3) holds true.

2. We then group together the terms that are raised to a constant power, and collect terms for each of the variables $x_{\pi(1)}, \ldots, x_{\pi(l-t)}$; see the derivation step marked by $(**)$.

3. Finally, we divide both sides by the product of all constant powers.

Example 3.3.9 will illustrate the process.

By substitution into Proposition 3.3.1 it is immediately seen that the demonstration of the formula TRUE corresponds to proving knowledge of a DL-representation of h with respect to $(g_1, \ldots, g_l)$. According to the proof of Proposition 3.3.1, this property holds in general.

Corollary 3.3.2. *Regardless of the formula demonstrated by $\mathcal{P}$, the proof of knowledge in Proposition 3.3.1 is also a proof of knowledge of a DL-representation of h with respect to $(g_1, \ldots, g_l)$.*

The importance of this simple result will become clear in Section 5.5.2, where we show how to discourage certificate lending, and in Section 6.3, where we show how to lift the demonstration technique to the smartcard setting.

Consider now a setting in which $\widetilde{\mathcal{V}}$ requests $\mathcal{P}$ to demonstrate a plurality of formulae of the form (3.3), not necessarily all the same. Clearly, with each new formula that is demonstrated for the same h, $\widetilde{\mathcal{V}}$ learns additional information about $\mathcal{P}$'s attributes.

Definition 3.3.3. *In an adaptively chosen formula attack, $\widetilde{\mathcal{V}}$ may select at the start of each new protocol execution which formula is to be demonstrated by $\mathcal{P}$. Protocol executions may be arbitrarily interleaved, in any way dictated by $\widetilde{\mathcal{V}}$. In case $\widetilde{\mathcal{V}}$ requests a formula that does not apply to $\mathcal{P}$'s attributes, $\mathcal{P}$ informs $\widetilde{\mathcal{V}}$ of this fact either by not responding before a time-out or by sending a predetermined fixed message; otherwise $\mathcal{P}$ demonstrates the formula to $\widetilde{\mathcal{V}}$. In either case, $\widetilde{\mathcal{V}}$ learns the status of the formula, namely whether it is true or false with respect to $\mathcal{P}$'s attributes.*

We are interested in determining whether $\widetilde{\mathcal{V}}$ can learn more about $\mathcal{P}$'s attributes than what can be learned from only the status of the requested formulae and $\widetilde{\mathcal{V}}$'s a priori information (the probability distribution from which $\mathcal{P}$'s attributes have been drawn). That is, do protocol executions leak additional information about $\mathcal{P}$'s attributes?

The following proposition provides a sufficient condition to guarantee that whatever $\widetilde{\mathcal{V}}$ can compute about $\overline{\mathcal{P}}$'s attributes, it can also compute using only its a priori information and the status of the requested formulae.

Proposition 3.3.4. *Let $\overline{\mathcal{P}}$ only demonstrate formulae in which x_l does not appear, using a proof of knowledge as described in Proposition 3.3.1 with the property that it is statistically witness-indistinguishable. For any distribution of $(x_1, \ldots, x_{l-1})$, whatever information $\widetilde{\mathcal{V}}$ in an adaptively chosen formula attack can compute about $(x_1, \ldots, x_{l-1})$ can also be computed using merely its a priori information and the status of the formulae requested.*

Proof. Without loss of generality we concentrate on the formulae that $\mathcal{P}$ demonstrates by means of a proof of knowledge. Consider first the demonstration of a single formula. If $x_{\pi(j)}$ does not appear in the formula, for some $j \in \{1, \ldots, l - t\}$, then the j-th column in the matrix on the left-hand side of system (3.2) contains all zeros, and it follows that

$$\prod_{i=1}^{t} g_{\pi(l-t+i)}^{-\alpha_{ij}} = 1.$$

As a consequence, in Proposition 3.3.1 the number $g_{\pi(j)}$ appears separately in the tuple with respect to which $\mathcal{P}$ proves knowledge of a DL-representation. Since in our case x_l does not appear in the formulae demonstrated, it follows that, in a single formula demonstration, $\mathcal{P}$ proves knowledge of a DL-representation $(y_1, \ldots, y_j, x_l)$ of a number in G_q with respect to a tuple $(g_1^*, \ldots, g_j^*, g_l)$, for some integer $j \geq 0$ and numbers $g_1^*, \ldots, g_j^*$ in G_q that depend on the formula demonstrated. The set $\{y_1, \ldots, y_j\}$ is a subset of $\{x_1, \ldots, x_{l-1}\}$. Since g_l is a generator of G_q, for any tuple $(y_1, \ldots, y_j) \in (\mathbb{Z}_q)^j$ there is exactly one x_l such that $(y_1, \ldots, y_j, x_l)$ is the DL-representation that $\mathcal{P}$ proves knowledge of. Because the proof of knowledge is witness-indistinguishable, and x_l has been chosen at random by $\mathcal{P}$, it follows that no information is revealed about $y_1, \ldots, y_j$. Consequently, no information is leaked about $(x_1, \ldots, x_{l-1})$ beyond the status of the formula.

To complete the proof, we apply Proposition 2.4.5, according to which the (arbitrarily interleaved) demonstration of many formulae, each by means of a witness-indistinguishable proof, is also witness-indistinguishable.   □

The witness-indistinguishability condition in Proposition 3.3.4 is not only sufficient, but also necessary. For example, if $l \geq 3$ and $t < l - 1$, and $\mathcal{P}$ performs the proof of knowledge by disclosing $x_{\pi(l-t)}$ and proving knowledge of a DL-representation of

$$\Big(\prod_{i=1}^{t} g_{\pi(l-t+i)}^{b_i}\Big)^{-1} h \big(g_{\pi(l-t)} \prod_{i=1}^{t} g_{\pi(l-t+i)}^{-\alpha_{i,l-t}}\big)^{-x_{\pi(l-t)}}$$

with respect to

$$\Big(g_{\pi(1)} \prod_{i=1}^{t} g_{\pi(l-t+i)}^{-\alpha_{i1}}, \ \ldots, \ g_{\pi(l-t-1)} \prod_{i=1}^{t} g_{\pi(l-t+i)}^{-\alpha_{i,l-t-1}}\Big),$$

then obviously $\mathcal{V}$ learns information that may not have been computable from its a priori information and the status of the formula. From this counterexample it is also seen that it does not suffice for the proof of knowledge in Proposition 3.3.4 to be witness-hiding.

A practical implementation of the proof of knowledge in Proposition 3.3.4 can be realized by substituting the proof of knowledge described in Section 2.4.3; according to Proposition 2.4.8 it is perfectly witness-indistinguishable. An important benefit of using this protocol is that the resulting expressions can be expanded, so that $\mathcal{P}$ and $\mathcal{V}$ can use a single precomputed table for simultaneous repeated squaring, regardless of the formulae demonstrated. Other advantages of this particular choice of protocol will become clear in Sections 3.5, 6.3, and 6.4.

The resulting (generic) protocol steps are as follows:

Step 1. $\mathcal{P}$ generates at random $l - t$ numbers, $w_1, \ldots, w_{l-t} \in \mathbb{Z}_q$, and computes

$$a := \prod_{i=1}^{l-t} g_{\pi(i)}^{w_i} \prod_{i=1}^{t} g_{\pi(l-t+i)}^{-\sum_{j=1}^{l-t} \alpha_{ij} w_j}.$$

$\mathcal{P}$ then sends the initial witness a to $\mathcal{V}$.

Step 2. $\mathcal{P}$ computes a set of responses, responsive to $\mathcal{V}$'s challenge $c \in \mathbb{Z}_s$, as follows:

$$r_i := cx_{\pi(i)} + w_i \bmod q \quad \forall i \in \{1, \ldots, l-t\}.$$

$\mathcal{P}$ then sends $(r_1, \ldots, r_{l-t})$ to $\mathcal{V}$.

$\mathcal{V}$ computes

$$r_{l-t+i} := b_i c - \sum_{j=1}^{l-t} \alpha_{ij} r_j \bmod q \quad \forall i \in \{1, \ldots, t\},$$

and accepts if and only if the verification relation

$$\prod_{i=1}^{l} g_{\pi(i)}^{r_i} h^{-c} = a$$

holds.

For later reference, in Sections 5.4 and 6.3, this protocol is depicted in Figure 3.1. The exponents in the expressions in Step 1 and in the verification relation, respectively, can be rapidly computed from the matrix of coefficients in (3.2), by taking the inner products of the matrix rows and the random numbers, and of the matrix rows and the responses, respectively. Note that the communication complexity of the protocol decreases as the number of "AND" connectives increases.

As with the proof of knowledge in Section 2.4.3, the above protocol description is generic in the sense that the binary size of s and the process of generating c have not been specified. To obtain a proof of knowledge, c should be generated in a substantially random manner and become known to $\mathcal{P}$ only after it has computed its initial witness.

The following property will be of importance in Section 3.5.

Proposition 3.3.5. *The protocol obtained by implementing the proof of knowledge in Proposition 3.3.4 by means of the proof of knowledge described in Section 2.4.3 is honest-verifier zero-knowledge.*

$\boxed{\mathcal{P}}$ $\qquad\qquad\qquad\qquad\qquad\qquad\qquad\qquad$ $\boxed{\mathcal{V}}$

SYSTEM PARAMETERS

$$(q, g_1, \ldots, g_l) := I_{\text{DLREP}}(1^k)$$

KEY SET-UP

Attributes: $x_1, \ldots, x_{l-1} \in \mathbb{Z}_q$

$x_l \in_{\mathcal{R}} \mathbb{Z}_q$

Secret key: $(x_1, \ldots, x_l)$

Public key: $\qquad\qquad\qquad h := \prod_{i=1}^{l} g_i^{x_i}$

PROTOCOL

$w_1, \ldots, w_{l-t} \in_{\mathcal{R}} \mathbb{Z}_q$

$$a := \prod_{i=1}^{l-t} g_{\pi(i)}^{w_i} \prod_{i=1}^{t} g_{\pi(l-t+i)}^{-\sum_{j=1}^{l-t} \alpha_{ij} w_j}$$

$$\xrightarrow{\quad a \quad}$$

$$\xleftarrow{\quad c \quad}$$

$\forall i \in \{1, \ldots, l-t\} :$

$\quad r_i := c x_{\pi(i)} + w_i \bmod q$

$$\xrightarrow{\quad r_1, \ldots, r_{l-t} \quad}$$

$$\forall i \in \{1, \ldots, t\} :$$

$$r_{l-t+i} := b_i c - \sum_{j=1}^{l-t} \alpha_{ij} r_j \bmod q$$

$$\prod_{i=1}^{l} g_{\pi(i)}^{r_i} h^{-c} \overset{?}{=} a$$

Figure 3.1: Generic protocol for demonstrating formula (3.3).

Proof. To simulate the view of the honest verifier, the simulator picks the challenge $c \in \mathbb{Z}_s$ according to the same distribution as the honest verifier. It then selects $r_1, \ldots, r_{l-t}$ at random from $\mathbb{Z}_q$, and computes $r_{l-t+1}, \ldots, r_l$ as would $\mathcal{V}$ in the protocol. Finally, it computes a such that the verification relation holds true:

$$a := \prod_{i=1}^{l} g_{\pi(i)}^{r_i} h^{-c}.$$

It is easy to check that the resulting view, $(a, c, r_1, \ldots, r_{l-t})$, is identically distributed to the view of the honest verifier. $\square$

Corollary 3.3.2 suggests that all the considerations in Sections 2.4.3 and 2.5.3 apply. Special care must be taken, though, because both h and the tuple with respect to which knowledge of a DL-representation is demonstrated depend on the particular formula that is demonstrated. This does not pose any problems for the zero-knowledge proof mode, which in light of the techniques that will be introduced in Section 6.3 is best realized by prepending a move in which V commits to its challenge. Caution must be exercised in case of signed proofs, though. Details follow.

To obtain a signed proof, $\mathcal{V}$'s challenge c is generated as a sufficiently strong one-way hash of at least a, in accordance with the Fiat-Shamir technique described in Section 2.5.2. To enable provability in the random oracle model, we will from now on always assume implicitly that the hash function produces outputs linear in k. The signed proof consists of $(a, (r_1, \ldots, r_{l-t}))$ or of $(c, (r_1, \ldots, r_{l-t}))$, and if the protocol is non-interactive then $\mathcal{P}$ can omit sending either a or c to $\mathcal{V}$, since $\mathcal{V}$ can recover it. If a message m is hashed along, then the signed proof also serves as a digital signature of $\mathcal{P}$ on m. Proposition 3.3.4 still applies, since the hashing does not affect the property of witness-indistinguishability; signed proofs unconditionally hide all attribute information that was not explicitly disclosed. The unforgeability of signed proofs is guaranteed computationally, as follows.

Proposition 3.3.6. *Suppose that the proof of knowledge in Proposition 3.3.4 is realized by substituting the witness-indistinguishable proof of knowledge described in Section 2.4.3, and that $\mathcal{V}$'s challenge is formed by hashing at least a. If the DL function used to implement $\mathcal{P}$'s commitment is one-way, then non-interactively issued signed proofs are provably unforgeable in the random oracle model, regardless of the formula(e) demonstrated and the distribution of $(x_1, \ldots, x_{l-1})$.*

The proof follows by application of Proposition 2.5.2, in light of Corollary 3.3.2 and Proposition 3.3.5. We stress that Proposition 3.3.6 holds even in case of an adaptively chosen formula attack (and, if messages are hashed along, an adaptively chosen message attack), as do all the other unforgeability results in this chapter.

Assuming that $\mathcal{P}$ performs no more than polylogarithmically many protocol executions, and that the status of the formulae requested by $\mathcal{V}$ still leaves non-negligible uncertainty about $(x_1, \ldots, x_{l-1})$, it can be shown that Proposition 3.3.6 holds true even for interactively issued signed proofs. However, once $\mathcal{V}$ has requested sufficiently many formulae to be able to determine $(x_1, \ldots, x_{l-1})$ with overwhelming probability, it is unclear how to prove unforgeability in the random oracle model; we in effect end up with the question of whether interactively issued Schnorr signatures are unforgeable, which is believed true but has yet to be proved. To prove unforgeability of interactively issued signed proofs in general, we must relate the security proof to the construction of Proposition 2.5.5.

Proposition 3.3.7. *Let $l \geq 3$, let x_{l-1} be the outcome of a random coin flip by $\mathcal{P}$, and let $\mathcal{P}$ only demonstrate formulae in which both x_{l-1} and x_l do not appear. Suppose that the proof of knowledge in Proposition 3.3.1 is realized by substituting the witness-indistinguishable proof of knowledge described in Section 2.4.3, and that $\mathcal{V}$'s challenge is formed by hashing at least a. If the DL function used to implement $\mathcal{P}$'s commitment is one-way, and $\mathcal{P}$ performs no more than polylogarithmically many formula demonstrations, then interactively issued signed proofs are provably unforgeable in the random oracle model, regardless of the formula(e) demonstrated and the distribution of $(x_1, \ldots, x_{l-2})$.*

The proof follows from Proposition 2.5.3. It is not hard to show that the result holds even for an unbiased coin flip, if only the uncertainty about the outcome is non-negligible.[1] Note that x_{l-1} need not take on the values 0 and 1; any set of values, of any size, will do, if only x_{l-1} does not take on one particular value with overwhelming probability.

By blinding its challenge, $\mathcal{V}$ can perfectly blind the signed proof, in the manner described in Section 2.5. Since this proof mode is of no use in this book, we omit the details.

Propositions 3.3.6 and 3.3.7 tell us that the number of signed proofs computable by $\widehat{\mathcal{V}}$ cannot exceed the number of protocol executions performed by $\overline{\mathcal{P}}$, except with negligible probability. For some applications this is all we need, but in other applications it is not. An entirely different (and new) issue is the *unmodifiability* of signed proofs: it should be infeasible to construct a signed proof for a formula that does in fact not apply to $\mathcal{P}$'s representation. Unless special precaution is taken, a signed proof convinces only that $\mathcal{P}$ knows a DL-representation of h with respect to $(g_1, \ldots, g_l)$. As an example, if $h = g_1^{x_1} g_2^{x_2}$, and formulae of the form $x_2 = b \bmod q$ are to be demonstrated, for arbitrary $b \in \mathbb{Z}_q$, then $\widehat{\mathcal{P}}$ can set $a := g_1^{w_1} g_2^{w_2}$, for random w_1 and w_2, and $b := x_2 + w_2/\mathcal{H}_{q,g_2}(m, a) \bmod q$. In case the signed proof is to be issued interactively, this requires $\widehat{\mathcal{P}}$ to conspire with $\mathcal{V}$, because normally the formula will be determined prior to executing the protocol. If, on the other hand, $\mathcal{P}$

---

[1] In a practical implementation one would likely not bother to introduce the extra coin flip x_{l-1}, since the benefit that comes from it appears to be only of a theoretical nature; the unforgeability property of interactively issued signed proofs is believed to hold even if it is omitted.

is to non-interactively issue a signed proof for demonstrating a formula of its own choice, then it does not need the assistance of $\mathcal{V}$.

One measure to ensure that a signed proof convinces of which formula has been demonstrated is to restrict all the matrix entries (the α_{ij}'s and the b_i's) that specify the formulae requested to sets V such that $|V|/q$ is negligible in k (e.g., sets of size $\sqrt{q}$). The set V may differ for each formula coefficient. This measure, however, restricts the range of formulae that $\mathcal{P}$ can demonstrate. The following measure does not have this drawback.

Proposition 3.3.8. *Non-interactively (interactively) issued signed proofs are provably unmodifiable in the random oracle model, subject to the conditions of Proposition 3.3.6 (Proposition 3.3.7), in case a uniquely identifying description of the formula is hashed along when forming $\mathcal{V}$'s challenge.*

To form a uniquely identifying description of the formula (3.3), one can concatenate, in a predetermined order, the α_{ij}'s and the b_i's. In case t and l are not fixed as part of the system, they must be part of the formula description as well.

In other words, when presented with h, a formula description F, an (optional) message m, and a signed proof $(c, r_1, \ldots, r_{l-t})$, any verifier can convince itself that the signed proof has been computed by a prover (possibly a group of parties) that applied its knowledge of a DL-representation of h, and that the prover demonstrated that its DL-representation satisfies F. To this end, the verifier must compute $r_{l-t+1}, \ldots, r_l$ in the manner specified in Figure 3.1 and verify that

$$c = \mathcal{H}_{q,g_l}\left(m, F, \prod_{i=1}^{l} g_{\pi(i)}^{r_i} h^{-c}\right).$$

In practice, one may prefer to apply both measures in combination, that is, to hash along the formula description as well as to restrict all the formula coefficients to small sets.

It is important to note that unmodifiability does not exclude the possibility for $\mathcal{V}$ to end up with a signed proof that convinces only of a part of the formula demonstrated by $\mathcal{P}$. In particular, by hashing along the formula TRUE (if $\mathcal{P}$ allows this) and lumping together $\mathcal{P}$'s responses, $\mathcal{V}$ can hide almost entirely the formula that has been demonstrated. This property enables $\mathcal{V}$ to protect its own privacy in applications in which it routinely submits its protocol transcripts to a central authority. Details will be provided in Section 5.3.

Preferably, h is hashed along as well when forming $\mathcal{V}$'s challenge. Micali and Reyzin [269] show in a general setting that this defeats attacks in practical implementations whereby the hash function is designed by an adversary in an attempt to enable forgery in an otherwise secure signature scheme. More importantly for our purposes, hashing h along is mandatory in situations where h is not fixed but may be chosen in a fairly arbitrary manner by $\mathcal{P}$; this is the case when our showing protocol techniques are combined with certificate issuing protocols in which the receiver is in control of generating its public key. For this reason we will from now on always hash along h in our protocol descriptions. As noted in Section 2.5.2, from the point of view of security it is strongly recommended anyway to hash along any other data that the verifier of a signed proof must apply.

To illustrate the preceding techniques, we now present a practical example.

Example 3.3.9. *Suppose* $\mathcal{P}$ *has three attributes* $x_1, x_2, x_3 \in \mathbb{Z}_q$, *selected according to an arbitrary probability distribution, and is to demonstrate by means of a non-interactively issued signed proof to* $\mathcal{V}$ *that the following formula holds:*

$$(x_1 + 2x_2 - 10x_3 = 13) \text{ AND } (x_2 - 4x_3 = 5).$$

Rewriting this formula in the form (3.2), we get the formula

$$(x_1 = 2x_3 + 3) \text{ AND } (x_2 = 4x_3 + 5).$$

To demonstrate this formula, $\mathcal{P}$ *generates a random* $x_4 \in \mathbb{Z}_q$, *and forms the commitment* $h := \prod_{i=1}^{4} g_i^{x_i}$. *If the formula holds true, then by substitution we get*

$$
\begin{aligned}
h &= g_1^{x_1} g_2^{x_2} g_3^{x_3} g_4^{x_4} \\
&= g_1^{2x_3+3} g_2^{4x_3+5} g_3^{x_3} g_4^{x_4},
\end{aligned}
$$

and by collecting the constant powers, as well as the variable powers for each of x_2, x_3, *we obtain*

$$h = (g_1^3 g_2^5)(g_1^2 g_2^4 g_3)^{x_3} g_4^{x_4}.$$

Finally, by dividing both sides by $g_1^3 g_2^5$, *we arrive at*

$$(g_1^3 g_2^5)^{-1} h = (g_1^2 g_2^4 g_3)^{x_3} g_4^{x_4}.$$

Consequently, $\overline{\mathcal{P}}$ *can prove knowledge of a DL-representation of* $h/(g_1^3 g_2^5)$ *with respect to* $(g_1^2 g_2^4 g_3, g_4)$. *According to Proposition 3.3.1, this is also sufficient to convince* $\mathcal{V}$. *By substituting the proof of knowledge described in Section 2.4.3, and expanding the resulting expressions, we obtain the protocol depicted in Figure 3.2. Here,* m *denotes an arbitrary message agreed on between the parties and* F *denotes a description uniquely identifying the formula demonstrated. The message is optional, and typically its inclusion serves primarily to protect against replay; hereto* m *should contain a random number, a counter, or a sufficiently accurate estimate of the time and date. Other information, such as an identifier of* $\mathcal{V}$ *or a public key to be used for session encryption, may be incorporated as well.*

The security of the protocol for $\overline{\mathcal{P}}$ *follows from the fact that* x_4 *has been chosen at random and does not appear in the formula demonstrated. Specifically, assuming that the underlying DL function is one-way, it follows from Propositions 3.3.4*

$\boxed{\mathcal{P}}$ $\hspace{7cm}$ $\boxed{\mathcal{V}}$

SYSTEM PARAMETERS

$$(q, g_1, g_2, g_3, g_4) := I_{\text{DLREP}}(1^k)$$

KEY SET-UP

Attributes: $x_1, x_2, x_3 \in \mathbb{Z}_q$
$x_4 \in_{\mathcal{R}} \mathbb{Z}_q$
Secret key: $(x_1, \ldots, x_4)$
Public key: $\qquad\qquad\qquad\qquad h := \prod_{i=1}^{4} g_i^{x_i}$
Additional information: $\qquad\qquad \mathcal{H}_{q,g_4}(\cdot)$

PROTOCOL

$w_1, w_2 \in_{\mathcal{R}} \mathbb{Z}_q$
$a := g_1^{2w_1} g_2^{4w_1} g_3^{w_1} g_4^{w_2}$
$c := \mathcal{H}_{q,g_4}(h, m, F, a)$
$r_1 := cx_3 + w_1 \bmod q$
$r_2 := cx_4 + w_2 \bmod q$

$$\xrightarrow{\quad c, r_1, r_2 \quad}$$

$$c \overset{?}{=} \mathcal{H}_{q,g_4}(h, m, F,$$
$$g_1^{2r_1+3c} g_2^{4r_1+5c} g_3^{r_1} g_4^{r_2} h^{-c})$$

Figure 3.2: Protocol for Example 3.3.9.

and 3.3.8 that the signed proof is unforgeable and unmodifiable in the random oracle model. Moreover, it does not leak more information about (x_1, x_2, x_3) than the validity of the formula; this holds even if $\overline{\mathcal{P}}$ demonstrates arbitrarily many other formulae involving only x_1, x_2, x_3, and $\widetilde{\mathcal{V}}$ can adaptively choose in each protocol execution which formula is to be demonstrated and which message is to be signed. As a consequence, $\overline{\mathcal{P}}$ is ensured that the data disclosed in all its showing protocol executions is no more than the aggregate of the information explicitly disclosed in each individual execution.

In accordance with the proof of Proposition 3.3.4, the powers of g_4 are cleanly "separated" from the other products of powers, because x_4 does not appear in the formula demonstrated. In particular, the computations corresponding to the powers of g_4 can all be performed by proving knowledge of the discrete logarithm of $g_4^{x_4}$ with respect to g_4, using the Schnorr proof of knowledge. This property, which can easily be seen to hold in general, will be of major importance in Sections 6.3 and 6.4, where it is shown how to lift the techniques of this chapter to the smartcard setting.

3.3.2   Technique based on the RSAREP function

To base the proof technique on the hardness of inverting the RSA function, consider $\mathcal{P}$ having to demonstrate the system of linear relations (3.2). As described in Section 3.2, in this case $\mathcal{P}$ commits to the attributes $(x_1, \ldots, x_l)$ by means of $h := g_1^{x_1} \cdots g_l^{x_l} x_{l+1}^v$, where x_{l+1} is chosen at random from $\mathbb{Z}_n^*$.

The proof of the following proposition is similar to that of Proposition 3.3.1.

Proposition 3.3.10. *$\mathcal{P}$ can prove knowledge of an RSA-representation of*

$$(\prod_{i=1}^{t} g_{\pi(l-t+i)}^{b_i})^{-1} h$$

with respect to

$$\left(g_{\pi(1)} \prod_{i=1}^{t} g_{\pi(l-t+i)}^{-\alpha_{i1}}, \; \cdots, \; g_{\pi(l-t)} \prod_{i=1}^{t} g_{\pi(l-t+i)}^{-\alpha_{i,l-t}}, \; v \right)$$

if and only if it knows a set of attributes that satisfies the formula.

The RSA-representation $\overline{\mathcal{P}}$ can prove knowledge of is $(x_{\pi(1)}, \ldots, x_{\pi(l-t)}, x_{l+1})$.

Corollary 3.3.11. *Regardless of the formula demonstrated by $\mathcal{P}$, the proof of knowledge in Proposition 3.3.10 is also a proof of knowledge of an RSA-representation of h with respect to $(g_1, \ldots, g_l, v)$.*

The proof of the following result is similar to that of Proposition 3.3.4.

Proposition 3.3.12. *Let $\mathcal{P}$ demonstrate formulae using a proof of knowledge as described in Proposition 3.3.10 with the extra property that it is statistically witness-indistinguishable. For any distribution of $(x_1, \ldots, x_l)$, whatever information $\tilde{\mathcal{V}}$ in an adaptively chosen formula attack can compute about $(x_1, \ldots, x_l)$ can also be computed using merely its a priori information and the status of the formulae requested.*

As in the case of the DLREP function, it is beneficial to implement the proof of knowledge in Proposition 3.3.10 using the witness-indistinguishable proof of knowledge of Section 2.4.4. The resulting expressions can be expanded, so that $\mathcal{P}$ and $\mathcal{V}$ can use a single precomputed table for simultaneous repeated squaring, regardless of the formulae demonstrated. This is straightforward, and so we refrain from a detailed stepwise description of the resulting protocol. For later reference, in Sections 5.4 and 6.3, the protocol is depicted in Figure 3.3. Note that $\mathcal{V}$ may alternatively apply the $\mathrm{mod}\ v$ operator to each of $r_{l-t+1}, \ldots, r_l$, and multiply the corresponding "junk" factor,

$$\prod_{i=1}^{t} g_{\pi(l-t+i)}^{(b_i c - \sum_{j=1}^{l-t} \alpha_{ij} r_j)\,\mathrm{div}\,v},$$

into r_{l+1} before applying the verification relation.

It is easy to see that the protocol is honest-verifier zero-knowledge. The following three propositions are straightforward analogues of results stated for the DLREP-based setting, and can be proved in a similar manner.

Proposition 3.3.13. *Suppose that the proof of knowledge in Proposition 3.3.12 is realized by substituting the witness-indistinguishable proof of knowledge described in Section 2.4.4, and that $\mathcal{V}$'s challenge is formed by hashing at least a. If the RSA function used to implement $\mathcal{P}$'s commitment is one-way, then non-interactively issued signed proofs are unforgeable in the random oracle model, regardless of the formula(e) demonstrated and the distribution of $(x_1, \ldots, x_l)$.*

Proposition 3.3.14. *Let $l \geq 2$, let x_l be the outcome of a random coin flip by $\mathcal{P}$, and let $\mathcal{P}$ only demonstrate formulae in which x_l does not appear. Suppose that the proof of knowledge in Proposition 3.3.10 is realized by substituting the witness-indistinguishable proof of knowledge described in Section 2.4.4, and that $\mathcal{V}$'s challenge is formed by hashing at least a. If the RSA function used to implement $\mathcal{P}$'s commitment is one-way, and $\mathcal{P}$ does not perform more than polylogarithmically many formula demonstrations, then interactively issued signed proofs are provably unforgeable in the random oracle model, regardless of the formula(e) demonstrated and the distribution of $(x_1, \ldots, x_{l-1})$.*

The remarks made about the coin flip in Proposition 3.3.7 apply here as well.

Proposition 3.3.15. *Non-interactively (interactively) issued signed proofs are provably unmodifiable in the random oracle model, subject to the conditions of Proposition 3.3.13 (Proposition 3.3.14), in case a uniquely identifying description of the formula is hashed along when computing $\mathcal{V}$'s challenge.*

$$\boxed{\mathcal{P}} \hspace{8cm} \boxed{\mathcal{V}}$$

SYSTEM PARAMETERS

$$(n, v, g_1, \ldots, g_l) := I_{\text{RSAREP}}(1^k)$$

KEY SET-UP

Attributes: $x_1, \ldots, x_l \in \mathbb{Z}_v$
$x_{l+1} \in_{\mathcal{R}} \mathbb{Z}_n^*$
Secret key: $(x_1, \ldots, x_l, x_{l+1})$
Public key: $\hspace{4cm} h := \prod_{i=1}^{l} g_i^{x_i} x_{l+1}^v$

PROTOCOL

$w_1, \ldots, w_{l-t} \in_{\mathcal{R}} \mathbb{Z}_v$
$w_{l+1} \in_{\mathcal{R}} \mathbb{Z}_n^*$
$a := \prod_{i=1}^{l-t} g_{\pi(i)}^{w_i} \prod_{i=1}^{t} g_{\pi(l-t+i)}^{-\sum_{j=1}^{l-t} \alpha_{ij} w_j} w_{l+1}^v$

$$\xrightarrow{\hspace{2cm} a \hspace{2cm}}$$
$$\xleftarrow{\hspace{2cm} c \hspace{2cm}}$$

$\forall i \in \{1, \ldots, l-t\}:$
$r_i := c x_{\pi(i)} + w_i \bmod v$
$r_{l+1} := \prod_{j=1}^{l-t} (g_{\pi(j)} \prod_{i=1}^{t} g_{\pi(l-t+i)}^{-\alpha_{ij}})^{(c x_{\pi(j)} + w_j) \operatorname{div} v} x_{l+1}^c w_{l+1}$

$$\xrightarrow{\hspace{1cm} r_1, \ldots, r_{l-t}, r_{l+1} \hspace{1cm}}$$

$\hspace{4cm} \forall i \in \{1, \ldots, t\}:$
$\hspace{4cm} r_{l-t+i} := b_i c - \sum_{j=1}^{l-t} \alpha_{ij} r_j$
$\hspace{4cm} \prod_{i=1}^{l} g_{\pi(i)}^{r_i} r_{l+1}^v h^{-c} \stackrel{?}{=} a$

Figure 3.3: Generic protocol for demonstrating formula (3.3), with v replacing q.

As with the DLREP function, the alternative measure of restricting all the matrix entries used to specify the Boolean formulae to sets V such that $|V|/q$ is negligible in k, instead of hashing along F, restricts the range of formulae that $\mathcal{P}$ can demonstrate.

Example 3.3.16. *Suppose that $\mathcal{P}$ has three attributes $x_1, x_2, x_3 \in \mathbb{Z}_v$, and is to demonstrate by means of an interactively issued signed proof to $\mathcal{V}$ that the formula in Example 3.3.9 holds. By applying the technique of Proposition 3.3.10, substituting the proof of knowledge described in Section 2.4.4 and expanding the resulting expressions, we obtain the protocol depicted in Figure 3.4. Assuming that the underlying RSA function is one-way, and $\mathcal{P}$ performs no more than polylogarithmically many protocol executions, in the random oracle model the signed proof is unforgeable and unmodifiable. Moreover, it does not leak more information about (x_1, x_2, x_3) than the validity of the formula; this holds even if $\overline{\mathcal{P}}$ demonstrates arbitrarily many other formulae about its attributes.*

As in Example 3.3.9, m denotes an (optional) message agreed on between the parties and F denotes a description uniquely identifying the formula demonstrated. Examples of data that could be included in m are a nonce to protect against replay, an identifier of $\mathcal{V}$, a public key to be used for session encryption, and a free-form message.

When forming c, the description of any other formula that is implied by F may be hashed along instead of F itself. In addition, if the protocol is performed interactively, $\mathcal{V}$ can blind a. In Section 5.3 we will show how this enables $\mathcal{V}$ to unconditionally hide (any part of) the formula that has been demonstrated. However, $\mathcal{P}$ and $\mathcal{V}$ cannot form a signed proof for a formula that does not apply to $\mathcal{P}$'s RSA-representation, according to the property of unmodifiability.

A notable aspect of the protocol is that the computations for the numbers that are raised to the power v can all be performed by proving knowledge of the v-th root of x_5^v, using the Guillou-Quisquater proof of knowledge. More generally, the computations involving x_4 and x_5 can be performed by proving knowledge of an RSA-representation of $g_4^{x_4} x_5^v$ with respect to (g_4, v). This clean separation can easily be seen to hold in general, and will be of major importance in Sections 6.3 and 6.4.

3.4 Formulae with one "NOT" connective

We now show how to demonstrate satisfiable formulae from proposition logic with zero or more "AND" connectives, exactly one "NOT" connective, and no other connectives.

3.4.1 Technique based on the DLREP function

Any consistent system consisting of zero or more independent linear relations and one linear inequality (i.e., a linear relation where "=" is replaced by "$\neq$") can be

$$\boxed{\mathcal{P}} \qquad\qquad\qquad\qquad \boxed{\mathcal{V}}$$

SYSTEM PARAMETERS

$$(q, g_1, g_2, g_3, g_4, g_5) := I_{\text{RSAREP}}(1^k)$$

KEY SET-UP

Attributes: $x_1, x_2, x_3 \in \mathbb{Z}_q$
$x_4 \in_\mathcal{R} \{0, 1\}$
$x_5 \in_\mathcal{R} \mathbb{Z}_n^*$
Secret key: $(x_1, \ldots, x_4, x_5)$
Public key: $\qquad\qquad\qquad\qquad h := \prod_{i=1}^4 g_i^{x_i} x_5^v$
Additional information: $\qquad\quad \mathcal{H}_{n,v}(\cdot)$

PROTOCOL

$w_1, w_2 \in_\mathcal{R} \mathbb{Z}_v$
$w_3 \in_\mathcal{R} \mathbb{Z}_n^*$
$a := g_1^{2w_1} g_2^{4w_1} g_3^{w_1} g_4^{w_2} w_3^v$

$$\xrightarrow{\qquad a \qquad}$$
$$c := \mathcal{H}_{n,v}(h, m, F, a)$$
$$\xleftarrow{\qquad c \qquad}$$

$r_1 := cx_3 + w_1 \bmod v$
$r_2 := cx_4 + w_2 \bmod v$
$r_3 := (g_1^2 g_2^4 g_3)^{(cx_3 + w_1)\,\mathrm{div}\,v} g_4^{(cx_4 + w_2)\,\mathrm{div}\,v} x_5^c w_3$

$$\xrightarrow{\qquad r_1, r_2, r_3 \qquad}$$
$$c \overset{?}{=} \mathcal{H}_{n,v}(h, m, F,$$
$$g_1^{2r_1 + 3c} g_2^{4r_1 + 5c} g_3^{r_1} g_4^{r_2} r_3^v h^{-c})$$

Figure 3.4: Protocol for Example 3.3.16.

written as a system of linear relations by introducing a non-zero difference term, $\epsilon \in \mathbb{Z}_q^*$. Using Gaussian elimination, the system can be represented by the matrix equation

$$
\begin{pmatrix}
\alpha_{11} & \cdots & \alpha_{1,l-t} & 1 & 0 & \cdots & 0 \\
\alpha_{21} & \cdots & \alpha_{2,l-t} & 0 & 1 & \cdots & 0 \\
\vdots & & \vdots & \vdots & \vdots & \ddots & \vdots \\
\alpha_{t1} & \cdots & \alpha_{t,l-t} & 0 & 0 & \cdots & 1
\end{pmatrix}
\begin{pmatrix}
x_{\pi(1)} \\
x_{\pi(2)} \\
\vdots \\
x_{\pi(l)}
\end{pmatrix}
=
\begin{pmatrix}
b_1 - f_1\epsilon \\
b_2 - f_2\epsilon \\
\vdots \\
b_t - f_t\epsilon
\end{pmatrix}, \quad (3.4)
$$

where $t \geq 1$. (Example 3.4.7 will clarify the process.) The coefficients α_{ij} are elements of $\mathbb{Z}_q$, and $f_1, \ldots, f_t$ are numbers in $\mathbb{Z}_q$, not all equal to 0 mod q. Clearly, it can always be ensured that f_1, say, is equal to 1. We may assume that $t \leq l$, because if $t = l+1$ then $\mathcal{V}$ can verify the applicability of the formula without communicating with $\mathcal{P}$.

Our technique for demonstrating the Boolean formula that corresponds to the system (3.4) is based on the following result. Recall that $\mathcal{P}$ commits to the attributes $(x_1, \ldots, x_l)$ by means of $h := \prod_{i=1}^{l} g_i^{x_i}$.

Proposition 3.4.1. *$\mathcal{P}$ can prove knowledge of a DL-representation of*

$$
\prod_{i=1}^{t} g_{\pi(l-t+i)}^{f_i}
$$

with respect to

$$
\left(\prod_{i=1}^{t} g_{\pi(l-t+i)}^{b_i} h^{-1}, \ g_{\pi(1)} \prod_{i=1}^{t} g_{\pi(l-t+i)}^{-\alpha_{i1}}, \ \ldots, \ g_{\pi(l-t)} \prod_{i=1}^{t} g_{\pi(l-t+i)}^{-\alpha_{i,l-t}} \right)
$$

if and only if it knows a set of attributes that satisfies the system (3.4).

Proof. If $(x_1, \ldots, x_l)$ satisfies system (3.4), then

$$
\begin{aligned}
h &= \prod_{i=1}^{l} g_{\pi(i)}^{x_{\pi(i)}} \\
&= \left(\prod_{i=1}^{l-t} g_{\pi(i)}^{x_{\pi(i)}} \right) \left(\prod_{i=1}^{t} g_{\pi(l-t+i)}^{b_i - f_i\epsilon - \sum_{j=1}^{l-t} \alpha_{ij} x_{\pi(j)}} \right) \\
&= \left(\prod_{i=1}^{t} g_{\pi(l-t+i)}^{b_i} \right) \left(g_{\pi(1)} \prod_{i=1}^{t} g_{\pi(l-t+i)}^{-\alpha_{i1}} \right)^{x_{\pi(1)}} \cdots \left(g_{\pi(l-t)} \prod_{i=1}^{t} g_{\pi(l-t+i)}^{-\alpha_{i,l-t}} \right)^{x_{\pi(l-t)}} \cdot \\
&\quad \left(\prod_{i=1}^{t} g_{\pi(l-t+i)}^{-f_i} \right)^{\epsilon}.
\end{aligned}
$$

By dividing both sides of the equation by h, as well as by $(\prod_{i=1}^{t} g_{\pi(l-t+i)}^{-f_i})^{\epsilon}$, we see that $(\prod_{i=1}^{t} g_{\pi(l-t+i)}^{f_i})^{\epsilon}$ equals

$$((\prod_{i=1}^{t} g_{\pi(l-t+i)}^{b_i})h^{-1})(g_{\pi(1)} \prod_{i=1}^{t} g_{\pi(l-t+i)}^{-\alpha_{i1}})^{x_{\pi(1)}} \cdots (g_{\pi(l-t)} \prod_{i=1}^{t} g_{\pi(l-t+i)}^{-\alpha_{i,l-t}})^{x_{\pi(l-t)}}.$$

Since $\epsilon \neq 0 \bmod q$, both sides can be raised to the power δ, where δ denotes $\epsilon^{-1} \bmod q$. From this we see that the DL-representation that $\overline{\mathcal{P}}$ can prove knowledge of is

$$(\delta, x_{\pi(1)}\delta \bmod q, \ldots, x_{\pi(l-t)}\delta \bmod q).$$

To prove the converse, suppose that $\widehat{\mathcal{P}}$ convinces $\overline{\mathcal{V}}$ with non-negligible success probability. There exists a polynomial-time knowledge extractor $\mathcal{K}$ that outputs with non-negligible success probability a DL-representation $(y_0, \ldots, y_{l-t})$. From the fact that $\prod_{i=1}^{t} g_{\pi(l-t+i)}^{f_i}$ equals

$$(\prod_{i=1}^{t} g_{\pi(l-t+i)}^{b_i} h^{-1})^{y_0} (g_{\pi(1)} \prod_{i=1}^{t} g_{\pi(l-t+i)}^{-\alpha_{i1}})^{y_1} \cdots (g_{\pi(l-t)} \prod_{i=1}^{t} g_{\pi(l-t+i)}^{-\alpha_{i,l-t}})^{y_{l-t}}$$

it follows that

$$h^{y_0} = \prod_{i=1}^{l-t} g_{\pi(i)}^{y_{l-t}} \prod_{i=1}^{t} g_{\pi(l-t+i)}^{b_i y_0 - f_i - \sum_{j=1}^{l-t} \alpha_{ij} y_j}.$$

If $y_0 = 0 \bmod q$ then

$$(y_1, \ldots, y_{l-t}, -f_1 - \sum_{j=1}^{l-t} \alpha_{1j} y_j \bmod q, \ldots, -f_t - \sum_{j=1}^{l-t} \alpha_{tj} y_j \bmod q) \quad (3.5)$$

is a DL-representation of 1 with respect to $(g_{\pi(1)}, \ldots, g_{\pi(l)})$, and two cases can be distinguished:

- If this is the trivial DL-representation, then $y_1, \ldots, y_{l-t}, f_1, \ldots, f_t$ must all be zero, in addition to y_0. But this is a contradiction, because $t \geq 1$ and at least one of $f_1, \ldots, f_t$ is unequal to 0 mod q, by virtue of the presence of one "NOT" connective.

- If this is a non-trivial DL-representation of 1, then $< \widehat{\mathcal{P}}, \overline{\mathcal{V}}>$ has computed a DL-representation of 1 other than the trivial one. (If $\mathcal{P}$ does not know a representation of h then $\mathcal{K}$ can be used directly to compute DL-representations.) According to Proposition 2.3.3 this contradicts the assumption that the DL function is one-way.

Therefore, $y_0 \neq 0 \bmod q$, and it follows that $(y_1 y_0^{-1}, \ldots, y_{l-t} y_0^{-1}, b_1 - f_1 y_0^{-1} - y_0^{-1} \sum_{j=1}^{l-t} \alpha_{1j} y_j, \ldots, b_t - f_t y_0^{-1} - y_0^{-1} \sum_{j=1}^{l-t} \alpha_{tj} y_j)$ is a DL-representation of h with respect to $(g_{\pi(1)}, \ldots, g_{\pi(l)})$. This must be the DL-representation $(x_{\pi(1)}, \ldots, x_{\pi(l)})$, for the same reason as in the proof of Proposition 3.3.1.

It remains to check that the DL-representation satisfies the formula (3.4). From the left-hand side of the matrix equation (3.4) it follows, for all $i \in \{1, \ldots, t\}$, that

$$
\begin{aligned}
\sum_{j=1}^{l-t} \alpha_{ij} x_{\pi(j)} + x_{\pi(l-t+i)} &= \sum_{j=1}^{l-t} \alpha_{ij} (y_j y_0^{-1}) + b_i - f_i y_0^{-1} - y_0^{-1} \sum_{j=1}^{l-t} \alpha_{ij} y_j \\
&= y_0^{-1} \sum_{j=1}^{l-t} \alpha_{ij} y_j + b_i - f_i y_0^{-1} - y_0^{-1} \sum_{j=1}^{l-t} \alpha_{ij} y_j \\
&= b_i - f_i y_0^{-1} \bmod q.
\end{aligned}
$$

Since $y_0 \neq 0 \bmod q$, this is equal to the i-th entry in the vector on the righthand side; note that we have $y_0^{-1} = \epsilon \bmod q$. This completes the proof. □

As in the case of Proposition 3.3.1, the expressions appearing in this proposition are fairly intimidating, but the process of deriving them is simple. In addition to the two steps of substitution and regrouping by collecting terms, we now also collect the terms that are raised to the power ϵ and move the resulting expression to the left-hand side. Example 3.4.7 will illustrate the process.

The following property is implicit in the proof of Proposition 3.4.1, and will be of major importance in Sections 5.5.2 and 6.3.

Corollary 3.4.2. *Regardless of the formula demonstrated by $\mathcal{P}$, the proof of knowledge in Proposition 3.4.1 is also a proof of knowledge of a DL-representation of h with respect to $(g_1, \ldots, g_l)$.*

We now extend the category of adaptively chosen formula attacks defined in Definition 3.3.3. This time $\tilde{\mathcal{V}}$ may request the demonstration of formulae of the form (3.3) as well as of the form (3.4).

Proposition 3.4.3. *Let $\overline{\mathcal{P}}$ only demonstrate formulae in which x_l does not appear, using a proof of knowledge as described in Proposition 3.4.1 with the property that it is statistically witness-indistinguishable. For any distribution of $(x_1, \ldots, x_{l-1})$, whatever information $\tilde{\mathcal{V}}$ in an adaptively chosen formula attack can compute about $(x_1, \ldots, x_{l-1})$ can also be computed using merely its a priori information and the status of the formulae requested.*

Proof. Consider first the demonstration of a single formula. If x_l does not appear in the formula (3.4), then in Proposition 3.4.1 the generator g_l appears separately in the tuple with respect to which $\mathcal{P}$ proves knowledge of a DL-representation. In particular, $\mathcal{P}$ proves knowledge of a DL-representation $(\epsilon^{-1} \bmod q, y_1, \ldots, y_j, x_l \epsilon^{-1} \bmod$

q) of a number in G_q with respect to a tuple $(g_0^*, \ldots, g_j^*, g_l)$, for some $j \in \{0, \ldots, l-1\}$ and numbers $g_0^*, \ldots, g_j^*$ in G_q that depend on the formula demonstrated. The set $\{y_1, \ldots, y_j\}$ is a subset of

$$\{x_1\epsilon^{-1} \bmod q, \ldots, x_{l-1}\epsilon^{-1} \bmod q\}.$$

Clearly, $x_l\epsilon^{-1} \bmod q$ is uniformly distributed over $\mathbb{Z}_q$, because x_l has been chosen at random by $\mathcal{P}$ and $\epsilon^{-1} \neq 0 \bmod q$. Since g_l is a generator of G_q, for any tuple $(y_1, \ldots, y_j) \in (\mathbb{Z}_q)^j$ and for any $\epsilon \in \mathbb{Z}_q^*$ there is exactly one x_l such that $(\epsilon^{-1} \bmod q, y_1, \ldots, y_j, x_l\epsilon^{-1} \bmod q)$ is the DL-representation that $\mathcal{P}$ proves knowledge of. Because the proof of knowledge is witness-indistinguishable, and x_l has been chosen at random by $\mathcal{P}$, it follows that no information is revealed about $(x_1, \ldots, x_{l-1})$ beyond the status of the formula. In particular, no information about ϵ leaks.

The rest of proof is as in Proposition 3.3.4. $\qquad\square$

A practical implementation of the proof of knowledge in Proposition 3.4.3 can be realized by substituting the perfect witness-indistinguishable proof of knowledge described in Section 2.4.3, and expanding the resulting expressions. The resulting (generic) protocol steps are as follows:

Step 1. $\mathcal{P}$ generates at random $l - t + 1$ numbers, $w_0, \ldots, w_{l-t} \in \mathbb{Z}_q$, and computes

$$a := h^{-w_0} \prod_{i=1}^{l-t} g_{\pi(i)}^{w_i} \prod_{i=1}^{t} g_{\pi(l-t+i)}^{b_i w_0 - \sum_{j=1}^{l-t} \alpha_{ij} w_j}.$$

$\mathcal{P}$ then sends the initial witness a to $\mathcal{V}$.

Step 2. Let $\delta := \epsilon^{-1} \bmod q$. $\mathcal{P}$ computes a set of responses, responsive to $\mathcal{V}$'s challenge $c \in \mathbb{Z}_s$, as follows:

$$\begin{aligned}
r_0 &:= c\delta + w_0 \bmod q, \\
r_i &:= cx_{\pi(i)}\delta + w_i \bmod q \quad \forall i \in \{1, \ldots, l-t\}.
\end{aligned}$$

$\mathcal{P}$ then sends $(r_0, \ldots, r_{l-t})$ to $\mathcal{V}$.

$\mathcal{V}$ computes

$$r_{l-t+i} := b_i r_0 - f_i c - \sum_{j=1}^{l-t} \alpha_{ij} r_j \bmod q \quad \forall i \in \{1, \ldots, t\},$$

and accepts if and only if the verification relation

$$\prod_{i=1}^{l} g_{\pi(i)}^{r_i} h^{-r_0} = a$$

$$\boxed{\mathcal{P}} \qquad\qquad\qquad\qquad \boxed{\mathcal{V}}$$

SYSTEM PARAMETERS

$$(q, g_1, \ldots, g_l) := I_{\text{DLREP}}(1^k)$$

KEY SET-UP

Attributes: $x_1, \ldots, x_{l-1} \in \mathbb{Z}_q$

$x_l \in_{\mathcal{R}} \mathbb{Z}_q$

Secret key: $(x_1, \ldots, x_l)$

Public key: $\qquad\qquad\qquad h := \prod_{i=1}^{l} g_i^{x_i}$

PROTOCOL

$w_0, \ldots, w_{l-t} \in_{\mathcal{R}} \mathbb{Z}_q$

$$a := h^{-w_0} \prod_{i=1}^{l-t} g_{\pi(i)}^{w_i} \prod_{i=1}^{t} g_{\pi(l-t+i)}^{b_i w_0 - \sum_{j=1}^{l-t} \alpha_{ij} w_j}$$

$$\xrightarrow{\quad a \quad}$$
$$\xleftarrow{\quad c \quad}$$

$\delta := \epsilon^{-1} \bmod q$

$r_0 := c\delta + w_0 \bmod q$

$\forall i \in \{1, \ldots, l - t\} :$

$\quad r_i := c x_{\pi(i)} \delta + w_i \bmod q$

$$\xrightarrow{\quad r_0, \ldots, r_{l-t} \quad}$$

$$\forall i \in \{1, \ldots, t\} :$$
$$r_{l-t+i} := b_i r_0 - f_i c - \sum_{j=1}^{l-t} \alpha_{ij} r_j \bmod q$$
$$\prod_{i=1}^{l} g_{\pi(i)}^{r_i} h^{-r_0} \stackrel{?}{=} a$$

Figure 3.5: Generic protocol for demonstrating formula (3.4).

holds.

For later reference, in Sections 5.4 and 6.3, the protocol is depicted in Figure 3.5. As with the proof of knowledge in Section 2.4.3, the protocol description is generic in the sense that the binary size of s and the process of generating c have not yet been specified.

The following proposition will be of importance in Section 3.5, and can be proved in a manner similar to the proof of Proposition 3.3.5.

Proposition 3.4.4. *The protocol obtained by implementing the proof of knowledge in Proposition 3.4.3 by means of the proof of knowledge described in Section 2.4.3 is honest-verifier zero-knowledge.*

As suggested by Corollary 3.4.2, the propositions of Section 2.4.3 apply, with the obvious modifications. Special care must be taken with respect to signed proofs, though. By way of example, consider $h := g_1^{x_1} g_2^{x_2}$, and assume that a formula of the form $x_1 \neq \alpha x_2 + \beta \bmod q$ must be demonstrated. The verification relation is

$$g_1^{\alpha r_1 + \beta r_2 - c} g_2^{r_1} = h^{r_2} a.$$

Now, suppose that c is formed by hashing a and possibly h but not a description of the formula. In sharp contrast to the situation in Section 3.3.1, where signed proofs for which the formula description is not hashed along still serve as proofs of knowledge of a DL-representation of h, the triple (c, r_1, r_2) does not serve as a signed proof of knowledge of a DL-representation of h with respect to (g_1, g_2). To come up with (h, a) and (c, r_1, r_2) that meet the verification relation, one can pick any $h \in G_q$, set $a := h^{-r_2} g_1^{w_1} g_2^{w_2}$ for any $(r_2, w_1, w_2) \in \mathbb{Z}_q \times \mathbb{Z}_q \times \mathbb{Z}_q^*$, set $c := \mathcal{H}_{q, g_2}(h, a)$, set $r_1 := w_2$, and compute $\alpha := (w_1 + c - \beta r_2) r_1^{-1} \bmod q$ for any $\beta \in \mathbb{Z}_q$. To get around this, a description of the demonstrated formula must be hashed along. (The alternative is to restrict the matrix entries used to specify the formula to sets V such that $|V|/q$ is negligible in k.) In the following two propositions, F denotes a unique description of the formula demonstrated.

Proposition 3.4.5. *Suppose that the proof of knowledge in Proposition 3.4.3 is realized by substituting the witness-indistinguishable proof of knowledge described in Section 2.4.3, and that $\mathcal{V}$'s challenge is formed by hashing at least (a, F). If the DL function that is used to implement $\mathcal{P}$'s commitment is one-way, then non-interactively issued signed proofs are provably unforgeable and unmodifiable in the random oracle model, regardless of the formula(e) demonstrated and the distribution of $(x_1, \ldots, x_{l-1})$.*

The proof follows by application of Proposition 2.5.2, in light of Corollary 3.4.2 and Proposition 3.4.4.

Proposition 3.4.6. *Let $l \geq 3$, let x_{l-1} be the outcome of a random coin flip by $\mathcal{P}$, and let $\mathcal{P}$ only demonstrate formulae in which both x_{l-1} and x_l do not appear.*

Suppose that the proof of knowledge in Proposition 3.4.1 is realized by substituting the witness-indistinguishable proof of knowledge described in Section 2.4.3, and that $\mathcal{V}$'s challenge is formed by hashing at least (a, F). If the DL function used to implement $\mathcal{P}$'s commitment is one-way, and $\mathcal{P}$ performs no more than polylogarithmically many formula demonstrations, then interactively issued signed proofs are provably unforgeable and unmodifiable in the random oracle model, regardless of the formula(e) demonstrated and the distribution of $(x_1, \ldots, x_{l-2})$.

As before, if h is not fixed but may be chosen in a substantially arbitrary manner by $\mathcal{P}$, then h should be hashed along when forming $\mathcal{V}$'s challenge.

According to the unmodifiability property, $\mathcal{P}$ and $\mathcal{V}$ cannot construct a signed proof for a formula that does in fact not apply to $\mathcal{P}$'s DL-representation. On the other hand, as we will show in Section 5.3, it is possible for $\mathcal{V}$ to obtain a signed proof for any formula F' implied by F, while being convinced itself of F.

We end with a practical example.

Example 3.4.7. *Suppose $\mathcal{P}$ has three attributes $x_1, x_2, x_3 \in \mathbb{Z}_q$, and is to demonstrate by means of a non-interactively issued signed proof to $\mathcal{V}$ that the following formula holds:*

$$\mathsf{NOT}(x_1 + 3x_2 + 5x_3 = 7) \ \mathsf{AND} \ (3x_1 + 10x_2 + 18x_3 = 23).$$

With ϵ denoting $7 - (x_1 + 3x_2 + 5x_3) \bmod q$, this formula is equivalent to the statement that there exists an $\epsilon \neq 0$ such that

$$(x_1 = 1 + 4x_3 - 10\epsilon) \ \mathsf{AND} \ (x_2 = 2 - 3x_3 + 3\epsilon).$$

To demonstrate this formula, $\mathcal{P}$ generates a random $x_4 \in \mathbb{Z}_q$, and forms the commitment $h := \prod_{i=1}^{4} g_i^{x_i}$. If the formula holds true, then by substitution we get

$$
\begin{aligned}
h &= g_1^{x_1} g_2^{x_2} g_3^{x_3} g_4^{x_4} \\
&= g_1^{1+4x_3-10\epsilon} g_2^{2-3x_3+3\epsilon} g_3^{x_3} g_4^{x_4},
\end{aligned}
$$

and by regrouping in three manners (according to constants, variables, and ϵ), we obtain

$$h = (g_1^1 g_2^2)(g_1^4 g_2^{-3} g_3)^{x_3} g_4^{x_4} (g_1^{-10} g_2^3)^\epsilon.$$

Finally, we divide both sides by h, as well as by $(g_1^{-10} g_2^3)^\epsilon$, and raise both sides to the power $\epsilon^{-1} \bmod q$, arriving at

$$g_1^{10} g_2^{-3} = (g_1^1 g_2^2 h^{-1})^{1/\epsilon} (g_1^4 g_2^{-3} g_3)^{x_3/\epsilon} g_4^{x_4/\epsilon}.$$

Therefore, $\overline{\mathcal{P}}$ can prove knowledge of a DL-representation of $g_1^{10} g_2^{-3}$ with respect to the triple $(g_1^1 g_2^2 h^{-1}, g_1^4 g_2^{-3} g_3, g_4)$. According to Proposition 3.4.1, this is also

$$\boxed{\mathcal{P}} \qquad\qquad\qquad\qquad\qquad\qquad \boxed{\mathcal{V}}$$

SYSTEM PARAMETERS

$$(q, g_1, g_2, g_3, g_4) := I_{\text{DLREP}}(1^k)$$

KEY SET-UP

Attributes: $x_1, x_2, x_3 \in \mathbb{Z}_q$
$x_4 \in_{\mathcal{R}} \mathbb{Z}_q$
Secret key: $(x_1, \ldots, x_4)$
Public key: $\qquad\qquad\qquad\qquad h := \prod_{i=1}^{4} g_i^{x_i}$
Additional information: $\qquad\qquad \mathcal{H}_{q,g_4}(\cdot)$

PROTOCOL

$w_1, w_2, w_3 \in_{\mathcal{R}} \mathbb{Z}_q$
$a := g_1^{w_1 + 4w_2} g_2^{2w_1 - 3w_2} g_3^{w_2} g_4^{w_3} h^{-w_1}$
$c := \mathcal{H}_{q,g_4}(h, m, F, a)$
$\epsilon := 7 - (x_1 + 3x_2 + 5x_3) \bmod q$
$\delta := \epsilon^{-1} \bmod q$
$r_1 := c\delta + w_1 \bmod q$
$r_2 := cx_3\delta + w_2 \bmod q$
$r_3 := cx_4\delta + w_3 \bmod q$

$$\xrightarrow{\quad c, r_1, r_2, r_3 \quad}$$

$$c \stackrel{?}{=} \mathcal{H}_{q,g_4}(h, m, F,$$
$$g_1^{r_1 + 4r_2 - 10c} g_2^{2r_1 - 3r_2 + 3c} g_3^{r_2} g_4^{r_3} h^{-r_1})$$

Figure 3.6: Protocol for Example 3.4.7.

sufficient to convince $\mathcal{V}$. *By substituting the proof of knowledge described in Section 2.4.3, and expanding the resulting expressions, we obtain the protocol depicted in Figure 3.6.*

The security of the protocol for $\overline{\mathcal{P}}$ *follows from the fact that* x_4 *has been chosen at random and does not appear in the formula demonstrated. Specifically, assuming that the underlying DL function is one-way, in the random oracle model the signed proof is unforgeable and unmodifiable. Moreover, it does not leak more information about* (x_1, x_2, x_3) *than the validity of the formula; this holds even if* $\overline{\mathcal{P}}$ *demonstrates arbitrarily many other formulae (with* x_4 *not appearing in any of these).*

A noteworthy aspect of the protocol is that the computations corresponding to the powers of g_4 *can all be performed by proving knowledge of the discrete logarithm of* $(g_4^{x_4})^{1/\epsilon}$ *with respect to* g_4, *using the Schnorr proof of knowledge, because* x_4 *does not appear in the formula demonstrated. This property can easily be seen to hold in general, and will be of great importance in Sections 6.3 and 6.4.*

3.4.2 Technique based on the RSAREP function

To base the technique on the hardness of inverting the RSA function, consider $\mathcal{P}$ having to demonstrate formula (3.4), with "mod v" replacing "mod q," and $\epsilon \in \mathbb{Z}_v^*$. Recall that $\mathcal{P}$ commits to $(x_1, \ldots, x_l)$ by means of $h := g_1^{x_1} \cdots g_l^{x_l} x_{l+1}^v$.

Proposition 3.4.8. $\mathcal{P}$ *can prove knowledge of an RSA-representation of*

$$\prod_{i=1}^{t} g_{\pi(l-t+i)}^{f_i}$$

with respect to

$$\left(\prod_{i=1}^{t} g_{\pi(l-t+i)}^{b_i} h^{-1}, \ g_{\pi(1)} \prod_{i=1}^{t} g_{\pi(l-t+i)}^{-\alpha_{i1}}, \ \cdots, \ g_{\pi(l-t)} \prod_{i=1}^{t} g_{\pi(l-t+i)}^{-\alpha_{i,l-t}}, v \right)$$

if and only if it knows a set of attributes that satisfies the system (3.4).

Proof. If $(x_1, \ldots, x_l)$ satisfies the system (3.4), then by regrouping expressions it is seen that

$$\left(\prod_{i=1}^{t} g_{\pi(l-t+i)}^{f_i} \right)^{\epsilon}$$

equals

$$\left(\prod_{i=1}^{t} g_{\pi(l-t+i)}^{b_i} h^{-1} \right) \left(g_{\pi(1)} \prod_{i=1}^{t} g_{\pi(l-t+i)}^{-\alpha_{i1}} \right)^{x_{\pi(1)}} \cdots \left(g_{\pi(l-t)} \prod_{i=1}^{t} g_{\pi(l-t+i)}^{-\alpha_{i,l-t}} \right)^{x_{\pi(l-t)}} x_{l+1}^v.$$

Because inequality holds, $\epsilon \neq 0 \bmod v$ and so $\mathcal{P}$ can compute integers $e, f \in \mathbb{Z}$ such that $e\epsilon + fv = 1$, by using the extended Euclidean algorithm. (This can be always be done, because v is prime.) It follows that

$$\left(e \bmod v, ex_{\pi(1)} \bmod v, \dots, ex_{\pi(l-t)} \bmod v, z \right)$$

is the RSA-representation sought for, where z denotes the expression

$$(\prod_{i=1}^{t} g_{\pi(l-t+i)}^{b_i} h^{-1})^{e\,\mathrm{div}\,v} \prod_{j=1}^{l-t} \left(g_{\pi(j)} \prod_{i=1}^{t} g_{\pi(l-t+i)}^{-\alpha_{ij}} \right)^{(ex_{\pi(j)})\,\mathrm{div}\,v} x_{l+1}^{e} (\prod_{i=1}^{t} g_{\pi(l-t+i)}^{f_i})^{f}.$$

The proof of the converse is similar to the second part of the proof of Proposition 3.4.1, with the additional application of normalizations where needed. $\qquad\square$

The protocol can be efficiently implemented by using the proof of knowledge described in Section 2.4.4 and expanding the resulting expressions. The direct analogue of Proposition 3.4.3 can be proved, as well as the unforgeability and unmodifiability of signed proofs (assuming at least a and F are hashed along when forming c). Since the necessary adaptations are straightforward, a further description is omitted.

3.5 Atomic formulae connected by "OR" connectives

We now show how $\mathcal{P}$ can demonstrate Boolean formulae in which subformulae, of either one of the two forms discussed in the previous sections, are connected by zero or more "OR" connectives.

3.5.1 Technique based on the DLREP function

The following definition defines the basic building block for the technique in this section.

Definition 3.5.1. *An* atomic *formula is one in which linear relations over $\mathbb{Z}_q$ are connected by zero or more "AND" connectives and at most one "NOT" connective.*

Any atomic formula can be described either by system (3.2) or by system (3.4). Consequently, any atomic formula applying to $\mathcal{P}$'s attributes can be demonstrated using either the method described in Section 3.3 or that described in Section 3.4.

Consider now the situation in which $\mathcal{P}$ is to demonstrate a satisfiable Boolean formula F of the form

$$F = F_1 \text{ OR } \dots \text{ OR } F_j, \tag{3.6}$$

for some $j \geq 1$ that may be polynomial in the security parameter k. Each of $F_1, \dots, F_j$ is an atomic formula. If F holds true for $\mathcal{P}$'s attributes, then at least one of the j atomic subformulae holds true, but $\tilde{\mathcal{V}}$ should not be able to learn which one(s). Suppose that (at least) F_t holds true, for some $t \in \{1, \ldots, j\}$.

In the following protocol for demonstrating F, it is assumed that atomic formulae are demonstrated by substituting the witness-indistinguishable proof of knowledge described in Section 2.4.3 into the proof of knowledge in either Proposition 3.3.1 or Proposition 3.4.1 (whichever is appropriate):

Step 1. Using the honest-verifier zero-knowledge simulator that exists according to Proposition 3.3.5 or 3.4.4, $\mathcal{P}$ generates $j-1$ transcripts of subformulae demonstrations for $F_1, \ldots, F_{t-1}, F_{t+1}, \ldots, F_j$. For each $i \in \{1, \ldots, j\} \setminus \{t\}$, the simulated proof for formula F_i involves a random *self-chosen* challenge that we denote by c_i, an initial witness, and one or more self-chosen responses. For subformula F_t, $\mathcal{P}$ generates an initial witness in the manner specified by the standard protocol for demonstrating an atomic formula (to prepare for a genuine proof). $\mathcal{P}$ then sends all j initial witnesses, referred to as its *initial witness set*, to $\mathcal{V}$.

Step 2. $\mathcal{V}$ generates a random challenge $c \in \mathbb{Z}_s$, and sends it to $\mathcal{P}$.

Step 3. $\mathcal{P}$ forms j response sets, as follows. $\mathcal{P}$ computes $c_t := c - \sum_{i \neq t} c_i \bmod s$. Responsive to challenge c_t, $\mathcal{P}$ computes its responses corresponding to the demonstration of F_t, in the manner described in Step 2 of the protocol in either Section 3.3 or Section 3.4 (whichever is appropriate). For each of the remaining $j-1$ subformulae, $\mathcal{P}$ uses the self-chosen responses from the simulated formulae demonstrations prepared in Step 1. $\mathcal{P}$ then sends all j response sets and $(c_1, \ldots, c_j)$ to $\mathcal{V}$.

$\mathcal{V}$ verifies that $c = \sum_{i=1}^{j} c_i \bmod s$. If this verification holds, then for each of the j atomic subformulae it applies the verification relation for that subformula. Specifically, $\mathcal{V}$ verifies the demonstration of F_i by applying the verification relation that applies in the standard protocol for demonstrating F_i, using the i-th initial witness and response set provided by $\mathcal{P}$ and the challenge c_i. $\mathcal{V}$ accepts if and only if the j challenges sum up correctly and all j verification relations hold; together, these $j + 1$ verification relations make up the verification process for the demonstration of F.

Note that the protocol encompasses the protocols of Sections 3.3 and 3.4 as special cases.

Proposition 3.5.2. *In the protocol for demonstrating F, assume that $\mathcal{P}$ only demonstrates formulae F in which x_l does not appear. The following properties hold:*

(a) The protocol is complete and sound.

(b) The protocol is a proof of knowledge of a DL-representation of h with respect to the tuple $(g_1, \ldots, g_l)$.

(c) For any distribution of $(x_1, \ldots, x_{l-1})$, whatever information $\tilde{\mathcal{V}}$ in an adaptively chosen formula attack[2] can compute about $(x_1, \ldots, x_{l-1})$ can also be computed using merely its a priori information and the status of the formulae requested.

Proof. We only sketch the proof here; the details are easy to fill in.

(a) Completeness is verified straightforwardly. Soundness follows from the condition that the c_i's have to sum up to $\mathcal{V}$'s challenge c, so that $\mathcal{P}$ cannot simulate the demonstration for all j subformulae. For at least one subformula $\mathcal{P}$ has to use a challenge that it cannot anticipate: it must perform a genuine proof of knowledge for that subformula. Because the demonstration of an atomic subformula is a sound proof of knowledge, $\mathcal{P}$ can do this only if the subformula indeed holds true for its attributes; in other words, if F holds true.

(b) The soundness of the protocol for demonstrating F implies that at least one of the atomic subformulae holds true for $\mathcal{P}$'s attributes. According to Corollaries 3.3.2 and 3.4.2, the proof of knowledge for this atomic subformula is also a proof of knowledge of a DL-representation of h with respect to $(g_1, \ldots, g_l)$.

(c) The third claim follows from the perfect simulatability of the $j-1$ subformulae demonstrations and the fact that the relation $\sum_{i=1}^{j} c_i = c \bmod s$ reveals no information on which $j-1$ challenges have been self-chosen by $\mathcal{P}$, regardless of the manner in which c is formed. ☐

Care must be taken in a practical implementation that the subformula for which a genuine proof is performed cannot be deduced by timing the delay between sending $\mathcal{V}$'s challenge and receiving the j response sets.

To obtain a signed proof, $\mathcal{V}$'s challenge c should be generated as a sufficiently strong one-way hash of at least the j initial witnesses, a description of F, and an (optional) message m. If h is not fixed, then it should be hashed along as well. The signed proof consists of $(c_1, \ldots, c_j)$ and the j response sets, or of the j initial witnesses and the j response sets. If the protocol is performed non-interactively then $\mathcal{P}$ need not send either its initial witness set or its j challenges to $\mathcal{V}$, since they can be recovered by $\mathcal{V}$.

Proposition 3.5.3. *In Proposition 3.5.2, if the DL function used to implement $\mathcal{P}$'s commitment is one-way, and $\mathcal{V}$'s challenge is formed by hashing at least all j initial witnesses and F, then non-interactively issued signed proofs are provably unforgeable and unmodifiable in the random oracle model, regardless of the formula(e) demonstrated and the distribution of $(x_1, \ldots, x_{l-1})$.*

Proposition 3.5.4. *Let $l \geq 3$, let x_{l-1} be the outcome of a random coin flip by $\mathcal{P}$, and let $\mathcal{P}$ only demonstrate formulae in which both x_{l-1} and x_l do not appear. If the DL function used to implement $\mathcal{P}$'s commitment is one-way, $\mathcal{V}$'s challenge is formed by*

---

[2]This time, $\mathcal{V}$ may request the demonstration of any Boolean formula of the form (3.6).

hashing at least all j initial witnesses and F, and $\mathcal{P}$ performs no more than polylog-arithmically many formula demonstrations, then interactively issued signed proofs are provably unforgeable and unmodifiable in the random oracle model, regardless of the formula(e) demonstrated and the distribution of $(x_1, \ldots, x_{l-2})$.

Again, the remarks made about the coin flip in Proposition 3.3.7 apply here as well.

If $j \geq 2$ in formula (3.6) the protocol is non-trivially witness-indistinguishable, and in Proposition 3.5.4 we can omit the requirement that x_{l-1} be random and do not appear in the formulae demonstrated by $\mathcal{P}$.

The protocol for demonstrating F admits several variations. For example:

- The relation $\sum_{i=1}^{j} c_i = c \bmod s$ can be replaced by any other relation with the property that, for any c, the selection of any $j - 1$ challenges uniquely determines the remaining challenge. For example, for s a prime one can use $\prod_{i=1}^{j} c_i = c \bmod s$ or, if s is a power of 2, $\oplus_{i=1}^{j} c_i = c$, where $\oplus$ denotes the bitwise exclusive-or operator.

- Instead of simulating all but one of the subformula demonstrations, $\mathcal{P}$ could perform a genuine proof of knowledge for all subformulae that hold true and simulate the demonstration only for those that do not hold true.

Both variations bring no noteworthy performance gain, and we will see in Section 6.3 that they are disadvantageous when lifting the formulae demonstration techniques to the smartcard setting. Moreover, in Sections 5.3 and 5.4.2 we will show that the relation $\sum_{i=1}^{j} c_i = c \bmod q$ can be exploited to improve efficiency and privacy in applications where $\mathcal{V}$ must relay signed proofs to the CA. For these reasons we will not consider the two variations any further.

Example 3.5.5. *Suppose $\mathcal{P}$ has three attributes $x_1, x_2, x_3 \in \mathbb{Z}_q$, and is to demonstrate by means of a non-interactively issued signed proof to $\mathcal{V}$ that the following formula holds:*

$$\Big((x_1 + 2x_2 - 10x_3 = 13) \text{ AND } (x_2 - 4x_3 = 5)\Big) \text{ OR}$$
$$\Big(\text{NOT}(x_1 + 3x_2 + 5x_3 = 7) \text{ AND } (3x_1 + 10x_2 + 18x_3 = 23)\Big)$$

Assume for concreteness that

$$(x_1 + 2x_2 - 10x_3 = 13) \text{ AND } (x_2 - 4x_3 = 5)$$

holds, and that

$$\text{NOT}(x_1 + 3x_2 + 5x_3 = 7) \text{ AND } (3x_1 + 10x_2 + 18x_3 = 23)$$

does not necessarily hold. To demonstrate the formula, $\mathcal{P}$ generates a random $x_4 \in \mathbb{Z}_q$, and forms the commitment $h := \prod_{i=1}^{4} g_i^{x_i}$. As we have seen in Example 3.3.9, to demonstrate the first subformula $\mathcal{P}$ proves knowledge of a DL-representation of $h/(g_1^3 g_2^5)$ with respect to $(g_1^2 g_2^4 g_3, g_4)$. According to Example 3.4.7, the second subformula requires a proof of knowledge of a DL-representation of $g_1^{10} g_2^{-3}$ with respect to $(g_1 g_2^2 h^{-1}, g_1^4 g_2^{-3} g_3, g_4)$; $\mathcal{P}$ simulates this demonstration, using a self-chosen challenge and self-chosen responses. The resulting protocol is depicted in Figure 3.7. Here, m denotes an (optional) message and F denotes a description uniquely identifying the formula demonstrated. The signed proof consists of $(c_1, c_2, r_1, r_2, r_3, r_4, r_5)$. Assuming that the underlying DL function is one-way, in the random oracle model the signed proof is unforgeable and unmodifiable. Moreover, it does not leak more information about (x_1, x_2, x_3) than the validity of the formula; this holds even if $\mathcal{P}$ demonstrates arbitrarily many other formulae.

3.5.2   Technique based on the RSAREP function

Adaptation to the difficulty of inverting the RSA function poses no particular difficulties, and is therefore omitted.

3.6   Demonstrating arbitrary Boolean formulae

We are now prepared for the final step: demonstrating arbitrary satisfiable Boolean formulae.

3.6.1   Technique based on the DLREP function

Suppose $\mathcal{P}$ is to demonstrate an arbitrary Boolean formula that applies to its attributes. Without loss of generality, we assume that F is of the conjunctive normal form,

$$F = F_1 \text{ AND } \ldots \text{ AND } F_j, \tag{3.7}$$

for some $j \geq 1$ that may be polynomial in k, where each of $F_1, \ldots, F_j$ are atomic subformulae of the form (3.6). The indices j here and in formula (3.6) do not bear any relation to one another. Likewise, each subformula may be composed of an arbitrary and distinct number of subformulae. The issue of writing an arbitrary Boolean formula in the form (3.7) is outside of the scope of this book.

Our technique for demonstrating F is as follows. F holds true for $\mathcal{P}$'s attributes if and only if $F_1, \ldots, F_j$ all hold true. To demonstrate F, $\mathcal{P}$ demonstrates each of $F_1, \ldots, F_j$ by means of the proof of knowledge described in the previous section, subject to the following two constraints:

- All j protocol executions are performed in parallel; and

$$\boxed{\mathcal{P}} \qquad\qquad\qquad\qquad \boxed{\mathcal{V}}$$

SYSTEM PARAMETERS

$$(q, g_1, g_2, g_3, g_4) := I_{\text{DLREP}}(1^k)$$

KEY SET-UP

Attributes: $x_1, x_2, x_3 \in \mathbb{Z}_q$

$x_4 \in_{\mathcal{R}} \mathbb{Z}_q$

Secret key: $(x_1, \ldots, x_4)$

Public key: $\qquad\qquad h := \prod_{i=1}^{4} g_i^{x_i}$

Additional information: $\qquad \mathcal{H}_{q,g_4}(\cdot)$

PROTOCOL

$w_1, w_2, c_2, r_3, r_4, r_5 \in_{\mathcal{R}} \mathbb{Z}_q$

$a_1 := g_1^{2w_1} g_2^{4w_1} g_3^{w_1} g_4^{w_2}$

$a_2 := g_1^{r_3 + 4r_4 - 10c_2} g_2^{2r_3 - 3r_4 + 3c_2} g_3^{r_4} g_4^{r_5} h^{-r_3}$

$c := \mathcal{H}_{q,g_4}(h, m, F, a_1, a_2)$

$c_1 := c - c_2 \bmod s$

$r_1 := c_1 x_3 + w_1 \bmod q$

$r_2 := c_1 x_4 + w_2 \bmod q$

$$\xrightarrow{\quad c_1, c_2, (r_1, r_2, r_3, r_4, r_5) \quad}$$

$$c := c_1 + c_2 \bmod s$$

$$c \stackrel{?}{=} \mathcal{H}_{q,g_4}(h, m, F, g_1^{2r_1 + 3c_1} g_2^{4r_1 + 5c_1} g_3^{r_1} g_4^{r_2} h^{-c_1},$$
$$g_1^{r_3 + 4r_4 - 10c_2} g_2^{2r_3 - 3r_4 + 3c_2} g_3^{r_4} g_4^{r_5} h^{-r_3})$$

Figure 3.7: Protocol for Example 3.5.5.

- $\mathcal{V}$'s challenge is the same in all j protocol executions.

$\mathcal{V}$ accepts if and only if it accepts $\mathcal{P}$'s demonstration of each of the j subformulae. Although the two constraints are not strictly necessary, they are preferable in light of efficiency and, more importantly, for the purpose of lifting the protocol to the smartcard setting, as we will see in Section 6.3. Also, the constraints are desirable for the purpose of forming signed proofs.

The following proposition follows straightforwardly from Proposition 3.5.2 and the fact that using the same challenge for all subformulae does not increase $\widehat{\mathcal{P}}$'s cheating probability.

Proposition 3.6.1. *In the protocol for demonstrating F, assume that $\mathcal{P}$ only demonstrates formulae F in which x_l does not appear. The following properties hold:*

(a) *The protocol is complete and sound.*

(b) *The protocol is a proof of knowledge of a DL-representation of h with respect to the tuple $(g_1, \ldots, g_l)$.*

(c) *For any distribution of $(x_1, \ldots, x_{l-1})$, whatever information $\widetilde{\mathcal{V}}$ in an adaptively chosen formula attack [3] can compute about $(x_1, \ldots, x_{l-1})$ can also be computed using merely its a priori information and the status of the formulae requested.*

The proof is straightforward. (A description of what is essentially the knowledge extractor required to prove soundness is contained in the proof of Proposition 5.4.1.)

To obtain a signed proof, $\mathcal{V}$'s challenge c should be generated as a sufficiently strong one-way hash of the j initial witness sets, a description of F, and an (optional) message m. In case h is not fixed a priori, it should be hashed along as well. The signed proof consists all $\mathcal{P}$'s challenge and response sets, or equivalently of all $\mathcal{P}$'s initial witness sets and response sets. (As before, instead of hashing along a description of F one may alternatively restrict all the matrix entries to sets V such that $|V|/q$ is negligible in k.)

Proposition 3.6.2. *In Proposition 3.6.1, if the DL function used to implement $\mathcal{P}$'s commitment is one-way, and $\mathcal{V}$'s challenge is formed by hashing at least all initial witnesses and F, then non-interactively issued signed proofs are provably unforgeable and unmodifiable in the random oracle model, regardless of the formula(e) demonstrated and the distribution of $(x_1, \ldots, x_{l-1})$.*

Proposition 3.6.3. *Let $l \geq 3$, let x_{l-1} be the outcome of a random coin flip by $\mathcal{P}$, and let $\mathcal{P}$ only demonstrate formulae F in which both x_{l-1} and x_l do not appear. If the DL function used to implement $\mathcal{P}$'s commitment is one-way, $\mathcal{V}$'s challenge is formed by hashing at least all initial witnesses and F, and $\mathcal{P}$ performs no more than*

---

[3] This time, $\mathcal{V}$ may request the demonstration of any Boolean formula of the form (3.7).

polylogarithmically many formula demonstrations, then interactively issued signed proofs are provably unforgeable and unmodifiable in the random oracle model, regardless of the formula(e) demonstrated and the distribution of $(x_1, \ldots, x_{l-2})$.

The remarks about the coin flip in Proposition 3.3.7 apply here as well.

We now posses all the machinery for $\mathcal{P}$ to demonstrate the example formula (3.1) in Section 3.1.

Example 3.6.4. *Suppose* $\mathcal{P}$ *has three attributes* $x_1, x_2, x_3 \in \mathbb{Z}_q$, *selected according to an arbitrary probability distribution, and is to demonstrate by means of a non-interactively issued signed proof to* $\mathcal{V}$ *that the example formula (3.1) holds true. Assume for concreteness that*

$$(x_1 + 2x_2 - 10x_3 = 13) \text{ AND } (x_2 - 4x_3 = 5)$$

holds. In Example 3.5.5 we have seen how to demonstrate the subformula appearing before the third "AND" connective. In accordance with Section 3.4, $\mathcal{P}$ *demonstrates the remaining part by proving knowledge of a DL-representation of* g_1 *with respect to* $(g_1^5 h^{-1}, g_1^8 g_2, g_1^{-11} g_3, g_4)$. *By merging the two protocols in accordance with the technique described in this section, we obtain the protocol depicted in Figure 3.8. As before,* m *denotes a message and* F *denotes a description uniquely identifying formula (3.1). Examples of data that could be included in* m *are a nonce to protect against replay, an identifier of* $\mathcal{V}$, *a public key to be used for session encryption, and a free-form message. The signed proof consists of* $(c_1, c_2, r_1, \ldots, r_9)$. *Assuming that the underlying DL function is one-way, in the random oracle model the signed proof is unforgeable and unmodifiable. Moreover, it does not leak more information about* (x_1, x_2, x_3) *than the validity of the formula; this holds even if* $\mathcal{P}$ *demonstrates arbitrarily many other formulae about its attributes.*

The performance estimates at the end of Section 3.1 are readily obtained. Namely, according to Section 2.2.2, 200-bit challenges and responses suffice for long-term security. Both $\mathcal{P}$ *and* $\mathcal{V}$, *to perform their computations in* G_q, *can use a precomputed table that contains the 31 products of the numbers in the non-empty subsets of* $\{g_1, \ldots, g_4, h\}$. *Performance can be pushed to the limit by using an elliptic curve implementation with 20-byte base numbers, but beware of the reservations expressed in Section 2.2.2. Also, the computational burden for* $\mathcal{V}$ *can be reduced by a factor of almost 3 by having* $\mathcal{P}$ *send along* (a_1, a_2, a_3) *(one of* c_1, c_2 *may be left out) and applying batch-verification, in the manner described in Section 2.5.3.*

3.6.2 Technique based on the RSAREP function

Again, adaptation to the difficulty of inverting the RSA function poses no particular difficulties.

$$\boxed{\mathcal{P}} \hspace{6cm} \boxed{\mathcal{V}}$$

SYSTEM PARAMETERS

$$(q, g_1, g_2, g_3, g_4) := I_{\text{DLREP}}(1^k)$$

KEY SET-UP

Attributes: $x_1, x_2, x_3 \in \mathbb{Z}_q$

$x_4 \in_{\mathcal{R}} \mathbb{Z}_q$

Secret key: $(x_1, \ldots, x_4)$

Public key: $\hspace{2cm} h := \prod_{i=1}^{4} g_i^{x_i}$

Additional information: $\hspace{1cm} \mathcal{H}_{q,g_4}(\cdot)$

PROTOCOL

$w_1, \ldots, w_6, c_2, r_3, r_4, r_5 \in_{\mathcal{R}} \mathbb{Z}_q$

$a_1 := g_1^{2w_1} g_2^{4w_1} g_3^{w_1} g_4^{w_2}$

$a_2 := g_1^{r_3 + 4r_4 - 10c_2} g_2^{2r_3 - 3r_4 + 3c_2} g_3^{r_4} g_4^{r_5} h^{-r_3}$

$a_3 := g_1^{5w_3 + 8w_4 - 11w_5} g_2^{w_4} g_3^{w_5} g_4^{w_6} h^{-w_3}$

$c := \mathcal{H}_{q,g_4}(h, m, F, a_1, a_2, a_3)$

$c_1 := c - c_2 \bmod s$

$r_1 := c_1 x_3 + w_1 \bmod q$

$r_2 := c_1 x_4 + w_2 \bmod q$

$\delta := \epsilon^{-1} \bmod q$

$r_6 := c\delta + w_3 \bmod q$

$r_7 := cx_2\delta + w_4 \bmod q$

$r_8 := cx_3\delta + w_5 \bmod q$

$r_9 := cx_4 + w_6 \bmod q$

$$\xrightarrow{\hspace{1cm} c_1, c_2, (r_1, \ldots, r_9) \hspace{1cm}}$$

$c := c_1 + c_2 \bmod s$

$c \overset{?}{=} \mathcal{H}_{q,g_4}(h, m, F,$

$\hspace{1cm} g_1^{2r_1 + 3c_1} g_2^{4r_1 + 5c_1} g_3^{r_1} g_4^{r_2} h^{-c_1},$

$\hspace{1cm} g_1^{r_3 + 4r_4 - 10c_2} g_2^{2r_3 - 3r_4 + 3c_2} g_3^{r_4} g_4^{r_5} h^{-r_3},$

$\hspace{1cm} g_1^{5r_6 + 8r_7 - 11r_8 - c} g_2^{r_7} g_3^{r_8} g_4^{r_9} h^{-r_6})$

Figure 3.8: Protocol for Example 3.6.4.

3.7   Optimizations and extensions

Modulo a small constant factor, the communication and computation complexity of our proof techniques for atomic formulae are the same as for proofs with full disclosure. In the latter case, $\mathcal{P}$ would simply transmit $(x_1, \ldots, x_l)$ to $\mathcal{V}$, and digitally sign $\mathcal{V}$'s challenge message using the Schnorr or Guillou-Quisquater signature scheme, say. Thus, our selective disclosure techniques for atomic formulae achieve privacy essentially for free.

This extreme efficiency does not hold when our techniques are used to demonstrate formulae of the form (3.6) or (3.7), although the increase in communication and computation complexity is only linear in the number of logical connectives. We now describe a slight optimization of our techniques for these two cases. To demonstrate an atomic formula, our techniques have $\mathcal{P}$ demonstrate knowledge of a secret key corresponding to a public key, where the definition of the public key and of what constitutes a secret key both depend on the formula demonstrated; see Propositions 3.3.1 and 3.4.1. In this interpretation, "complex" propositions of the form

"I know a secret key corresponding to public key h and it satisfies formula F"

(with h fixed a priori and F atomic) are mapped to simple propositions of the form

"I know a secret key corresponding to public key h_i,"

where the "distorted" public key h_i is not fixed a priori but derived from h in a formula-dependent manner, and the definition of what constitutes a secret key corresponding to h_i also depends on F. Cramer, Damgård, and Schoenmakers [123] show how to demonstrate monotone Boolean formulae over such simple propositions.[4] Since the witness-indistinguishable proof of knowledge in Section 2.4.3 satisfies their requirements [123, Corollary 14], their technique can be applied here. The idea is to dictate the restrictions, according to which $\mathcal{P}$ generates its self-chosen challenges from the challenge message, in accordance with a secret-sharing construction due to Benaloh and Leichter [25] for the access structure defined by the "dual" of the formula. Since this technique does not require F to be expressed in the conjunctive normal form (3.7), the resulting proof of knowledge may be more compact. On the downside, lifting the optimized demonstration protocols to the smartcard setting (see Chapter 6) is not always possible without significantly increasing the complexity of the protocol. Therefore, we will not consider this optimization any further.

Another optimization is for $\mathcal{V}$ to batch-process all the verification relations, one for each atomic (sub)subformula, in the manner described in Section 2.5.3. Batch-verification may also be applied to the verification of multiple protocol executions.

It is possible to use our showing protocol techniques in such a manner that $\mathcal{P}$ can rapidly demonstrate possession of t out of u "qualitative" attributes, for any

---

[4]De Santis, Di Crescenzo, Persiano, and Yung [334] independently devised a similar technique.

$t \leq u \leq l$. Namely, if each of $x_1, \ldots, x_u$ is guaranteed to be either 1 or 0, then $\mathcal{P}$ can simply demonstrate that $\sum_{i=1}^{u} x_i = t \bmod q$. In Chapter 5 we will see that the guarantee that each x_i is either 0 or 1 can come from a CA that encodes the attribute values into $\mathcal{P}$'s key pair.

The atomic propositions for which Boolean formulae can be demonstrated can be extended beyond linear relations:

- A technique of Damgård [127] can be adapted to our scenario in order to demonstrate polynomial relations. Demonstration of

$$x_1^{\gamma_1} + \beta_2 x_2^{\gamma_2} + \cdots + \beta_k x_l^{\gamma_l} = \beta_1 \bmod q$$

requires $\mathcal{P}$ to spawn in the order of $\sum_{i=1}^{l} \gamma_i$ auxiliary commitments, and to perform two basic proofs of knowledge for each of these. (Either a proof of knowledge of a representation or a proof of equality of two secrets; the latter can be handled using a protocol of Chaum and Pedersen [109] that will also be used in Section 4.5.2.) This is practical only for low-degree polynomials.[5]

- Brickell, Chaum, Dåmgard, and van de Graaf [63] show how to demonstrate that a secret is contained in an interval. Their technique, which can be adapted to our scenario, is not very practical because it requires polynomially many repetitions of a three-move protocol with binary challenges. Moreover, the interval for which $\mathcal{P}$ must perform the proof must be three times larger than the interval one is interested in, to avoid leakage of information (so that $\mathcal{P}$ is actually demonstrating a different statement).

An improvement is due to Schoenmakers [342]. With $h = g_1^{x_1} g_2^{\alpha}$, say, to demonstrate that $x_1 \in \{0, \ldots, 2^t - 1\}$ the prover discloses t auxiliary commitments

$$h_0 := g_1^{b_1} g_2^{\alpha_1}, \ldots, h_{t-1} := g_1^{b_t} g_2^{\alpha_t}.$$

The b_i's satisfy $\sum_{i=0}^{t-1} b_i 2^i = x_1$ and the α_i's are chosen at random subject to the condition

$$\alpha = \sum_{i=0}^{t-1} \alpha_i 2^i \bmod q.$$

The prover proves that each $b_i \in \{0, 1\}$, using our technique in Section 3.5, and the verifier in addition checks that

$$\prod_{i=0}^{t-1} h_i^{2^i} = h.$$

Generalization to arbitrary intervals is accomplished by proving that x_1 is in the intersection of two appropriately shifted intervals, each of length a power

---

[5]Fujisaka and Okamoto [179] proposed another technique that is equally impractical and less elegant.

of 2. This technique requires the prover to spawn a number of auxiliary commitments that is linear in the size of the interval, and to perform essentially two Schnorr proofs of knowledge for each of these.

Demonstrating an atomic proposition in both cases involves a serious amount of overhead, and the practical relevance of demonstrating polynomial relations is unclear. Therefore we will not consider these techniques any further.

3.8 Bibliographic notes

The technique in Section 3.3 for demonstrating a single linear relation is due to Brands [54]. The general techniques for demonstrating arbitrary Boolean propositions, for atomic propositions that are linear relations, originate from Brands [45], with a summary in Brands [55]. None of the formal security statements and their proofs have appeared elsewhere previously, nor have the examples.

The suggestion in Section 3.7 to adapt a technique of Damgård [127] to demonstrate polynomial relations is due to Brands [55], and was later on used by Camenisch and Stadler [70, 73]. They [74] also rediscovered the simple technique in Section 5.2.2 for demonstrating properties of the attributes encoded into different key pairs, due to Brands [46, page 22] (see also Brands [54]); the resulting proof system is significantly less practical and flexible, though.

The techniques in this chapter have numerous applications that do not necessarily involve digital certificates. For example, the techniques in Sections 3.3 and 3.4 can be used to improve the undeniable signature scheme of Chaum, van Heijst, and Pfitzmann [111, 112]. The technique in Section 3.5, which was inspired by a technique of Schoenmakers [340] to prove knowledge of a secret key corresponding to at least one of two public keys, has been applied by Cramer, Franklin, Schoenmakers, and Yung [124] and Cramer, Gennaro, and Schoenmakers [125] to design "key escrow" electronic voting schemes (see the Epilogue). Other applications that need not involve digital certificates but could benefit from our showing protocol techniques include fair exchange of digital signatures, incremental signing, digital watermarking, private information retrieval, and distributed database querying. In the remaining chapters we will confine ourselves to applications involving digital certification.

Chapter 4

Restrictive Blind Issuing Protocols

In this chapter we introduce a new notion, called restrictive blinding, to enable the CA to encode attributes into certified key pairs that are unlinkable and untraceable in all other respects. We design various practical restrictive blind certificate issuing protocols, for DLREP-based certificates as well as for RSAREP-based certificates, and analyze their security. This chapter builds on Chapter 2, but may be read independently of Chapter 3. In Chapter 5 we will show how to combine the issuing and showing protocol techniques.

4.1 Restrictive blinding

Informally, a *restrictive blind* certificate scheme is a digital certificate scheme (see Section 2.6) with the following properties:

- If $\mathcal{V}$ and $\mathcal{P}$ both follow the protocol, then $\mathcal{V}$ obtains a certified key pair

$$(s, p, \mathsf{cert}(p)).$$

  The pair (s, p) is a key pair of $\mathcal{V}$, and $\mathsf{cert}(p)$ is $\mathcal{P}$'s (secret-key or public-key) digital certificate on $\mathcal{V}$'s public key p.

- The certified public key $(p, \mathsf{cert}(p))$ obtained by $\overline{\mathcal{V}}$ by interacting with $\widetilde{\mathcal{P}}$ is statistically independent from $\widetilde{\mathcal{P}}$'s view in the protocol execution.

- If $\mathcal{P}$ follows the protocol, then $\widehat{\mathcal{V}}$ cannot forge certified key pairs.

- If $\widehat{\mathcal{V}}$ obtains a certified key pair $(s, p, \mathsf{cert}(p))$, then with overwhelming probability the secret key s contains at least one attribute encoded by $\overline{\mathcal{P}}$.

The last property is the hardest to formalize. To understand the meaning of "encoding at least one attribute," consider by way of example a scenario in which $\mathcal{V}$ is to receive $\mathcal{P}$'s certificate on a public key defined by the RSAREP function (see Section 2.3.3). If $\mathcal{P}$ is to encode $(x_1, \ldots, x_l)$ into the secret key $\mathcal{V}$ will know for the public key $\prod_{i=1}^{l} g_i^{x_i} x_{l+1}^v$ it will end up with, then $\mathcal{V}$ must be unable to modify these l attributes as part of its blinding operations; we say that part of $\mathcal{V}$'s secret key (the first l positions) is *blinding-invariant*. Note that $\mathcal{P}$'s ability to encode $(x_1, \ldots, x_l)$ into $\mathcal{V}$'s secret key does not contradict the requirement that $\mathcal{V}$ is able to blind its certified public key $(p, \mathsf{cert}(p))$, assuming that $\mathcal{V}$ can generate x_{l+1} at random from $\mathbb{Z}_n^*$. The difficulty resides in how to meet all four properties.

In general, $\mathcal{P}$ may encode attributes into $\mathcal{V}$'s secret key in an arbitrary fashion. All that matters is that the blinding-invariant part of $\mathcal{V}$'s secret key can be described by a polynomial-time computable (non-constant) function from the space of secret keys into the space of attributes. For example, suppose that $\widehat{\mathcal{V}}$ can obtain $\mathcal{P}$'s certificate on a public key of the form $\prod_{i=1}^{l} g_i^{\alpha x_i + \beta} x_{l+1}^v$, for random blinding factors $\alpha, \beta \in \mathbb{Z}_v$, but not on other forms. Then $\mathcal{P}$ can still encode $l - 2$ attributes in an independent manner into $\mathcal{V}$'s secret key, since $x_i^* := (x_i - x_l)(x_{l-1} - x_l)^{-1} \bmod v$ remains unchanged for all $i \in \{1, \ldots, l - 2\}$). (More generally, the invariance applies under linear transformations.) For another example, see Proposition 4.3.15. If, on the other hand, $\widehat{\mathcal{V}}$ can obtain $\mathcal{P}$'s certificate on a public key of the form $\prod_{i=1}^{l} g_i^{x_i + \alpha_i} x_{l+1}^v$, for random blinding factors $\alpha_1, \ldots, \alpha_l \in \mathbb{Z}_v$, then $\mathcal{P}$ cannot encode anything into $\mathcal{V}$'s secret key.

$\mathcal{P}$ need not necessarily know the attributes it encodes into $\mathcal{V}$'s secret key; knowing a one-way image may suffice, as we will see in Section 5.2.1. This generalization enables $\mathcal{P}$ to "update" previously encoded attributes without knowing their current values. For this reason, in the definition of restrictive blinding we will not be concerned with who determines, knows, or generates the attributes that are to be encoded; of importance is only the existence of a blinding-invariant part in the secret key that $\mathcal{V}$ will end up with.

We are now prepared for a formal definition.

Definition 4.1.1. *A restrictive blind certificate scheme is a digital certificate scheme with the following additional properties:*

- *(Blinding of the certified public key) If $\mathcal{V}$ follows the protocol and accepts, then $\mathcal{V}$ obtains a certified key pair $(s, p, \mathsf{cert}(p))$ such that the certified public key $(p, \mathsf{cert}(p))$ is statistically independent from $\widetilde{\mathcal{P}}$'s view in the protocol execution.*

- *(Blinding-invariant part) There exists a non-constant function $\{\mathrm{Inv}_i(\cdot)\}_{i \in V}$ that can be evaluated in polynomial time, such that the following two properties hold if $\mathcal{P}$ follows the protocol:*

- Let s denote the secret key of the certified key pair obtained by $\overline{\mathcal{V}}$. Then $\mathrm{Inv}_i(s) = \mathsf{tuple}$, where tuple is the attribute tuple encoded by $\overline{\mathcal{P}}$.

- Let $s_1, \ldots, s_{t^*}$ denote the secret keys of any t^* certified key pairs obtained by $\widehat{\mathcal{V}}$ after engaging in $t \geq t^*$ protocol executions, and let tuple_j denote the attribute tuple $\overline{\mathcal{P}}$ intended to encode into $\mathcal{V}$'s certified key pair in the j-th protocol execution, for all $j \in \{1, \ldots, t\}$. For all $j^* \in \{1, \ldots, t^*\}$, there exists $j \in \{1, \ldots, t\}$ such that the following two properties hold with overwhelming probability:

  * $\mathrm{Inv}_i(s_{j^*}) = \mathsf{tuple}_j$.
  * The multiplicity of $\mathrm{Inv}_i(s_{j^*})$ is no greater than the multiplicity of tuple_j.

We will say that a restrictive blind certificate issuing protocol execution is performed *with respect to* $(x_1, \ldots, x_l)$ if $(x_1, \ldots, x_l)$ is the attribute tuple that $\mathcal{P}$ intends to encode into $\mathcal{V}$'s certified key pair in that particular protocol execution.

The second part of the definition may seem overly complex, but is needed to capture the case where $\mathcal{V}$ consists of a plurality of receivers. Namely, operating under the assumption that an adversary can passively monitor the protocol executions of honest receivers, it must be infeasible for the adversary to benefit from this information by being able to compute a certified key pair for which the secret key encodes an attribute tuple that $\mathcal{P}$ intended to encode only in the secret key of one of the monitored honest receivers.[1] It is not hard to see that the definition captures this scenario, regardless of how protocol executions are interleaved. Note that there is no problem if $\widehat{\mathcal{V}}$ can swap attribute tuples that $\mathcal{P}$ encodes in different protocol executions with $\mathcal{V}$.

Definition 4.1.1 encompasses both public-key certificates and secret-key certificates. Note that restrictive blinding of secret-key certificates is not a special case of Chaum's blind signature paradigm [91, 92, 93, 94, 95, 96, 99, 100]: $\mathcal{P}$'s certificate is not a digital signature on $\mathcal{V}$'s public key but only on $\mathcal{V}$'s secret key, which by definition cannot be blinded.

The notion of restrictive blinding also differs from Chaum's notion of one-show blinding [90, 98]. The latter concerns a property of an issuing protocol in combination with a showing protocol, while restrictive blinding is a property of the issuing protocol only. In particular, restrictive blinding has nothing to do with restricting the number of times a certificate may be shown. One special use of restrictive blinding is to construct practical one-show blind signature schemes (see Section 5.4), but its general applicability is much broader.

Definition 4.1.1 describes the strongest possible case of blinding; not even a CA with unlimited resources can create a correlation between the certified public keys

---

[1]In a practical situation, session encryption can prevent monitoring of protocol executions, but the security of the session encryption method depends not only on the receiver. Moreover, as a general design principle it is undesirable to make the security of two different building blocks, that serve different goals, depend on each other.

it issues and its views in the issuing protocol. A weaker flavor would be one where linking is merely computationally infeasible, but as explained in Section 1.3.5 this is unsatisfactory.

In practical applications, it will often be desirable that $\mathcal{V}$'s secret key cannot be computed by a party that gets to learn $\mathcal{V}$'s certified public key and also knows $\tilde{\mathcal{P}}$'s view in the originating issuing protocol. This property is not part of the definition, but holds for all the constructions in this chapter.

Two generic approaches are known to design restrictive blind certificate schemes:

- One can use any "ordinary" blind signature issuing protocol, and have the receiver use a zero-knowledge proof to prove to the issuer that it has properly encoded the attributes into its "challenge" message, before the issuer returns its final response. According to Goldreich, Micali, and Wigderson [191], zero-knowledge proofs exist for all languages in the complexity class NP.

- Techniques from the field of secure multi-party computations can be used, along the lines of Juels, Luby, and Ostrovsky [224]. (See also Damgård [126] and Pfitzmann and Waidner [303].)

Both approaches result in highly impractical protocols. A more efficient approach is to run polynomially many copies of an ordinary blind signature protocol in parallel, and have the signer complete a randomly chosen run of the protocol only when the receiver shows correct formation of the "challenge" messages it submitted in all the other protocol runs. This approach is still far from practical, though, and in fact does not qualify: the attributes cannot be encoded in polynomial time with overwhelming success probability. Note also that the improved issuing protocol of Chaum's ad hoc one-show blind signature scheme [98, 90] does not meet Definition 4.1.1.

The objective of this chapter is to design secure restrictive blind issuing protocols that are truly practical, and that enable the CA to encode polynomially many attributes without affecting the size of certified public keys.

4.2 Practical constructions

In this section we design four practical restrictive blind certificate schemes. The first two of these are based on the DLREP function, the latter two on the RSAREP function. All schemes are for issuing secret-key certificates. We will extensively analyze the schemes in the next section.

In Chapter 5 we will combine the showing protocols of the previous chapter with the issuing protocols designed here. Because the receiver in the issuing protocol will be the prover (signer) in the showing protocol, in the rest of this chapter we denote the CA by $\mathcal{P}_0$ and the receiver by $\mathcal{V}_0$, to avoid confusion with the $(\mathcal{P}, \mathcal{V})$ notation used in Chapter 3.

4.2.1 Restrictive blinding based on the DLREP function

DLREP-based scheme I

Let (I_{DL}, D_{DL}) be any invulnerable instance generator for the DL function, and let (q, g_0) denote the output of I_{DL} on input 1^k. $\mathcal{P}_0$ feeds (q, g_0) to D_{DL} to obtain x_0, and computes $h_0 := g_0^{x_0}$. $\mathcal{P}_0$ then generates $l \geq 1$ random numbers $y_1, \ldots, y_l \in \mathbb{Z}_q$, for some l of its own choice, and computes $g_i := g_0^{y_i}$, for all $i \in \{1, \ldots, l\}$. The system parameters are (q, g_0). The public key of $\mathcal{P}_0$ is

$$h_0, (g_1, \ldots, g_l),$$

and its secret key is

$$x_0, (y_1, \ldots, y_l).$$

In addition, a correlation-intractable hash function $\mathcal{H}(\cdot) = \{\mathcal{H}_i(\cdot)\}_{i \in \{(q,g_0)\}}$, such that $\mathcal{H}_{q,g_0}(\cdot)$ maps its outputs into $\mathbb{Z}_s$ (for some s superpolynomial in k), is decided on. A concise description of $\mathcal{H}_{q,g_0}(\cdot)$ is published along with the public key. Although not made explicit in the notation, $\mathcal{H}_{q,g_0}(\cdot)$ may (and preferably does) depend also on $\mathcal{P}_0$'s public key and any other information specified before protocol executions take place. (Alternatively, in each application of the hash function all such static information is hashed along.) We will address the issue of selecting $\mathcal{H}(\cdot)$ in Section 4.3.3 when analyzing the security of the scheme.

The restrictive blind issuing protocol $(\mathcal{P}_0, \mathcal{V}_0)$ is a proof of knowledge such that $\mathcal{V}_0$ obtains a blinded public key, $h' \in G_q$, and a blinded certificate $(c'_0, r'_0) \in \mathbb{Z}_s \times \mathbb{Z}_q$ of $\mathcal{P}_0$ on h'. The pair (c'_0, r'_0) is defined to be a certificate of $\mathcal{P}_0$ on h' if and only if the verification relation

$$c'_0 = \mathcal{H}_{q,g_0}(h', g_0^{r'_0}(h_0 h')^{-c'_0})$$

holds. The secret key of $\mathcal{V}_0$ is a DL-representation, $(x_1, \ldots, x_l, \alpha_1)$, of h' with respect to $(g_1, \ldots, g_l, g_0)$. The numbers $x_1, \ldots, x_l \in \mathbb{Z}_q$ are encoded by $\mathcal{P}_0$ into $\mathcal{V}_0$'s secret key, and in particular are known to $\mathcal{P}_0$; they form the blinding-invariant part of $\mathcal{V}_0$'s secret key. Because $\mathcal{V}_0$ generates α_1 at random, only $\mathcal{V}_0$ knows a secret key corresponding to h' (see Proposition 2.3.3). Moreover, h' is statistically uncorrelated to $(x_1, \ldots, x_l)$, regardless of the distribution of $(x_1, \ldots, x_l)$.

With h denoting $\prod_{i=1}^l g_i^{x_i}$, an execution of the certificate issuing protocol with respect to $(x_1, \ldots, x_l)$ is defined as follows:

Step 1. $\mathcal{P}_0$ generates a random number $w_0 \in \mathbb{Z}_q$, and sends $a_0 := g_0^{w_0}$ to $\mathcal{V}_0$.

Step 2. $\mathcal{V}_0$ generates three random numbers $\alpha_1, \alpha_2, \alpha_3 \in \mathbb{Z}_q$. $\mathcal{V}_0$ computes $h' := hg_0^{\alpha_1}$, $c'_0 := \mathcal{H}_{q,g_0}(h', g_0^{\alpha_2}(h_0 h)^{\alpha_3} a_0)$, and sends $c_0 := c'_0 + \alpha_3 \bmod q$ to $\mathcal{P}_0$.

Step 3. $\mathcal{P}_0$ sends $r_0 := c_0(x_0 + \sum_{i=1}^l x_i y_i) + w_0 \bmod q$ to $\mathcal{V}_0$.

$\mathcal{V}_0$ accepts if and only if $g_0^{r_0}(h_0 h)^{-c_0} = a_0$. If this verification holds, $\mathcal{V}_0$ computes $r'_0 := r_0 + \alpha_2 + c'_0 \alpha_1 \bmod q$.

We restrict $\mathcal{P}_0$ in the following manner. It may perform protocol executions with respect to the same $(x_1, \ldots, x_l)$ in parallel, but must perform executions that involve different attribute tuples sequentially. (The reason for this restriction will be clarified in Section 4.3.3. In Section 4.4 we will show how to get around the restriction.) The resulting scheme is depicted in Figure 4.1.

When forming c'_0 in Step 2, $\mathcal{V}_0$ may hash along additional information, such as a public key to be used for session encryption in a showing protocol or one or more initial witnesses for the showing protocol. The advantages of including the latter will become clear in Section 5.4.

DLREP-based scheme II

The following variation of DLREP-based scheme I is somewhat less efficient, but as Proposition 4.3.7 will show admits a better proof of unforgeability in the random oracle model. The required modifications are minimal, and so we only describe these:

- $\mathcal{P}_0$ generates an additional random number $f \in G_q$, which it publishes along with the other public key data. It also generates an additional random number $t \in \{0, 1\}$, serving as additional secret key information to $\mathcal{P}_0$, and forms h_0 according to $h_0 := g_0^{x_0} f^t$. No further changes are needed in the key set-up.

- A certificate of $\mathcal{P}_0$ on h' is redefined to be a triple, $(c'_0, r'_0, r'_1) \in \mathbb{Z}_s \times \mathbb{Z}_q \times \mathbb{Z}_q$ such that

$$c'_0 = \mathcal{H}_{q,g_0}(h', g_0^{r'_0} f^{r'_1}(h_0 h')^{-c'_0})$$

  The definition of a key pair for $\mathcal{V}_0$ is not changed, nor is that of the blinding-invariant part.

- In Step 1 of the certificate issuing protocol, $\mathcal{P}_0$ generates an additional random number $w_1 \in \mathbb{Z}_q$, and forms a_0 according to $a_0 := g_0^{w_0} f^{w_1}$. In Step 2 of the protocol, $\mathcal{V}_0$ generates an additional random number $\alpha_4 \in \mathbb{Z}_q$, and multiplies f^{α_4} into the second argument to $\mathcal{H}_{q,g_0}(\cdot)$ when computing c'_0. In Step 3 of the protocol, $\mathcal{P}_0$ computes an additional response, r_1, according to $r_1 := c_0 t + w_1 \bmod q$, and sends this along to $\mathcal{V}_0$. Finally, $\mathcal{V}_0$ accepts if and only if $g_0^{r_0} f^{r_1}(h_0 h)^{-c_0} = a_0$, and in addition blinds r_1 to $r'_1 := r_1 + \alpha_4 \bmod q$.

The requirement that $\mathcal{P}_0$ may not interleave protocol executions with respect to different attribute tuples still applies.

The resulting scheme is depicted in Figure 4.2.

$$\boxed{\mathcal{P}_0} \qquad\qquad\qquad\qquad\qquad\qquad \boxed{\mathcal{V}_0}$$

SYSTEM PARAMETERS

$$(q, g_0) := I_{\mathrm{DL}}(1^k)$$

KEY SET-UP

$x_0 := D_{\mathrm{DL}}(q, g_0)$
$y_1, \ldots, y_l \in_{\mathcal{R}} \mathbb{Z}_q$
Secret key: $x_0, (y_1, \ldots, y_l)$
$h_0 := g_0^{x_0}$
$g_i := g_0^{y_i} \ \forall i \in \{1, \ldots, l\}$
Public key: $\qquad\qquad\qquad h_0, (g_1, \ldots, g_l)$
Additional information: $\qquad\quad \mathcal{H}_{q,g_0}(\cdot)$

PROTOCOL

$w_0 \in_{\mathcal{R}} \mathbb{Z}_q$
$a_0 := g_0^{w_0}$

$$\xrightarrow{\quad a_0 \quad}$$

$\qquad\qquad\qquad\qquad \alpha_1, \alpha_2, \alpha_3 \in_{\mathcal{R}} \mathbb{Z}_q$
$\qquad\qquad\qquad\qquad h' := h g_0^{\alpha_1}$
$\qquad\qquad\qquad\qquad c_0' := \mathcal{H}_{q,g_0}(h', g_0^{\alpha_2}(h_0 h)^{\alpha_3} a_0)$
$\qquad\qquad\qquad\qquad c_0 := c_0' + \alpha_3 \bmod q$

$$\xleftarrow{\quad c_0 \quad}$$

$r_0 := c_0(x_0 + \sum_{i=1}^{l} x_i y_i) + w_0 \bmod q$

$$\xrightarrow{\quad r_0 \quad}$$

$\qquad\qquad\qquad\qquad g_0^{r_0}(h_0 h)^{-c_0} \overset{?}{=} a_0$
$\qquad\qquad\qquad\qquad r_0' := r_0 + \alpha_2 + c_0' \alpha_1 \bmod q$

Figure 4.1: DLREP-based scheme I.

$\boxed{\mathcal{P}_0}$ $\boxed{\mathcal{V}_0}$

SYSTEM PARAMETERS

$$(q, g_0) := I_{\text{DL}}(1^k)$$

KEY SET-UP

$x_0 := D_{\text{DL}}(q, g_0)$
$t \in_{\mathcal{R}} \{0, 1\}$
$y_1, \ldots, y_l \in_{\mathcal{R}} \mathbb{Z}_q$
Secret key: $(x_0, t), (y_1, \ldots, y_l)$
$f \in_{\mathcal{R}} G_q$
$h_0 := g_0^{x_0} f^t$
$g_i := g_0^{y_i} \ \forall i \in \{1, \ldots, l\}$
Public key: $(f, h_0), (g_1, \ldots, g_l)$
Additional information: $\mathcal{H}_{q,g_0}(\cdot)$

PROTOCOL

$w_0, w_1 \in_{\mathcal{R}} \mathbb{Z}_q$
$a_0 := g_0^{w_0} f^{w_1}$

$\xrightarrow{\quad a_0 \quad}$

$\alpha_1, \alpha_2, \alpha_3, \alpha_4 \in_{\mathcal{R}} \mathbb{Z}_q$
$h' := h g_0^{\alpha_1}$
$c_0' := \mathcal{H}_{q,g_0}(h', g_0^{\alpha_2}(h_0 h)^{\alpha_3} f^{\alpha_4} a_0)$
$c_0 := c_0' + \alpha_3 \mod q$

$\xleftarrow{\quad c_0 \quad}$

$r_0 := c_0(x_0 + \sum_{i=1}^{l} x_i y_i) + w_0 \mod q$
$r_1 := c_0 t + w_1 \mod q$

$\xrightarrow{\quad r_0, r_1 \quad}$

$g_0^{r_0} f^{r_1} (h_0 h)^{-c_0} \overset{?}{=} a_0$
$r_0' := r_0 + \alpha_2 + c_0' \alpha_1 \mod q$
$r_1' := r_1 + \alpha_4 \mod q$

Figure 4.2: DLREP-based scheme II.

4.2.2   Restrictive blinding based on the RSAREP function

RSAREP-based scheme I

Let $(I_{\text{RSA}}, D_{\text{RSA}})$ be any invulnerable instance generator for the RSA function, and let (n, v) denote the output of I_{RSA} on input 1^k. We assume that I_{RSA} outputs the prime factorization (p, q) of n as "side information" for $\mathcal{P}_0$. $\mathcal{P}_0$ feeds (n, v) to D_{RSA} to obtain x_0, and computes $h_0 := x_0^v$. $\mathcal{P}_0$ then generates $l \geq 1$ random numbers $g_1, \ldots, g_l \in \mathbb{Z}_n^*$.
The system parameters are (n, v). The public key of $\mathcal{P}_0$ is

$$h_0, (g_1, \ldots, g_l),$$

and its secret key is the prime factorization of n. In addition, a one-way hash function $\mathcal{H}(\cdot) = \{\mathcal{H}_i(\cdot)\}_{i \in \{(n,v)\}}$, such that $\mathcal{H}_{n,v}(\cdot)$ maps its outputs into $\mathbb{Z}_s$ (for some s superpolynomial in k), is decided on. A concise description of $\mathcal{H}_{n,v}(\cdot)$ is published along with the public key. Although not made explicit in the notation, its specification may depend on $\mathcal{P}_0$'s public key and any other information specified before protocol executions take place. We will address the issue of selecting $\mathcal{H}(\cdot)$ in Section 4.3.3.

Our restrictive blind issuing protocol $(\mathcal{P}_0, \mathcal{V}_0)$ is a proof of knowledge such that $\mathcal{V}_0$ obtains a blinded public key, $h' \in \mathbb{Z}_n^*$, and a blinded certificate $(c_0', r_0') \in \mathbb{Z}_s \times \mathbb{Z}_n^*$ of $\mathcal{P}_0$ on h'. The pair (c_0', r_0') is defined to be a certificate of $\mathcal{P}_0$ on h' if and only if the verification relation

$$c_0' = \mathcal{H}_{n,v}(h', (r_0')^v (h_0 h')^{-c_0'})$$

holds. The secret key of $\mathcal{V}_0$ is an RSA-representation, $(x_1, \ldots, x_l, \alpha_1)$, of h' with respect to $(g_1, \ldots, g_l, v)$. The numbers $x_1, \ldots, x_l \in \mathbb{Z}_v$ are encoded by $\mathcal{P}_0$ into $\mathcal{V}_0$'s secret key; they form the blinding-invariant part of $\mathcal{V}_0$'s secret key. Because $\mathcal{V}_0$ generates α_1 at random, h' is uncorrelated to $(x_1, \ldots, x_l)$, regardless of the distribution of $(x_1, \ldots, x_l)$.

With h denoting $\prod_{i=1}^{l} g_i^{x_i}$, an execution of the certificate issuing protocol with respect to $(x_1, \ldots, x_l)$ is defined as follows:

Step 1. $\mathcal{P}_0$ generates a random number $a_0 \in \mathbb{Z}_n^*$, and sends it to $\mathcal{V}_0$.

Step 2. $\mathcal{V}_0$ generates two random numbers $\alpha_1, \alpha_2 \in \mathbb{Z}_n^*$ and a random number $\alpha_3 \in \mathbb{Z}_v$. $\mathcal{V}_0$ computes $h' := h\alpha_1^v$, $c_0' := \mathcal{H}(h', \alpha_2^v (h_0 h)^{\alpha_3} a_0)$, and sends $c_0 := c_0' + \alpha_3 \mod v$ to $\mathcal{P}_0$.

Step 3. $\mathcal{P}_0$ sends $r_0 := ((h_0 h)^{c_0} a_0)^{1/v}$ to $\mathcal{V}_0$. (Note that $\mathcal{P}_0$ can compute v-th roots of arbitrary numbers in $\mathbb{Z}_n^*$, because it knows the prime factorization of n.)

$\mathcal{V}_0$ accepts if and only if $r_0^v (h_0 h)^{-c_0} = a_0$. If this verification holds, $\mathcal{V}_0$ computes

$$r_0' := r_0 \alpha_2 \alpha_1^{c_0'} (h_0 h)^{(c_0' + \alpha_3) \operatorname{div} v}.$$

As with both DLREP-based schemes, $\mathcal{P}_0$ may perform protocol executions with respect to the same $(x_1, \ldots, x_l)$ in parallel, but may not interleave executions that involve different attribute tuples. (In Section 4.4 we will show how to get around this restriction.) The resulting scheme is depicted in Figure 4.3.

When forming c_0' in Step 2, $\mathcal{V}_0$ may hash along additional information, such as a public key for session encryption or one or more initial witnesses for a subsequent showing protocol. Inclusion of the latter will be pursued further in Section 5.4.

RSAREP-based scheme II

The following variation of RSAREP-based scheme I is somewhat less efficient, but admits a better proof of unforgeability in the random oracle model. The modifications to RSAREP-based scheme I are the following:

- $\mathcal{P}_0$ generates an additional random number $f \in \mathbb{Z}_n^*$, which it publishes along with its other public key data. No further changes are needed in the key set-up.

- A certificate of $\mathcal{P}_0$ on h' is redefined to be a triple, $(c_0', r_0', r_1') \in \mathbb{Z}_s \times \mathbb{Z}_n^* \times \mathbb{Z}_v$ such that

$$c_0' = \mathcal{H}_{n,v}(h', (r_0')^v f^{r_1'}(h_0 h')^{-c_0'})$$

The definition of a key pair for $\mathcal{V}_0$ is not changed, nor is that of the blinding-invariant part.

- In Step 2 of the protocol, $\mathcal{V}_0$ generates an additional random number $\alpha_4 \in \mathbb{Z}_v$, and multiplies f^{α_4} into the second argument to $\mathcal{H}_{n,v}(\cdot)$ when computing c_0'. In Step 3 of the protocol, $\mathcal{P}_0$ generates a random number $r_1 \in \mathbb{Z}_v$, computes r_0 according to $r_0 := ((h_0 h)^{c_0} a_0 / f^{r_1})^{1/v}$, and sends r_0 along to $\mathcal{V}_0$. Finally, $\mathcal{V}_0$ accepts if and only if $r_0^v f^{r_1}(h_0 h)^{-c_0} = a_0$, and computes

$$r_0' := r_0 \alpha_2 \alpha_1^{c_0'}(h_0 h)^{(c_0' + \alpha_3) \operatorname{div} v} f^{(r_1 + \alpha_4) \operatorname{div} v}$$

and $r_1' := r_1 + \alpha_4 \bmod v$.

The requirement that $\mathcal{P}_0$ may not interleave protocol executions with respect to different attribute tuples still applies.

The resulting scheme is depicted in Figure 4.4.

4.2.3   Comparison

The constructions based on the DLREP function and on the RSAREP function follow exactly the same design principle. This may not be readily clear from the descriptions, because $\mathcal{P}_0$ in the RSAREP-based variants makes use of trapdoor information, which is not available in the DLREP-based variants. To appreciate the underlying design principle, observe that $\mathcal{P}_0$ need not make use of trapdoor information in the

$$\boxed{\mathcal{P}_0} \qquad\qquad\qquad \boxed{\mathcal{V}_0}$$

SYSTEM PARAMETERS

$$(n, v) := I_{\mathrm{RSA}}(1^k)$$

KEY SET-UP

Secret key: factorization of n
$h_0, g_1, \ldots, g_l \in_{\mathcal{R}} \mathbb{Z}_n^*$
Public key: $\qquad\qquad\qquad h_0, (g_1, \ldots, g_l)$
Additional information: $\qquad\qquad \mathcal{H}_{n,v}(\cdot)$

PROTOCOL

$a_0 \in_{\mathcal{R}} \mathbb{Z}_n^*$

$$\xrightarrow{\quad a_0 \quad}$$

$$\alpha_1, \alpha_2 \in_{\mathcal{R}} \mathbb{Z}_n^*$$
$$\alpha_3 \in_{\mathcal{R}} \mathbb{Z}_v$$
$$h' := h\alpha_1^v$$
$$c_0' := \mathcal{H}_{n,v}(h', \alpha_2^v(h_0 h)^{\alpha_3} a_0)$$
$$c_0 := c_0' + \alpha_3 \bmod v$$

$$\xleftarrow{\quad c_0 \quad}$$

$$r_0 := ((h_0 h)^{c_0} a_0)^{1/v}$$

$$\xrightarrow{\quad r_0 \quad}$$

$$r_0^v (h_0 h)^{-c_0} \stackrel{?}{=} a_0$$
$$r_0' := r_0 \alpha_2 \alpha_1^{c_0'} (h_0 h)^{(c_0' + \alpha_3) \operatorname{div} v}$$

Figure 4.3: RSAREP-based scheme I.

$$\boxed{\mathcal{P}_0} \qquad\qquad\qquad\qquad\qquad \boxed{\mathcal{V}_0}$$

SYSTEM PARAMETERS

$$(n, v) := I_{\mathrm{RSA}}(1^k)$$

KEY SET-UP

Secret key: factorization of n
$f, h_0, g_1, \ldots, g_l \in_{\mathcal{R}} \mathbb{Z}_n^*$
Public key: $\qquad\qquad\qquad (f, h_0), (g_1, \ldots, g_l)$
Additional information: $\qquad \mathcal{H}_{n,v}(\cdot)$

PROTOCOL

$a_0 \in_{\mathcal{R}} \mathbb{Z}_n^*$

$$\xrightarrow{\quad a_0 \quad}$$

$$\alpha_1, \alpha_2 \in_{\mathcal{R}} \mathbb{Z}_n^*$$
$$\alpha_3, \alpha_4 \in_{\mathcal{R}} \mathbb{Z}_v$$
$$h' := h\alpha_1^v$$
$$c_0' := \mathcal{H}_{n,v}(h', \alpha_2^v (h_0 h)^{\alpha_3} f^{\alpha_4} a_0)$$
$$c_0 := c_0' + \alpha_3 \bmod v$$

$$\xleftarrow{\quad c_0 \quad}$$

$r_1 \in_{\mathcal{R}} \mathbb{Z}_v$
$r_0 := ((h_0 h)^{c_0} a_0 / f^{r_1})^{1/v}$

$$\xrightarrow{\quad r_0, r_1 \quad}$$

$$f^{r_1} r_0^v (h_0 h)^{-c_0} \overset{?}{=} a_0$$
$$r_0' := r_0 \alpha_2 \alpha_1^{c_0'} (h_0 h)^{(c_0' + \alpha_3)\,\mathrm{div}\,v} f^{(r_1 + \alpha_4)\,\mathrm{div}\,v}$$
$$r_1' := r_1 + \alpha_4 \bmod v$$

Figure 4.4: RSAREP-based scheme II.

RSAREP-based schemes. In RSAREP-based scheme I, we hereto make the following modifications:

- Instead of generating $h_0, g_1, \ldots, g_l$ at random, $\mathcal{P}_0$ generates $l + 1$ random numbers $x_0, y_1, \ldots, y_l$ from $\mathbb{Z}_n^*$, and computes $h_0 := x_0^v$ and $g_i := y_i^v$, for all $i \in \{1, \ldots, l\}$. (More generally, $\mathcal{P}_0$ may set $x_0 := D_{\text{RSA}}(n, v)$.)

- In Step 1 of the issuing protocol, $\mathcal{P}_0$ generates a_0 according to $a_0 := w_0^v$, for a random $w_0 \in \mathbb{Z}_n^*$.

- In Step 3 of the issuing protocol, $\mathcal{P}_0$ computes r_0 as follows:

$$r_0 := (x_0 \prod_{i=1}^{l} y_i^{x_i})^{c_0} w_0.$$

The resulting scheme is depicted in Figure 4.5. Similar modifications can be made to RSAREP-based scheme II. With these modifications, it is easily seen that the DLREP-based and the RSAREP-based schemes are all based on the same design principle:

> $\mathcal{P}_0$ interactively issues a signed proof of knowledge of a secret key corresponding to the joint public key $h_0 h$, using one of the proofs of knowledge described in Sections 2.4.3 and 2.4.4. $\mathcal{V}_0$ blinds not only a_0 and $\mathcal{P}_0$'s response(s), but also h.

In all four schemes, $h_0 h$ or h may be thought of as the auxiliary common input m^* in Definition 2.5.1. Note that for both DLREP-based scheme II and RSAREP-based scheme II the issuing protocols are provably witness-hiding. (In particular, even after $\overline{\mathcal{P}}_0$ has performed polynomially many protocol executions, arbitrarily interleaved and possibly with respect to all valid attribute tuples, its secret key provably cannot leak.)

Not using the trapdoor information in the RSAREP-based schemes has several advantages:

- Multiple provers can all operate with respect to the same (n, v), generated by a trusted party or by means of a secure multi-party protocol (see Boneh and Franklin [39] and Poupard and Stern [309]).

- The binary sizes of v and c may be much smaller than the binary sizes of the prime factors of n. This reduces $\mathcal{P}_0$'s computational burden.

- $\mathcal{P}_0$ can be split into many sub-provers that all hold a share of the public key, and that must all contribute to issue a certified key pair to $\mathcal{V}_0$. Using RSAREP-based scheme I, for instance, the i-th sub-prover could hold $h_{0i} := x_{0i}^v$, with $\prod_{i=1}^{l} h_{0i} = h_0$, and could be in charge of generating y_i. The contribution of the i-th sub-prover to the issuing protocol would be an initial witness $a_{0i} :=$

$$\boxed{\mathcal{P}_0} \qquad\qquad\qquad\qquad \boxed{\mathcal{V}_0}$$

SYSTEM PARAMETERS

$$(n, v) := I_{\mathrm{RSA}}(1^k)$$

KEY SET-UP

$x_0 := D_{\mathrm{RSA}}(n, v)$
$y_1, \ldots, y_l \in_{\mathcal{R}} \mathbb{Z}_n^*$
Secret key: $x_0, (y_1, \ldots, y_l)$
$h_0 := x_0^v$
$g_i := y_i^v \; \forall i \in \{1, \ldots, l\}$
Public key: $\qquad\qquad h_0, (g_1, \ldots, g_l)$
Additional information: $\qquad \mathcal{H}_{n,v}(\cdot)$

PROTOCOL

$w_0 \in_{\mathcal{R}} \mathbb{Z}_n^*$
$a_0 := w_0^v$

$$\xrightarrow{\quad a_0 \quad}$$

$$\alpha_1, \alpha_2 \in_{\mathcal{R}} \mathbb{Z}_n^*$$
$$\alpha_3 \in_{\mathcal{R}} \mathbb{Z}_v$$
$$h' := h\alpha_1^v$$
$$c_0' := \mathcal{H}_{n,v}(h', \alpha_2^v (h_0 h)^{\alpha_3} a_0)$$
$$c_0 := c_0' + \alpha_3 \bmod v$$

$$\xleftarrow{\quad c_0 \quad}$$

$r_0 := (x_0 \prod_{i=1}^{l} y_i^{x_i})^{c_0} w_0$

$$\xrightarrow{\quad r_0 \quad}$$

$$r_0^v (h_0 h)^{-c_0} \overset{?}{=} a_0$$
$$r_0' := r_0 \alpha_2 \alpha_1^{c_0'} (h_0 h)^{(c_0' + \alpha_3)\,\mathrm{div}\,v}$$

Figure 4.5: RSAREP-based scheme I without use of trapdoor information.

w_{0i}^v and a response $r_{0i} := (x_{0i} y_i^{x_i})^{c_0} w_{0i}$; the product of all the individual witnesses is the initial witness expected by $\mathcal{V}_0$, and likewise for the responses.

The technique of sharing $\mathcal{P}_0$'s secret key can also be applied to the DLREP-based issuing protocols (and the other protocols that will be described later in this chapter). It is even possible to extend the technique to provide for arbitrary secret sharing, requiring one of several predetermined subsets to cooperate in order to perform the role of $\mathcal{P}_0$. For relevant secret-sharing techniques, see Pedersen [299], Cerecedo, Matsumoto, and Imai [84], Gennaro, Jarecki, Krawczyk, and Rabin [184], and Takaragi, Miyazaki, and Takahashi [369]. Also, the number of entities that share $\mathcal{P}_0$'s secret key could be increased so that multiple entities are needed to approve each attribute. In a practical implementation, the sub-provers could take the form of tamper-resistant computing devices stored in independently guarded locations. This not only provides optimal protection against (insider and outsider) theft and extortion of $\mathcal{P}_0$'s secret key, but it can also ensure that different device operators must approve the same attributes that are to be encoded into a certified key pair.[2]

Using the trapdoor information in the RSAREP-based schemes also has a couple of advantages:

- It avoids the exponentiation in Step 1 of the protocol.

- $\mathcal{P}_0$ does not need to remember or reconstruct in Step 3 a secret number that it generated in Step 1, which is an advantage when implementing the protocol. ($\mathcal{P}_0$ still needs to access its secret key, of course.) The protocol can even be turned into a two-move protocol by having $\mathcal{V}_0$ form a_0 by feeding at least an identifier for $\mathcal{V}_0$ and a nonce into a sufficiently strong one-way function. ($\mathcal{V}_0$ must send the nonce along with its challenge to $\mathcal{P}_0$, so that $\mathcal{P}_0$ can check its freshness.)

- $\mathcal{P}_0$ can perform the issuing protocol without knowing $(x_1, \ldots, x_l)$; it merely needs to know h. This property enables $\mathcal{P}_0$ to recertify a previously certified public key, without knowing its blinding-invariant part. During the process, $\mathcal{P}_0$ can even update one or more of the x_i values. (Details will be provided in Section 5.2.1.)

In the RSAREP-based schemes, $\mathcal{V}_0$ cannot verify by itself that v is co-prime to $\varphi(n)$. However, if the prime v is not co-prime to $\varphi(n)$, then $\widetilde{\mathcal{P}}_0$ cannot respond to $\mathcal{V}$'s challenge c_0 with probability at least $1 - 1/v$. In other words, $\overline{\mathcal{V}}_0$ becomes convinced with overwhelming probability of the proper formation of (n, v) by engaging in a single execution of the certificate issuing protocol.

---

[2]Issuer fraud is a serious threat, as witnessed for instance by the 250 employees of the Department of Motor Vehicles of California who in 1998 were found to have issued over 25 000 genuine-looking but fraudulent licenses in a two-year period.

In Step 2 of all four certificate schemes, $\mathcal{V}_0$ can perform all the required exponentiations in a preprocessing stage; its real-time computational burden in each protocol amounts to one modular multiplication and one application of the hash function. This makes the schemes highly practical.

The main advantage of the DLREP-based variants over the RSAREP-based variants is that the computation of $\mathcal{P}_0$'s response(s) does not involve any exponentiations. In highly demanding applications, this enables the CA to serve more receivers using cheaper equipment, especially when using an elliptic curve implementation with short system parameters.

4.3 Analysis

In this section we analyze the certificate schemes of the previous section. We will prove that all four schemes are restrictive blind certificate schemes, under plausible cryptographic assumptions.

To avoid unnecessary duplication of security statements and proof reductions, a detailed analysis is provided only of RSAREP-based scheme I. The analysis of the other three schemes is highly similar, and so for these we merely point out the differences.

Throughout this section it is assumed that the system parameters, (q, g_0) and (n, v), respectively, are properly formed.

4.3.1 Completeness

The statements in this section hold for any choice of $\mathcal{H}(\cdot)$.

Proposition 4.3.1. *When interacting with* $\overline{\mathcal{P}}_0$, $\overline{\mathcal{V}}_0$ *in RSAREP-based scheme I accepts.*

Proof. This follows immediately from the manner in which $\mathcal{P}_0$ computes r_0 in Step 3 and the verification relation applied by $\mathcal{V}_0$. $\square$

Proposition 4.3.2. *For any* $\widetilde{\mathcal{P}}_0$, *if* $\overline{\mathcal{V}}_0$ *in RSAREP-based scheme I accepts, then*

$$(x_1, \ldots, x_l, \alpha_1),\ h',\ (c_0', r_0')$$

is a certified key pair.

Proof. Clearly, $(x_1, \ldots, x_l, \alpha_1)$ is an RSA-representation of h' with respect to the tuple $(g_1, \ldots, g_l, v)$. To show that (c_0', r_0') is a certificate of $\mathcal{P}_0$ on h', note that $\overline{\mathcal{V}}_0$ in Step 2 of the issuing protocol computes $c_0' := \mathcal{H}_{n,v}(h', \alpha_2^v (h_0 h)^{\alpha_3} a_0)$. It therefore suffices to prove that $(r_0')^v (h_0 h')^{-c_0'} = \alpha_2^v (h_0 h)^{\alpha_3} a_0$ for the assignments made by $\overline{\mathcal{V}}_0$. This can be seen as follows:

$$
\begin{aligned}
(r_0')^v (h_0 h')^{-c_0'} &= (r_0 \alpha_2 \alpha_1^{c_0'} (h_0 h)^{(c_0' + \alpha_3)\,\mathrm{div}\,v})^v (h_0 h \alpha_1^v)^{-c_0'} \\
&= (r_0 \alpha_2 (h_0 h)^{(c_0' + \alpha_3)\,\mathrm{div}\,v})^v (h_0 h)^{-c_0'} \\
&= r_0^v \alpha_2^v (h_0 h)^{v\,((c_0' + \alpha_3)\,\mathrm{div}\,v)} (h_0 h)^{-c_0'} \\
&\overset{(\star)}{=} ((h_0 h)^{c_0} a_0)\, \alpha_2^v (h_0 h)^{v((c_0' + \alpha_3)\,\mathrm{div}\,v)} (h_0 h)^{-c_0'} \\
&= (h_0 h)^{(c_0' + \alpha_3 \bmod v) + v\,((c_0' + \alpha_3)\,\mathrm{div}\,v)} a_0 \alpha_2^v (h_0 h)^{-c_0'} \\
&= (h_0 h)^{c_0' + \alpha_3} \alpha_2^v (h_0 h)^{-c_0'} a_0 \\
&= \alpha_2^v (h_0 h)^{\alpha_3} a_0 .
\end{aligned}
$$

The substitution $(\star)$ is allowed because $\overline{\mathcal{V}}_0$ accepts only if $r_0^v (h_0 h)^{-c_0} = a_0$. $\quad\square$

In a like manner, the direct analogues of these two propositions can be proved for the other three certificate schemes in Section 4.2.

4.3.2 Privacy for the receiver

The statements in this section address the protocol $(\widetilde{\mathcal{P}}_0, \overline{\mathcal{V}}_0)$, and hold for any choice of $\mathcal{H}(\cdot)$.

Lemma 4.3.3. *In RSAREP-based scheme I, for any properly formed system parameters, any certified public key, any $(x_1, \ldots, x_l)$, and any possible view of $\widetilde{\mathcal{P}}_0$ in an execution of the issuing protocol with respect to $(x_1, \ldots, x_l)$ in which $\overline{\mathcal{V}}_0$ accepts, there is exactly one set of random choices that $\overline{\mathcal{V}}_0$ could have made in that execution of the issuing protocol such that $\overline{\mathcal{V}}_0$ would end up with a certified key pair containing that particular certified public key.*

Proof. Consider any tuple $(x_1, \ldots, x_l)$ and any certified public key h', (c_0', r_0'). With h denoting $\prod_{i=1}^{l} g_i^{x_i}$, the response r_0 of $\widetilde{\mathcal{P}}_0$ is such that $r_0^v (h_0 h)^{-c_0} = a_0$, since $\overline{\mathcal{V}}_0$ accepts. Define the following two sets:

$$
\begin{aligned}
\mathrm{Views}\,(\widetilde{\mathcal{P}}_0) &= \{(a_0, c_0, r_0) \mid a_0, r_0 \in \mathbb{Z}_n^* \text{ and } c_0 \in \mathbb{Z}_v \text{ such that} \\
&\qquad r_0^v (h_0 h)^{-c_0} = a_0\} \\
\mathrm{Choices}\,(\mathcal{V}_0) &= \{(\alpha_1, \alpha_2, \alpha_3) \mid \alpha_1, \alpha_2 \in \mathbb{Z}_n^* \text{ and } \alpha_3 \in \mathbb{Z}_v\}.
\end{aligned}
$$

We will show that for all $\widetilde{\mathcal{P}}_0$-view $\in \mathrm{Views}\,(\widetilde{\mathcal{P}}_0)$ exactly one triple $(\alpha_1, \alpha_2, \alpha_3) \in \mathrm{Choices}\,(\mathcal{V}_0)$ exists such that $\widetilde{\mathcal{P}}_0$-view corresponds to an execution of the issuing protocol in which $\overline{\mathcal{V}}_0$ receives the certified public key $(h', (c_0', r_0'))$.

Suppose that $\widetilde{\mathcal{P}}_0$-view corresponds to the issuing of $h', (c'_0, r'_0)$. We determine the numbers $\alpha_1, \alpha_2, \alpha_3$ that must have been chosen by $\overline{\mathcal{V}}_0$. First, α_1 is determined from h, h' as

$$\alpha_1 := (h' \, h^{-1})^{1/v}.$$

Note that α_1 exists and is uniquely defined, since v is co-prime to $\varphi(n)$. Next, α_3 is determined from c_0, c'_0 according to

$$\alpha_3 := c_0 - c'_0 \bmod v.$$

Finally, the choices for α_1 and α_3, together with r_0, r'_0 and c'_0, uniquely determine α_2 as

$$\alpha_2 := r'_0 (r_0 \alpha_1^{c'_0} (h_0 h)^{(c'_0 + \alpha_3) \, \mathrm{div} \, v})^{-1}.$$

For these choices of the three variables all the assignments and verifications in the execution of the issuing protocol would be satisfied by definition, except maybe for the assignment

$$c'_0 := \mathcal{H}_{n,v}(h', \, \alpha_2^v (h_0 h)^{\alpha_3} a_0)$$

that must have been made by $\overline{\mathcal{V}}_0$. To prove that this assignment holds as well, note that

$$c'_0 = \mathcal{H}_{n,v}(h', (r'_0)^v (h_0 h')^{-c'_0})$$

by definition of a certified public key. Therefore the proof is complete if

$$(r'_0)^v (h_0 h')^{-c'_0} = \alpha_2^v (h_0 h)^{\alpha_3} a_0$$

for the choices for α_1, α_2, and α_3 made above. This can be derived exactly as in the proof of Proposition 4.3.2, considering that the substitution $(\star)$ is allowed here because $\widetilde{\mathcal{P}}_0$-view $\in$ Views $(\widetilde{\mathcal{P}}_0)$. $\square$

Lemma 4.3.3 does not necessarily hold in the case of improperly formed system parameters. In particular, if v is not co-prime to $\varphi(n)$ then a substantial part of the views of $\widetilde{\mathcal{P}}_0$ cannot be matched with a substantial part of the certified public keys. This is not a problem, though, as we saw in Section 4.2.3.

Proposition 4.3.4. *For any properly formed system parameters in RSAREP-based scheme I, if $\mathcal{V}_0$ follows the issuing protocol and accepts, then it obtains a certified key pair comprising a perfectly blinded certified public key, regardless of the behavior of $\mathcal{P}_0$.*

Proof. This is an immediate consequence of Lemma 4.3.3 and the fact that $\overline{\mathcal{V}}_0$ generates its triples $(\alpha_1, \alpha_2, \alpha_3)$ at random from Choices $(\mathcal{V}_0)$. $\square$

The same result can be proved for the other three certificate schemes described in Section 4.2.

In Chapter 5 we will make the connection with the showing protocols in Chapter 3 and show that that the above privacy result holds even when $\overline{\mathcal{V}}_0$ selectively discloses any property of the encoded attributes. That is, any certificate that $\overline{\mathcal{V}}_0$ shows in the showing protocol execution could have originated (with uniform probability) from any of the issuing protocol executions in which $\widetilde{\mathcal{P}}_0$ encoded attributes that satisfy the formula disclosed by $\overline{\mathcal{V}}_0$.

4.3.3   Security for the Certificate Authority

In this section we address the protocol $(\overline{\mathcal{P}}_0, \widehat{\mathcal{V}}_0)$, by analyzing the properties of unforgeability and restrictive blinding.

Unforgeability

We study the unforgeability of RSAREP-based scheme I in the strongest possible attack model. All our unforgeability results hold even if $\widehat{\mathcal{V}}_0$ can engage in polynomially many executions of the issuing protocol, can arbitrarily interleave protocol executions, and may select an arbitrary attribute tuple $(x_1, \ldots, x_l)$ at the start of each new protocol execution.

The following lemma holds for any choice of $\mathcal{H}(\cdot)$.

Lemma 4.3.5. *If the Guillou-Quisquater proof of knowledge with $s := v$ is witness-hiding, then $\widehat{\mathcal{V}}_0$ in RSAREP-based scheme I cannot output with non-negligible success probability a non-trivial RSA-representation of 1 with respect to $(g_1, \ldots, g_l, v)$.*

Proof. Suppose that $\widehat{\mathcal{V}}_0$, after engaging in t executions of the issuing protocol, outputs a non-trivial RSA-representation of 1 with respect to $(g_1, \ldots, g_l, v)$, with non-negligible probability ϵ. We construct a polynomial-time interactive algorithm $\widehat{\mathcal{V}}$ for extracting the witness of $\overline{\mathcal{P}}$ in the Guillou-Quisquater proof of knowledge, as follows.

Let (n, v) denote the system parameters in the Guillou-Quisquater proof of knowledge, and h_{GQ} the public key of $\overline{\mathcal{P}}$. $\widehat{\mathcal{V}}$ simulates $\overline{\mathcal{P}}_0$ with the help of the protocol executions of $\overline{\mathcal{P}}$, by performing the following steps:

Step A. (Simulate the key set-up for $\overline{\mathcal{P}}_0$.) Select a random index $j \in \{1, \ldots, l\}$ and $l + 1$ random numbers $x_0, y_1, \ldots, y_l \in \mathbb{Z}_n^*$. Set $h_0 := x_0^v$, $g_i := y_i^v$, for all $i \in \{1, \ldots, l\} \setminus \{j\}$, and $g_j := h_{\mathrm{GQ}} y_j^v$. The simulated public key of $\overline{\mathcal{P}}_0$ is $h_0, (g_1, \ldots, g_l)$.

Step B. (Simulate $\overline{\mathcal{P}}_0$ in issuing protocol executions with respect to $(x_1, \ldots, x_l)$.)

> **Step 1.** Receive a from $\overline{\mathcal{P}}$. Generate a random number $\alpha \in \mathbb{Z}_n^*$ and pass $a_0 := a^{x_j} \alpha^v \bmod n$ on to $\widehat{\mathcal{V}}_0$.

Step 2. Receive c_0 from $\widehat{\mathcal{V}}_0$, and pass $c := c_0$ on to $\overline{\mathcal{P}}$.

Step 3. Receive r from $\overline{\mathcal{P}}$, and pass

$$r_0 := r^{x_j} (x_0 \prod_{i=1}^{l} y_i^{x_i})^{c_0} \alpha$$

on to $\widehat{\mathcal{V}}_0$.

Repeat this simulation until t executions of the issuing protocol have been performed.

Step C. Check if $\widehat{\mathcal{V}}_0$ has output a non-trivial RSA-representation, $(u_1, \ldots, u_l, u_{l+1})$, of 1. If not, then halt.

Step D. If $u_j = 0 \bmod v$, then halt.

Step E. Compute integers $e, f \in \mathbb{Z}$ such that $eu_j + fv = 1$, using the extended Euclidean algorithm. (This can always be done, because v is a prime.) Compute

$$h_{\mathrm{GQ}}^{f}(\prod_{i=1}^{l} y_i^{u_i} u_{l+1})^{-e}$$

and output the result.

It is easy to see that the public key in Step A is generated with the same probability distribution as that by which $\overline{\mathcal{P}}_0$ generates its public key. Note that this is the case regardless of the probability distribution of h_{GQ}.

The response that is computed by $\widehat{\mathcal{V}}$ in the simulated issuing protocol is the same as the response that $\overline{\mathcal{P}}_0$ would compute:

$$
\begin{aligned}
r_0^{v} &= (r^{x_j}(x_0 \prod_{i=1}^{l} y_i^{x_i})^{c_0} \alpha)^{v} \\
&= (r^{v})^{x_j}(x_0^{v} \prod_{i=1}^{l}(y_i^{v})^{x_i})^{c_0} \alpha^{v} \\
&\overset{(\star)}{=} (h_{\mathrm{GQ}}^{c} a)^{x_j} \alpha^{v} x_0^{v c_0}(\prod_{i \in \{1,\ldots,l\} \backslash \{j\}} g_i^{x_i})^{c_0} y_j^{v c x_j} \\
&= (h_{\mathrm{GQ}} y_j^{v})^{c x_j}(a^{x_j} \alpha^{v}) h_0^{c_0}(\prod_{i \in \{1,\ldots,l\} \backslash \{j\}} g_i^{x_i})^{c_0} \\
&= (g_j^{x_j})^{c_0} a_0 h_0^{c_0}(\prod_{i \in \{1,\ldots,l\} \backslash \{j\}} g_i^{x_i})^{c_0} \\
&= (h_0 h)^{c_0} a_0,
\end{aligned}
$$

where the substitution $(\star)$ is allowed because the response of $\overline{\mathcal{P}}$ satisfies $r^v h_{\mathrm{GQ}}^{-c} = a$. Since α is chosen at random from $\mathbb{Z}_n^*$, a_0 is randomly distributed over $\mathbb{Z}_n^*$ regardless of x_j. From this it follows that the view of $\widehat{\mathcal{V}}_0$ in the simulated issuing protocol has the same distribution as when $\widehat{\mathcal{V}}_0$ interacts with $\overline{\mathcal{P}}_0$, regardless of the probability distributions of $(x_1, \ldots, x_l)$, its challenges, and h_{GQ}. Therefore $\widehat{\mathcal{V}}$ moves from Step C to Step D with probability ϵ.

Because j is chosen at random by $\widehat{\mathcal{V}}$, and is uncorrelated to the view of $\widehat{\mathcal{V}}_0$ in the issuing protocol, $u_j \neq 0 \bmod v$ in Step D with probability at least $1/l$. (Not all u_i can be zero, because v is co-prime to $\varphi(n)$.)

The output of $\widehat{\mathcal{V}}$ in Step E is equal to $h_{\mathrm{GQ}}^{1/v}$:

$$
\begin{aligned}
(h_{\mathrm{GQ}}^f (\prod_{i=1}^{l} y_i^{u_i} u_{l+1})^{-e})^v
&= h_{\mathrm{GQ}}^{fv} (\prod_{i=1}^{l} (y_i^v)^{u_i} u_{l+1}^v)^{-e} \\
&= h_{\mathrm{GQ}}^{1-eu_j} y_j^{u_j v} (\prod_{i \in \{1,\ldots,l\} \setminus \{j\}} g_i^{u_i} u_{l+1}^v)^{-e} \\
&= h_{\mathrm{GQ}} (h_{\mathrm{GQ}} y_j^v)^{-eu_j} (\prod_{i \in \{1,\ldots,l\} \setminus \{j\}} g_i^{u_i} u_{l+1}^v)^{-e} \\
&= h_{\mathrm{GQ}} (g_j^{u_j})^{-e} (\prod_{i \in \{1,\ldots,l\} \setminus \{j\}} g_i^{u_i} u_{l+1}^v)^{-e} \\
&= h_{\mathrm{GQ}} (\prod_{i=1}^{l} g_i^{u_i} u_{l+1}^v)^{-e} \\
&= h_{\mathrm{GQ}} 1^{-e} \\
&= h_{\mathrm{GQ}}.
\end{aligned}
$$

In all, the probability that $\widehat{\mathcal{V}}$ can compute the secret key of $\overline{\mathcal{P}}$ is at least ϵ/l. Since l is polynomial in k, this probability is non-negligible if ϵ is non-negligible. This contradicts the assumption. $\qquad\square$

Note that the reduction is tight only if l is a (small) constant; it is not clear how to achieve tightness for arbitrary l polynomial in k.

We are now prepared for the main result.

Proposition 4.3.6. *If Assumption 2.5.9 is true, then a hash function $\mathcal{H}(\cdot)$ exists such that RSAREP-based scheme I is unforgeable.*

Proof. Take $\mathcal{H}(\cdot)$ equal to the hash function $\mathcal{H}^*(\cdot)$ defined in Assumption 2.5.9. Suppose that $\widehat{\mathcal{V}}_0$ obtains $t+1$ certified key pairs with non-negligible success probability ϵ after engaging in t executions of the certificate issuing protocol, for some $t \geq 0$. We construct a polynomial-time (interactive) algorithm $\widehat{\mathcal{V}}$ that can forge signatures in the interactive Guillou-Quisquater signature scheme.

Let (n, v) denote the system parameters in the Guillou-Quisquater proof of knowledge, and h_{GQ} the public key of $\overline{\mathcal{P}}$. $\widehat{\mathcal{V}}$ simulates $\overline{\mathcal{P}}_0$ with the help of the protocol executions of $\overline{\mathcal{P}}$, by performing the following steps:

Step A. (Simulate the key set-up for $\overline{\mathcal{P}}_0$.) Generate a random number $x_0 \in \mathbb{Z}_n^*$ and set $h_0 := h_{\text{GQ}} x_0^v$. Generate l random numbers $y_1, \ldots, y_l \in \mathbb{Z}_n^*$, and compute $g_i := y_i^v$, for all $i \in \{1, \ldots, l\}$. The simulated public key of $\overline{\mathcal{P}}_0$ is $h_0, (g_1, \ldots, g_l)$.

Step B. (Simulate $\overline{\mathcal{P}}_0$ in issuing protocol executions with respect to $(x_1, \ldots, x_l)$.)

Step 1. Receive a from $\overline{\mathcal{P}}$, and pass $a_0 := a$ on to $\widehat{\mathcal{V}}_0$.

Step 2. Receive c_0 from $\widehat{\mathcal{V}}$, and pass $c := c_0$ on to $\overline{\mathcal{P}}$.

Step 3. Receive r from $\overline{\mathcal{P}}$, and pass $r_0 := r(x_0 \prod_{i=1}^l y_i^{x_i})^{c_0}$ on to $\widehat{\mathcal{V}}_0$.

Repeat this simulation until t executions of the issuing protocol have been performed.

Step C. Check if $\widehat{\mathcal{V}}$ has $t+1$ distinct certified key pairs on its tapes. If not, then halt.

Step D. For each of these $t + 1$ certified key pairs, $((x_1, \ldots, x_l, \alpha_1), h', (c_0', r_0'))$, compute $c^* := c_0'$, $r^* := r_0'(x_0 \prod_{i=1}^l y_i^{x_i} \alpha_1)^{-c_0'}$, and $m := h'$, and output the signed message $(m, (c^*, r^*))$.

It is easy to see that the public key in Step A is generated with the same probability distribution as that by which $\overline{\mathcal{P}}_0$ generates its public key. The response that is computed by $\widehat{\mathcal{V}}$ in the simulated issuing protocol is the same as the response that $\overline{\mathcal{P}}_0$ would compute:

$$
\begin{aligned}
r_0^v &= \left(r(x_0 \prod_{i=1}^l y_i^{x_i})^{c_0}\right)^v \\
&= r^v x_0^{c_0 v}\left((\prod_{i=1}^l (y_i^v)^{x_i})^{c_0}\right) \\
&\overset{(\star)}{=} (h_{\text{GQ}}^c a) x_0^{cv}\left(\prod_{i=1}^l g_i^{x_i}\right)^{c_0} \\
&= (h_{\text{GQ}} x_0^v)^c a h^{c_0} \\
&= (h_0 h)^{c_0} a_0,
\end{aligned}
$$

where the substitution $(\star)$ is allowed because the response of $\overline{\mathcal{P}}$ satisfies $r^v h_{\text{GQ}}^{-c} = a$. It follows that the view of $\widehat{\mathcal{V}}_0$ in the simulated issuing protocol has the same distribution as when $\widehat{\mathcal{V}}_0$ interacts with $\overline{\mathcal{P}}_0$, regardless of the probability distributions of its challenges, $(x_1, \ldots, x_l)$, and h_{GQ}. Therefore, $\widehat{\mathcal{V}}$ moves from Step C to Step D with probability ϵ.

We next show (i) that the output of $\widehat{\mathcal{V}}$ consists of $t + 1$ messages with corresponding Guillou-Quisquater signatures, and (ii) that these signed messages are all distinct with overwhelming probability. Property (i) follows from

$$
\begin{aligned}
c^* &= c_0' \\
&\stackrel{(\star)}{=} \mathcal{H}_{n,v}(h', (r_0')^v (h_0 h')^{-c_0'}) \\
&\stackrel{(\star\star)}{=} \mathcal{H}_{n,v}(m, (r^*)^v h_{\mathrm{GQ}}^{-c^*}).
\end{aligned}
$$

The substitution $(\star)$ is allowed by definition of a certificate, and substitution $(\star\star)$ follows from

$$
\begin{aligned}
(r_0')^v (h_0 h')^{-c_0'} &= (r^*(x_0 \prod_{i=1}^{l} y_i^{x_i} \alpha_1)^{c_0'})^v (h_0 \prod_{i=1}^{l} g_i^{x_i} \alpha_1^v)^{-c_0'} \\
&= (r^*)^v x_0^{c_0' v} (\prod_{i=1}^{l} (y_i^v)^{x_i} \alpha_1^v)^{c_0'} h_0^{-c_0'} (\prod_{i=1}^{l} g_i^{x_i} \alpha_1^v)^{-c_0'} \\
&= (r^*)^v (h_0 x_0^{-v})^{-c_0'} \\
&= (r^*)^v h_{\mathrm{GQ}}^{-c^*}.
\end{aligned}
$$

To prove property (ii), consider any two certified key pairs,

$$
(x_1, \ldots, x_l, \alpha_1), \ h', \ (c_0', r_0')
$$

and

$$
(x_1^*, \ldots, x_l^*, \alpha_1^*), \ h^*, \ (c_0^*, r_0^*).
$$

The corresponding signed messages, as computed by $\widehat{\mathcal{V}}$ in Step D, are equal to

$$
h', (c_0', r_0'((h')^{1/v})^{-c_0'})
$$

and

$$
h^*, (c_0^*, r_0^*((h^*)^{1/v})^{-c_0^*}).
$$

Suppose that these two signed messages are the same. From $h' = h^*$ and $c_0' = c_0^*$ it follows that $r_0' = r_0^*$. Furthermore, if $(x_1, \ldots, x_l, \alpha_1)$ and $(x_1^*, \ldots, x_l^*, \alpha_1^*)$ are not the same, then

$$
(x_1 - x_1^* \bmod v, \ldots, x_l - x_l^* \bmod v, \prod_{i=1}^{l} g_i^{(x_i - x_i^*) \operatorname{div} v} \alpha_1 / \alpha_1^*)
$$

is a non-trivial RSA-representation of 1. According to Lemma 4.3.5, this contradicts Assumption 2.5.9. Consequently, if the two signed messages are the same, then the two certified key pairs are the same, and therefore property (ii) holds as well.

To complete the proof, observe that an execution of the simulated issuing protocol constitutes exactly one execution of the protocol with $\overline{\mathcal{P}}$. In all, $\hat{\mathcal{V}}$ can compute $t + 1$ Guillou-Quisquater signed messages from t protocol executions with $\overline{\mathcal{P}}$ with probability ϵ. If ϵ is non-negligible, this contradicts Assumption 2.5.9. $\square$

Similar reductions can be made for the other three certificate schemes in Section 4.2. Because DLREP-based scheme II and RSAREP-based scheme II are non-trivially witness-indistinguishable, we get the following results by application of Proposition 2.5.3.

Proposition 4.3.7. *Assume that $\mathcal{P}_0$ performs no more than polylogarithmically many protocol executions, and that the binary size of the outputs of $\mathcal{H}_{g,g_0}(\cdot)$ is linear in k. If $(I_{\text{DL}}, D_{\text{DL}})$ is invulnerable for the DL function, then DLREP-based scheme II is unforgeable in the random oracle model, for any distribution of $(x_1, \ldots, x_l)$.*

Proposition 4.3.8. *Assume that $\mathcal{P}_0$ performs no more than polylogarithmically many protocol executions, and that the binary size of the outputs of $\mathcal{H}_{n,v}(\cdot)$ is linear in k. If $(I_{\text{RSA}}, D_{\text{RSA}})$ is invulnerable for the RSA function, then RSAREP-based scheme II is unforgeable in the random oracle model, for any distribution of $(x_1, \ldots, x_l)$.*

These results hold even in case $\mathcal{V}_0$ may arbitrarily interleave the protocol executions and $\mathcal{P}_0$ encodes different attribute tuples of $\mathcal{V}_0$'s choice.

Blinding-invariance

To study the restrictive blinding property, we slightly weaken the attack model by assuming that $(x_1, \ldots, x_l)$ is formed independently of h_0. In most applications this requirement is naturally met, especially if $\mathcal{P}_0$ selects $(x_1, \ldots, x_l)$.

The following assumption states that the only manner to generate a pair $h, (c, r)$ for which $c = \mathcal{H}_{n,v}(h, r^v h^{-c})$ is by forming h as the v-th power of some known $x \in \mathbb{Z}_n^*$. That is, if an algorithm could output such a transcript, then with "modest" extra effort it could also compute $h^{1/v} \bmod n$.

Assumption 4.3.9. *There exists a hash function $\mathcal{H}^*(\cdot) = \{\mathcal{H}_i^*(\cdot)\}_{i \in \{n,v\}}$ and an expected polynomial-time algorithm $\mathcal{K}$, such that for any polynomial-time algorithm A, for all constants $c > 0$, and for all sufficiently large k,*

$$\left| \mathsf{P}_k\Big(A(n,v) = (h,c,r) \text{ such that } c = \mathcal{H}_{n,v}^*(h, r^v h^{-c}) \mid (n,v) := I_{\text{RSA}}(1^k) \Big) \right.$$
$$\left. - \mathsf{P}_k\Big(\mathcal{K}((n,v),(h,c,r);A) = \beta \in \mathbb{Z}_n^* \text{ such that } \beta^v = h \Big) \right| < 1/k^c.$$

This assumption can be proved in the random oracle model by using the oracle replay technique of Pointcheval and Stern [307].[3]

Proposition 4.3.10. *If Assumption 4.3.9 holds, then a hash function $\mathcal{H}(\cdot)$ exists such that the following holds for all $l \geq 1$ and all $(x_1, \ldots, x_l)$. Let $(x_1, \ldots, x_l)$ be formed independently of $h_0, (g_1, \ldots, g_l)$, and be the same in all protocol executions of RSAREP-based scheme I. If $\widehat{\mathcal{V}}_0$, after engaging in polynomially many protocol executions with respect to $(x_1, \ldots, x_l)$, outputs a certified key pair comprising a secret key $(x_1^*, \ldots, x_l^*, \alpha_1)$, then*

$$(x_1^*, \ldots, x_l^*) = (x_1, \ldots, x_l)$$

with overwhelming probability.

Proof. Suppose that $\widehat{\mathcal{V}}_0$, after t protocol executions, outputs with non-negligible success probability ϵ a certified key pair comprising a secret key $(x_1^*, \ldots, x_l^*, \alpha_1)$ for which $(x_1^*, \ldots, x_l^*)$ differs from $(x_1, \ldots, x_l)$. Using a proper choice for $\mathcal{H}(\cdot)$, we show how to use algorithm $\mathcal{K}$ in Assumption 4.3.9 to construct a polynomial-time algorithm A for inverting the RSA function, thereby obtaining a contradiction.

Let $(I_{\text{RSA}}, D_{\text{RSA}})$ denote any invulnerable instance generator for the RSA function. On input k, this instance generator outputs a triple (n, v, x). Algorithm A, on input $(n, v, h_{\text{RSA}} := x^v)$, performs the following steps:

Step A. (Simulate the key set-up for $\overline{\mathcal{P}}_0$.) Generate l random numbers, $r_1, \ldots, r_l \in \mathbb{Z}_v$, and l random numbers, $s_1, \ldots, s_l \in \mathbb{Z}_n^*$. Set

$$g_i := h_{\text{RSA}}^{r_i} s_i^v \quad \forall i \in \{1, \ldots, l\}.$$

With h denoting $\prod_{i=1}^{l} g_i^{x_i}$, generate a random number $x_0 \in \mathbb{Z}_n^*$, and compute $h_0 := x_0^v h^{-1}$. (Since $(x_1, \ldots, x_l)$ is generated independently of h_0, we may assume that it is generated before $(h_0, g_1, \ldots, g_l)$ is generated.) The simulated public key of $\overline{\mathcal{P}}_0$ is $h_0, (g_1, \ldots, g_l)$. In addition, define $\mathcal{H}(\cdot)$ according to

$$\mathcal{H}_{n,v} : (a, b) \mapsto \mathcal{H}_{n,v}^*(h_0 a, b),$$

for all $a, b \in \mathbb{Z}_n^*$, where $\mathcal{H}^*(\cdot)$ is the hash function in Assumption 4.3.9.

Step B. (Simulate $\overline{\mathcal{P}}_0$ in issuing protocol executions with respect to $(x_1, \ldots, x_l)$.)

Step 1. Generate a random number $w_0 \in \mathbb{Z}_n^*$. Compute $a_0 := w_0^v$, and send a_0 to $\widehat{\mathcal{V}}_0$.

---

[3]Because A is non-interactive, it is unclear how to formalize knowledge extraction outside of the random oracle model. The intuition is that if A would keep a "history" tape that contains a copy of everything it has written on its work tape (but with previous contents never overwritten), then $\mathcal{K}$ should be able to extract knowledge from A by looking at the history tape and A's input tape and random tape.

Step 2. Receive c_0 from $\widehat{\mathcal{V}}_0$.

Step 3. Compute $r_0 := x_0^{c_0} w_0$, and send r_0 to $\widehat{\mathcal{V}}_0$.

Repeat this simulation until t executions of the issuing protocol with $\widehat{\mathcal{V}}_0$ have been performed.

Step C. Check if $\widehat{\mathcal{V}}_0$ has output a certified key pair $(x_1^*, \ldots, x_l^*, \alpha_1), h', (c_0', r_0')$ for which $(x_1^*, \ldots, x_l^*)$ does not equal $(x_1, \ldots, x_l)$. If this is not the case, then halt.

Step D. If $\sum_{i=1}^{l} r_i(x_i - x_i^*) = 0 \bmod v$, then halt.

Step E. Run algorithm $\mathcal{K}$ on input (n, v) and $(h', (c_0', r_0'))$, using $< A, \widehat{\mathcal{V}}_0 >$ as a black-box algorithm. If $\mathcal{K}$ does not output $\beta \in \mathbb{Z}_n^*$ such that $\beta^v = h' \bmod n$, then halt.

Step F. Using the extended Euclidean algorithm, compute integers $e, f \in \mathbb{Z}$ satisfying

$$e\Big(\sum_{i=1}^{l} r_i(x_i - x_i^*)\Big) + fv = 1.$$

(This can always be done, because v is prime.) Compute

$$h_{\text{RSA}}^f (\alpha_1 x_0 \beta^{-1} \prod_{i=1}^{l} s_i^{x_i - x_i^*})^e,$$

and output the result.

By definition of the key generation of A in Step A, the public key in Step A is simulated with the same probability distribution as that by which $\overline{\mathcal{P}}_0$ generates its public key, regardless of the distribution of h_{RSA} and $(x_1, \ldots, x_l)$. The response that is computed by A in the simulated issuing protocol is the same as the response that $\overline{\mathcal{P}}_0$ would compute:

$$
\begin{aligned}
r_0^v &= (x_0^{c_0} w_0)^v \\
&= (x_0^v)^{c_0} w_0^v \\
&= (h_0 h)^{c_0} a_0.
\end{aligned}
$$

It follows that the view of $\widehat{\mathcal{V}}_0$ in the simulated issuing protocol has the same distribution as that provided by $\overline{\mathcal{P}}_0$, regardless of the probability distribution by which $\widehat{\mathcal{V}}_0$ generates its challenges. Therefore, Step D is reached by supposition with probability ϵ.

The tuple $(r_1, \ldots, r_l)$ is unconditionally hidden from $\widehat{\mathcal{V}}_0$, due to the randomness of the s_i's and the fact that v is co-prime to $\varphi(n)$, and it is therefore independent of

$(x_1^*, \ldots, x_l^*)$. Because $(r_1, \ldots, r_l)$ is also independent of $(x_1, \ldots, x_l)$, the transition from Step D to Step E takes place with probability $1 - 1/v$.

Because of the definition of $\mathcal{H}(\cdot)$, we can infer from Assumption 4.3.9 that the output β of $\mathcal{K}$ in Step E satisfies

$$\beta^v = h_0 h' = h_0 \prod_{i=1}^{l} g_i^{x_i^*} \alpha_1^v$$

with non-negligible probability. Therefore, the transition from Step E to Step F takes place with non-negligible probability.

According to the key pair construction in Step A we also have

$$x_0^v = h_0 h = h_0 \prod_{i=1}^{l} g_i^{x_i}.$$

From these two relations we get

$$
\begin{aligned}
(x_0 \beta^{-1})^v &= \prod_{i=1}^{l} g_i^{x_i - x_i^*} (\alpha_1^v)^{-1} \\
&= \prod_{i=1}^{l} (h_{\mathrm{RSA}}^{r_i} s_i^v)^{x_i - x_i^*} (\alpha_1^v)^{-1} \\
&= h_{\mathrm{RSA}}^{\sum_{i=1}^{l} r_i (x_i - x_i^*)} \left(\prod_{i=1}^{l} s_i^{x_i - x_i^*} \alpha_1^{-1} \right)^v
\end{aligned}
$$

and so

$$\left(\alpha_1 x_0 \beta^{-1} \prod_{i=1}^{l} s_i^{x_i^* - x_i} \right)^v = h_{\mathrm{RSA}}^{\sum_{i=1}^{l} r_i (x_i - x_i^*)}.$$

From this it follows that the output of A in Step F is equal to $h_{\mathrm{RSA}}^{1/v}$, with overwhelming probability:

$$
\begin{aligned}
\left(h_{\mathrm{RSA}}^{f} (\alpha_1 x_0 \beta^{-1} \prod_{i=1}^{l} s_i^{x_i - x_i^*})^e \right)^v &= h_{\mathrm{RSA}}^{fv} \left((\alpha_1 x_0 \beta^{-1} \prod_{i=1}^{l} s_i^{x_i - x_i^*})^v \right)^e \\
&= h_{\mathrm{RSA}}^{1 - e(\sum_{i=1}^{l} r_i (x_i - x_i^*))} (h_{\mathrm{RSA}}^{\sum_{i=1}^{l} r_i (x_i - x_i^*)})^e \\
&= h_{\mathrm{RSA}}.
\end{aligned}
$$

The overall success probability of A is $(1 - 1/v)\epsilon$ times the (non-negligible) success probability of algorithm $\mathcal{K}$. If ϵ is non-negligible, then $(I_{\mathrm{RSA}}, D_{\mathrm{RSA}})$ is not invulnerable for the RSA function. Therefore $(x_1^*, \ldots, x_l^*) = (x_1, \ldots, x_l)$ with overwhelming probability. □

The result holds regardless of the fashion in which protocol executions with respect to the same attribute tuple are interleaved.

The hash function defined in the proof of Proposition 4.3.10 is not the same as that in the proof of Proposition 4.3.6. In practice, any sufficiently strong one-way hash function should suffice for both propositions. (Another approach is to adjust Assumption 4.3.9.)

A similar result can be proved for the other three certificate schemes described in Section 4.2. In all four schemes, $\mathcal{P}_0$ is effectively proving knowledge of a representation of the joint public key $h_0 h$, by means of a protocol that we know from Section 2.4 to be honest-verifier zero-knowledge. Since c_0 as formed by $\overline{\mathcal{V}}_0$ is randomly distributed, wiretappers cannot infer anything from the protocol executions of honest receivers. More generally, the blinding-invariance property remains valid even if $\widehat{\mathcal{V}}_0$ can wiretap the issuing as well as the showing protocol executions of honest parties, assuming that these use their certified key pairs only in zero-knowledge showing protocols.

The following negative result shows that Proposition 4.3.10 cannot easily be generalized.

Proposition 4.3.11. *If $\overline{\mathcal{P}}_0$ performs protocol executions in parallel with respect to different attribute tuples, then $\widehat{\mathcal{V}}_0$ can obtain a certified key pair for which the putative restrictive blinding-invariant part is not equal to any of these tuples.*

Proof. Suppose that $\overline{\mathcal{P}}_0$ performs its protocol executions with respect to $t > 1$ different attribute tuples, $(x_{11}, \ldots, x_{l1}), \ldots, (x_{1t}, \ldots, x_{lt})$. In the following attack, $\mathcal{V}_0$ engages in parallel in t protocol executions, each with respect to one of the tuples. Assume without loss of generality that the j-th protocol execution is with respect to the tuple $(x_{1j}, \ldots, x_{lj})$ and let $h_j := \prod_{i=1}^{l} g_i^{x_{ij}}$, for all $j \in \{1, \ldots, t\}$.[4]

Step 1. $\widehat{\mathcal{V}}_0$ obtains t numbers, $a_{01}, \ldots, a_{0t} \in \mathbb{Z}_n^*$ from $\overline{\mathcal{P}}_0$, by engaging in Step 1 of all t protocol executions.

Step 2. $\widehat{\mathcal{V}}_0$ chooses t numbers, $\alpha_1, \ldots, \alpha_t \in \mathbb{Z}_v$, subject to $\sum_{i=1}^{t} \alpha_i = 1 \bmod v$. $\mathcal{V}_0$ computes

$$h' := \prod_{i=1}^{t} h_i^{\alpha_i}$$

and

$$c_0' := \mathcal{H}_{n,v}(h', \prod_{i=1}^{t} a_{0i}).$$

For all $i \in \{1, \ldots, t\}$, $\widehat{\mathcal{V}}_0$ then computes $c_{0i} := \alpha_i c_0' \bmod v$ and sends c_{0i} to $\overline{\mathcal{P}}_0$ in Step 2 of the i-th protocol execution.

---

[4]The ordering of protocol executions assumed here follows for instance from the time order in which $\mathcal{V}_0$ processes the first message of each protocol execution.

Step 3. $\widehat{\mathcal{V}}_0$ obtains t numbers, $r_{01}, \ldots, r_{0t} \in \mathbb{Z}_n^*$ from $\overline{\mathcal{P}}_0$, by engaging in Step 3 of all t protocol executions.

If $\widehat{\mathcal{V}}_0$ accepts in all t protocol executions, it computes

$$r_0' := \prod_{i=1}^{t} r_{0i} (h_0 h_i)^{(\alpha_i c_0') \operatorname{div} v} h_0^{-((\sum_{i=1}^{t} \alpha_i) \operatorname{div} v)}.$$

(The additional operations needed to blind the certified key pair have been left out only for reason of clarity; they are easy to incorporate.)

If the t responses of $\mathcal{P}_0$ are all correct, then (c_0', r_0') is a certificate of $\mathcal{P}_0$ on h':

$$
\begin{aligned}
(r_0')^v &= \left(\prod_{i=1}^{t} r_{0i} (h_0 h_i)^{(\alpha_i c_0') \operatorname{div} v} h_0^{-((\sum_{i=1}^{t} \alpha_i) \operatorname{div} v)} \right)^v \\
&= \prod_{i=1}^{t} r_{0i}^v (h_0 h_i)^{v((\alpha_i c_0') \operatorname{div} v)} h_0^{-v((\sum_{i=1}^{t} \alpha_i) \operatorname{div} v)} \\
&= \prod_{i=1}^{t} (h_0 h_i)^{c_{0i}} a_{0i} (h_0 h_i)^{v((\alpha_i c_0') \operatorname{div} v)} h_0^{-v((\sum_{i=1}^{t} \alpha_i) \operatorname{div} v)} \\
&= \prod_{i=1}^{t} (h_0 h_i)^{\alpha_i c_0' \bmod v} a_{0i} (h_0 h_i)^{v((\alpha_i c_0') \operatorname{div} v)} h_0^{-v((\sum_{i=1}^{t} \alpha_i) \operatorname{div} v)} \\
&= \prod_{i=1}^{t} (h_0 h_i)^{\alpha_i c_0'} a_{0i} h_0^{-v((\sum_{i=1}^{t} \alpha_i) \operatorname{div} v)} \\
&= (h_0^{\sum_{i=1}^{t} \alpha_i})^{c_0'} \prod_{i=1}^{t} h_i^{\alpha_i c_0'} a_{0i} h_0^{-v((\sum_{i=1}^{t} \alpha_i) \operatorname{div} v)} \\
&= (h_0^{\sum_{i=1}^{t} \alpha_i \bmod v})^{c_0'} \prod_{i=1}^{t} (h_i^{\alpha_i})^{c_0'} a_{0i} \\
&= h_0^{c_0'} (h')^{c_0'} \prod_{i=1}^{t} a_{0i} \\
&= (h_0 h')^{c_0'} \prod_{i=1}^{t} a_{0i}.
\end{aligned}
$$

From

$$h' = \prod_{j=1}^{l} g_j^{\sum_{i=1}^{t} \alpha_i x_{ij}}$$

it is clear that $\widehat{\mathcal{V}}_0$ can obtain a certified key pair for which the secret key does not contain any of the t attribute tuples with respect to which the protocol executions have been performed. □

In fact, if $t > l$ then $\widehat{\mathcal{V}}_0$ can target any attribute tuple it desires, assuming a certain linear independence property; see Proposition 4.3.15 for details.

The attack in the proof of Proposition 4.3.11 requires $\widehat{\mathcal{V}}_0$ to engage in parallel executions of the issuing protocol, because each of the t challenges of $\widehat{\mathcal{V}}_0$ depends on all t initial witnesses. In case $\overline{\mathcal{P}}_0$ does not perform protocol executions with respect to different attribute tuples in parallel, it seems that $\widehat{\mathcal{V}}_0$ can only obtain certified key pairs that comprise one of the t tuples with respect to which the protocol executions have been performed. This isolation property is formalized by the following assumption.

Assumption 4.3.12. *There exists a hash function* $\mathcal{H}(\cdot)$ *such that the following holds for all* $l, t \geq 1$*. Let* t *attribute tuples,*

$$(x_{11}, \ldots, x_{l1}), \ldots, (x_{1t}, \ldots, x_{lt}),$$

be formed. Let $(x_1^*, \ldots, x_l^*, \alpha)$ *denote the secret key of a certified key pair computed by* $\widehat{\mathcal{V}}_0$ *in RSAREP-based scheme I after engaging in polynomially many protocol executions with respect to tuples* $(x_{1i}, \ldots, x_{li})$*,* $i \in \{1, \ldots, t\}$ *of its own choice (possibly adaptively chosen). If* $\overline{\mathcal{P}}_0$ *does not perform protocol executions with respect to distinct attribute tuples in parallel, then with overwhelming probability there exists* $i \in \{1, \ldots, t\}$ *such that* $(x_1^*, \ldots, x_l^*) = (x_{1i}, \ldots, x_{li})$*. More generally, the second property in Definition 4.1.1 holds.*

For DLREP-based scheme II and RSAREP-based scheme II, the analogous assumption can be proved in the random oracle model, provided that $\mathcal{P}_0$ performs no more than polylogarithmically many protocol executions. Note that the assumption does not forbid protocol executions with respect to the same attribute tuple to be performed in parallel.

4.3.4 Additional properties

$\mathcal{P}_0$ knows the numbers $(x_1, \ldots, x_l)$ that end up in the secret key of $\overline{\mathcal{V}}_0$. Once $\mathcal{P}_0$ gets to see h' and for some reason (for instance because x_1 is an identifier that $\mathcal{V}_0$ discloses in the showing protocol) is able to link it to the protocol execution in which it was certified, it can compute $h'/h = \alpha_1^v$. According to Proposition 4.3.4, α_1 is uncorrelated to the view of $\widetilde{\mathcal{P}}_0$ in $(\widetilde{\mathcal{P}}_0, \overline{\mathcal{V}}_0)$. In Section 2.2.3 we have seen that if any D_{RSA} leads to a one-way RSA function, then a random choice for α_1 certainly will. From this we get the following result.

Corollary 4.3.13. *If* $(I_{\text{RSA}}, D_{\text{RSA}})$ *is invulnerable for the RSA-function, and does not output the factorization of* n *as side information, then* $\widehat{\mathcal{P}}_0$ *cannot compute the secret* *key of* $\overline{\mathcal{V}}_0$ *from the certified public key of* $\overline{\mathcal{V}}_0$ *even if* $\widehat{\mathcal{P}}_0$ *knows the encoded attribute tuple* $(x_1, \ldots, x_l)$.

Therefore, only $\mathcal{V}_0$ can feasibly perform a (signed) proof of knowledge of a secret key corresponding to its certified public key(s). Note that the interests of $\mathcal{P}_0$ and $\mathcal{V}_0$ are aligned, because $(I_{\mathrm{RSA}}, D_{\mathrm{RSA}})$ needs to be invulnerable to guarantee the unforgeability of certified key pairs. If the issuing protocol is combined with one of the RSAREP-based showing protocols of Chapter 3, and $\mathcal{V}_0$ does not disclose at least part of the encoded attribute tuple, then not even $\widehat{\mathcal{P}}_0$ will be able to determine $\mathcal{V}_0$'s secret key. The latter property is desirable to achieve non-repudiation, especially in the case of limited-show certificates; see Section 5.5.3 for details.

A similar result holds for the other three certificate schemes constructed in Section 4.2. The DLREP-based schemes have the advantage that a trapdoor is not known to exist, so that $\mathcal{P}_0$ may generate the system parameters by itself.

The following property clarifies the nature of the certificate scheme.

Proposition 4.3.14. *RSAREP-based scheme I is a secret-key certificate scheme.*

Proof. We construct a polynomial-time simulation algorithm S that generates certified public keys with the same probability distribution as that according to which they are generated in the issuing protocol between $\overline{\mathcal{P}}_0$ and $\overline{\mathcal{V}}_0$. On given as input $n, v, h_0, (g_1, \ldots, g_l)$ and $\mathcal{H}_{n,v}(\cdot)$, S generates two random numbers $\alpha_2, \alpha_3 \in \mathbb{Z}_n^*$, computes $h := h_0^{-1}\alpha_2^v$, $c_0 := \mathcal{H}_{n,v}(h, \alpha_3^v)$ and $r_0 := \alpha_2^{c_0}\alpha_3$, and outputs the pair $h, (c_0, r_0)$. The output of S is a certified public key:

$$
\begin{aligned}
c_0 &= \mathcal{H}_{n,v}(h, \alpha_3^v) \\
&= \mathcal{H}_{n,v}(h, (r_0\alpha_2^{-c_0})^v) \\
&= \mathcal{H}_{n,v}(h, r_0^v(\alpha_2^v)^{-c_0}) \\
&= \mathcal{H}_{n,v}(h, r_0^v(h_0 h)^{-c_0}).
\end{aligned}
$$

Since v is co-prime to $\varphi(n)$, and α_2 and α_3 in Step 1 are chosen at random from $\mathbb{Z}_n^*$, the output distribution of A is identical to that of certified public keys issued to $\overline{\mathcal{V}}_0$ by $\overline{\mathcal{P}}_0$. $\qquad\square$

The other three schemes described in Section 4.2 are secret-key certificate schemes as well. For the advantages of this property, see Section 2.6 and Section 5.2.2.

For any of the certificate schemes in Section 4.2, a limited degree of parallelization can be achieved without any modifications. Observe that the crux of the proof of Proposition 4.3.10 is that $(\mathcal{P}_0, \mathcal{V}_0)$ is a proof of knowledge of the v-th root of $h_0 h$, but not of the v-th root of h_0. Elaborating on this observation, we can obtain the following result.

Proposition 4.3.15. *There exists a hash function* $\mathcal{H}(\cdot)$ *such that the following holds. Let* $(x_1^*, \ldots, x_l^*, \alpha)$ *denote the secret key of a certified key pair computed by* $\widehat{\mathcal{V}}_0$ *in*

RSAREP-based scheme I after engaging in polynomially many protocol executions (that may be arbitrarily interleaved) with respect to attribute tuples $(x_{1i}, \ldots, x_{li})$, *for* $i \in \{1, \ldots, t\}$, *of its own choice, subject to the restriction that the tuples are formed independently of* h_0. *If Assumption 4.3.9 holds, then for all* $l, t \geq 1$, *with overwhelming probability* $(1, x_1^*, \ldots, x_l^*)$ *is contained in the linear span of the* t *vectors* $(1, x_{1i}, \ldots, x_{li})$, *for* $i \in \{1, \ldots, t\}$. *In particular, if* $t \leq l$ *the second property in Definition 4.1.1 holds.*

In other words, if $\mathcal{P}_0$ performs protocol executions with respect to up to $t \leq l$ independent tuples in parallel, it can still encode $l - t + 1$ attributes into the secret key of each certified key pair that $\widehat{\mathcal{V}}_0$ ends up with. The same holds for the DLREP-based schemes. This immunization technique is not very practical, though, because the degree of parallelization depends on l and the number of attributes to be encoded. In the next section we show how to guarantee security in the presence of arbitrary parallelization.

4.4   Parallelization of protocol executions

Whether or not the measure of not running protocol executions with respect to different attribute tuples in parallel poses a performance bottleneck depends on the application at hand. Sequential protocol executions need not be inefficient, because $\mathcal{P}_0$ can send out a_0 for a new protocol execution as soon as it has received the challenge c_0 for the current protocol execution. To prevent queuing, $\mathcal{P}_0$ should abort an execution of the issuing protocol if a predetermined time lag between the transmittal of a_0 and the reception of c_0 is exceeded; the receiver must then try again in a later protocol execution. Assuming that requests for protocol executions arrive in accordance with a Poisson process, this strategy is the M/D/1 model with feedback known from queueing theory. The feedback may be purposely limited by $\mathcal{P}_0$, to shut out parties that frequently exceed the permitted time lag. Furthermore, executions of the certificate issuing protocol can be scheduled to take place at a convenient time and can be repeated if necessary. Also, remember that protocol executions with respect to the same attribute tuple may always be performed in parallel.

The ability to arbitrarily interleave protocol executions offers two benefits in highly demanding applications:

- The role of $\mathcal{P}_0$ can be performed by distributed processors that need not communicate or synchronize; they merely need access to the same secret key.

- Receivers can go off-line between Step 1 and Step 2, in principle for as long as they please. $\mathcal{P}_0$ in Step 1 could even send to $\mathcal{V}_0$ an authenticated encryption of the random bits it used to form its initial witness, and have $\mathcal{V}_0$ return it in Step 2. (Obviously, $\mathcal{P}_0$ must prevent replay.) In the RSAREP-based protocols

$\mathcal{V}_0$ may even form a_0 on its own as the output of a sufficiently strong one-way function, as pointed out in Section 4.2.3.

In the following two sections we describe two techniques to "immunize" the certificate schemes of Section 4.2 against parallel mode attacks. Both immunizations admit arbitrary parallelization, and do not affect the definition of the system parameters and $\mathcal{P}_0$'s public key; only the definition of a certificate changes slightly.

4.4.1 Masking the initial witness

Our first immunization technique aims to destroy the multiplicative relation in the initial witnesses that is exploited by $\mathcal{V}_0$ in Step 2 of the parallel mode attack of Proposition 4.3.11. It applies to both DLREP-based schemes and to both RSAREP-based schemes.

Concretely, to enable full parallelization of protocol executions in RSAREP-based scheme I, we have $\mathcal{P}_0$ send $f_{n,v}(a_0)$ instead of a_0 in Step 1 of the issuing protocol. The function $\{f_i(\cdot)\}_{i \in \{(n,v)\}}$ must satisfy the following two requirements:

1. For random $a_0, b_0 \in \mathbb{Z}_n^*$, it is easy to compute $f_{n,v}(a_0 b_0)$ from $f_{n,v}(a_0)$ and b_0.

2. For random $a_0, b_0 \in \mathbb{Z}_n^*$, it is infeasible to compute a triple

$$\alpha \neq 0 \bmod v, \beta \neq 0 \bmod v, f_{n,v}(a_0^\alpha b_0^\beta)$$

from $f_{n,v}(a_0)$ and $f_{n,v}(b_0)$.

The first requirement ensures that $\mathcal{V}_0$ can retrieve certified public keys in exactly the same manner as in the original issuing protocol, while the second requirement prevents parallel mode attacks based on the exploitation of multiplicative properties. The second requirement may be weakened by having $\mathcal{P}_0$ time the delay between sending out a_0 and receiving c_0, aborting when a predetermined time bound is exceeded; it then suffices that triples $\alpha \neq 0 \bmod v, \beta \neq 0 \bmod v, f_{n,v}(a_0^\alpha b_0^\beta)$ cannot be computed within the imposed time bound. Note that we do not require that the computation of $f_{n,v}(a_0^\alpha)$ from $f_{n,v}(a_0)$ be infeasible.

Correspondingly, the following modifications must be made to RSAREP-based scheme I:

- The pair (c_0', r_0') is redefined to be a certificate of $\mathcal{P}_0$ on h' if and only if

$$c_0' = \mathcal{H}_{n,v}(h', f_{n,v}((r_0')^v (h_0 h')^{-c_0'})).$$

- In Step 1 of the issuing protocol, $\mathcal{P}_0$ sends $f_{n,v}(a_0)$ instead of a_0.

- In Step 2 of the issuing protocol, $\mathcal{V}_0$ computes c'_0 according to

$$c'_0 := \mathcal{H}_{n,v}(h', f_{n,v}(\alpha_2^v(h_0 h)^{\alpha_3} a_0)).$$

$\mathcal{V}_0$ can compute c'_0 by virtue of the first requirement for $f(\cdot)$.

- $\mathcal{V}_0$ accepts if and only if $f_{n,v}(r_0^v(h_0 h)^{-c_0})$ is equal to the number provided by $\mathcal{P}_0$ in Step 1.

Note that the definition of a key pair for $\mathcal{V}_0$ is not affected; only the definition of a certificate is changed. The resulting scheme is depicted in Figure 4.6.

Proposition 4.4.1. *If $f(\cdot)$ is one-to-one, then the immunized RSAREP-based scheme I is at least as secure as the original scheme.*

The proof is trivial: the security of the immunized scheme is easily seen to reduce to that of the original scheme in case it is feasible to invert $f(\cdot)$.

Assumption 4.4.2. *There exists a function $f(\cdot)$ and a hash function $\mathcal{H}(\cdot)$ such that the issuing protocol of the immunized RSAREP-based scheme I is restrictive blind with blinding-invariant part $(x_1, \ldots, x_l)$, even when protocol executions with respect to different attribute tuples are arbitrarily interleaved.*

A concrete suggestion for a one-to-one function $f(\cdot)$ satisfying our two requirements is the following. Let M be a random prime such that n divides $M - 1$, and let F be a random element of order n in $\mathbb{Z}_M^*$. Define

$$f_{n,v} : a_0 \to F^{a_0} \bmod M \quad \forall a_0 \in \mathbb{Z}_n^*.$$

It is easy to see that the first requirement for $f(\cdot)$ is met. Whether the second requirement is met depends on the hardness of the *Diffie-Hellman problem* [136]; this is the problem of computing g^{ab}, on input (g, g^a, g^b) for random a, b and a random group element g of large order. It is widely believed that there exist groups in which the ability to solve the Diffie-Hellman problem is polynomial-time equivalent to the ability to compute discrete logarithms; see Maurer and Wolf [258] for partial evidence.

Proposition 4.4.3. *Suppose there exist positive integers (α, β) and a polynomial-time algorithm that, on given as input a randomly chosen tuple (n, M, F) of the specified format and a pair $(F^{a_0} \bmod M, F^{b_0} \bmod M)$ for randomly chosen a_0, b_0 in $\mathbb{Z}_n^*$, outputs $F^{a_0^\alpha b_0^\beta} \bmod M$ with non-negligible success probability. Then the Diffie-Hellman problem in groups $\mathbb{Z}_M^*$, with M of the specified form, is tractable.*

The proof of this proposition makes use of standard techniques, and is therefore omitted.

Proposition 4.4.3 does not suffice to prove the second requirement, because it pertains only to algorithms that compute $F^{a_0^\alpha b_0^\beta} \bmod M$ for fixed (α, β). Nevertheless, it provides evidence in favor of $f(\cdot)$ meeting the second requirement.

$$\boxed{\mathcal{P}_0} \qquad\qquad\qquad\qquad \boxed{\mathcal{V}_0}$$

SYSTEM PARAMETERS

$$(n, v) := I_{\mathrm{RSA}}(1^k)$$

KEY SET-UP

Secret key: factorization of n

$h_0, g_1, \ldots, g_l \in_{\mathcal{R}} \mathbb{Z}_n^*$

Public key: $\qquad\qquad\qquad h_0, (g_1, \ldots, g_l)$

Additional information: $\qquad \mathcal{H}_{n,v}(\cdot), f_{n,v}(\cdot)$

PROTOCOL

$a_0 \in_{\mathcal{R}} \mathbb{Z}_n^*$

$a_0^* := f_{n,v}(a_0)$

$$\xrightarrow{\quad a_0^* \quad}$$

$\alpha_1, \alpha_2 \in_{\mathcal{R}} \mathbb{Z}_n^*$

$\alpha_3 \in_{\mathcal{R}} \mathbb{Z}_v$

$h' := h\alpha_1^v$

$c_0' := \mathcal{H}_{n,v}(h', f_{n,v}(\alpha_2^v (h_0 h)^{\alpha_3} a_0))$

$c_0 := c_0' + \alpha_3 \bmod v$

$$\xleftarrow{\quad c_0 \quad}$$

$r_0 := ((h_0 h)^{c_0} a_0)^{1/v}$

$$\xrightarrow{\quad r_0 \quad}$$

$f_{n,v}(r_0^v (h_0 h)^{-c_0}) \overset{?}{=} a_0^*$

$r_0' := r_0 \alpha_2 \alpha_1^{c_0'} (h_0 h)^{(c_0' + \alpha_3) \operatorname{div} v}$

Figure 4.6: Immunization I of RSAREP-based scheme I.

This immunization technique also applies to the other three certificate schemes described in Section 4.2. Its drawback is decreased performance: $\mathcal{V}_0$ cannot precompute the application of $f_{n,v}(\cdot)$ in Step 2, and certificates are larger and more costly to verify. Furthermore, an elliptic curve implementation of the immunized DLREP-based schemes seems out of the question.

4.4.2 Swapping exponents in the verification relation

The second immunization technique applies to both DLREP-based schemes as well as to RSAREP-based scheme II, and fully preserves their efficiency. On the downside, it does not apply to RSAREP-based scheme I, and it is unclear how to prove unforgeability in the random oracle model.

The required modifications are the result of swapping the position of the challenge with that of (one of) the response(s) in the verification relation. In the case of DLREP-based scheme I, the certificate verification relation

$$c_0' = \mathcal{H}_{q,g_0}(h', g_0^{r_0'}(h_0 h')^{-c_0'}),$$

becomes

$$c_0' = \mathcal{H}_{q,g_0}(h', g_0^{c_0'}(h')^{r_0'}).$$

The secret key of $\mathcal{V}_0$ is redefined to be a DL-representation of h' with respect to $(g_1, \ldots, g_l, h_0)$, instead of with respect to $(g_1, \ldots, g_l, g_0)$. No changes are needed to the process of generating the system parameters. The issuing protocol is modified correspondingly, as follows:

Step 1. $\mathcal{P}_0$ generates a random number $w_0 \in \mathbb{Z}_q$, and sends $a_0 := g_0^{w_0}$ to $\mathcal{V}_0$.

Step 2. $\mathcal{V}_0$ generates three random numbers $\alpha_1 \in \mathbb{Z}_q^*$ and $\alpha_2, \alpha_3 \in \mathbb{Z}_q$. $\mathcal{V}_0$ computes $h' := (h_0 h)^{\alpha_1}$, $c_0' := \mathcal{H}_{q,g_0}(h', g_0^{\alpha_2}(h_0 h)^{\alpha_3} a_0)$, and sends $c_0 := c_0' - \alpha_2 \bmod q$ to $\mathcal{P}_0$.

Step 3. $\mathcal{P}_0$ sends $r_0 := (w_0 - c_0)/(x_0 + \sum_{i=1}^l x_i y_i) \bmod q$ to $\mathcal{V}_0$.[5]

$\mathcal{V}_0$ accepts if and only if $g_0^{c_0}(h_0 h)^{r_0} = a_0$. If this verification holds, $\mathcal{V}_0$ computes $r_0' := (r_0 + \alpha_3)/\alpha_1 \bmod q$. The resulting scheme is depicted in Figure 4.7.

It is easy to verify that the protocol is complete, and that (c_0', r_0') is a secret-key certificate of $\mathcal{P}_0$ on h'. Excluding public keys h' that are equal to 1, the following result can be proved in a manner similar to the proof of Proposition 4.3.4.

---

[5]To guarantee that $\mathcal{P}_0$ can always perform Step 3, the attribute tuple that is encoded must satisfy $(x_0 + \sum_{i=1}^l x_i y_i) \neq 0 \bmod q$. Since finding a tuple for which equality hold should be infeasible for $\mathcal{V}_0$ there is no need to check for this.

$$\boxed{\mathcal{P}_0} \qquad\qquad\qquad\qquad \boxed{\mathcal{V}_0}$$

SYSTEM PARAMETERS

$$(q, g_0) := I_{\text{DL}}(1^k)$$

KEY SET-UP

$x_0 := D_{\text{DL}}(q, g_0)$

$y_1, \ldots, y_l \in_{\mathcal{R}} \mathbb{Z}_q$

Secret key: $x_0, (y_1, \ldots, y_l)$

$h_0 := g_0^{x_0}$

$g_i := g_0^{y_i} \ \forall i \in \{1, \ldots, l\}$

Public key: $h_0, (g_1, \ldots, g_l)$

Additional information: $\mathcal{H}_{q,g_0}(\cdot)$

PROTOCOL

$w_0 \in_{\mathcal{R}} \mathbb{Z}_q$

$a_0 := g_0^{w_0}$

$$\xrightarrow{\ a_0\ }$$

$\alpha_1 \in \mathbb{Z}_q^*$

$\alpha_2, \alpha_3 \in_{\mathcal{R}} \mathbb{Z}_q$

$h' := (h_0 h)^{\alpha_1}$

$c_0' := \mathcal{H}_{q,g_0}(h', g_0^{\alpha_2}(h_0 h)^{\alpha_3} a_0)$

$c_0 := c_0' - \alpha_2 \bmod q$

$$\xleftarrow{\ c_0\ }$$

$r_0 := (w_0 - c_0)/(x_0 + \sum_{i=1}^{l} x_i y_i) \bmod q$

$$\xrightarrow{\ r_0\ }$$

$g_0^{c_0}(h_0 h)^{r_0} \stackrel{?}{=} a_0$

$r_0' := (r_0 + \alpha_3)/\alpha_1 \bmod q$

Figure 4.7: Immunization II of DLREP-based scheme I.

Proposition 4.4.4. *For any properly formed system parameters in the immunized DLREP-based scheme I, if $\mathcal{V}_0$ follows the issuing protocol and accepts, then it obtains a certified key pair comprising a perfectly blinded certified public key, regardless of the behavior of $\widetilde{\mathcal{P}}_0$.*

Obtaining a certificate on $h' = 1$ seems infeasible; it implies the ability to compute a number $c_0 \in \mathbb{Z}_q$ such that $\mathcal{H}_{q,g_0}(1, g_0^{c_0}) = c_0$. However, there is no need to make an assumption to this effect, since this case can be recognized and declared invalid.

While it would seem that the unforgeability of the modified certificate scheme can be proved in a manner similar to the proof of Proposition 4.3.6, this is not the case. Nevertheless, unforgeability is believed to hold for the modified scheme as well.

We now arrive at the crucial difference with DLREP-based scheme I. The parallel mode attack described in the proof of Proposition 4.3.11 does not apply, because $\mathcal{V}_0$ in Step 2 has to solve linear relations in terms of the responses of $\mathcal{P}_0$, which it cannot anticipate at that time.

Assumption 4.4.5. *There exists a hash function $\mathcal{H}(\cdot)$ such that in the immunized DLREP-based scheme I the following holds for all $l, t \geq 1$. Let t attribute tuples,*

$$(x_{11}, \ldots, x_{l1}), \ldots, (x_{1t}, \ldots, x_{lt}),$$

be formed. Suppose that $\widehat{\mathcal{V}}_0$, after engaging in polynomially many protocol executions (arbitrarily interleaved) with respect to tuples $(x_{1i}, \ldots, x_{li})$, $i \in \{1, \ldots, t\}$ of its own choice (possibly adaptively chosen), outputs a certified key pair comprising a secret key $(x_1^*, \ldots, x_l^*, \alpha_1)$. With overwhelming probability, there exists $i \in \{1, \ldots, t\}$ such that $(x_1^*, \ldots, x_l^*) = (\alpha_1 x_{1i} \bmod q, \ldots, \alpha_1 x_{li} \bmod q)$. More generally, the second property in Definition 4.1.1 holds.

Assuming that public keys equal to 1 are declared invalid, it follows that $\alpha_1 \neq 0$, and so

$$(x_1^*/\alpha_1 \bmod q, \ldots, x_l^*/\alpha_1 \bmod q) = (x_{1i}, \ldots, x_{li}).$$

The following argument gives some insight as to why the assumption should hold. If we restrict ourselves in Assumption 4.4.5 to protocol executions that involve the same $(x_1, \ldots, x_l)$, which is formed independently of h_0, then the proof of Proposition 4.3.10 applies in virtually the same manner, assuming the DL-based analogue to Assumption 4.3.9. Therefore, attacks must exploit the parallel nature of the issuing protocol with respect to different attribute tuples, if they are to have a non-negligible success probability. In the following, we consider only "algebraic" attacks on the parallel version of the issuing protocol. We restrict ourselves to the case $l = 1$; it is easy to prove that if Assumption 4.4.5 holds for $l = 1$ then it also holds for general l. Furthermore, we consider only two parallel executions of the issuing protocol, each with respect to a different blinding-invariant number; the argument can easily be generalized. Finally, we assume that $\widehat{\mathcal{V}}_0$ cannot compute with non-negligible probability of success a non-trivial representation of 1 with respect to (g_0, g_1, h_0). (It is easy to prove that $\log_{g_0} h_0$ and $\log_{g_0} g_1$ do not leak.)

Denote by x_{10} and $x_{11} \neq x_{10} \bmod q$, respectively, the putative blinding-invariant parts corresponding to each of the parallel two executions of the certificate issuing protocol. The goal of $\widehat{\mathcal{V}}_0$ is to obtain a certified public key $h' \neq 1, (c_0, r_0)$ and a secret key (β_0, β_1) for h' such that

$$\beta_0 \neq x_{10}\beta_1 \bmod q \quad \text{and} \quad \beta_0 \neq x_{11}\beta_1 \bmod q.$$

Knowing (c_0, r_0) such that

$$c_0 = \mathcal{H}_{q,g_0}(h', g_0^{c_0}(h')^{r_0})$$

is equivalent to knowing (a_0, r_0) such that

$$g_0^{\mathcal{H}_{q,g_0}(h', a_0)}(h')^{r_0} = a_0.$$

Therefore, the attack target is a triple (β_0, β_1), $h' = g_1^{\beta_0} h_0^{\beta_1}$, (a_0, r_0) such that $g_0^{c_0}(g_1^{\beta_0} h_0^{\beta_1})^{r_0} = a_0$, where c_0 denotes $\mathcal{H}_{q,g_0}(g_1^{\beta_0} h_0^{\beta_1}, a_0)$. Raising the verification relations for each of the two protocol executions to the powers γ_0 and γ_1, respectively, and multiplying the results, we obtain

$$g_0^{\gamma_0 c_{00}+\gamma_1 c_{01}} h_0^{\gamma_0 r_{00}+\gamma_1 r_{01}} g_1^{\gamma_0 x_{10} r_{00}+\gamma_1 x_{11} r_{01}} = a_{00}^{\gamma_0} a_{01}^{\gamma_1}.$$

$\widehat{\mathcal{V}}_0$ must determine a pair β_0, β_1, and numbers $\gamma_0, \gamma_1, c_{00}, c_{01}$ for which the information provided by $\mathcal{P}_0$ can be combined into a pair (a_0, r_0) such that

$$g_0^{c_0} g_1^{\beta_0 r_0} h_0^{\beta_1 r_0} = a_0,$$

where $c_0 = \mathcal{H}_{q,g_0}(g_1^{\beta_0} h_0^{\beta_1}, a_0)$.

Assume first that $\widehat{\mathcal{V}}_0$ computes $a_0 := a_{00}^{\gamma_0} a_{01}^{\gamma_1}$, for $\gamma_0, \gamma_1 \neq 0 \bmod q$ that need not be explicitly known at the time c_{00} and c_{01} have to be provided. $\widehat{\mathcal{V}}_0$ must ensure that

$$g_0^{\gamma_0 c_{00}+\gamma_1 c_{01}} h_0^{\gamma_0 r_{00}+\gamma_1 r_{01}} g_1^{\gamma_0 x_{10} r_{00}+\gamma_1 x_{11} r_{01}} = g_0^{c_0} g_1^{\beta_0 r_0} h_0^{\beta_1 r_0}.$$

Assume furthermore that γ_0 and γ_1 are computable by $\widehat{\mathcal{V}}_0$ once the attack has been completed successfully (a plausible assumption given the algebraic nature of the attack). It follows from the assumption that $\widehat{\mathcal{V}}_0$ cannot compute a non-trivial representation of 1 with respect to (g_0, g_1, h_0) that $\widehat{\mathcal{V}}_0$ has to (implicitly) solve the following three relations,

$$\gamma_0 x_{10} r_{00} + \gamma_1 x_{11} r_{01} = \beta_0 r_0 \bmod q,$$
$$\gamma_0 r_{00} + \gamma_1 r_{01} = \beta_1 r_0 \bmod q,$$
$$\gamma_0 c_{00} + \gamma_1 c_{01} = c_0 \bmod q,$$

for $(\gamma_0, \gamma_1, \beta_0, \beta_1, c_{00}, c_{01})$ and r_0. It seems that $(\gamma_0, \gamma_1, \beta_0, \beta_1, c_{00}, c_{01})$ must be committed to before r_{00} and r_{01} are provided; only r_0 can be computed afterwards. Since r_0 can be computed by $\widehat{\mathcal{V}}_0$ after r_{00} and r_{01} have been received, it may seem that there are many workable choices for $\gamma_0, \gamma_1, \beta_0, \beta_1$. This is not true, however, since $\widehat{\mathcal{V}}_0$ has to solve, in terms of $\gamma_0, \gamma_1, \beta_0, \beta_1$, a single relation that does not involve r_0 but does involve r_{00} and r_{01}. Multiplying both sides of $\gamma_0 r_{00} + \gamma_1 r_{01} = \beta_1 r_0 \bmod q$ by $\beta_0/\beta_1 \bmod q$, and subtracting the result from $\gamma_0 x_{10} r_{00} + \gamma_1 x_{11} r_{01} = \beta_0 r_0 \bmod q$, we get

$$(\gamma_0 (x_{10} - \beta_0/\beta_1)) r_{00} + (\gamma_1 (x_{11} - \beta_0/\beta_1)) r_{01} = 0 \bmod q.$$

Because r_{00} and r_{01} cannot be anticipated, and because $\beta_0/\beta_1 \bmod q$ cannot be equal to both x_{10} and x_{11}, the only workable non-zero choices for $\gamma_0, \gamma_1, \beta_0, \beta_1$ seem to be to take $\gamma_0 = A_{00} r_{00}^{-1} \bmod q$ and $\gamma_1 = A_{01} r_{01}^{-1} \bmod q$, or $\gamma_0 = A_{00} r_{01} \bmod q$ and $\gamma_1 = A_{01} r_{00} \bmod q$, for some suitable constants A_{00} and A_{01} that may depend on β_0 and β_1. To argue that $\widehat{\mathcal{V}}_0$ cannot compute $a := a_{00}^{\gamma_0} a_{01}^{\gamma_1}$ for such a choice for γ_0, γ_1, we focus on the third relation, $\gamma_0 c_{00} + \gamma_1 c_{01} = c_0 \bmod q$. (After all, it is not completely inconceivable that a can be computed in this way before r_{00} and r_{01} become known, since r_{00} and r_{01} are known to satisfy the two verification relations.) Even if a could be computed, the fact that c_0 is the outcome of a sufficiently strong one-way hash function applied to a_0 implies that its value cannot be expressed in terms of r_{00} and r_{01}. (Note that $c_0 = \mathcal{H}_{q,g_0}(g_1^{\beta_0} h_0^{\beta_1}, a_{00}^{\gamma_0} a_{01}^{\gamma_1})$ should imply, by virtue of the strength of the hash-function, that c_0 cannot be chosen as an algebraic function of $\beta_0, \beta_1, \gamma_0, \gamma_1$; this trivially holds in the random oracle model.) Consequently, $\gamma_0 c_{00} + \gamma_1 c_{01} = c_0 \bmod q$ can only be solved for values c_{00} and c_{01} that are expressed in terms of r_{00}, r_{01}. Because c_{00} and c_{01} have to be provided by $\widehat{\mathcal{V}}_0$ before r_{00} and r_{01} become known, workable choices for γ_0 and γ_1 should be infeasible.

We assumed in this argument that $\widehat{\mathcal{V}}_0$ computes $a_0 := a_{00}^{\gamma_0} a_{01}^{\gamma_1}$. The information contained in

$$g_0^{\gamma_0 c_{00} + \gamma_1 c_{01}} h_0^{\gamma_0 r_{00} + \gamma_1 r_{01}} g_1^{\gamma_0 x_{10} r_{00} + \gamma_1 x_{11} r_{01}}$$

can be combined into $g_0^{c_0}(g_1^{\beta_0} h_0^{\beta_1})^{r_0}$ in a more general way. The most general form seems to be $a_0 := a_{00}^{\gamma_0} a_{01}^{\gamma_1} g_0^{\delta_0} g_1^{\delta_1} h_0^{\delta_2}$ for smart choices for $\delta_0, \delta_1, \delta_2$. Assuming again that it is infeasible to compute with non-negligible probability of success a non-trivial representation of 1 with respect to (g_0, g_1, h_0), we can derive three relations similar to those previously displayed. From the first two of these we can again derive one relation that involves r_{00} and r_{01} but not r_0, and that relation must be solved (implicitly) for $\gamma_0, \gamma_1, \beta_0, \beta_1$. The only way to arrive at a relation in which γ_0 and γ_1 are not expressions in terms of r_{00}, r_{01} (for which the preceding argument applies) seems to be to choose δ_0, δ_1 such that $\gamma_0 r_{00} + \gamma_1 r_{01} + \delta_1 = \beta_0 r_0 \bmod q$ and $\gamma_0 x_{10} r_{00} + \gamma_1 x_{11} r_{01} + \delta_0 = \beta_1 r_0 \bmod q$ are linearly dependent in r_0; in that case r_0 cannot be made to drop out of the equations. Such choices for δ_0, δ_1 seem to require expressions in terms of r_{00} and r_{01} that cannot be anticipated.

This completes our argument as to why Assumption 4.4.5 should hold. Unfortunately, it is unclear how to prove Assumption 4.4.5, even in the random oracle model.

A similar immunization applies to DLREP-based scheme II; we simply swap the position of the challenge in the verification relation with that of one of the two responses. The immunization technique does not apply to RSAREP-based scheme I, since it does not have a response that appears as an exponent in the verification relation. It can be applied to RSAREP-based scheme II, though, but not without a twist. Redefine a certificate of $\mathcal{P}_0$ on $h' \in \mathbb{Z}_n^*$ to be a triple, $(c_0', r_0', r_1') \in \mathbb{Z}_s \times \mathbb{Z}_n^* \times \mathbb{Z}_v$ such that

$$c_0' = \mathcal{H}_{n,v}(h', (r_0')^v f^{c_0'}(h')^{-r_1'}).$$

$\mathcal{V}_0$'s secret key now is an RSA-representation of h' with respect to $(g_1, \dots, g_l, h_0, v)$. In the modified issuing protocol, $\mathcal{V}_0$ can blind $h = \prod_{i=1}^l g_i^{x_i}$ to $h' = (h_0 h)^\beta \alpha_1^v$, for arbitrary $\beta \in \mathbb{Z}_v$ and $\alpha_1 \in \mathbb{Z}_n^*$. While in an application this general blinding form must be taken into account, for unlinkability it suffices for $\mathcal{V}_0$ to simply fix $\beta = 1$, say, and use a random α_1. The resulting issuing protocol is depicted in Figure 4.8. (Alternatively, $\mathcal{P}_0$ can perform this protocol without using the factorization of n, similar as described in Section 4.2.3. The protocol can be converted into a two-move protocol in the manner pointed out in Section 4.2.3.) Now, from h' one cannot infer that $\beta \neq 0 \bmod v$, yet this choice must be prevented. We can get around this by having $\mathcal{V}_0$ in the showing protocol demonstrate that $\beta \neq 0 \bmod v$, as part of the formula it is demonstrating: see Section 5.1.1 for details.

4.5   Other certificate schemes

The certificate schemes in Sections 4.2 and 4.4 are all based on the digital signature schemes discussed in Sections 2.5.3 and 2.5.4. As in many areas of cryptography, it is of interest to have alternatives based on different underlying assumptions, instead of placing all bets on one horse. In this section we describe two such alternatives. Both alternatives are believed to be secure even when protocol executions with respect to different attribute tuples are arbitrarily interleaved.

4.5.1   DSA-like certificates

The system parameter generation and the key set-up for this scheme are the same as for DLREP-based scheme I. It is preferable that $\mathcal{H}(\cdot)$ do not map arguments to zero, but since this event should have negligible probability anyway there is no need to make an assumption to this effect.

For $a \in G_q$, let $\bar{a}$ denote $a \bmod q$. In the DSA [277], a signature standard originally proposed in 1994 by the U.S. National Institute of Standards and Technology, a signature on a message m with respect to a public key $h_0 = g_0^{x_0}$ is a pair

$$\boxed{\mathcal{P}_0} \qquad\qquad\qquad \boxed{\mathcal{V}_0}$$

SYSTEM PARAMETERS

$$(n, v) := I_{\text{RSA}}(1^k)$$

KEY SET-UP

Secret key: factorization of n

$f, h_0, g_1, \ldots, g_l \in_{\mathcal{R}} \mathbb{Z}_n^*$

Public key: $\qquad\qquad (f, h_0), (g_1, \ldots, g_l)$

Additional information: $\qquad \mathcal{H}_{n,v}(\cdot)$

PROTOCOL

$a_0 \in_{\mathcal{R}} \mathbb{Z}_n^*$

$$\xrightarrow{\quad a_0 \quad}$$

$\alpha_1, \alpha_2 \in_{\mathcal{R}} \mathbb{Z}_n^*$

$\alpha_3, \alpha_4 \in_{\mathcal{R}} \mathbb{Z}_v$

$h' := h_0 h \alpha_1^v$

$c_0' := \mathcal{H}_{n,v}(h', \alpha_2^v f^{-\alpha_3}(h')^{-\alpha_4} a_0)$

$c_0 := c_0' + \alpha_3 \bmod v$

$$\xleftarrow{\quad c_0 \quad}$$

$r_1 \in_{\mathcal{R}} \mathbb{Z}_v$

$r_0 := ((h_0 h)^{r_1} a_0 / f^{c_0})^{1/v}$

$$\xrightarrow{\quad r_0, r_1 \quad}$$

$f^{c_0} r_0^v (h_0 h)^{-r_1} \stackrel{?}{=} a_0$

$r_0' := r_0 \alpha_1^{r_1} \alpha_2 f^{-((c_0' + \alpha_3)\operatorname{div} v)} (h')^{-((r_1 + \alpha_4)\operatorname{div} v)}$

$r_1' := r_1 + \alpha_4 \bmod v$

Figure 4.8: Immunization II of RSAREP-based scheme II.

$(\overline{a_0}, r_0) \in \mathbb{Z}_q \times \mathbb{Z}_q$ such that

$$(g_0^{\mathcal{H}_{q,g_0}(m)/r_0} h_0^{\overline{a_0}/r_0}) \bmod q = \overline{a_0}.$$

The DSA makes the following specific choices: G_q is constructed using the subgroup construction, q is a 160-bit prime, and $\mathcal{H}_{q,g_0}(\cdot)$ is set equal to SHA-I [276].

We modify the DSA scheme by applying a cyclic left shift to the role of the exponents, $(\mathcal{H}_{q,g_0}(m), r_0, \overline{a_0})$, in the DSA verification relation.[6] A certificate of $\mathcal{P}_0$ on a public key $h' \neq 1$ is defined to be a pair $(\overline{a_0'}, r_0') \in \mathbb{Z}_q \times \mathbb{Z}_q$ such that

$$(g_0^{\overline{a_0'}/c_0'} (h')^{r_0'/c_0'}) \bmod q = \overline{a_0'},$$

where $c_0' = \mathcal{H}_{g,g_0}(h_0, \overline{a_0'})$. The presence of $\overline{a_0'}$ in $\mathcal{H}_{q,g_0}(h_0, \overline{a_0'})$ is not mandatory, but is believed preferable. The secret key of $\mathcal{V}_0$ is a DL-representation of h' with respect to $(g_1, \ldots, g_l, h_0)$.

Let h denote $\prod_{i=1}^{l} g_i^{x_i}$. The issuing protocol is as follows:

Step 1. $\mathcal{P}_0$ generates a random number $w_0 \in \mathbb{Z}_q$, and sends $a_0 := g_0^{w_0}$ to $\mathcal{V}_0$.

Step 2. $\mathcal{V}_0$ generates a random number $\alpha_1 \in \mathbb{Z}_q^*$ and two random numbers $\alpha_2, \alpha_3 \in \mathbb{Z}_q$. It computes $h' := (h_0 h)^{\alpha_1}$, $a_0' := a_0^{\alpha_2}(h_0 h)^{\alpha_3}$, and $c_0' := \mathcal{H}_{q,g_0}(h', \overline{a_0'})$. Finally, $\mathcal{V}_0$ sends $c_0 := c_0' \alpha_2 \overline{a_0} \overline{a_0'}^{-1} \bmod q$ to $\mathcal{P}_0$.

Step 3. $\mathcal{P}_0$ sends $r_0 := (x_0 + \sum_{i=1}^{l} x_i y_i)^{-1}(c_0 w_0 - \overline{a_0}) \bmod q$ to $\mathcal{V}_0$. (To guarantee that $\mathcal{P}_0$ can always perform Step 3, $(x_1, \ldots, x_l)$ must satisfy $(x_0 + \sum_{i=1}^{l} x_i y_i) \neq 0 \bmod q$.)

$\mathcal{V}_0$ accepts if and only if $g_0^{\overline{a_0}/c_0}(h_0 h)^{r_0/c_0} = a_0$. If this verification holds, $\mathcal{V}_0$ computes $r_0' := \alpha_1^{-1}(r_0 \overline{a_0}^{-1} a_0' + c_0' \alpha_3) \bmod q$. The resulting scheme is depicted in Figure 4.9.

It is easy to verify that the protocol is a proof of knowledge (the probability that the inverses of $\overline{a_0}$ and $\overline{a_0'}$ are defined is overwhelming) and that $(\overline{a_0'}, r_0')$ is a secret-key certificate of $\mathcal{P}_0$ on h'. As with the schemes in Section 4.4.2, it is unclear how to reduce the unforgeability of the underlying signature scheme to that of the new scheme, but unforgeability is believed to hold nevertheless. Furthermore, if $\mathcal{V}_0$ follows the issuing protocol and accepts then it obtains a certified key pair comprising a perfectly blinded certified public key.

Assumption 4.4.5 should apply here as well. Following the argument in Section 4.4.2, we arrive at three relations that differ only in that $\gamma_0 c_{00} + \gamma_1 c_{01} = c_0 \bmod q$ is replaced by $\gamma_0 \overline{a_{00}} + \gamma_1 \overline{a_{01}} = a_0 \bmod q$, where $a_0 = a_{00}^{\gamma_0 c_{00}} a_{01}^{\gamma_1 c_{01}}$.

---

[6]Camenisch, Piveteau, and Stadler [72] applied another shift of the exponents, in order to construct an ordinary DSA-like blind signature scheme in Chaum's sense. Their shift does not give rise to a restrictive blind certificate scheme that is secure in parallel mode.

$$\boxed{\mathcal{P}_0} \qquad\qquad\qquad \boxed{\mathcal{V}_0}$$

SYSTEM PARAMETERS

$$(q, g_0) := I_{\mathrm{DL}}(1^k)$$

KEY SET-UP

$x_0 := D_{\mathrm{DL}}(q, g_0)$
$y_1, \ldots, y_l \in_{\mathcal{R}} \mathbb{Z}_q$
Secret key: $x_0, (y_1, \ldots, y_l)$
$h_0 := g_0^{x_0}$
$g_i := g_0^{y_i} \ \forall i \in \{1, \ldots, l\}$
Public key: $\qquad\qquad\qquad\qquad h_0, (g_1, \ldots, g_l)$
Additional information: $\qquad\qquad \mathcal{H}_{q, g_0}(\cdot)$

PROTOCOL

$w_0 \in_{\mathcal{R}} \mathbb{Z}_q$
$a_0 := g_0^{w_0}$

$$\xrightarrow{\quad a_0 \quad}$$

$\qquad\qquad\qquad\qquad \alpha_1 \in_{\mathcal{R}} \mathbb{Z}_q^*$
$\qquad\qquad\qquad\qquad \alpha_2, \alpha_3 \in_{\mathcal{R}} \mathbb{Z}_q$
$\qquad\qquad\qquad\qquad h' := (h_0 h)^{\alpha_1}$
$\qquad\qquad\qquad\qquad a_0' := a_0^{\alpha_2}(h_0 h)^{\alpha_3}$
$\qquad\qquad\qquad\qquad c_0' := \mathcal{H}_{q, g_0}(h', \overline{a_0'})$
$\qquad\qquad\qquad\qquad c_0 := c_0' \alpha_2 \overline{a_0} \overline{a_0'}^{-1} \bmod q$

$$\xleftarrow{\quad c_0 \quad}$$

$r_0 := (x_0 + \sum_{i=1}^{l} x_i y_i)^{-1}(c_0 w_0 - \overline{a_0}) \bmod q$

$$\xrightarrow{\quad r_0 \quad}$$

$\qquad\qquad\qquad\qquad g_0^{\overline{a_0}/c_0}(h_0 h)^{r_0/c_0} \stackrel{?}{=} a_0$
$\qquad\qquad\qquad\qquad r_0' := \alpha_1^{-1}(r_0 \overline{a_0}^{-1} \overline{a_0'} + c_0' \alpha_3) \bmod q$

Figure 4.9: DSA-like scheme.

The latter relation seems even harder to handle, although it is unclear how to prove this intuition.

A drawback of this DSA-like certificate scheme over the immunized DLREP-based scheme I in Section 4.4.2 is that $\mathcal{V}_0$ cannot precompute the exponentiation $a_0^{\alpha_2}$ in Step 2.

Although the DSA makes the explicit choice $G_q \subset \mathbb{Z}_p^*$, an elliptic curve implementation may be used instead. Indeed, the elliptic curve analog of the DSA, called the ECDSA, has been adopted as a standard by ISO, by ANSI, by IEEE, and by NIST; see Johnson and Menezes [223] for an overview. Since numbers in G_q are represented by coordinate pairs, and base numbers occur also as exponents, a secure mapping is needed from base numbers to numbers in $\mathbb{Z}_q$. One solution is to use the first coordinate; this is the approach taken in the ECDSA.

4.5.2 Certificates based on Chaum-Pedersen signatures

The following scheme differs from all the other certificate schemes in this chapter in that public-key certificates are issued, not secret-key certificates. The system parameter generation and the key set-up for this scheme are the same as for DLREP-based scheme I.

Chaum and Pedersen [109] presented a digital signature scheme that can be viewed as an entangled application of two Schnorr protocol executions; it is an optimization of a protocol due to Chaum, Evertse, and van de Graaf [108, Protocol 4]. A signature on a message m with respect to a public key $h_0 = g_0^{x_0}$ is a triple $(z, c_0, r_0) \in G_q \times \mathbb{Z}_s \times \mathbb{Z}_q$ such that

$$c_0 = \mathcal{H}_{q,g_0}(m, z, g^{r_0}h_0^{-c_0}, m^{r_0}z^{-c_0}).$$

Chaum and Pedersen defined G_q using the subgroup construction, but an elliptic curve implementation is permitted as well. They also described how to construct a blind issuing protocol for their signatures. The interactive Chaum-Pedersen protocol is a Fiat-Shamir type proof of knowledge of both $\log_{g_0} h_0$ and $\log_m z$ that also demonstrates that these two discrete logarithms are equal. For the purpose of ordinary blind signatures, though, the Chaum-Pedersen scheme does not have advantages over the Schnorr signature scheme.

The situation is different for the restrictive blind certificate scheme that we will now construct from their signature scheme by applying our techniques. Define a certificate of $\mathcal{P}_0$ on a public key $h' \neq 1$ to be a triple, $(z', c_0', r_0') \in G_q \times \mathbb{Z}_s \times \mathbb{Z}_q$ such that

$$c_0' = \mathcal{H}_{q,g_0}(h', z', g_0^{r_0'}h_0^{-c_0'}, (h')^{r_0'}(z')^{-c_0'}).$$

The secret key of $\mathcal{V}_0$ is a DL-representation $(x_1, \ldots, x_l, \alpha_1)$ of h' with respect to $(g_1, \ldots, g_l, h_0)$, with $\mathcal{P}_0$ encoding $x_1, \ldots, x_l \in \mathbb{Z}_q$ into $\mathcal{V}_0$'s secret key. As before, let h denote $\prod_{i=1}^l g_i^{x_i}$. $\mathcal{V}_0$ this time needs to know $z := (h_0 h)^{x_0}$. Hereto $\mathcal{P}_0$ must either compute z for $\mathcal{V}_0$ or publish $(g_1^{x_0}, \ldots, g_l^{x_0}, h_0^{x_0})$ along with its public key; in the latter case, $\mathcal{V}_0$ can compute z by itself.

The issuing protocol is as follows:

Step 1. $\mathcal{P}_0$ generates a random number $w_0 \in \mathbb{Z}_q$, and sends $a_0 := g_0^{w_0}$ and $b_0 := (h_0 h)^{w_0}$ to $\mathcal{V}_0$.

Step 2. $\mathcal{V}_0$ generates a random number $\alpha_1 \in \mathbb{Z}_q^*$ and two random numbers $\alpha_2, \alpha_3 \in \mathbb{Z}_q$. $\mathcal{V}_0$ computes $h' := (h_0 h)^{\alpha_1}$, $z' := z^{\alpha_1}$, $a_0' := h_0^{\alpha_2} g_0^{\alpha_3} a_0$, $b_0' := (z')^{\alpha_2} (h')^{\alpha_3} b_0^{\alpha_1}$, $c_0' := \mathcal{H}_{q, g_0}(h', z', a_0', b_0')$, and sends $c_0 := c_0' + \alpha_2 \bmod q$ to $\mathcal{P}_0$.

Step 3. $\mathcal{P}_0$ sends $r_0 := c_0 x_0 + w_0 \bmod q$ to $\mathcal{V}_0$.

$\mathcal{V}_0$ accepts if and only if $g_0^{r_0} h_0^{-c_0} = a_0$ and $(h_0 h)^{r_0} z^{-c_0} = b_0$. If this verification holds, then $\mathcal{V}_0$ computes $r_0' := r_0 + \alpha_3 \bmod q$. (Alternatively, $\mathcal{V}_0$ first computes r_0' and then checks whether $(g_0 h')^{r_0'} (h_0 z')^{-c_0'} = a_0' b_0'$.) The resulting scheme is depicted in Figure 4.10.

It is easy to verify that the protocol is a Fiat-Shamir type proof of knowledge, and that (z', r_0', c_0') is a certificate of $\mathcal{P}_0$ on h' if $\mathcal{V}_0$ accepts. The witness-hiding property can be argued in the same manner as with the Schnorr proof of knowledge, but no proof is known. The unforgeability of certificates follows directly from the unforgeability of blind Chaum-Pedersen signatures and the fact that $\widehat{\mathcal{V}_0}$ cannot know two different DL-representations of the same public key. Proving the latter fact is trivial: $\mathcal{P}_0$ can perform the protocol without knowing a non-trivial DL-representation of 1 with respect to $(g_1, \ldots, g_l, h_0)$, and in particular it may generate $g_1, \ldots, g_l$ at random.

Excluding public keys h' equal to 1, it can be shown that $\overline{\mathcal{V}_0}$ obtains a certified key pair comprising a perfectly blinded certified public key. Finally, Assumption 4.4.5 is believed to apply.

This certificate scheme has several drawbacks in comparison to DLREP-based schemes I and II and their immunization described in Section 4.4.2:

- Certificates are larger and more costly to verify.

- $\mathcal{V}_0$'s computation of $b_0^{\alpha_1}$ in Step 2 of the issuing protocol cannot be preprocessed.

- It is not clear how to prove the property of restrictive blinding even when only sequential protocol executions involving the same attribute tuple are considered.

- The scheme is a public-key certificate scheme; certified public keys cannot be simulated.

$$\boxed{\mathcal{P}_0} \qquad\qquad\qquad\qquad \boxed{\mathcal{V}_0}$$

SYSTEM PARAMETERS

$$(q, g_0) := I_{\mathrm{DL}}(1^k)$$

KEY SET-UP

$x_0 := D_{\mathrm{DL}}(q, g_0)$

$y_1, \ldots, y_l \in_{\mathcal{R}} \mathbb{Z}_q$

Secret key: $x_0, (y_1, \ldots, y_l)$

$h_0 := g_0^{x_0}$

$g_1, \ldots, g_l \in_{\mathcal{R}} G_q$

Public key: $h_0, (g_1, \ldots, g_l)$

Additional information: $\mathcal{H}_{q,g_0}(\cdot), z := (h_0 h)^{x_0}$

PROTOCOL

$w_0 \in_{\mathcal{R}} \mathbb{Z}_q$

$a_0 := g_0^{w_0}$

$b_0 := (h_0 h)^{w_0}$

$$\xrightarrow{\quad a_0, b_0 \quad}$$

$\alpha_1 \in \mathbb{Z}_q^*$

$\alpha_2, \alpha_3 \in \mathbb{Z}_q$

$h' := (h_0 h)^{\alpha_1}$

$z' := z^{\alpha_1}$

$a_0' := h_0^{\alpha_2} g_0^{\alpha_3} a_0$

$b_0' := (z')^{\alpha_2} (h')^{\alpha_3} b_0^{\alpha_1}$

$c_0' := \mathcal{H}_{q,g_0}(h', z', a_0', b_0')$

$c_0 := c_0' + \alpha_2 \bmod q$

$$\xleftarrow{\quad c_0 \quad}$$

$r_0 := c_0 x_0 + w_0 \bmod q$

$$\xrightarrow{\quad r_0 \quad}$$

$g_0^{r_0} h_0^{-c_0} \stackrel{?}{=} a_0$

$(h_0 h)^{r_0} z^{-c_0} \stackrel{?}{=} b_0$

$r_0' := r_0 + \alpha_3 \bmod q$

Figure 4.10: Scheme based on Chaum-Pedersen signatures.

On the upside, $\mathcal{P}_0$ can perform the issuing protocol without knowing $(x_1, \ldots, x_l)$. This has several advantages:

- $\mathcal{P}_0$ can certify attributes without needing to know them. Hereto $\mathcal{V}_0$ forms h as its commitment to attributes $x_1, \ldots, x_{l-1}$ (the number x_l must be generated at random to unconditionally hide the $l - 1$ attributes) and at the start of the issuing protocol presents this to $\mathcal{P}_0$ together with a proof of knowledge of a DL-representation with respect to $(g_1, \ldots, g_l)$.

- More generally, $\mathcal{P}_0$ can certify attributes of which it knows no more than a property demonstrated by $\mathcal{V}_0$. $\mathcal{V}_0$ can demonstrate this property when presenting h by using the showing protocol techniques, for instance by sending along a signed proof.

- $\mathcal{P}_0$ can recertify previously certified attributes without knowing their values; see Section 5.2.1 for details. (It cannot update their values, though; for this an RSAREP-based issuing protocol is needed.)

- It is possible to protect against framing attempts by parties with unlimited computing resources; see Section 5.5.3 for details.

Whether these advantages are desirable depends on the application at hand.

Another advantage is that the delegation strategy (see Section 2.6) is excluded altogether, because public-key certificates are used. This is not the case for the certificate issuing schemes based on secret-key certificates, as Section 5.1.2 will show.

4.6   Bibliographic notes

The notion of restrictive blinding in Section 4.1 originates from Brands [46, 48]. Definition 4.1.1 appears here for the first time.

The four certificate schemes in Section 4.2 originate from Brands [54]. The case $l = 2$ of DLREP-based scheme I was introduced by Brands [49] for the purpose of withdrawing electronic coins with embedded identifiers in an off-line electronic cash system. The case $l = 1$ of RSAREP-based scheme I was analyzed by Brands [51]. The security proofs presented in Section 4.3.3 are stronger than those in [49, 51], in that the reductions are based on any invulnerable instance generator instead of one specific distribution.

The immunization technique described in Section 4.4.1 is due to Brands [50]. The immunized DLREP-based schemes in Section 4.4.2 are a generalization of a withdrawal protocol devised by Schoenmakers [341] in the context of electronic cash.

The immunization described in Section 4.4.2 of RSAREP-based scheme II, which is based on a new twist, appears here for the first time; previously, the immunization technique of Schoenmakers was believed not to apply to RSAREP-based schemes.

The DSA-based certificate scheme described in Section 4.5.1 has not previously appeared in the academic literature.

Brands [46, 48] introduced the special case $l = 2$ of the scheme in Section 4.5.2, for the purpose of designing an off-line electronic cash scheme. Cramer and Pedersen [122] subsequently used this scheme to modify a protocol by Chaum and Pedersen [109]; the slightly more general form used by them was already considered by Brands [46, page 27 & 28]. Radu, Govaerts, and Vandewalle [316] proposed a variation to make the scheme provably witness-hiding, but their variation does not improve the overall security of the scheme.

Chapter 5

Combining Issuing and Showing Protocols

In this chapter we show how to seamlessly combine the showing protocol techniques of Chapter 3 with the issuing protocol techniques of Chapter 4, without adding complexity and without compromising security or privacy. We develop additional privacy techniques, for both certificate holders and certificate verifiers, and design limited-show certificates that reveal all the encoded attributes in case of fraud. We also design software-only techniques that enable the CA to discourage a variety of frauds.

5.1 Integration

Consider a PKI with one CA, many certificate holders (provers), and many verifiers. To gain access to a secure "service" provided by a verifier $\mathcal{V}$, $\mathcal{P}$ must demonstrate to $\mathcal{V}$ its possession of a certificate of the CA on attributes that meet certain criteria. The CA will issue a certificate to $\mathcal{P}$ only after the latter has authenticated itself or proved its right to obtain such a certificate. Clearly, the CA can non-interactively issue an ordinary digital signature on a public key h of $\mathcal{P}$ constructed as described in Chapter 3, but this does not offer any privacy with respect to the CA. In this section we show how to combine the showing protocol techniques of Chapter 3 with the issuing protocol techniques of Chapter 4.

5.1.1 Making the match

The case of DLREP-based scheme I or II or the immunization in Section 4.4.1

Suppose that the CA (playing the role of $\mathcal{P}_0$) uses DLREP-based scheme I or II, or their immunization described in Section 4.4.1. $\mathcal{P}$ (playing the role of $\mathcal{V}_0$) obtains a certificate of the CA on a public key h' of the form

$$g_1^{x_1} \cdots g_l^{x_l} g_0^{\alpha_1},$$

where $x_1, \ldots, x_l \in \mathbb{Z}_q$ are the encoded attributes and $\alpha_1 \in \mathbb{Z}_q$ is a random number chosen by $\mathcal{P}$. $\mathcal{P}$ can subsequently demonstrate to $\mathcal{V}$ a property about the encoded attributes, in the manner described in Chapter 3. The perfect fit of the issuing and showing protocols is illustrated by the dual role now played by the blinding factor α_1: it ensures that h' is uncorrelated to the view of the CA in the issuing protocol, and also that $\mathcal{P}$ in the showing protocol does not reveal anything about the encoded attributes beyond the validity of the formula it demonstrates (see Proposition 3.6.1(c)).

It is not hard to prove the following generalization of Proposition 4.3.4.

Proposition 5.1.1. *Suppose that $\mathcal{P}$ follows the issuing protocol and uses the resulting certified key pair in a showing protocol execution in which it demonstrates some property of the encoded attributes. The view that $\widetilde{\mathcal{V}}$ can obtain could have originated (with uniform probability) from any one of the issuing protocol executions in which $\widetilde{\mathcal{P}}_0$ encoded attributes that $\widetilde{\mathcal{P}}_0$ knows satisfy this particular property.*

This result applies even when $\widetilde{\mathcal{P}}_0$ and $\widetilde{\mathcal{V}}$ conspire throughout, and applies also to the other protocol combinations considered in this section.

The case of the other DLREP-based schemes in Chapter 4

The match between the showing protocol techniques and the other DLREP-based issuing protocols described in Chapter 4 seems more problematic at first. $\mathcal{P}$ obtains a certificate on a public key h' of the form

$$(g_1^{x_1} \cdots g_l^{x_l} h_0)^{\alpha_1},$$

where $\alpha_1 \in \mathbb{Z}_q^*$ is a random number chosen by $\mathcal{P}$. The blinding factor this time spreads across all exponents. This does not limit the applicability of our showing protocol techniques in any way, though. There are two approaches:

- If $\alpha_1 \neq 0 \bmod q$ (which is required) then

$$h_0^{-1} = g_1^{x_1} \cdots g_l^{x_l} (h')^{-1/\alpha_1},$$

and so $\mathcal{P}$ can demonstrate Boolean formulae for the DL-representation that it knows of h_0^{-1} with respect to $(g_1, \ldots, g_l, h')$. Although h' is not a fixed generator specified by the CA, the security properties are not adversely affected. Namely, the ability to prove knowledge of a DL-representation of h_0^{-1} with respect to $(g_1, \ldots, g_l, h')$ implies the ability to prove knowledge of a DL-representation of h' with respect to $(g_1, \ldots, g_l, h_0)$. Proposition 3.6.1(b) is easily seen to apply. The showing protocol techniques and results in Chapter 3 apply without change, because the distribution of $-1/\alpha_1 \bmod q$ is statistically indistinguishable from the uniform distribution over $\mathbb{Z}_q$. Note that $\mathcal{P}$'s ability to demonstrate a Boolean formula, and thus to prove knowledge of a DL-representation of h_0^{-1} with respect to $(g_1, \ldots, g_l, h')$, implicitly demonstrates that $\alpha_1 \neq 0 \bmod q$ (much as in Section 3.4.1).

- The above twist of considering DL-representations of h_0^{-1} with respect to $(g_1, \ldots, g_l, h')$ is not necessary. Consider $h' = g_1^{x_1 \alpha_1} \cdots g_l^{x_l \alpha_1} h_0^{\alpha_1}$. Let $z_0 := \alpha_1$, and let z_i denote $x_i \alpha_1 \bmod q$, for all $i \in \{1, \ldots, l\}$. $\mathcal{V}$ can verify that $\alpha_1 \neq 0 \bmod q$ by checking that $h' \neq 1$, and so demonstrating that $x_1 = \beta x_2 + \gamma \bmod q$, say, is equivalent to demonstrating that $z_1 = \beta z_2 + \gamma z_0 \bmod q$. This we can handle by using our demonstration technique for linear relations. It is easy to see that any Boolean formula can be handled in this manner.

As will be shown in Section 5.1.2, both approaches have unique security implications with respect to the delegation strategy in case they are combined with a secret-key certificate issuing protocol that admits arbitrary parallelization.

The second approach results exactly in the first approach if we have $\mathcal{P}$ in addition demonstrate that $z_0 \neq 0$, as part of the formula it is to demonstrate. In the example, the formula would become $(z_1 = \beta z_2 + \gamma z_0)$ AND NOT$(z_0 = 0)$. Of course, $\mathcal{V}$ in that case need no longer check that $h' \neq 1$.

Since $\mathcal{P}_0$ in the issuing protocol in Section 4.5.2 need not know the attributes it encodes, certificate holders can enjoy even greater privacy.

The case of RSAREP-based scheme I or II or the immunization in Section 4.4.1

To encode attributes $x_1, \ldots, x_l \in \mathbb{Z}_v$ into a certified key pair for $\mathcal{P}$, the CA and $\mathcal{P}$ engage in RSAREP-based scheme I or II or their immunization described in Section 4.4.1. $\mathcal{P}$ obtains a certificate of the CA on a public key h' of the form

$$g_1^{x_1} \cdots g_l^{x_l} \alpha_1^v,$$

where $\alpha_1 \in \mathbb{Z}_n^*$ is a random number chosen by $\mathcal{P}$, playing the same dual role as in the case of the DLREP-based schemes. The rest is clear.

The case of the immunized RSAREP-based scheme II in Section 4.4.2

Finally, in the second immunization of RSAREP-based scheme II, described in Section 4.4.2, $\mathcal{P}$ obtains a certificate on a public key h' of the form

$$g_1^{x_1 \beta} \cdots g_l^{x_l \beta} h_0^\beta \alpha_1^v.$$

In the showing protocol, $\mathcal{P}$ must demonstrate that $\beta \neq 0 \bmod v$. If $\beta \neq 0 \bmod v$, then the RSA-representation $\mathcal{P}$ knows of h_0^{-1} with respect to $((h')^{-1}, g_1, \ldots, g_l, v)$ is

$$(e \bmod v, x_1, \ldots, x_l, z),$$

where $e, f \in \mathbb{Z}$ satisfy $e\beta + fv = 1$, and z is the product of α_1^e and the powers of $l+2$ junk factors resulting from normalization. It is easy to see that proving knowledge of an RSA-representation of h_0^{-1} with respect to $((h')^{-1}, g_1, \ldots, g_l, v)$ suffices to demonstrate $\beta \neq 0 \bmod v$; this is a simple application of the technique described in Section 3.4.2. Therefore, according to the equivalent of Proposition 3.6.1(b) for the RSAREP function, $\mathcal{P}$ demonstrates $\beta \neq 0 \bmod v$ as a by-product of demonstrating any Boolean formula for the RSA-representation it knows of h_0^{-1} with respect to $((h')^{-1}, g_1, \ldots, g_l, v)$. Alternatively, and more efficiently, $\mathcal{P}$ simply demonstrates that $\beta = 1 \bmod v$ as part of the formula it is demonstrating; there is no need to hide β.

Remarks

In many PKIs, only the ability to demonstrate Boolean formulae involving the attributes (i.e., not the more general form of linear relations) is required. In these PKIs the CA can encode attributes that contain more than $|q|$ or $|v|$ bits of information, such as digitally encoded photographs. Consider by way of example a certificate on a DLREP-based public key of the form

$$g_1^{\mathcal{F}_{q,g_l}(x_1)} \cdots g_{l-1}^{\mathcal{F}_{q,g_l}(x_{l-1})} g_l^{x_l}.$$

Assuming that $\mathcal{F}_{q,g_l}(\cdot)$ is a collision-intractable hash function with outputs smaller than q, $\mathcal{P}$ can demonstrate that $x_i = \beta$, for some $\beta \in \mathbb{N}$, by demonstrating that $\mathcal{F}_{q,g_l}(x_i) = \mathcal{F}_{q,g_l}(\beta)$. Likewise, demonstrating that $x_i \neq \beta$ can be done by demonstrating that $\mathcal{F}_{q,g_l}(x_i) \neq \mathcal{F}_{q,g_l}(\beta)$. The usefulness of this variation is limited if the CA sees the attributes it encodes, because attributes with large entropy are in effect identifiers that facilitate tracing and linking when disclosed; however, as we will show in Section 5.2.1, the CA can encode attributes without knowing their values.

In another variation, following Merkle [267] (see also Section 5.4.3), attributes are incorporated in a hash tree. For example, with x_2 chosen at random from $\mathbb{Z}_q$, the number x_1 in $g_1^{x_1} g_2^{x_2}$, could be the root of a Merkle hash tree. To reveal some of the attributes in the tree, $\mathcal{P}$ discloses node values from which the root value can be reconstructed. This approach improves efficiency (and enables limited selective disclosure, assuming $\mathcal{P}$ hashes along a random salt for each attribute to prevent an exhaustive search), but many of the techniques in this book no longer apply.

For efficiency reasons, in practice $\mathcal{V}_0$ may prefer to skip the verification of $\mathcal{P}_0$'s response(s) in the issuing protocol. $\widetilde{\mathcal{P}}_0$ cannot leak more than a single bit of information to $\mathcal{V}$, owing to $\widehat{\mathcal{V}}_0$'s blinding operations. Because $\mathcal{V}$ cannot determine whether $\widetilde{\mathcal{P}}_0$ or $\widehat{\mathcal{V}}_0$ is the source of incorrect certificate data supplied in the showing protocol, it has no choice but to reject incorrect data. Therefore, if $\mathcal{P}_0$'s response in the issuing protocol is incorrect then $\mathcal{V}_0$ will find out in the showing protocol.

From now on we will always assume that the public key h' of the certificate holder is hashed along when determining $\mathcal{V}$'s challenge c in a signed proof.

5.1.2   Coping with delegation

As noted in Section 2.6, care must be taken when the CA issues secret-key certificates. $\mathcal{P}$ may be able to use a simulated certified public key in the showing protocol and delegate part of the requested action to the CA in an execution of the issuing protocol.

Example 5.1.2. *Consider the immunized DLREP-based certificate scheme I in Section 4.4.2. To simulate a certified public key, $\widehat{\mathcal{P}}$ generates a number $\beta \in \mathbb{Z}_q$, sets $h' := g_0^\beta$, and computes a corresponding certificate. To issue a signed proof of the formula* TRUE, *say, $\widehat{\mathcal{P}}$ must be able to come up with $a \in G_q$ and $r_1, \ldots, r_{l+1} \in \mathbb{Z}_q$ such that*

$$\prod_{i=1}^{l} g_i^{r_i} h_0^{r_{l+1}} = (h')^c a \quad and \quad c = \mathcal{H}_{q,g_l}(h', a, \ldots).$$

Hereto $\widehat{\mathcal{P}}$ engages in an execution of the certificate issuing protocol with the CA, *in the following manner. Upon receiving a_0, $\widehat{\mathcal{P}}$ sets $a := a_0$, $c := \mathcal{H}_{q,g_l}(h', a, \ldots)$, and sends the challenge $c_0 := -\beta c \bmod q$ to the* CA. *Upon receiving r_0 from the* CA, *$\widehat{\mathcal{P}}$ sets $r_i := x_i r_0 \bmod q$, for all $i \in \{1, \ldots, l\}$, and $r_{l+1} := r_0$. (Additional blinding operations can be applied to a, c_0, and $r_0, \ldots, r_{l+1}$.) It is easy to verify that the result convinces $\widehat{\mathcal{V}}$. Note that this works also if the hash function in the showing protocol is different from that used in the issuing protocol.*

The delegation strategy in this example is without security consequences, because $\widehat{\mathcal{P}}$ demonstrates a formula that pertains to the attributes $(x_1, \ldots, x_l)$ that the CA "encodes" in the protocol execution to which $\widehat{\mathcal{P}}$ delegates the cryptographic action. In effect, $\mathcal{P}$ simply follows a shortcut that circumvents the need to compute a as a product of powers of $g_1, \ldots, g_l, h_0$. In most circumstances this shortcut is not preferable: it requires an online connection with the CA at the time of the showing protocol execution; simulated certified public keys cannot be reused; and, for interactive showing protocols, timing of issuing and showing protocol executions would reveal the link between them.

When using the certificate issuing protocol in Section 4.5.2, the possibility of delegation simply does not arise, because public-key certificates are issued. Whenever delegation is harmless, though, there is no reason to prefer public-key certificates. In fact, secret-key certificates are preferable for reason of their greater efficiency, provable security, and privacy. (The privacy benefits will be clarified in Section 5.2.2.) In the remainder of this section we examine for all the secret-key certificate issuing protocols in Chapter 4 whether $\widehat{\mathcal{P}}$ can abuse delegation to demonstrate a formula that does not apply to the attributes that the CA encodes in the issuing protocol execution with $\widehat{\mathcal{P}}$. We will show that in many situations the delegation strategy is not possible at all, and in those cases where it cannot be prevented it can easily be rendered harmless.

The case of the four issuing schemes in Section 4.2

Assumption 5.1.3. *For any of the four secret-key certificate schemes in Section 4.2, if $\overline{\mathcal{V}}$ accepts a formula demonstration by $\widehat{\mathcal{P}}$, then $\widehat{\mathcal{P}}$ must have engaged in an issuing protocol execution in which the CA encoded an attribute tuple that satisfies the formula.*

In other words, delegation may be feasible, but it does not enable $\widehat{\mathcal{P}}$ to pretend to have attributes for which it cannot (at the same moment) obtain a certificate from the CA. We now argue why this should be true.

Consider first DLREP-based certificate scheme I in Section 4.2.1. According to the DL-based analogue to Assumption 4.3.9, the only way to simulate a certified public key is to set $h' := h_0^{-1} g_0^\beta$, for some $\beta \in \mathbb{Z}_q$. Assume for the moment that the CA uses the same attribute tuple $(x_1, \ldots, x_l)$ in all protocol executions. In the same manner as in Proposition 4.3.10, the role of the CA in these protocol executions with $\mathcal{P}$ can be simulated by generating a random $\gamma \in \mathbb{Z}_q$ and setting $h_0 := h^{-1} g_0^\gamma$, on input $l+1$ random numbers $g_0, \ldots, g_l \in G_q$. Now, the demonstration of a Boolean formula by means of the showing protocol techniques of Chapter 3 is a proof of knowledge of a DL-representation $(y_0, \ldots, y_l)$ of h' with respect to $(g_0, g_1, \ldots, g_l)$; see Proposition 3.6.1(b). (For signed proofs, the validity of Proposition 3.6.1(b) follows from the DL-based analogue to Assumption 4.3.9.) From the four relations

$$
\begin{aligned}
h &= g_1^{x_1} \cdots g_l^{x_l} \\
h' &= h_0^{-1} g_0^\beta \\
h_0 &= h^{-1} g_0^\gamma \\
h' &= g_0^{y_0} g_1^{y_1} \cdots g_l^{y_l},
\end{aligned}
$$

we get

$$
g_0^{\beta - \gamma} g_1^{x_1 - y_1} \cdots g_l^{x_l - y_l} = 1.
$$

Thus, a polynomial-time collision-finding algorithm for the DLREP function can be constructed, unless $\beta = \gamma \bmod q$ and $y_i = x_i \bmod q$, for all $i \in \{1, \ldots, l\}$. Therefore, any choice for β should result in $\widehat{\mathcal{P}}$ demonstrating a property for a DL-representation

$$
(\beta - \gamma \bmod q, x_1, \ldots, x_l)
$$

of h' with respect to $(g_0, g_1, \ldots, g_l)$. This is the same as what $\overline{\mathcal{P}}$ can demonstrate by simply following the issuing and the showing protocol.

When issuing protocol executions are run with respect to different attribute tuples, the CA can no longer be simulated by setting $h_0 := h^{-1} g_0^\gamma$. However, the fact that these protocol executions cannot be run in parallel is believed to ensure that the security argument remains valid; the situation is reminiscent of that in Section 4.3.3.

The security argument can be easily generalized to the scenario considered by Proposition 4.3.15, which provides a limited degree of parallelization of protocol executions with respect to different attribute tuples.

Interestingly, DLREP-based certificate scheme I seems to admit delegation only when the challenge c_0 in the verification relation of the issuing protocol appears at the same position as $\mathcal{V}$'s challenge c in the verification relation of the showing protocol. In particular, delegation is believed to be infeasible for atomic formulae without a "NOT" connective: the verification relations for these formulae have $\mathcal{V}$'s challenge situated as an exponent of the "wrong" base number.

The same considerations apply to the other three secret-key certificate schemes in Section 4.2.

The case of the immunized DLREP-based scheme I in Section 4.4.2

In case all protocol executions involve the same attribute tuple, the security argument for DLREP-based scheme I this time results in the relation

$$g_0^{\beta - y_0\gamma} g_1^{y_0 x_1 - y_1} \cdots g_l^{y_0 x_l - y_l} = 1.$$

Consequently, any choice for β should result in $\widehat{\mathcal{P}}$ demonstrating a property for a DL-representation

$$((\beta/\gamma)x_1 \bmod q, \ldots, (\beta/\gamma)x_l \bmod q, \beta/\gamma \bmod q)$$

of h' with respect to $(g_1, \ldots, g_l, h_0)$; this is the same as what $\overline{\mathcal{P}}$ can demonstrate by simply following the issuing and the showing protocol. On the basis of this, it seems that any delegation strategy with undesirable security consequences must exploit the ability of $\widehat{\mathcal{P}}$ to engage in parallel in two (or more) issuing protocol executions with respect to distinct attribute tuples.

Consider now the following parallel delegation strategy, involving two parallel issuing protocol executions with respect to different tuples. The verification relation in the i-th issuing protocol execution, for $i \in \{0, 1\}$, is

$$g_0^{c_{0i}} = (h_0 g_1^{x_{1i}} \cdots g_l^{x_{li}})^{r_{0i}} a_{0i}.$$

$\widehat{\mathcal{P}}$ can combine the information obtained in the two issuing protocol executions into information that satisfies the combined verification relation

$$h_0^{-(\gamma_0 r_{00} + \gamma_1 r_{01})} g_0^{\gamma_0 c_{00} + \gamma_1 c_{01}} \prod_{i=1}^{l} g_i^{-(\gamma_0 x_{i0} r_{00} + \gamma_1 x_{i1} r_{01})} = a_{00}^{\gamma_0} a_{01}^{\gamma_1},$$

for some $\gamma_0, \gamma_1 \in \mathbb{Z}_q$ of its own choice. According to the DL-based analogue to Assumption 4.3.9, the only way to simulate a certified public key is to set $h' := g_0^{\beta}$, for some $\beta \in \mathbb{Z}_q$. According to Figure 3.1, the verification relation in the showing protocol for an atomic formula without a "NOT" connective is of the form

$$h_0^{r_0} (g_0^{\beta})^{-c} \prod_{i=1}^{l} g_i^{r_i} = a.$$

Consequently, $\widehat{\mathcal{P}}$ in the issuing protocol executions can choose c_{00} and c_{01} subject to $\gamma_0 c_{00} + \gamma_1 c_{01} = -\beta c \bmod q$. With $a := a_{00}^{\gamma_0} a_{01}^{\gamma_1}$, $\widehat{\mathcal{P}}$ can use the responses in the two issuing protocol executions to satisfy the verification relation in the showing protocol, by setting $r_0 := -(\gamma_0 r_{00} + \gamma_1 r_{01}) \bmod q$ and, for all $i \in \{1, \ldots, l\}$, $r_i := -(\gamma_0 x_{i0} r_{00} + \gamma_1 x_{i1} r_{01}) \bmod q$. Now, if the showing protocol execution is to demonstrate the formula TRUE, $\widehat{\mathcal{P}}$ does not gain anything by this strategy. For any other atomic formula without a "NOT" connective, the responses $r_1, \ldots, r_l$ must satisfy at least one linear relation. Since the responses r_{00}, r_{01} are outside of $\widehat{\mathcal{P}}$'s control, in the sense that they should be as unpredictable as two independent random variables, $\widehat{\mathcal{P}}$ can satisfy this linear relation only if it may select the formula coefficients by itself. In that case, the parallel delegation strategy enables $\widehat{\mathcal{P}}$ to pretend to have certified attributes that it in fact has never been issued.

Either of the following two measures is believed to suffice to make the parallel delegation strategy harmless:

- A description of the formula F is hashed along when forming $\mathcal{V}$'s challenge in the showing protocol. With $c = \mathcal{H}_{q,g_l}(g_0^\beta, a_{00}^{\gamma_0} a_{01}^{\gamma_1}, F, \ldots)$, it should be infeasible to determine c as an algebraic function of $\beta, \gamma_0, \gamma_1$ and the formula coefficients. (This is provably true in the random oracle model.) Therefore, it seems that $\widehat{\mathcal{P}}$, upon receiving (a_{00}, a_{01}), has no choice but to select $(\beta, \gamma_0, \gamma_1)$ and the formula coefficients before forming c. The rest of the security argument is similar to that in Section 4.4.2 for the restrictive blinding property of the immunized DLREP-based scheme I; the only workable choices seem to be those that result in formulae that $\overline{\mathcal{P}}$ can demonstrate by following the issuing and showing protocols.

- All the matrix entries (coefficients) that specify the Boolean formulae are restricted to sets V such that $|V|/q$ is negligible in k. (The set V may differ for each formula coefficient.) The idea is that it should be infeasible to come up with $(\beta, \gamma_0, \gamma_1)$ and admissible formula coefficients (favorable to $\widehat{\mathcal{P}}$) that satisfy the linear relations. (Note that $c = \mathcal{H}_{q,g_l}(g_0^\beta, a_{00}^{\gamma_0} a_{01}^{\gamma_1}, \ldots)$ must be satisfied as well.) For security reasons, it is recommendable to apply this measure in combination with the preceding measure.

These measures were also recommended in Chapter 3 to guarantee unmodifiability of signed proofs for atomic formulae without a "NOT" connective. (Recall, though, that they are not always necessary to guarantee unforgeability of signed proofs.)

For atomic formulae that contain one "NOT" connective, the delegation strategy (be it the sequential or the parallel variant) is believed to be infeasible altogether, without any additional measures; $\mathcal{V}$'s challenge in the verification relations for these formulae is an exponent of the wrong base numbers. As we have seen in Section 5.1.1, in the showing protocol $\mathcal{P}$ must demonstrate anyway that $\alpha_1 \neq 0$; in case it does so as part of the formula that it is demonstrating to $\mathcal{V}$, the whole formula demonstration will always include a "NOT" connective. In other words, the issue of delegation can be circumvented altogether by requiring that $\mathcal{P}$ always demonstrate Boolean formulae for the DL-representation it knows of h_0^{-1} with respect to $(g_1, \ldots, g_l, h')$, rather than having $\mathcal{V}$ check that $h' \neq 1$ and having $\mathcal{P}$ demonstrate formulae without "NOT" connectives.

The case of the remaining secret-key certificate schemes

The observations with respect to the immunized DLREP-based scheme I in Section 4.4.2 apply also to the immunized RSAREP-based scheme II in Section 4.4.2 and to the DSA-like scheme in Section 4.5.1.

Finally, in the case of the immunized issuing protocols described in Section 4.4.1, the application of the function $f(\cdot)$ to the CA's initial witness in the issuing protocol is believed to make the delegation infeasible altogether.

5.2 Privacy improvements for certificate holders

In this section we describe various techniques to improve privacy for certificate holders.

5.2.1 Issuing protocol techniques

Users are free to obtain a single batch of certificates from the CA and to thereafter never again retrieve new ones. In effect, a certified public key is a *digital pseudonym*. All communications and transactions conducted using the same pseudonym are linkable. In applications such as online discussion groups, this allows certificate holders to build a reputation with respect to each of their pseudonyms. For reason of privacy, however, it will often be desirable to use each certificate only a limited number of times. In applications where there is no need to build a reputation, single use is optimal. It also has advantages in other respects, as we have seen in Section 1.1.

Issuing many certificates to each applicant does not significantly raise the burden for the CA, if only identifiers and other attributes need not be verified out-of-band each time. The following two methods facilitate the recurring issuance of certificates to the same certificate applicant:

- (Account-based method) The certificate applicant opens an *account* with the CA, and registers under a person identifier (see Section 1.1.2) or a pseudonym. The account holder uses an account key (or, if a digital pseudonym is used, the secret key of the pseudonym) to authenticate its requests for new certificates. Standard authentication techniques can protect against replay and, if desired, ensure non-repudiation.

If the attributes of each account holder are recorded in a database entry associated with the account, then the CA need not verify them more than once. Account holders can minimize the information the CA can learn about their certificate showing behavior by retrieving certificates in batches.

- (Account-less method) The certificate holder proves the right to retrieve new certificates by showing to the CA a previously retrieved certificate (not necessarily of the same type or issued by the same CA). In this manner, the CA can be assured of the authenticity of relevant attributes (identity or otherwise) without needing to keep an account database.

  This model does away with the account database by having each user port his or her own database entries, digitally certified by the CA for security. At the very least, the account-less method is natural for *refreshing* previously issued certificates. More generally, it fits well with the philosophy behind digital certificates to minimize the reliance on central databases; see Section 1.1.3.

In many PKIs it is more efficient to issue many short-lived certificates than to issue a few long-lived certificates and apply online certificate validation. By front-loading the handling of certificates and issuing certificates in batches, the CA greatly reduces the number of accesses to a central database. Also, certificate issuing can easily be scheduled, and in case of a communication or computation fault the same actions can be repeated until successful. Note that even in a PKI with long-lived certificates, the CA must be prepared to reissue certificates; certificates may be lost, stolen, or corrupted, and must be refreshed upon expiry.

The account-based method allows certificate holders to remain anonymous in the issuing protocol, by registering under a pseudonym and using an anonymous channel to retrieve certificates. Unlinkability of certificate retrievals can be achieved by opening multiple anonymous accounts. Full unlinkability, however, is feasible only when using the account-less approach. Hereto certificate applicants must be able to obtain attribute certificates that can be used to authenticate their right to retrieve new certificates.

The account-less approach also enables a certificate holder to anonymously have a previously issued certificate recertified by the CA. Anonymous refreshing of a certificate can be accomplished using any of the RSAREP-based certificate issuing schemes or the DLREP-based scheme described in Section 4.5.2. Suppose in the DLREP-based scheme that the CA is presented with $h' := (g_1^{x_1} \cdots g_l^{x_l} h_0)^{\alpha_1}$, a certificate on h', and (optionally) a signed proof (or another kind of proof) that discloses some property of the attributes (to enable $\mathcal{P}_0$ to certify unknown attributes that it knows satisfy a certain property) or at least authenticates the request. If the CA agrees to use h' in the new issuing protocol execution (in the role of $h_0 h$), the certificate holder can obtain a certificate on $(h')^\beta = (h_0 h)^{\alpha_1 \beta}$, for a random $\beta \neq 0 \mod q$. The associativity of raising numbers in G_q to a power ensures that the encoded attributes remain intact. Note that different CAs, each with their own signing key, can perform different recertification stages, assuming they all operate in the same group G_q.

The CA can *update* the attributes of anonymous certificate holders before recertifying them, without knowing the current attribute values. Consider hereto RSAREP-based scheme I. $\mathcal{V}_0$ receives a certificate on a public key h' of the form $g_1^{x_1} \ldots g_l^{x_l} \alpha_1^v$, for a random $\alpha_1 \in \mathbb{Z}_n^*$. Before recertification, the CA multiplies h' by $\prod_{i=1}^{l} g_i^{u_i}$, where $u_1, \ldots, u_l \in \mathbb{Z}_v$ represent the update values. This technique applies also to RSAREP-based scheme II and the immunized RSAREP-based schemes described in Section 4.4. The updating technique does not work when a hash function $\mathcal{F}(\cdot)$ is applied to the attributes (as described at the end of Section 5.1.1), and does not work for the DLREP-based schemes.

A special application of anonymous updating is to prevent the CA from learning the entire set of attributes of a certificate applicant. Attributes that can be assigned to a certificate applicant without requiring the applicant to disclose his or her identity can be encoded in successive anonymous executions of the issuing protocol, in each of which the certificate issued in the previous protocol execution is updated. To prevent linking by timing, there must be ample time between successive updates. Having different CAs certify different attributes further improves privacy.

5.2.2 Showing protocol techniques

To limit the privacy-invading powers of parties who build profiles from lists of certified public keys (obtained from certificate repositories or compiled by monitoring network traffic), one can use secret-key certificates and have certificate holders perform only zero-knowledge proofs. In this manner, nobody is able to obtain digitally signed evidence about the attributes of PKI participants.

Secret-key certificates can also reduce the scope for discrimination on the basis of (the lack of) one's right to participate in a PKI. Certified public keys obtained from a CA in one PKI can be combined with simulated certified public keys for other PKIs in an execution of the showing protocol, to prove knowledge of a secret key (more generally, an attribute property) for at least one of the certified public keys; the "OR" technique of Cramer, Damgård, and Schoenmakers [123] applies straightforwardly to our showing protocol techniques.

Instead of performing a zero-knowledge proof or issuing a signed proof, $\mathcal{P}$ in the showing protocol can also issue a *designated-verifier proof*. This notion, due to Chaum [102], guarantees that $\mathcal{P}$'s proof is convincing only to a designated verifier; this reduces the scope for privacy-invasive practices. (See Jakobsson, Sako, and Impagliazzo [219] and Krawczyk and Rabin [241] for improved constructions.) The idea is for $\mathcal{P}$ to perform its demonstration by proving knowledge of a secret key corresponding to its own public key or to one of the designated verifier, using a witness-indistinguishable proof of knowledge. Hereto our showing protocol techniques can be straightforwardly combined with the "OR" technique of Cramer, Damgård, and

Schoenmakers [123]. The resulting protocol transcript does not convince anyone but the verifier, because the verifier can generate transcripts with indistinguishable probability distribution. An inherent drawback of designated-verifier proofs is that $\mathcal{V}$ must be prevented from using a secret key that is known only to a group of verifiers. To overcome this attack, verifiers must either make a physical appearance in a Faraday cage (to have their public key certified) or a trusted party must securely issue a secret key to each verifier (e.g., by providing a smartcard that stores the key); both approaches have obvious drawbacks. In most PKIs either a signed proof or a zero-knowledge proof will be the preferred choice.

Our showing protocol techniques enable certificate holders to demonstrate properties of attributes that have been encoded into different certified key pairs. Limiting the number of attributes per certificate reduces the need to have attributes recertified (attributes with clearly distinct lifetimes can be encoded into different certified key pairs), improves efficiency,[1] and improves privacy when attributes are certified by different CAs. Any Boolean formula pertaining to the attributes in an arbitrary number of certified public keys can be demonstrated by applying our showing protocol techniques to the appropriate product of powers of the public keys, provided that the attributes specified in atomic formulae are all exponents of the same generator. For example, in the DLREP-based setting, with $h = \prod_{i=1}^{l} g_i^{x_i}$ and $h^* = \prod_{i=1}^{l} g_i^{x_i^*}$, demonstrating that $\alpha_1 x_1 + x_1^* = \alpha_2 \bmod q$, say, can be done by proving knowledge of a DL-representation of $h^{\alpha_1} h^* g_1^{-\alpha_2}$ with respect to $(g_2, \ldots, g_l)$. Depending on the certificate issuing scheme, for each public key an additional proof of knowledge of a representation may need to be performed, for security reasons. To prove knowledge of a representation of each of many public keys $h_1, \ldots, h_t$, knowledge of a representation of the product $h_1 \prod_{i=2}^{t} h_i^{\alpha_i}$ may be proved, for $\alpha_2, \ldots, \alpha_t$ generated at random from a large set. Either the α_i's are generated by application of a sufficiently strong one-way hash function to $h_1, \ldots, h_t$ and the initial witness of the prover, or the protocol is performed interactively and $\mathcal{V}$ generates the α_i's at random after receiving the initial witness.

This technique can be applied not only by a single certificate holder, but also by multiple certificate holders who wish to jointly demonstrate that their combined attributes meet certain criteria, without pooling their attributes. It can even be applied to certificates issued by different CAs, assuming all CAs operate in the same group; in DLREP-based scheme I, for instance, each CA may have its own x_0, but G_q and at least some of the generators should be the same.

The technique is less practical when $\mathcal{P}$ is to demonstrate a formula that involves attributes that are exponents of different g_i's in different certified key pairs. Auxiliary

---

[1] Attributes that are rarely shown in combination are best encoded into different certified key pairs. Other approaches to shorten certificates include: use of elliptic curve implementations, removing information from certificates, using better data encoding rules, and ensuring that certificate verifiers can derive the certificate holder's public key from its identifier and the CA's public key (Certicom's applies this approach in its "bullet" certificates).

commitments must then be spawned and additional relations must be proved, much as described in Section 3.7. In many PKIs, though, only the ability to demonstrate Boolean formulae involving the attributes (i.e., not the more general form of linear relations) is of interest; for these formulae, our showing protocol techniques readily apply to the attributes encoded into (arbitrarily many) different certified key pairs.

In some PKIs it is desirable that certificate holders can anonymously prove to be the originator of several showing protocol executions. This gives them the power to control the degree to which their communications and transactions can be linked. If the CA encodes into each certified key pair an attribute x_1 (possibly a random number) that is unique to the certificate applicant (applicants may provide $g_1^{x_1}$ or other suitable commitments to hide their x_1 from the CA), certificate holders can provide indisputable linking information for arbitrarily many public keys, $h_1, \ldots, h_t$, as follows. After the initial witnesses have been fixed, $\mathcal{V}$ generates t numbers, $\alpha_1, \ldots, \alpha_t$, at random from a set $V \subseteq \mathbb{Z}_q$, subject to the condition $\sum_{i=1}^{t} \alpha_i = 0 \bmod q$. It is easy to show that if $\mathcal{P}$ can prove knowledge of a representation of $\prod_{i=1}^{t} h_i^{\alpha_i}$ with respect to a tuple that does not contain g_1, then the probability of successful cheating is at most $1/|V|$. The α_i's may be generated as the output of a sufficiently strong one-way hash function to $\mathcal{P}$'s initial witnesses. The same technique applies to the RSAREP-based protocols.

A special application of the latter technique are credential systems in which certificate holders are to build pseudonymous reputations in the showing protocol. Using our techniques, certificate holders can establish digital pseudonyms with organizations; the pseudonyms can be thought of as anonymous accounts. To ensure that certificates can be shown only to organizations at which one has a pseudonym, we have the CA (or different CAs) encode a key holder identifier (e.g., a random number) into each pseudonym and attribute certificate. With $h = g_1^I g_0^\alpha$, say, denoting a person's pseudonym at an organization, and $h^* = g_1^{I^*} \prod_{i=2}^{l} g_i^{x_i}$ an attribute certificate, Boolean formulae of h^*/h with respect to tuples in which g_1 does not appear can be demonstrated only if $I = I^* \bmod q$. Seperate proofs of knowledge of a representation of h^* and h may be needed; for h this would naturally be done when registering or using the pseudonym with the organization.

Using our techniques it is also straightforward for several certificate holders to jointly demonstrate that their showing protocol executions did not all originate from the same certificate holder, or for one certificate holder to show that he or she was not involved in a fraudulent transaction; see Section 5.5.1 for details on the latter.

5.3   Privacy improvements for certificate verifiers

In many PKIs, certificate verifiers (must) submit their showing protocol transcripts to the CA (or another central authority), either online or off-line. This enables the CA to detect fraud with limited-show certificates, to keep track of the number of customers served by $\mathcal{V}$, to gather statistics on how often a certain attribute property is disclosed, or to perform other administrative tasks.

For competitive or other reasons, $\mathcal{V}$ may want to hide from the CA all or part of the formulae demonstrated. On the other hand, with the possible exception of closed PKIs in which verifiers are tamper-resistant terminals representing the security interests of the CA, the CA is unlikely to trust verifiers with truthfully submitting summary indications of the required information. That is, $\widehat{\mathcal{V}}$ should not be able to provide false information to the CA.

As an example application, consider an untraceable electronic coin system with "earmarks." Each electronic coin is a certified key pair encoding an attribute x_1 that specifies (at least) the expiry date and the denomination of the coin, and attributes $x_2, \ldots, x_l$ that specify personal data (such as age, gender, hobbies, income, marital status, and perhaps the identity of the coin holder). To make a payment, the payer discloses x_1 to the shop. Depending on the conditions, the payer may in addition decide to disclose some of $x_2, \ldots, x_l$, for example to get a discount. To get its account credited, the shop deposits the coin to the bank. The shop is required to deposit a signed proof (to enable the bank to detect and trace double-spending) that discloses x_1 (to enable the bank to determine the redeemable amount), but the personal data that the shop acquired from the payer is none of the bank's business.

We now show how $\mathcal{V}$ can obtain a signed proof that hides all or part of the formula demonstrated by $\mathcal{P}$, while $\mathcal{V}$ itself becomes convinced of the entire formula.

Consider first the case in which $\mathcal{P}$ interactively demonstrates to $\mathcal{V}$ an atomic formula F of the form (3.2), in the manner depicted in Figure 3.1 and subject to the conditions of Proposition 3.3.7. Let F^* be any atomic formula obtained from F by pruning "AND" connectives from F (i.e., by deleting rows from the left-hand side matrix in (3.2)). We claim that $\mathcal{V}$ can obtain a signed proof that serves as self-authenticating evidence that F^* applies to $\mathcal{P}$'s DL-representation but that unconditionally hides all other information about F. The basic idea is for $\mathcal{V}$ to hash along a description of F^* instead of F when determining c, and to make it appear as if some of $r_{l-t+1}, \ldots, r_l$ were provided by $\mathcal{P}$. For instance, the signed proof $(c, (r_1, \ldots, r_{l-t+1}))$ corresponds to the formula F^* that is the result of deleting the first row of the left-hand side matrix in (3.2), assuming that a description of F^* is hashed along instead of F when forming c. This signed proof does not unconditionally hide all other information about F, though, because r_{l+1} does not have an independent random distribution; for any choice of $l - t$ elements of the tuple $(b_1, \alpha_{11}, \ldots, \alpha_{1,l-t})$, the remaining element is uniquely defined. To take care of this aspect, $\mathcal{V}$ must randomize r_{l-t+1} by adding a random element $\beta \in \mathbb{Z}_q$; this must be compensated by hashing along $ag_{\pi(l-t+1)}^{\beta}$ instead of a when forming c.

More generally, with $\mathcal{P}$ demonstrating to $\mathcal{V}$ a formula F of the form (3.2), the following protocol steps result:

Step 1. (This step is identical to Step 1 of the protocol in Section 3.3.) $\mathcal{P}$ generates at random $l - t$ numbers, $w_1, \ldots, w_{l-t} \in \mathbb{Z}_q$, and computes

$$a := \prod_{i=1}^{l-t} g_{\pi(i)}^{w_i} \prod_{i=1}^{t} g_{\pi(l-t+i)}^{-\sum_{j=1}^{l-t} \alpha_{ij} w_j}.$$

$\mathcal{P}$ then sends the initial witness a to $\mathcal{V}$.

Step 2. $\mathcal{V}$ decides on F^* by deleting rows from the left-hand side matrix in (3.2). Without loss of generality, we assume that F^* is the result of pruning the first $t^* \leq t$ rows.

$\mathcal{V}$ generates at random t^* blinding factors $\beta_1, \ldots, \beta_{t^*} \in \mathbb{Z}_q$, and computes $a^* := a \prod_{i=1}^{t^*} g_{\pi(l-t+i)}^{\beta_i}$. $\mathcal{V}$ then forms $c := \mathcal{H}_{q,g_l}(h, m, F^*, a^*)$, for some (optional) message m, and sends c to $\mathcal{P}$.

Step 3. (This step is identical to Step 2 of the protocol in Section 3.3.) $\mathcal{P}$ computes a set of responses, responsive to $\mathcal{V}$'s challenge $c \in \mathbb{Z}_s$, as follows:

$$r_i := c x_{\pi(i)} + w_i \bmod q \quad \forall i \in \{1, \ldots, l-t\}.$$

$\mathcal{P}$ then sends $(r_1, \ldots, r_{l-t})$ to $\mathcal{V}$.

As in the protocol in Section 3.3, $\mathcal{V}$ computes

$$r_{l-t+i} := b_i c - \sum_{j=1}^{l-t} \alpha_{ij} r_j \bmod q \quad \forall i \in \{1, \ldots, t\},$$

and accepts the demonstration of F if and only if the verification relation

$$\prod_{i=1}^{l} g_{\pi(i)}^{r_i} h^{-c} = a$$

holds. If $\mathcal{V}$ accepts, it computes $r_{l-t+i}^* := r_{l-t+i} + \beta_i \bmod q$, for all $i \in \{1, \ldots, t^*\}$, and outputs the signed proof

$$c, r_{\pi^{-1}(1)}, \ldots, r_{\pi^{-1}(l-t)}, r_{\pi^{-1}(l-t+1)}^*, \ldots, r_{\pi^{-1}(l-t+t^*)}^*.$$

The CA (or anyone else) accepts the signed proof if and only if

$$c = \mathcal{H}_{q,g_l}\left(h, m, F^*, \prod_{i=1}^{l-t} g_i^{r_{\pi^{-1}(i)}} \prod_{i=1}^{t^*} g_{l-t+i}^{r_{\pi^{-1}(i)}^*} h^{-c}\right).$$

Note that if $t^* = t$ then the signed proof hides F in its entirety.

According to Proposition 3.6.3, if $\mathcal{V}$'s challenge is formed by hashing at least h, any initial witnesses, and a unique description of a formula F, then a signed proof serves as self-authenticating evidence that $\mathcal{P}$ knows (knew) a representation of h, and that $\mathcal{P}$'s representation satisfies the formula F. It follows that $\mathcal{V}$ can hide an arbitrary part of the formula demonstrated, but cannot obtain a signed proof for a formula that does not apply to $\mathcal{P}$'s representation: F^* is implied by the formula F demonstrated by $\mathcal{P}$ in the showing protocol execution from which the signed proof resulted.

The same technique applies to atomic formulae of the form (3.4). Peculiarly, though, $\mathcal{V}$ can only obtain signed proofs for formulae F^* obtained by pruning linear equalities from F^*; it is unclear how to prune the linear inequality.

More generally, if $\mathcal{P}$ interactively demonstrates an arbitrary formula F of the form (3.7), then $\mathcal{V}$ can obtain a signed proof for any formula that is obtained by pruning one or more of the j subformulae of F. Hereto $\mathcal{V}$ simply omits hashing along the initial witness sets for those subformulae when forming c.

In sum, when $\mathcal{P}$ is interactively demonstrating to $\mathcal{V}$ a formula F of the form (3.7), $\mathcal{V}$ can obtain a signed proof for any formula F^* that is obtained from the formula F demonstrated by $\mathcal{P}$ by pruning "AND" connectives. The signed proof unconditionally hides all other information about F. How much $\mathcal{V}$ may hide in the signed proof it deposits to the CA could depend on the policies set by the latter.

In case $\mathcal{P}$ wants to prevent $\mathcal{V}$ from obtaining a signed proof for a formula other than the formula F it is demonstrating to $\mathcal{V}$, it must form c itself by hashing along a description of F. More generally, $\mathcal{P}$ can ensure that $\mathcal{V}$ obtains a signed proof that convinces of a formula F^* obtained from F by pruning "AND" connectives by hashing along a description of F^* itself (and possibly a^* instead of a, for blinding factors supplied by $\mathcal{V}$).

In case of disputes, it may be desirable that $\mathcal{V}$ can "open up" the signed proof to prove that $\mathcal{P}$ demonstrated F, not just F^*. Hereto $\mathcal{V}$ should form c by hashing along a commitment to (the hidden part of) F, and save the blinding factors it used in Step 2 (in order to reconstruct those responses of $\mathcal{P}$ that it blinded). $\mathcal{P}$ has leverage to settle disputes as well: it can always prove to the CA to be the originator of the signed proof, by revealing h and proving knowledge of a corresponding secret key.

An efficiency improvement is possible in case $\mathcal{P}$ demonstrates a formula F of the form (3.6) containing only atomic subformulae of the form (3.2), and $\mathcal{V}$ wants to obtain a signed proof that hides F entirely. Let $s := q$. With $\prod_{i=1}^{l} g_{\pi(i)}^{r_{it}} h^{-c_t} = a_t$ denoting the verification relation for the t-th atomic subformula, for $t \in \{1, \ldots, j\}$, we have

$$\prod_{i=1}^{l} g_{\pi(i)}^{\sum_{j=1}^{t} r_{ij}} h^{-c} = \prod_{i=1}^{t} a_i.$$

Consequently, c together with the responses in this compound verification relation form a signed proof for the formula TRUE. $\mathcal{V}$ must hash along $a := \prod_{i=1}^{t} a_i$ (instead of all a_i's) and a description of the formula TRUE when determining c. There is no need for blinding factors or interaction.

Our techniques thus far do not enable $\mathcal{V}$ to obtain a signed proof for any formula

F^* implied by F. To get around this limitation, $\mathcal{P}$ should submit two proofs to $\mathcal{V}$: a signed proof that discloses the minimal information required by the CA (perhaps just the formula TRUE) and a proof (not necessarily a signed proof) that discloses the formula $\mathcal{V}$ is interested in. A drawback of this approach is increased computation and communication complexity.

All the techniques in this section apply straightforwardly to the RSAREP-based showing protocols.

5.4 Limited-show certificates

In this section we show how to ensure that the CA (or another central party to which showing protocol transcripts are submitted) can compute all the attributes encoded into a certified key pair once the certificate is shown more than a predetermined number of times. Benefits of this technique will be explained in Section 5.5.

5.4.1 Static one-show certificates

Consider the setting in Chapter 3. Suppose that $\mathcal{P}$ engages in a showing protocol execution, demonstrating a Boolean formula F for its DL-representation of h with respect to $(g_1, \ldots, g_l)$. We do not care whether $\mathcal{P}$ gives a signed proof, a zero-knowledge proof, or otherwise. We claim the following.

Proposition 5.4.1. *Suppose that formulae are demonstrated using the showing protocol described in Section 3.6.1. If $\widehat{\mathcal{P}}$ demonstrates the same formula twice using the same public key, responsive to any two different challenges of $\mathcal{V}$ but with respect to the same initial witness (sets), then with overwhelming probability $\mathcal{P}$'s secret key can be efficiently computed from the two accepting views of $\overline{\mathcal{V}}$.*

Proof. To prove the claim, we consider the following four cases for the formula F that is demonstrated:

Case 1. F is an atomic formula consisting of zero or more "AND" connectives and no other connectives, in the form (3.3). Recall from Figure 3.1 that the verification relation in the protocol for demonstrating F is

$$\prod_{i=1}^{l} g_{\pi(i)}^{r_i} h^{-c} = a,$$

where a is the initial witness. The verification relation with respect to a challenge $c^* \neq c \bmod s$ is

$$\prod_{i=1}^{l} g_{\pi(i)}^{r_i^*} h^{-c^*} = a.$$

Division of the two relations results in

$$h^{c-c^*} = g_{\pi(1)}^{r_1-r_1^*} \cdots g_{\pi(l)}^{r_l-r_l^*},$$

and from $s \leq q$ it follows that

$$h = g_{\pi(1)}^{(r_1-r_1^*)/(c-c^*)} \cdots g_{\pi(l)}^{(r_l-r_l^*)/(c-c^*)}.$$

The DL-representation $((r_1 - r_1^*)/(c - c^*) \bmod q, \ldots, (r_l - r_l^*)/(c - c^*) \bmod q)$ can be efficiently computed from the two views of $\overline{\mathcal{V}}$. With overwhelming probability, this DL-representation is $\mathcal{P}$'s secret key, $(x_{\pi(1)}, \ldots, x_{\pi(l)})$. Namely, according to Corollary 3.3.2 $\mathcal{P}$ must know at least one secret key, and if this is different then $< \widehat{\mathcal{P}}, \overline{\mathcal{V}} >$ is a collision-finding algorithm for the DLREP function used to implement $\mathcal{P}$'s commitment; according to Proposition 2.3.3 this contradicts the assumption that the underlying DL function is one-way.

Case 2. F is an atomic formula consisting of zero or more "AND" connectives, one "NOT" connective, and no other connectives, in the form (3.4). Recall from Figure 3.5 that the verification relation in the protocol for demonstrating F is

$$\prod_{i=1}^{l} g_{\pi(i)}^{r_i} h^{-r_0} = a.$$

The verification relation with respect to a challenge $c^* \neq c \bmod s$ is

$$\prod_{i=1}^{l} g_{\pi(i)}^{r_i^*} h^{-r_0^*} = a.$$

Division of the two relations results in

$$h^{r_0-r_0^*} = g_{\pi(1)}^{r_1-r_1^*} \cdots g_{\pi(l)}^{r_l-r_l^*}.$$

If $r_0 = r_0^* \bmod q$, then

$$(r_1 - r_1^* \bmod q, \ldots, r_l - r_l^* \bmod q)$$

is a DL-representation of 1 with respect to $(g_{\pi(1)}, \ldots, g_{\pi(l)})$, and two cases can be distinguished:

- If this is a non-trivial DL-representation of 1, then $< \widehat{\mathcal{P}}, \overline{\mathcal{V}} >$ has found a DL-representation of 1 other than the trivial one. According to Proposition 2.3.3 this contradicts the assumption that the DL function is one-way.

- If this is the trivial DL-representation, then $r_i = r_i^* \bmod q$ for all $i \in \{1, \ldots, l\}$. Recall that $\mathcal{V}$ computes $(r_{l-t+1}, \ldots, r_l)$ from $(r_0, \ldots, r_{l-t})$ according to

$$r_{l-t+i} := b_i r_0 - f_i c - \sum_{j=1}^{l-t} \alpha_{ij} r_j \bmod q \quad \forall i \in \{1, \ldots, t\},$$

where $t \geq 1$. From the linearity of these t responses it follows that $f_i(c - c^*) = 0 \bmod q$, for all $i \in \{1, \ldots, t\}$. From $s \leq q$ it follows that $c \neq c^* \bmod q$, and so $f_1, \ldots, f_t$ are all zero. This contradicts the presence of one "NOT" connective.

Therefore, with overwhelming probability $r_0 \neq r_0^* \bmod q$. It follows that

$$((r_1 - r_1^*)/(r_0 - r_0^*) \bmod q, \ldots, (r_l - r_l^*)/(r_0 - r_0^*) \bmod q)$$

is a DL-representation of h with respect to $(g_{\pi(1)}, \ldots, g_{\pi(l)})$. The same argument as in Case 1 completes the proof.

Case 3. F is a formula connecting atomic subformulae by zero or more "OR" connectives and no other connectives, in the form (3.6). According to the protocol in Section 3.5, $\mathcal{V}$ accepts if and only if $c = \sum_{i=1}^{j} c_i \bmod s$ and the verification relations for all the atomic subformulae hold. Let c^* denote the challenge of $\mathcal{V}$ in the second protocol execution involving the same initial witness (set), and c_i^* the challenge used by $\widehat{\mathcal{P}}$ for the i-th subformulae in that protocol execution. We have $\sum_{i=0}^{t} c_i^* = c^* \bmod s$. From $c^* \neq c \bmod s$ it follows that there exists at least one i such that $c_i^* \neq c_i \bmod s$. This index i corresponds to an atomic subformula that $\widehat{\mathcal{P}}$ has demonstrated twice with respect to the same initial witness but different challenges. We are now in Case 1 or 2, and refer to these cases for the completion of the proof.

Case 4. F is an arbitrary Boolean formula, in the form (3.7). According to the protocol in Section 3.6, $\mathcal{V}$ accepts if and only if it accepts $\mathcal{P}$'s demonstration of each of the j subformulae. We can therefore consider $\widehat{\mathcal{P}}$'s demonstration of any one of these subformulae, and apply the proof of Case 3.

This completes the proof.   □

The same result can be proved for the RSAREP-based showing protocols.

Based on Proposition 5.4.1 it is straightforward to construct a showing protocol that protects $\mathcal{P}$'s privacy if and only if $\mathcal{P}$ does not use the same certified public key more than once. $\mathcal{P}$ must hereto commit already in the certificate issuing protocol to the initial witness (sets) that it will use in the showing protocol, so that the CA can certify these along. Specifically, for any of the restrictive blind certificate issuing protocols in Chapter 4, $\mathcal{P}$ (i.e., $\mathcal{V}_0$) must hash along its initial witness (sets) for the showing protocol when computing c'_0 in Step 2 of the issuing protocol.

It is natural to think of h (or h', in the notation used in the issuing protocols in Chapter 4) together with the initial witness (sets) of $\mathcal{P}$ as a one-time public key of $\mathcal{P}$. Any two showing protocol executions by $\mathcal{P}$, with respect to the same one-time public key but different challenges, reveal its secret key. In case $\mathcal{P}$ non-interactively issues signed proofs, the use of different challenges can be forced by having $\mathcal{P}$ hash along a unique message m when forming $\mathcal{V}$'s challenge; if the hash function used to form $\mathcal{V}$'s challenge is collision-intractable, it is infeasible to compute two different messages that are mapped to the same challenge, regardless of any additional inputs to the hash function. Note that m need not be generated at random: Proposition 5.4.1 does not require $\mathcal{V}$'s challenge to satisfy a particular probability distribution. In a practical implementation, m could be the concatenation of an identifier for $\mathcal{V}$ (e.g., a true name, a local name, a pseudonym, or a public key) and a nonce.[2]

The limited-show technique applies even if the certificate verifier uses the technique in Section 5.3 to hide (part of) the formulae demonstrated, regardless of the strategy of $\widehat{\mathcal{P}}$ and $\widehat{\mathcal{V}}$.

The proof of Proposition 5.4.1 makes use of the fact that $< \widehat{\mathcal{P}}, \overline{\mathcal{V}} >$ cannot compute a collision for the DL function used to implement $\mathcal{P}$'s commitment. When combining the showing protocol with a certificate issuing protocol, we must see to it that this remains true. For the certificate schemes in Section 4.2 and the immunization in Section 4.4.1, $\widehat{\mathcal{P}}$'s inability to learn a non-trivial representation of 1 follows from Lemma 4.3.5. (Recall that we needed this property to prove blinding-invariance.) For the public-key certificate scheme in Section 4.5.2 the property follows from the fact that the CA need not know a non-trivial DL-representation of 1 to perform the issuing protocol. The other schemes in Chapter 4 are believed to meet the desired property as well.

The delegation strategy is never an issue. $\widehat{\mathcal{P}}$ cannot use the delegation strategy to show a number of certificates that exceeds the number of issuing protocol executions it would need to engage in; "forgery" is not possible. In fact, even if a secret-key certificate issuing protocol is used that admits delegation, reuse of a simulated certified public key is not possible because the CA uses an independent random initial witness in each protocol execution.

The most obvious application of limited-show certificates is to implement certificates that by their very nature may be shown only a limited number of times, such as food stamps, subway tokens, and electronic coins. In Section 5.5 we will see that limited-show certificates are advantageous also to prevent fraud with other types of certificates, such as personal certificates.

---

[2]The nonce may be a sequence number, a random number provided by $\mathcal{V}$, or a sufficiently accurate estimate of the time and date of the demonstration; in the latter case the showing protocol can be non-interactive, assuming $\mathcal{P}$ can determine the time without the assistance of $\mathcal{V}$.

In many PKIs, only one encoded attribute need be computable in case of fraud. Of special interest is the case where one of the encoded attributes is an identifier of $\mathcal{P}$, which normally need not be shown but must be computable when a limited-show certificate is shown too many times. Instead of storing the entire protocol view, in this case it is more efficient to store those exponents that correspond, in the expanded form of the verification relation, to $h, g_1, \ldots, g_l$. For instance, to be able to compute $x_{\pi(i)}$ in case a formula of the form (3.3) is demonstrated twice, for some $i \in \{1, \ldots, l\}$, it suffices to store (c, r_i) in each showing protocol execution. According to Subsections 2.2.2 and 2.2.3, 25-byte exponents suffice for long-term security, which makes our one-show certificate technique highly practical.

In a typical PKI implementation, there will be many verifiers. To enable detection of reuse of a one-show certificate, verifiers should deposit (relevant data of) the transcripts of their showing protocol executions to the CA (or another central party), in a timely fashion. (Either in real-time during certificate validation or batched at a convenient moment later on.) Verifiers that the CA trusts (such as tamper-proof verifier devices issued by the CA) may accept zero-knowledge demonstrations and deposit only the minimal data needed by the CA, but all others must receive and deposit signed proofs on challenges for which a nonce has been hashed along. The latter group of verifiers must be incited to perform the deposit. How to accomplish this depends on the PKI at hand. Incentives may be either positive (e.g., a financial reward for each deposited transcript) or negative (e.g., a penalty in case audits reveal a discrepancy between the number of customers serviced and the number of transcripts deposited). In some applications, it may be in the best interest of the verifiers themselves to faithfully perform the deposit, for instance if a successful attack leads to damages to their own organization.

By making use of its knowledge of $y_i = \log_{g_l} g_i$, for all $i \in \{1, \ldots, l-1\}$, the CA can speed up the verification of transcripts of showing protocol executions. Instead of verifying whether

$$\prod_{i=1}^{l} g_i^{r_i} h^{-c} = a,$$

say, the CA can simply verify whether

$$g_l^{\sum_{i=1}^{l-1} y_i r_i + r_l} h^{-c} = a.$$

Also, the CA can apply batch-verification to verify one or multiple transcripts, as described in Section 2.5.3.

5.4.2 Dynamic one-show certificates

With the *static* one-show certificate technique in Section 5.4.1, $\mathcal{P}$ must anticipate in the certificate issuing protocol which formula it will demonstrate in the showing protocol. Depending on the application, this may or may not be a drawback. For instance, the design of a privacy-protecting electronic coin system may be such that each coin encodes two attributes, one to specify (at least) the coin expiry date and the coin denomination and the other to specify the identity of the coin owner; the formula for the showing protocol (payment) would always require the disclosure of just the first attribute. In many PKIs, however, the requirement that the formula must be anticipated is inconvenient or even unrealistic. Typically, the formula to be demonstrated will depend on the verifier or its service, and $\mathcal{P}$ does not know in advance which service of which verifier it will want to get access to. In the case of unlimited-show certificates, $\mathcal{P}$ can postpone the moment of computing its initial witness (sets) until Step 1 of the showing protocol, but this cannot be accomplished for limited-show certificates. We now show how to get around this. Again, we assume the setting of Chapter 3, and detail the technique only for the DLREP-based showing protocols.

Atomic formulae without "NOT" connectives

Consider first the case that $\mathcal{P}$ is to demonstrate an atomic formula of the form (3.3), using the showing protocol depicted in Figure 3.1. In Step 2 of the issuing protocol, instead of generating the initial witness in a formula-dependent manner, $\mathcal{P}$ simply computes $a := \prod_{i=1}^{l} g_i^{w_i}$, for random $w_1, \ldots, w_l \in \mathbb{Z}_q$. In the showing protocol, $\mathcal{P}$ in addition sends to $\mathcal{V}$ a set of t *correction factors*, $e_1, \ldots, e_t$, all in $\mathbb{Z}_q$. These serve to adjust a, in such a manner that the DL-representation known to $\mathcal{P}$ of the adjusted a is suitable to complete the demonstration in the same manner as in the original protocol. Specifically, the adjusted a is computed as

$$a / \prod_{i=1}^{t} g_{\pi(l-t+i)}^{e_i}.$$

By applying the protocol of Figure 3.1 and expanding the resulting terms, the following (generic) protocol steps result:

Step 1. $\mathcal{P}$ computes t correction factors, as follows:

$$e_i := w_{\pi(l-t+i)} + \sum_{j=1}^{l-t} \alpha_{ij} w_{\pi(j)} \bmod q \quad \forall i \in \{1, \ldots, t\}.$$

$\mathcal{P}$ then sends its one-time public key (h, a) and $(e_1, \ldots, e_t)$ to $\mathcal{V}$.

Step 2. $\mathcal{P}$ computes a set of responses, responsive to $\mathcal{V}$'s challenge $c \in \mathbb{Z}_s$, as follows:

$$r_i := c x_{\pi(i)} + w_{\pi(i)} \bmod q \quad \forall i \in \{1, \ldots, l-t\}.$$

$\mathcal{P}$ then sends $(r_1, \ldots, r_{l-t})$ to $\mathcal{V}$.

$\mathcal{V}$ computes

$$r_{l-t+i} := e_i + b_i c - \sum_{j=1}^{l-t} \alpha_{ij} r_j \bmod q \quad \forall i \in \{1, \ldots, t\},$$

and accepts if and only if

$$\prod_{i=1}^{l} g_{\pi(i)}^{r_i} h^{-c} = a.$$

Assuming s is large and c is generated in a substantially random manner and after the data in Step 1 has been sent, it is easy to prove that $\overline{\mathcal{V}}$ is convinced if and only if $\mathcal{P}$'s attributes satisfy the formula (3.3). Furthermore, all the considerations in Section 3.3.1 apply, with the obvious modifications. Notably, assuming that all the correction factors are hashed along as well when forming c, Propositions 3.3.6, 3.3.7, and 3.3.8 all hold.

Suppose now that $\mathcal{P}$ reuses the one-time public key (h, a), demonstrating a formula of the form (3.3) that need not be the same as in the first demonstration. Clearly, the proof of Case 1 in Proposition 5.4.1 applies as is. Consequently, if the two demonstrations are performed responsive to different challenges, then with overwhelming probability all the attributes of $\widehat{\mathcal{P}}$ can be efficiently computed from the two accepting views of $\mathcal{V}$.

$\mathcal{V}$ can limit the class of atomic formulae that $\mathcal{P}$ is able to demonstrate by imposing restrictions on the number, the position, or the form of the correction factors that $\mathcal{P}$ may use. Complete anticipation of the formula corresponds to the extreme case where $\mathcal{P}$ is not allowed to use any correction factors; this is the case of static one-show certificates. The CA can encode restrictions on the correction factors into one of the x_i's (e.g., as part of a CA policy attribute), which $\mathcal{P}$ must then disclose to $\mathcal{V}$ in the showing protocol as part of the formula it is demonstrating.

The technique in Section 5.3 can be applied as well. Only those correction factors that correspond to F^* should be hashed along when forming c. For dispute settlement, $\mathcal{V}$ should in addition hash along a commitment to both the hidden part of F and the remaining correction factors.

Arbitrary atomic formulae

The situation is slightly more complex in case $\mathcal{P}$ must be able to demonstrate any atomic formula. This time, we have $\mathcal{P}$ in Step 2 of the issuing protocol hash along an initial witness $a := h^{-w_0} \prod_{i=1}^{l} g_i^{w_i}$, for random $w_0, \ldots, w_l \in \mathbb{Z}_q$. To demonstrate a formula of the form (3.4), $\mathcal{P}$ in Step 1 of the showing protocol of Figure 3.5 must be allowed to reveal t correction factors, $(e_1, \ldots, e_t)$, to adjust a to

$$a / \prod_{i=1}^{t} g_{\pi(l-t+i)}^{e_i}.$$

To demonstrate a formula of the form (3.3), $\mathcal{P}$ in Step 1 of the showing protocol depicted in Figure 3.1 must this time be allowed to reveal $t + 1$ correction factors, to adjust a to

$$a/h^{e_0} \prod_{i=1}^{t} g_{\pi(l-t+i)}^{e_i},$$

because the exponent $-w_0$ of h must be canceled as well. For both cases, it is easy to describe the resulting protocol. This time, the proof of Case 1 in Proposition 5.4.1 does not apply, because $\mathcal{V}$'s challenge in the verification relation for the demonstration of an atomic formula with a "NOT" connective does not appear as a power of h. Specifically, the verification relation for an atomic formula of the form (3.4) is

$$\prod_{i=1}^{l-t} g_{\pi(i)}^{r_i} \prod_{i=1}^{t} g_{\pi(l-t+i)}^{e_i+b_i r_0 - f_i c - \sum_{j=1}^{l-t} \alpha_{ij} r_j} = h^{r_0} a$$

and that for an atomic formula of the form (3.3) with matrix coefficients α_{ij}^* is

$$\prod_{i=1}^{l-t^*} g_{\pi(i)}^{r_i^*} \prod_{i=1}^{t^*} g_{\pi(l-t^*+i)}^{e_i^*+b_i^* c^* - \sum_{j=1}^{l-t^*} \alpha_{ij}^* r_j^*} = h^{c^*+e_0^*} a.$$

If $r_0 = c^* + e_0^* \bmod q$, and cancellation takes place also for the exponents to all g_i's (otherwise a non-trivial DL-representation of 1 is obtained; cf. Case 2 of Proposition 5.4.1), then the DL-representation of h with respect to $(g_1, \ldots, g_l)$ cannot be computed even though c^* may differ from c. Indeed, if $\widehat{\mathcal{P}}$ is allowed to select $\mathcal{V}$'s challenge in an arbitrary manner, subject only to the condition that it has to be unique in each formula demonstration, it is not hard to construct a one-time public key (h, a), two atomic formulae, two different challenge messages, and two protocol transcripts for which total cancellation takes place.

We can get around this in a natural manner, by requiring $\mathcal{V}$'s challenge message to be a sufficiently strong hash of at least (h, a), a unique formula description, and the correction factors (in a unique order). Under this condition, which is needed anyway to prove the unforgeability and unmodifiability of signed proofs in the random oracle model (see Section 3.4.1), the following holds: if any two atomic formula demonstrations are performed responsive to different challenges, then with overwhelming probability all the attributes of $\widehat{\mathcal{P}}$ can be efficiently computed from the two accepting views of $\mathcal{V}$. Under the conditions of Proposition 3.3.6 and 3.3.7, respectively, this can be proved in the random oracle model for both non-interactively and interactively issued signed proofs.

Atomic formulae connected by "OR" connectives

Another treacherous aspect enters when $\mathcal{P}$ must be able to demonstrate any formula of the form (3.6), in such a manner that any two demonstrations involving the same one-time public key disclose all the encoded attributes. The simplest approach is for $\mathcal{P}$ to simulate all but one of the subformulae demonstrations, in the manner described in Section 3.5.1, and to hash along in Step 2 of the issuing protocol an initial witness formed in the same formula-independent manner as in the case of atomic formulae. This fails, however, because $\mathcal{V}$ can infer from a single showing protocol execution which subformula demonstration is genuine. Using the same a for each subformula demonstration, and providing random correction factors for those subformulae demonstrations that are simulated, does not work either: if $j \geq 2$ then $\mathcal{V}$ can compute $\mathcal{P}$'s representation from a single execution of the showing protocol. Yet another flawed approach is for $\mathcal{P}$ to use a one-time public key of the form $(h, a_1, \ldots, a_{j^*})$, where $j^* \geq j$: this requires $\mathcal{P}$ to know an upper bound on j, the number of "OR" connectives in the formula to be demonstrated.

All these problems can be avoided by introducing an extra constraint in the showing protocol described in Section 3.5.1. Let

$$a := h^{-w_0} \prod_{i=1}^{l} g_i^{w_i}$$

be the *master initial witness* that $\mathcal{P}$ in Step 2 of the issuing protocol incorporates into its one-time public key, and let a_i denote the initial witness used in the demonstration of subformula F_i, for all $i \in \{1, \ldots, j\}$. For each of the j subformula demonstrations, we have $\mathcal{P}$ reveal up to l correction factors to adjust the initial witness a_i for that subformula demonstration, as described previously. $\mathcal{P}$ could do without the use of correction factors in the $j - 1$ subformula demonstrations that are simulated, but they are needed to hide from $\mathcal{V}$ which subformula demonstration is genuine; the zero-knowledge simulator must generate the required number of correction factors at random (as many as would be needed in a genuine proof). The extra constraint is that the product of the j adjusted initial witnesses must equal the master initial witness, a. $\mathcal{P}$ can easily meet this constraint, since a_i in each of the $j - 1$ simulated subformulae demonstrations is generated in such a manner that $\mathcal{P}$ knows a DL-representation with respect to $(g_1, \ldots, g_l, h)$; therefore, $\mathcal{P}$ can determine the remaining set of correction factors (for the subformula that requires a genuine proof) by comparing the representation it knows of a with that of the product of the $j - 1$ adjusted initial witnesses. $\mathcal{V}$ must verify the extra constraint as part of its verification process.

To obtain a signed proof, $\mathcal{V}$'s challenge should be formed by hashing at least (h, a, F) and all correction factors (in a unique order). Under the conditions of Proposition 3.3.6 and 3.3.7, respectively, it can be proved in the random oracle model that both non-interactively and interactively issued signed proofs are unforgeable and unmodifiable. If the CA does not trust $\mathcal{V}$, the latter will need to relay the entire transcript of the showing protocol to the CA.

Why does this work? By aggregating the j verification relations (one for each subformula demonstration), $\mathcal{V}$ can obtain a compound verification relation of the form

$$\prod_{i=1}^{l} g_i^{y_i} = h^{y_0} a.$$

Each y_i, for $i \in \{0, \ldots, l\}$, is an arithmetic expression that involves subformulae coefficients, responses (at most one from each subformula demonstration), and perhaps correction factors and $\mathcal{V}$'s challenge. Suppose now that $\mathcal{P}$ reuses its one-time public key (h, a). This time, $\mathcal{V}$ obtains a compound verification relation

$$\prod_{i=1}^{l} g_i^{y_i^*} = h^{y_0^*} a.$$

From the two compound verification relations, the DL-representation that $\mathcal{P}$ knows of h can be extracted, unless $\widehat{\mathcal{P}}$ has managed to perform its two protocol executions in such a manner that $y_i = y_i^* \bmod q$ for all $i \in \{0, \ldots, l\}$. If $\mathcal{V}$'s challenge is formed by hashing at least (h, a, F) and all correction factors, then it is infeasible to effect this cancellation, assuming only that $\mathcal{V}$'s challenge differs in the two showing protocol executions; this result can be proved in the random oracle model.

An anomaly occurs in case none of the atomic subformulae involve a "NOT" connective. In this case, $\mathcal{V}$ need not hash along a description of F and the correction factors. If $\sum_{i=1}^{j} c_i = c \bmod q$, it follows from the constraint on the adjusted initial witnesses that $\mathcal{V}$ can obtain a compound relation of the form

$$\prod_{i=1}^{l} g_i^{y_i} = h^c a.$$

With c being a sufficiently strong hash of at least (h, a), the unforgeability of this compressed signed proof of knowledge of a DL-representation of h follows as in the case of Propositions 3.3.6 and 3.3.7. By applying the technique described in Section 5.3, $\mathcal{V}$ can unconditionally hide which formula F has been demonstrated (from the space of all formulae that connect atomic subformula without "NOT" connectives by zero or more "OR" connectives), yet $\mathcal{V}$ itself becomes convinced of F during the showing protocol. In case (h, a) is reused in a showing protocol execution involving a different c, the CA can extract $\mathcal{P}$'s DL-representation of h. Sending only $(h, c, y_1, \ldots, y_l)$ to the CA is preferable also for reason of efficiency.

Arbitrary Boolean formulae

Finally, consider the case where $\mathcal{P}$ must be able to demonstrate any formula F of the form (3.7). The one-show certificate technique for formulae of the form (3.6) applies here as well. This time, the product of all the adjusted initial witnesses, one for each atomic subsubformula in F, must equal the master initial witness, a. Aggregation of all the verification relations, one for each subformula demonstration, results in a compound verification relation of the form

$$\prod_{i=1}^{l} g_i^{y_i} = h^{y_0} a.$$

Assuming $\mathcal{V}$'s challenge is formed by hashing at least (h, a, F) and all correction factors, reuse of (h, a) with respect to a different c enables the computation of $\mathcal{P}$'s DL-representation of h. Again, this result can be proved in the random oracle model. Note that only (y_0, y_i) needs to be stored to be able to compute x_i from $\mathcal{P}$'s DL-representation upon reuse of (h, a), regardless of the formula demonstrated. To be able to detect reuse, in addition the CA must store a hash of $(h, a, \mathsf{cert}(h, a))$. A hash function that is second-preimage resistant may be used (i.e., for a random input, it is infeasible to find another input that maps to the same output). In practice, simply storing the 10 most significant bytes of h, say, should be adequate, assuming that it is agreed on that no certificate applicant retrieves multiple certificates on the same public key. According to Section 2.2.2, 25-byte exponents should suffice for long-term security, which makes our technique for dynamic one-show certificates highly practical: per showing protocol transcript a mere 60 bytes need to be stored, regardless of the formula demonstrated.

The dynamic one-show certificate technique can be applied in a straightforward manner to the RSAREP-based issuing and showing protocols. In this case, the CA will be able to compute $\mathcal{P}$'s attributes $(x_1, \dots, x_l)$ as well as x_{l+1} upon redemonstration of the same formula.

5.4.3 Increasing the threshold

There is nothing magical about a threshold value of 1. To ensure that $\mathcal{P}$'s representation can be computed if and only if $\widehat{\mathcal{P}}$ performs more than t demonstrations using the same certified public key, for a predetermined positive integer t, $\mathcal{P}$'s t-time public key should comprise t master initial witnesses. When performing the i-th execution of the showing protocol, using the same t-time public key, $\overline{\mathcal{P}}$ uses the i-th master initial witness. Alternatively, to obscure in the current showing protocol execution how many showing protocol executions have already been performed using the same public key, $\overline{\mathcal{P}}$ uses a master initial witness that it randomly chooses out of those not yet used. The pigeon-hole principle ensures that any $t + 1$ demonstrations lead to the reuse of a master initial witness. From the corresponding two views $\widehat{\mathcal{P}}$'s representation can be computed.

For large thresholds, it is more efficient to use Merkle's tree authentication technique [267]. Hereto $\mathcal{P}$ builds a binary tree with the master initial witnesses in the leaves. Each node value in the level just above the leaves is computed by compressing the entries in the leaves below it, using a collision-intractable hash function. All the other node values are computed by compressing the child node values. The value of the root node together with h' serves as the t-time public key; it must be hashed along in Step 2 of the issuing protocol. In the showing protocol, $\mathcal{P}$ must reveal the particular master initial witness it intends to use in the formula demonstration, together with $\lceil 2 \log t \rceil$ nodes to enable $\mathcal{V}$ to compute its way back to the root node and verify the certificate.

If $\mathcal{V}$ (or the CA) consents, t-show certificates can be turned on the spot into i-show certificates for any $i \in \{1, \ldots, t\}$, by fixing a subset of size i of master initial witnesses that may be used in the showing protocol. Also, a t-show certificate may be converted into an unlimited-show certificate, by allowing $\mathcal{P}$ in the showing protocol to use initial witnesses other than those comprised in its t-time public key. By way of example, consider the technique in Section 5.3 and suppose the CA is interested only in being able to trace certificate holders who show their certificates too many times. $\mathcal{P}$ supplies two proofs to $\mathcal{V}$: a signed proof demonstrating the formula TRUE and a proof demonstrating the formula $\mathcal{V}$ is interested in. The signed proof must use one of the (master) initial witnesses committed to in Step 2 of the issuing protocol, while the other proof may make use of freshly generated initial witnesses and need not be a signed proof.

5.5   Security improvements

In this section we introduce techniques to improve security, without resorting to smartcards or other tamper-resistant devices for certificate holders. Among others, we show how to discourage lending, copying, and discarding of certificates, and how to achieve non-repudiation for limited-show certificates. Most of these software-only techniques are based on the limited-show certification technique of Section 5.4. We also provide measures to protect against leakage and misuse of the CA's secret key.

5.5.1   Benefits of encoding identifiers

Certified key pairs that do not contain information that can be uniquely traced or linked to one person or to a select group are sometimes called *digital bearer certificates*. They are the digital equivalent of paper-based bearer certificates, such as currency and bearer bonds. Anyone may obtain them, show them, and pass them around. Bearer certificates are the opposite of *personal certificates*, which are generally issued only to parties that meet certain criteria. The simplest way for the CA to create digital bearer certificates is to issue blind signatures on public keys. An improved approach is to use restrictive blinding, to enable the CA to encode basic attributes (such as use limitations, expiry dates, and verifier policies) and to provide the ability of selective disclosure.

By definition, non-personal certificates must be limited-show certificates; otherwise everyone could simply use the same certificate. This requirement is at odds with the ability of computers to instantaneously copy digital certificates in large numbers at virtually no cost, and to freely distribute them over electronic networks at the speed of light. Fraud with digital bearer certificates and other limited-show certificates implemented in software-only devices can be prevented only by clearing all showing protocol executions online with a central party. For each authorization request, this party (typically the CA) must consult an online database that keeps track of the number of times a presented certificate has already been shown. Online clearing suffers from the drawbacks in Section 1.1.3. The scalability problem is even worse, since the process of checking the occurrence of a certificate in the database is inherently sequential; queries may not be performed in parallel, and the online database may not be distributed. In many PKIs, though, it suffices for the CA to strongly discourage fraud and to be able quickly contain it. Using our technique in Section 5.4, it is possible to realize these security goals and to do away with the need for online clearing. Hereto the CA must personalize all limited-show attribute certificates by encoding into each certified key pair an attribute identifying the certificate applicant. Consider the security benefits:

- A certificate holder who shows a limited-show certificate more times than allowed can be traced by computing the built-in identifier from the transcripts of the showing protocol executions. This enables the CA to stop the fraud by listing the abused certificate on a CRL and by blocking further retrieval of certificates from account. In addition, if the identifier can be linked to the identity of the certificate holder, it may be possible to sue for damages and to prevent the perpetrator from continuing to participate in the system. Of course, traceability of perpetrators often also serves as a powerful deterrent.

- This technique can be made to work even for anonymous accounts. Traced perpetrators can be prevented from opening new anonymous accounts, from which new limited-show certificates can be retrieved, by limiting the number of anonymous accounts to one per certificate applicant. Hereto a special entity should issue digital pseudonyms with an embedded identifier, that can each be used to open one anonymous account. If personal account pseudonyms are issued in such a manner that the recertification technique described in Section 5.2.1 applies, the limited-show property remains intact.

- The number of anonymous accounts need not be limited to one per certificate applicant. In case a traced perpetrator refuses to reveal any other anonymous accounts he or she may have opened, the CA can require all system participants (e.g., the next time they retrieve certificates) to demonstrate that the identifier built into their account pseudonym is not that of the perpetrator. Hereto the showing protocol technique in Section 3.4 can be used. This is not an extra burden, since applicants must use their account pseudonym anyway to authenticate account access requests.

- In the same manner, a perpetrator can be stopped from using any other digital certificates that may have been issued to him or her. For example, an administrator of a pseudonymous chat box can require each participant to digitally sign his or her next message in such a manner that the signed proof demonstrates that the pseudonym is not that of an identified misbehaving participant. (The alternative of issuing only one-show certificates is not always desirable.)

- More generally, to verify that t public keys, $h_1, \ldots, h_t$, are not all owned by the same certificate applicant, the verifier generates t numbers, $\alpha_1, \ldots, \alpha_t$ at random from a set V that is a subset of $\mathbb{Z}_q$, subject to the condition $\sum_{i=1}^{t} \alpha_i = 0 \bmod q$. Let attribute x_1 be unique to the certificate applicant. A cheating prover can prove knowledge of a DL-representation of g_1 with respect to a tuple that contains $\prod_{i=1}^{t} h_i^{\alpha_i}$ with success probability at most $1/|V|$, but an honest group of provers can always (jointly) convince the verifier. (The same technique applies to the RSAREP-based constructions.)

Stronger fraud discouragement without resorting to online clearing requires the use of smartcards or other tamper-resistant devices; for details, see the next chapter.

In sum, even though in regular communications and transactions there may be no need for certificate holders to show identifiers, it is beneficial the CA for to encode them anyway into their certified key pairs.

There is no need for the CA to encode globally unique identifiers; they should merely be unique within the domain of the PKI. Identifiers need not even be determined using an out-of-band method: an identifier may be a random number or a pseudonym known to the CA. In cases where a true name is to be used, the CA may require registrants to present an X.509 or other identity certificate; the CA can copy and paste the subject names from these certificates into the certificates it issues.

The current standards for identity certificates can easily be encapsulated. To encapsulate an X.509v3 certificate, for instance, the CA can take x_1 to be (a collision-intractable hash of) the concatenation of all the fields except the subject's X.500 name (i.e., the format version, serial number, the CA's certification algorithm identifier, the CA's X.500 name, the validity period, and the certificate holder's public key and the algorithm with which it is to be used), and x_2 the certificate holder's X.500 name. The remaining x_i's can specify additional attributes, such as X.509v3 extensions. In the certificate showing protocol, the certificate holder must disclose (the preimage of) x_1, and may be required to demonstrate properties about the other attributes. To ensure that the data encoded into x_1 does not serve as a unique identifier, the entropy of at least the validity period and any extension fields must be restricted. Furthermore, the serial number should be set to a hash of the (certified) public key, since this is what is posted on a CRL; alternatively, it is set to zero, since verifiers can compute the hash themselves if needed.[3]

---

[3]ANSI draft standard X9.68 for mobile devices proposes to shorten X.509 certificates by assigning to each certificate an implicit serial number formed by hashing the certificate; this matches our approach.

A non-technical objection to the inclusion of identifiers into certified key pairs is that organizations and other verifiers may incite certificate holders to disclose their built-in identifiers, for example by giving discounts to customers who disclose their identifiers or by refusing to serve anonymous certificate holders. Privacy legislation should be adopted that prohibits such discrimination in PKIs where there is no strict need for identification; PKI legislation is needed anyway, so this is not an unreasonable course of action. In Section 6.5.5 we will show how to make it technically infeasible for certificate holders to disclose their identifier attributes.

5.5.2 How to discourage lending

It should not be possible for certificate holder to lend (i.e., distribute copies of) their personal certificates, such as driver's licenses and diplomas, to others. To discourage lending of certified key pairs for personal certificates that are used in face-to-face situations, the CA could encode biometric identifiers into certified key pairs, such as digitized photographs, fingerprints, or retina scans. Privacy legislation should specify when identity disclosure may be required; preferably, verifiers may require disclosure of visual identifiers only in rare cases, sampled at random. Fairness can be enforced by using a cryptographic (biased) coin flipping protocol to determine whether a biometric identifier must be disclosed.

For improved security and privacy, the CA could encode into each certified key pair a plurality of personal characteristics, such as eye color, gender, height, and skin type. Each of these by itself is not a person identifier, but sufficiently many taken as a group are. In the showing protocol the verifier could then request the certificate holder to disclose a random subset of the built-in personal characteristics. Again, fairness can be achieved by means of (biased) coin flipping, to determine the size and the elements of the subset that must be disclosed.

Another measure for the CA to discourage lending of certified key pairs is to encode into each certified key pair an attribute that the certificate holder wants to remain confidential. Examples are the identity of the certificate holder (his or her reputation may be damaged when the borrower discloses the attribute), the secret key of a key pair used to sign messages (such as a PGP secret key), or a redeemable electronic token of significant value. (It should not be possible, though, for a certificate holder to revoke a key or a token within the period that lending is to be discouraged.) According to Proposition 3.6.1(b), the demonstration of any Boolean formula requires knowledge of the entire secret key. Consequently, the lender must reveal to the borrower all the attributes, including the confidential attribute, even though the borrower may be interested only in some of the other attributes. This measure may be combined with the previous measure, but applies also to personal certificates that are not restricted to face-to-face situations. By way of example, consider digital gender certificates needed to gain access to certain online discussion groups, or "over 18" certificates to gain access to adult-oriented Web sites. By encoding along the credit card data of the legitimate receiver into his or her certificates, the issuer can ensure that the receiver cannot lend (or give out copies of) the certificate without disclosing the credit card data; at the same time, privacy is not compromised because the receiver itself can hide the data when showing the certificate.[4] The CA need not know the confidential attributes it encodes: it can apply our updating or (re)certification technique described in Section 5.2.1 to a public key presented by the certificate applicant (corresponding to the secret the applicant wants to remain confidential).

Yet another measure to discourage lending is for the CA to issue all personal certificates in the form of limited-show certificates.[5] This subjects a lender to the risk that the borrower uses his or her certified key pair more times than allowed, which would result in the lender being traced (and held responsible). It also reduces the number of times the certificate holder can continue to use the certified key pair him or herself. This measure may be applied in conjunction with the measure in the previous paragraph, applies also to certificates that by their nature may be shown an unlimited number of times (before expiry), and works particularly well in conjunction with short validity periods (which are more natural for limited-show certificates; see Section 1.1.5).

Stronger protection against lending requires smartcards; see Section 6.5.3.

5.5.3 Non-repudiation

To prevent the CA from framing certificate holders by falsely claiming abuse of limited-show certificates, consider a variation of the DLREP-based scheme described in Section 4.5.2. Before issuing certified key pairs to $\mathcal{V}_0$, $\mathcal{P}_0$ requires $\mathcal{V}_0$ to provide $h^* := g_1^I$, for a random $I \in \mathbb{Z}_q$, and to prove knowledge of $\log_{g_1} h^*$ without revealing I; $\mathcal{V}_0$ can apply the Schnorr proof of knowledge or its zero-knowledge variation. In addition, $\mathcal{V}_0$ may be required to sign a statement to agree to the consequences of the use of h^*; this can be combined with the proof of knowledge by giving a signed proof of $\log_{g_1} h^*$. If the proof is convincing (it need only be performed once), $\mathcal{P}_0$ multiplies the desired g_i-powers into h^*, and uses the result as the number h in the issuing protocol to issue to $\mathcal{V}_0$ one or more limited-show certificates. If a certificate is shown more times than allowed, I can be computed. Assuming that (q, g_1, I) has been generated by an invulnerable instance generator, I serves as compact undeniable evidence of fraud.

The evidence can be made unconditionally convincing. Hereto the CA should

---

[4]This valuable property cannot be ensured by simply certifying a one-way hash structure of the attributes (such as the concatenation of one-way images of all the attribute values). The resulting certificates can be shown without needing to know all the attribute values themselves.

[5]To prevent linkability of showing protocol executions, certificate holders must use their certificates only a limited number of times anyway, and the CA might as well exploit this by issuing limited-show certificates with built-in identifiers. The burden of issuing 100 copies (and new ones when needed) is hardly greater than the burden of issuing a single copy, especially if the CA uses a DLREP-based issuing protocol that admits preprocessing of all exponentiations.

require $\mathcal{V}_0$ to register using a number h^* of the form $g_1^I g_2^\beta$, for an arbitrary I and a random $\beta \in \mathbb{Z}_q$. $\mathcal{V}_0$ must prove knowledge of a DL-representation of h^* with respect to (g_1, g_2); again, this need only be done once. In case of fraud, the CA can compute I, β, which serve as unconditionally undeniable evidence; assuming that $g_1, g_2 \neq 1$, the CA cannot frame $\mathcal{V}_0$, no matter how it generates the system parameters and its public key.

This non-repudiation technique works also in conjunction with anonymous accounts: h^* serves as the account pseudonym, which the certificate applicant must acquire from an account pseudonym issuer (possibly by showing an X.509 certificate or another type of identity certificate) and uses to authenticate account requests.

To apply the non-repudiation technique to an RSAREP-based certificate scheme, $\mathcal{V}_0$ should preferably register using a number h^* of the form $g_1^I \beta^v$.

5.5.4 How to discourage discarding

To discourage certificate holders from discarding certified key pairs that encode unfavorable attributes, the CA can encode favorable attributes into the same certified key pairs. For instance, information on late payments could be encoded into a membership certificate for a health club or the like, and marks for drunk driving into a driver's license certificate. Note that the updating technique described in Section 5.2.1 can be put to use here.

This measure does not work when the attributes encoded into the certified key pairs of a certificate applicant change over time and become less favorable to the applicant. To limit the ability of certificate holders to reuse old certified key pairs that encode attributes that are more favorable, the CA should encode short validity periods. Alternatively, or preferably in addition, the CA could issue only limited-show certificates.

The strongest possible protection in software-only implementations is to issue only one-show certificates, and to ensure that certificate holders cannot show more than one certificate at any time. This can be achieved by having the CA recertify (and update) one-show certificates only when they are shown in executions of the showing protocol. This requires all verifiers to have an online connection with the CA, and applies only to certificates for which the decision as to how to update attributes relies solely on the data disclosed in the showing protocol.

Stronger protection requires the use of smartcards or other tamper-resistant devices. These can be programmed to show certificates in the order in which they were retrieved, and can enter a suspension mode in case of tampering.

5.5.5 Guarding the secret key of the Certificate Authority

In this section we describe measures to guard the CA's secret key. Whether any or all of these measures are actually necessary depends on the PKI at hand.

Elementary measures

To enforce personnel to behave according to guidelines, organizational controls are needed. Examples are security clearance and background checks for new employees, auditing, strict manufacturing and software development procedures, separation of staff responsibilities, frequent change of assignments, and controlled initialization, personalization, and distribution of devices. A discussion of these and other controls is outside the scope of this book.

To raise the barrier to gaining access to the CA's secret key, it is best generated and stored within the confines of a tamper-resistant device and never revealed to the outside world (including the legitimate operators). This prevents CA personnel from being extorted or tempted to misuse the key themselves.[6] The device could even be programmed such as to restrain the rate of certificate issuing to a single person or location in a given time frame.

For CA devices, it is entirely cost-effective and feasible to achieve very strong tamper-resistance, because in contrast to smartcards there are no tight size and cost constraints. CA devices can be made tamper-evident, can be riveted at a secured location, and can maintain unmodifiable audit logs revealing the exact date and time of each task performed. Preferably, they meet at least security level 3 of FIPS 140-2 [275], a U.S. federal standard on the security of cryptographic modules and a de facto industry standard for commercial devices. Adherence to the Common Criteria for Information Technology Security Evaluations (a voluntary international process for developing test requirements, intended to replace ITSEC and other like standards) is recommendable as well.

In addition, it may be desirable to distribute the CA's secret key across multiple tamper-resistant devices, and to use secret-sharing techniques to enable designated subsets to perform the required cryptographic actions without leaking their respective shares.[7] Techniques for shared signature generation are well-known in the cryptographic literature, and can readily be adapted to the issuing protocols described in Chapter 4; see also Section 4.2.3. The secret key of each tamper-resistant device is best generated in a mutually random and verifiable manner between the device and its legitimate operators; this can be accomplished through standard cryptographic techniques.

To cope with cryptanalytic attacks on the CA's secret key, the system design should be based on strong underlying cryptographic primitives that have been publicly scrutinized by experts for decades (such as factoring or computing discrete log-

---

[6]Jakobsson and Yung [220], in the context of electronic cash, proposed to make each certificate fully traceable and clear each certificate showing online with a central party whenever the CA's secret key has leaked or coins have been extorted. This approach leads to severe system disruption, destroys privacy, does nothing to make extortion less attractive or to prevent it from reoccurring, and does not protect against insider abuse.

[7]CertCo and Spyrus, contracted in May 1997 by MasterCard and Visa to manufacture the CA system for SET [257], were the first to adopt this technique in practice.

arithms). The techniques in this book are believed to meet this criterion. Rather than using key sizes that are just a little beyond reach of currently known algorithms, key sizes should be as large as possible without causing a serious performance devaluation. In this respect, an elliptic curve implementation with keys that are not too short offers a distinct advantage. The CA should update to larger key sizes on a regular basis, and be prepared to do so in short term.

Stronger measures

When much is at stake, the CA should (in addition to the previous measures) enforce deposit of all showing protocol transcripts (not necessarily online), and continuously compare the number of certificates issued against that of certificates deposited. It appears that none of today's commercial certificate systems offer this provision, but this will likely change once the parallels between digital certificate systems and electronic cash systems are widely acknowledged.

This measure is not very effective in a large-scale PKI, because suspicion of forgery does not arise until the number of forged certificates approaches the number of issued certificates that have not yet been shown. The situation can be improved by taking into account the issued and disclosed attributes of each certificate. That is, for each attribute property disclosed the CA should maintain a separate category and compare a running count of each category with the number and combination of attributes issued. In an electronic coin system, for instance, the bank should monitor per coin denomination and per coin version.

In high-risk PKIs, the CA could encode random numbers from small sets into the attribute certificates it issues. Certificate holders are in full control over the secrecy of these attributes, but in case of strong suspicion of forgery, the CA can turn up the heat by requiring verifiers to demand certificate holders to reveal (part of) the encoded random numbers; the CA should then announce that it will no longer honor deposits from verifiers that do not abide by these rules. (Legislation should specify the conditions under which such a revision of deposit rules is legitimate.) In this way, the CA can dynamically shift between a positive list and a negative list approach; in the worst case, certificate holders are required to disclose a built-in identifier each time. (In this fashion, our techniques cover the entire range between privacy-protecting certificates and identity certificates.)

In a similar manner, the CA can dynamically set conditions for which types of certificates may be accepted off-line and which require its on-line approval.

Even stronger measures

In the presence of an attacker with "infinite" computing power, these measures are insufficient. A quantum computer, for instance, would be able to compute discrete logarithms and factorize in about the same time as it takes to exponentiate large numbers; see Shor [350]. Since forgery by an attacker with unlimited computing power can never be prevented, the primary defense line is to contain the damages.

The ultimate containment measure, if all else fails, is system suspension. The CA should make sure either that its certificate issuance is no longer accepted or that it can recognize and reject forged certificates during online certificate validation. The CA can still accept online executions of the certificate showing protocol by requiring certificate holders to disclose the identifiers that have been encoded into their certificates.

In addition, depending on the nature of the PKI, it may be necessary that all authentic outstanding digital certificates can be securely redeemed, to prevent a meltdown scenario. This fall-back mechanism must be secure even in the presence of an attacker with unlimited computing power. Preferably the fall-back mechanism can be implemented by means of a protocol that does not require certificate holders to show up in person at the CA. To this end, the software-only return protocol that will be described in Section 6.5.2 can be used.

5.6　Bibliographic notes

The techniques in Section 5.1.1 originate from Brands [54]. For an application, see Brands [46, 48]; here, the issuing protocol serves to issue electronic coins that encode an attribute representing the coin denomination (and possibly also an expiry date and other data that must always be disclosed to payees) and an identifier attribute that can be computed if and only if the coin is double-spent (using the static one-show blinding technique).

The discussion of the delegation strategy in Section 5.1.2 is based on Brands [53]. The parallel delegation strategy described for the case of the immunized DLREP-based scheme I in Section 4.4.2 was discovered by Schoenmakers [341, footnote 1]; the proposed measures to make this strategy ineffective are new, though. (In light of this Schoenmakers' remark on the insecurity of the second method of Brands [47] for exchange rates must be nuanced. In fact, in the issuing and showing protocol described by [47] the problem does not arise in the first place because parallel protocol executions by different account holders are excluded.)

The anonymous recertification and updating techniques in Section 5.2.1 were introduced by Brands [54], together with an application of the updating technique to anonymous accounts in the off-line electronic cash system of Brands [46, 48]. Subsequently, Brickell, Gemmell, and Kravitz [62, 240] applied the anonymous updating technique for the purpose of online change-making in the off-line electronic cash system of Brands [48].

The techniques described in Section 5.2.2 are all based on Brands [54]. The application to credential systems predates a credential system proposed by Chen [113], which has many drawbacks over our proposal: Chen's system offers only computational unlinkability, does not handle attribute certificates and selective disclosure, does not offer traceability of fraud with limited-show credentials, does not provide for smartcard extensions (whereas we can apply the techniques that will be developed in the next chapter), and uses an issuing protocol that is inferior to that described in Section 4.5.2.

The techniques in Section 5.3 appear here for the first time.

The static and dynamic limited-show certification techniques in Section 5.4 are based on Brands [45]. Some details have been filled in, and the formal security statements and their proofs are new.

Most of the security improvements in Section 5.5 originate from Brands [54]. The idea of discouraging lending of certified key pairs by encoding a special secret that the certificate holder wants to remain confidential (see Section 5.5.2) was inspired by the following remark by Garfinkel [180] about identity certificates: "While a few dozen guys might get together and share a single username and password for a cybersex site, there is no way that any of these clowns will let the others share his digital ID's secret key, which will also unlock his bank account and credit cards." The same observation has been used by Dwork, Lotspiech, and Naor [142], by Goldreich, Pfitzmann, and Rivest [192], by Sander and Ta-Shma [333] (to discourage lending in the electronic cash system of Brands [46, 48]), and by Lysyanskaya, Rivest, Sahai, and Wolf [253][8] in the context of digital pseudonyms. However, none of these publications consider the remote lending problem that we will address in Section 6.5.3.

The non-repudiation technique in Section 5.5.3 originates from Brands [46, 48], where it was applied in the context of off-line electronic cash.

---

[8]The techniques in this book offer a much better solution; the advantages are the same as the advantages over the credential system of Chen [113].

Chapter 6

Smartcard Integration

In this chapter we show how to implement our certificate issuing and showing protocol techniques in smartcards. We realize all the smartcard benefits listed in Section 1.1.6, without adding complexity and without downgrading security or privacy. We also show how to tune our protocols in the smartcard-enhanced setting to accommodate any degree of privacy desired.

6.1 Shortcomings of the smartcard-only paradigm

As we have seen in Section 1.1.6, smartcard-based implementations of PKI mechanisms offer numerous advantages over software-only implementations. Many of the benefits do not exist, though, when certificates are implemented entirely in smartcards. In this section we describe the shortcomings of smartcard-only implementations.

6.1.1 Privacy dangers

In a brochure [358], the Smart Card Forum states: "Smart card technology, if properly designed and implemented, can enhance both the fact and the perception of the individual's ability to exercise a much greater degree of control over personal information than is the case with any comparable delivery system." While it is true that smartcards enhance the perception of privacy, perception and fact are two very different things:

- The smartcard systems currently in use do nothing to prevent organizations from linking and tracing all communications and transactions by the same cardholder. For security reasons, they operate by transmitting in each transaction a unique card identifier that can be linked to central database entries that hold all kinds of identifiable personal data.

- A smartcard, or any other tamper-resistant device for that matter, operates as a black box to anyone but its manufacturer; its inner workings cannot be scrutinized or modified by its holder. (Most outsiders are not capable of breaking into smartcards to determine their internal behavior, and detected attempts to break in may result in criminal charges.) Smartcards can be programmed to operate as Trojan horses, offering convenience to their holders while at the same time covertly sending out their personal data.

The idea that government agencies may cause organizations to build in backdoors into devices is not far-fetched, as history reveals:

- In the early eighties the U.S. Justice Department misappropriated PROMIS, a software program developed by Inslaw Inc. that facilitated the integration of all sorts of databases. The U.S. intelligence community incorporated a backdoor and sold the modified version to intelligence organizations and banks in over 80 foreign countries; see Fricker [175], Kimery [231], Kunkin [243], Leon [248], and the Washington Weekly [372].

- In the mid eighties, the NSA worked together with Systematics, a major supplier of software for back office clearing and wire transfers, to introduce backdoors in much of the banking software supplied to U.S. financial institutions; see Grabbe [197] and Russell [332].

- In 1995, Der Spiegel and The Baltimore Sun reported that the NSA since 1957 had a secret deal with the Swiss cryptography company Crypto AG, under which Crypto AG built backdoor access into its encryption products; see Bamford [19, Chapter 8], Global Network Navigator [188], Strehle [364], the Baltimore Sun [371], and Madsen [254].

- In 1996, Walsh, a former deputy of the Australian Security Intelligence Organisation (ASIO, the Australian equivalent of the NSA), conducted an influential study [386] about Australian cryptography policy. In the uncensored version of the report, Walsh recommended: "Authority should be created for the AFP, the NCA and ASIO to alter proprietary software so that it performs additional functions to those specified by the manufacturer. [...] The software (or more rarely the hardware) may relate to communication, data storage, encoding, encryption or publishing devices. [...] some modifications may [...] create an intelligent memory, a permanent set of commands not specified in the program written by the manufacturer or a remote switching device with a capacity to issue commands at request. [...] In the event of an equipment or software malfunction or failure to perform to full specification, an investigation of a complaint could lead to discovery of the modification. The issue of liability of the Commonwealth may then potentially arise."

Covert data exchange between a tamper-resistant device and the outside world can take place through a number of channels. Two obvious channels are the following:

- The device can covertly send out or receive data by exploiting the van Eck effect or simply by sending out or receiving radio signals. We call this the *physical broadcast channel*. It is a particular problem in case of contactless smartcards, which can communicate over much larger distances than commonly believed. For instance, On Track Innovation Ltd. markets a contactless smartcard that it claims can communicate with a reader over a distance of up to 30 meters; the card can be remotely "revised, expanded and changed, and new applications can be added, without having to replace the card itself."

- Another channel becomes available when the device is engaged in a protocol execution with another device. Along with the data specified by the protocol, the device can leak out data. Alternatively, data can be leaked by changing the format of the messages as specified by the protocol; stop bits can be flipped, message fields set to values outside of specified ranges, and so on. We call this the *piggyback channel*.

The following channels are more surreptitious:

- In case a device engages in an interactive protocol, one or more bits of information can be leaked by halting during the protocol execution. For instance, by deciding whether or not to respond to a challenge before a time-out the device can leak one bit. More generally, in a protocol with t rounds, one of $t + 1$ preestablished messages can be leaked. This is called the *halting channel* (also known as the *stopping channel*).

- In a similar manner, a device can leak out bits of information by timing the delay before transmitting a message; this is called the *timing channel*. In contrast to the halting channel, this requires the device to have access to a timer. (This can be as simple as resetting a counter value in a chip register when a message is received, and sending out a response message when the counter reaches zero.) If messages are transmitted over a reliable channel with known performance characteristics, many bits can be leaked without noticeable delays.

- A related channel is the *computation error channel*. Here, a device deliberately causes one of its response messages to be incorrect. The fact whether or not a response is correct can be used to leak one bit of data, while an incorrect response can leak as many bits as its binary size.

Even more surreptitious are *subliminal channels*, first studied by Simmons [354, 355] in the setting of two prisoners who want to hatch an escape plan but can only communicate via a warden. Here, the data transmitted complies with all the range limitations, format specifications, and verification relations specified by the protocol, but the manner in which the data is formed does not. In particular, data is leaked in such a manner that not even an interposed observer can distinguish a legitimate protocol execution from one in which bits are leaked. Following Chaum [97], we distinguish two subliminal channels:

- Any data that is subliminally leaked by a device is called *outflow*. The data can be leaked by encoding covert message bits in any data that may be chosen by the device. If the device encrypts its covert messages under a random key known only to the receiving device, an observer with unlimited computing power will not be able to tell the difference with a truly random number.

- Any data that is subliminally leaked to a device is called *inflow*. In the showing protocols in Chapter 3, the verifier can encode a covert message into the part of its challenge message that serves to protect against replay, possibly encrypted under a mutually known key. Any other data that is hashed along and under the control of the verifier can also be misused to cause inflow.

Certificate holders will in general be more concerned about outflow than inflow. Outflow can reveal their device identifier, access control code, communication and transaction history, attributes, data from other applications running on the same device, and so on. The device does not need to know with whom it is communicating; it can simply leak out the data with each protocol execution, possibly encrypted under a key of the intended recipient. Outflow gives verifiers and other parties the power to discriminate against certificate holders and to follow certificate holders around in real time.

Outflow is particularly powerful when triggered by inflow. For example, a receiving device could transmit its device identifier, so that the smartcard can decide whether or not to leak data. New rule specifications can be uploaded dynamically by means of inflow, and the certificate holder's device can be queried in an arbitrary manner.

When outflow is prevented, inflow is less of a problem, but even then it poses dangers:

- Inflow messages can cause the smartcard to enter a state of suspension or to default in other ways. For example, an inflow message could say "If the device identifier is #134522, then abort." Errors can be made to occur that appear random to the device holder.

- In cases where the device is expected to send out at least one message, it can always respond to inflow queries by means of the halting channel.

- When the smartcard is returned to its issuer, either to be replaced or for another reason, the card issuer can read out all the inflow collected by the card during the time it was in the hands of its holder. (The card issuer may for instance make the card dump its memory contents by entering a special access code.) In this manner, the card issuer may be able to retroactively trace all the communications and transactions of the individual.

Inflow is most powerful when receiving devices are tamper-resistant as well.

The trend to store multiple applications on a single smartcard increases the scope for privacy invasion. It is impossible for anyone but the card issuing organizations to verify that different pieces of personal data are used only by the application for which they were collected.

The disparity between perception and fact makes the smartcard-only model extremely dangerous, especially since the interests of card issuers are not aligned with those of individuals. Even if the issuer and the manufacturer(s) of the smartcards could be trusted, implementing our issuing and showing protocol techniques entirely in tamper-resistant smartcards would not preserve privacy. Namely, most of today's smartcards can produce only pseudorandom numbers, on the basis of a random seed value that must be installed by (or under the supervision of) the issuer, to guarantee its uniqueness, randomness, and secrecy. Therefore, the issuer can compute all the pseudorandom numbers used by each device during its lifetime. Even if the issuer were to state that it does not know the seed values, or that its tamper-resistant devices produce random numbers by post-processing bits sampled from an internal "true" randomness source (such as a noise diode), this statement cannot be publicly verified. Also, the quality of a noise generator or other hardware methods for generating random numbers cannot be guaranteed.

Privacy concerns are one of the main reasons why smartcard implementations worldwide are stalling. As Schwartz [343] notes, "Ultimately, smart cards will not be able to succeed if consumers do not trust them. If the tracking ability of the cards weighs greater in the minds of consumers than convenience, the cards will not succeed in the market."

6.1.2   Other shortcomings

In addition to these serious privacy problems, there are other reasons to believe that the smartcard-only paradigm is inadequate and dangerous:

- Great care must be taken that the addition of complex circuitry and software does not introduce weaknesses in the tamper-resistance characteristics of the hardware. The cost of developing and incorporating new circuitry and software is much greater in the case of smartcards than in environments where tamper-resistance is not a concern. The ability to protect smartcards hinges on having enough capability and space for a software solution.

- With smartcard components already cramming for space, adding circuitry adversely affects smartcard reliability. A "dead" card at the very least inconveniences and frustrates its holder, and in many applications the consequences can be quite dramatic. If multiple applications are stored on the same card, its holder may all of a sudden be locked out of a number of services.

- Because of size constraints, there will always be serious limitations to the functionality that can be squeezed into a smartcard. The amount of smartcard memory needed to keep track of a detailed log of all uses of a certificate (for the convenience of its holder) is substantial. The display and keyboard sizes of a so-called "super smartcard" are adequate only for communication of the most rudimentary data.

- The smartcard must be relied on to protect the security interests of its holder. Since standard smartcards do not have their own display and keyboard, user identification data must be entered on a terminal communicating with the card, and this terminal must be trusted not to capture the user's identification data. Likewise, any results that the card wants to communicate to its holder must be displayed on the terminal. The result is that a variety of *fake-terminal attacks* become possible. Even with a super smartcard there is no way for cardholders to verify that the data entered into and displayed by their card is the same as that processed and output by the card.

- If the secret keys of certificate holders are generated inside a smartcard, there is no way to verify that they are generated in such a manner that others cannot guess them. In particular, as we have seen in the previous section, it is very hard to guarantee that the CA cannot reconstruct all the secret keys. This makes the legal status of digital signatures highly doubtful.

- Card issuers for security reasons will need to migrate to a new tamper-resistant chip design every couple of years. During the renewal period, the individual is unable to use his or her certified key pairs, and is inconvenienced by the loss of the functionality stored on the card.

In sum, smartcards are far from the most logical place to install additional circuitry and software intended to expand functionality for the card holder.

In spite of the pitfalls, the security advantages of smartcards are so great that smartcards should not be abandoned. We now examine how to overcome the shortcomings of the smartcard-only model and realize all the benefits described in Section 1.1.6.

6.2   Combining smartcards and software-only devices

A smartcard is not a stand-alone computing device; by its very nature, it can operate only in combination with another device. Indeed, most smartcards do not have their own power source. In many communication and transaction settings, smartcards are naturally used in conjunction with user-controlled software-only computing devices. For example, to use a smartcard over the Internet, it will have to be connected to a desktop computer, notebook, handheld, or otherwise.

The integration of smartcards and software-only computing devices (such as PCs, notebooks, and handhelds) is already well underway. Standardization efforts by major industry consortiums include the PC/SC Workgroup [297] and the OpenCard Framework[293]. Smartcard readers for PCs come in many forms: as a serial port add-on, embedded into the keyboard, as a device connected to the keyboard port, plugging into a floppy drive, combined with a modem, or as a PC Card. Prices are dropping rapidly owing to new design methods. In October 1998, Microsoft announced Smart Cards for Windows (subsequently renamed to Windows for Smart Cards), an 8-bit multi-application operating system for low-cost smart cards with 8 kilobytes of ROM, designed to extend the desktop computer environment into smartcard use.[1]

6.2.1 Benefits

Combining smartcards with user-controlled software-only computers offers many advantages:

- Fake terminal attacks can be prevented. If the user's computer has a keyboard and a display, the user can enter his or her password, PIN, or biometric using the keyboard, and can read out any transaction information from the computer's display; there is no need to rely on someone else's device for interacting with one's own smartcard.

- With a proper design, most of the computational and storage burden of the smartcard can be moved to the user-controlled computer, which can be much more powerful. In particular, high-strength public key cryptographic techniques may become entirely feasible using low-cost smartcards without cryptographic coprocessors. (See Section 6.5.1 for an example.)

- As a consequence of the fact that fake terminal attacks need not be prevented and sophisticated public-key cryptographic techniques are entirely feasible, verifiers do not need tamper-resistant terminals that represent the security interests of a CA.[2] This makes it much easier to become an acceptor of certificates.

- Any individual or software or hardware manufacturer can make or provide its own functional or other enhancements for the user's computer and sell them on the open market; this is an attractive feature for all parties alike.

---

[1] Users of Windows NT 5.0, for instance, can gain network access by presenting an X.509v3 certificate stored on a smartcard.

[2] In today's electronic purse systems and other off-line smartcard systems based on symmetric cryptography, verifier terminals must be strongly tamper-resistant to protect a master key that enables reconstruction of all smartcard secret keys.

- The user's computer can safeguard the secret keys of the user, and can make, store (for the purpose of non-repudiation), and verify any digital signatures. It can also keep its own chronological transaction log, and allow the user to review and print it. Special software could provide certificate management functions, such as help the user track his or her own transactions and categorize them. The transaction data could automatically flow into a software program, so that the user need never key in any data. For improved confidentiality, any sensitive data stored on the user's computer can be encrypted using a password-derived secret key.

- Schneier and Shostack [336] discuss the security ramifications of the fact that many different parties are involved with manufacturing and handling smart-cards. Among other measures, they argue that a prime candidate for improvement is to place the user interface under the control of the user. This fits perfectly with the model considered here.

Compact operating systems, open source code, independent code reviews, digital certification of source code and executables, open market availability, and anti-virus software all contribute to the trust that users can place in the software running on their own computer.

Ideally, desktop computers are used only as devices to communicate over the Internet and to run application software, and the user-controlled computer is in the form of a personal digital assistant (PDA) or similar handheld device. The handheld device enables its holder to port his or her certified key pairs, and is better suited as a medium to run trusted code. Access to the Internet by PDAs is on the rise. In 1998, Semico Research predicted that the sales of small portable computers will reach 7.5 billion dollars in the year 2003, and the Yankee Group estimated that by 2002 there will be over 21 million subscribers of mobile, wireless access to the Internet. Companies including Microsoft and 3COM have already announced smartcard enhancements for handheld devices.

By interposing their computer between the smartcard and the outside world, users can straightforwardly prevent certain data leakages:

- The user's computer can prevent the smartcard from covertly sending out data using physical broadcast. In cyberspace, there should rarely be a need to protect against the emission or reception of radio signals or electromagnetic radiation, especially when communications and transactions are untraceable. Communications and transactions in the physical world, however, require protection by means of physical shielding. General measures to protect against van Eck monitoring are expensive and mostly classified, but effective solutions are available for smartcards and other user devices. For instance, Cord Technologies, Inc. ships a low-cost electromagnetic shield slightly larger than a smartcard, which (according to its claims) closely approximates a Faraday Cage; by blocking low frequency magnetic fields and radiofrequency communication, it prevents an inserted chipcard from communicating with a card reader and from receiving the electrical power needed to operate. Handhelds and other software-only devices could have such protection built into their smartcard slots.

- Software on the user's computer can verify all the data passing to and from the smartcard. It can do range checks, check verification relations, and so on. Sniffer programs can intercept data sent to communication ports and compare this with specified data formats, allowing the user's computer to detect the existence of a piggyback channel.[3] More generally, software running on the user's computer can sift any data before passing it on, or simply halt a transmission in case data fields do not comply with the protocol specifications.

Thus, the integration of smartcards and other tamper-resistant user devices with user-controlled computers provides a natural environment to protect against data leakages that are efficiently detectable. From now on, we will assume that the smartcard-enhanced systems that we will develop prevent such data leakages.

6.2.2   How not to cope with subliminal channels

Simmons [354, 355] and Desmedt, Goutier, and Bengio [135, Section 5] showed how to use randomization to destroy subliminal channels, in a general setting. In 1988, Chaum [97] proposed very similar techniques to prevent inflow and outflow in the setting of consumer transactions, particularly electronic cash. Chaum's smartcard techniques [97, 103, 109] have numerous drawbacks, though, that make them unsuitable for practical use.

By far the most serious shortcoming relates to security: the systemic security breaks down completely when an attacker succeeds in compromising the tamper-resistance of a single smartcard. The problem is Chaum's reliance on blind signature protocols. Anyone who extracts the secret key of a smartcard can copy and lend out certificates at will. The blinding makes it hard or even impossible to detect the fraud, even if all the showing protocol executions involve the online participation of the CA. Even if fraud could be detected, its source cannot be traced and the fraud cannot be contained in any other way than by suspending the operation of the entire system: distribution of CRLs and online certificate validation do not help, because the attacker cannot be stopped from retrieving new certificates.

The security problem is worsened by the way in which Chaum encodes attribute information. Instead of having the CA encode attributes by cryptographic techniques (blind signatures cannot accomplish this), Chaum simply has the smartcard digitally sign statements about attributes the CA has stored in its memory. This flawed approach is central to all Chaum's work, as witnessed for instance by the following:

---

[3]In this manner, engineers in May 1995 discovered that Microsoft's Registration Wizard covertly sent the entire directory structure of the user's hard drive to Microsoft.

- Chaum [97, page 16] proposes that the tamper-resistant device "sign statements requested by C that T checks are true based on credential data it maintains." (Here, C denotes the user-controlled computer, and T the tamper-resistant device.)

- Chaum [88] states: "When the young Bob graduates with honors in medieval literature, for example, the university registrar gives his representative a digitally signed message asserting his academic credentials. When Bob applies to graduate school, [...] his representative asks its observer to sign a statement that he has a B.A. cum laude and that he qualifies for financial aid based on at least one of the university's criteria (but without revealing which ones). The observer, which has verified and stored each of Bob's credentials as they come in, simply checks its memory and signs the statement if it is true." (Chaum uses the terms "observer" and "representative" to refer to the smartcard and the user-controlled computer, respectively.)

- In the same manner, Chaum [88] deals with negative statements, such as felony convictions, license suspensions, or statements of pending bankruptcy: "Once the observer has registered a negative credential, an organization can find out about it simply by asking the observer (through the representative) to sign a message attesting to its presence or absence. Although a representative could muzzle the observer, it could not forge an assertion about the state of its credentials."

- In his smartcard-enhanced electronic cash systems [41, 103], Chaum gives each consumer smartcard the power to mint electronic money. Each smartcard stores electronic cash in the form of a counter value maintained in a chip register. For example, one hundred electronic dollars spendable up to cent granularity would be represented by a counter value of 10 000. To make a payment, a smartcard fills out the payable amount using a blinded electronic check and decreases its register value correspondingly.[4]

Consequently, the physical compromise of a single smartcard not only enables the attacker to anonymously flood the system with (copies of) untraceable certificates, but also to pretend to possess certificates for arbitrary attributes. Depending on the application, this can result in enormous damages. For instance, in a financial application the attacker may claim to have been issued digital bearer bonds worth huge sums of money, and may be able to impersonate people by assuming arbitrary identity attributes.

Chaum's blind trust in the tamper-proofness of smartcards is puzzling. Decades of experience have provided strong evidence that absolute tamper-proofness will

---

[4]Electronic purse systems based on symmetric cryptography also work this way, but the complete lack of privacy at least ensures that fraud can be contained.

likely never be fully realizable. Kocher [236], Anderson and Kuhn [12, 13], Boneh, DeMillo, and Lipton [38], and Biham and Shamir [29] discuss low-cost physical attacks that do not require direct physical access to the smartcard's internals. The most powerful non-invasive attack is Differential Power Analysis, due to Kocher, Jaffe, and Jun [237], in which the attacker gathers information correlated to secret keys by using statistical analysis and error correction techniques. Invasive physical attacks require days or weeks in a specialized laboratory and are much more costly to undertake, but they are also much harder to protect against. Microprobe workstations and other sophisticated equipment can be used to physically damage a smartcard chip in a controlled manner. See Kuhn [242, Section 1.2] and Kömmerling and Kuhn [239] for an overview of equipment to attack chips at the hardware level, and Biham and Shamir [30] for an invasive attack based on destroying a single wire of a carefully chosen memory cell using a laser beam. Even though manufacturers work hard to improve smartcard tamper-resistance, mass production smartcards will likely never be able to withstand invasive physical attacks for more than a couple of years following their release. New sophisticated apparatus will appear, and existing apparatus is being improved all the time. Organized crime can hire expertise comparable to that in national laboratories, and sophisticated tools are increasingly becoming accessible to hackers and undergraduate students at technical universities. Kömmerling and Kuhn [239] "see no really effective short-term protection against carefully planned invasive tampering involving focused ion-beam tools." They note that storage of secrets in battery-backed SRAM is highly effective to protect against invasive attacks (through zeroization), but this technology is not feasible for smartcards.

In a 1997 interview, Chaum [104] claimed: "On-line, software-only techniques sometimes become rather elaborate, whereas if you have a tamper-resistant device, you can do things in a relatively simple way." We now know, though, that the practice of relying solely on smartcard tamper-resistance is not acceptable. As Kocher, Jaffe, and Jun [237] point out with respect to Differential Power Analysis, the best way to deal with smartcard vulnerability is to design cryptographic systems under the assumption that secret key information will leak. In light of this, we will operate in this chapter under the assumption that smartcard tamper-resistance is a matter of economics. At the very least, we need the following security features:

- Each smartcard must have a unique independent secret key. (In practice, computational independence suffices, and so this principle is not violated by using diversified secret keys.)

- To guarantee that a smartcard design will be able to survive widespread physical compromise of smartcards, the design must provide for the ability to detect, trace and contain fraud even if all smartcards are compromised. That is, the smartcard-enhanced system should have all the security features of a secure software-only system. (This also facilitates a seamless migration path from software-only devices to a setting where certificate holders also hold smartcards, or vice versa.)

- Any sound smartcard system requires a strategy for migrating from one generation of smartcards to the next, to keep up with advances in smartcard tampering.

Chaum's smartcard techniques have yet another drawback: they cannot prevent the
smartcard from storing data that the CA can use retroactively to trace transactions,
once it gains access to the contents of the device. Any unique random number known
to both the smartcard and the verifier in the showing protocol execution can be used
to trace the transaction. Cramer and Pedersen [122] modified Chaum's protocols to
prevent the smartcard and the verifier from developing *common coin flips*, i.e., mutually known information that is statistically correlated, other than inflow and outflow.
A drawback of their protocol is that both the smartcard and the user's computer must
perform several real-time exponentiations that cannot be preprocessed, and the issuing protocol consists of 10 moves. More seriously, the modified protocol does
nothing to overcome the security problems of Chaum's techniques, and in fact de-
grades security even further. An anonymous extortioner in cyberspace can force an
individual to retrieve certificates for which the extortioner supplies the blinding factors, and can subsequently show these by requiring the victim to assist in performing
the showing protocol execution. The extortioner can blind any data from and to the
verifier before relaying it, and in this manner can remain untraceable at all times to
anyone including the victim.[5] When certificates represent money or other significant
value that verifiers can redeem from the CA, this *perfect crime* exposes certificate
holders to unacceptable risk.

In the remainder of this chapter we show how to overcome all these problems.

6.3   Secure smartcard integration

In this section we show how to overcome the security and efficiency shortcomings
described in the previous section. The goal is to ensure that the user-controlled computer cannot show a certificate without the assistance of the smartcard. This will lay
the foundation for the privacy techniques in Section 6.4.

6.3.1   Technique based on the DLREP function

We replace $\mathcal{P}$ in the showing protocols of Chapter 3 by $< \mathcal{S}, \mathcal{U} >$. $\mathcal{S}$ denotes the
smartcard and $\mathcal{U}$ the user's software-only computer. $\mathcal{S}$ and $\mathcal{U}$ must be configured
in such a manner that any protocol data to and from $\mathcal{S}$ flows through $\mathcal{U}$. The system

---

[5]A simpler form of this extortion strategy applies in the software-only setting, where the extortioner
needs the "assistance" of the victim only in the issuing protocol. In the special case of electronic cash, this
is known as "payee untraceability."

parameters and the public key h are generated as described in Section 3.2, and atomic propositions are demonstrated as depicted in Figures 3.1 and 3.5.

According to Proposition 3.6.1(b), the demonstration of a satisfiable Boolean formula is a proof of knowledge of a DL-representation of h with respect to $(g_1, \ldots, g_l)$. From this we immediately obtain the following result.

Proposition 6.3.1. *If* $(x_1, \ldots, x_l)$ *is shared between* $\mathcal{S}$ *and* $\mathcal{U}$ *in such a manner that* $\widehat{\mathcal{U}}$ *cannot compute with non-negligible success probability a DL-representation of* $h := \prod_{i=1}^{l} g_i^{x_i}$ *with respect to* $(g_1, \ldots, g_l)$, *then* $\mathcal{U}$ *cannot demonstrate any Boolean formula without the assistance of* $\mathcal{S}$.

Note that $\mathcal{S}$'s assistance is required even to demonstrate formulae in which its share of the DL-representation does not appear, and in particular to demonstrate the formula **TRUE**.

Any manner of sharing the DL-representation of h will do; all that matters is that $\widehat{\mathcal{U}}$ cannot compute the entire representation by itself. Not all sharing methods are equally suitable, though. Non-linear sharing makes it difficult for $\mathcal{S}$ to assist $\mathcal{U}$ in the showing protocol in any other manner than by providing to $\mathcal{U}$ its share of the representation. The resulting showing protocol would be insecure, since $\mathcal{U}$ can reuse h in subsequent formula demonstrations without needing $\mathcal{S}$'s assistance. The following construction shows how $(x_1, \ldots, x_l)$ may be shared securely and efficiently.

Proposition 6.3.2. *Suppose that* x_1 *is generated at random from* $\mathbb{Z}_q$, *and is known to* $\mathcal{S}$ *but not to* $\mathcal{U}$. *Regardless of the distribution of* $(x_2, \ldots, x_l)$, $< \mathcal{S}, \mathcal{U}>$ *can demonstrate to* $\mathcal{V}$ *any Boolean formula of the form (3.7) in which* x_1 *does not appear, in such a manner that:*

- *The only task that* $\mathcal{S}$ *performs in each formula demonstration is one execution of the Schnorr proof of knowledge, in which it proves knowledge of* x_1 *to* $\mathcal{U}$.

- *The view of* $\widetilde{\mathcal{V}}$ *when interacting with* $< \overline{\mathcal{S}}, \overline{\mathcal{U}}>$ *is the same as it would be when interacting with* $\overline{\mathcal{P}}$.

Proof. Let $h = h_{\mathcal{S}} h_{\mathcal{U}}$, where $h_{\mathcal{S}} = g_1^{x_1}$ and $h_{\mathcal{U}} = \prod_{i=2}^{l} g_i^{x_i}$. To show how the demonstration of a formula takes place, we consider four cases:

Case 1. F is an atomic formula consisting of zero or more "AND" connectives and no other connectives, in the form (3.3). We assume the permutation $\pi(\cdot)$ of $\{1, \ldots, l\}$ has 1 as a fixed point. If x_1 does not appear in the formula to be demonstrated by $< \mathcal{S}, \mathcal{U}>$, then the 1-st column in the matrix on the left-hand side of the system (3.2) contains all zeros.

To compute a in Step 1 of the showing protocol, $\mathcal{S}$ generates a random number $w_1 \in \mathbb{Z}_q$, computes $a_{\mathcal{S}} := g_1^{w_1}$, and sends $a_{\mathcal{S}}$ to $\mathcal{U}$. $\mathcal{U}$ generates $l - t - 1$

random numbers, $w_2, \ldots, w_{l-t} \in \mathbb{Z}_q$, and computes

$$a := a_{\mathcal{S}} \prod_{i=2}^{l-t} g_{\pi(i)}^{w_i} \prod_{i=1}^{t} g_{\pi(l-t+i)}^{-\sum_{j=2}^{l-t} \alpha_{ij} w_j} .$$

To compute the $l - t$ responses in Step 2, $\mathcal{U}$ sends $\mathcal{V}$'s challenge c to $\mathcal{S}$. $\mathcal{S}$ computes $r_{\mathcal{S}} := c x_1 + w_1 \bmod q$, and sends $r_{\mathcal{S}}$ to $\mathcal{U}$. $\mathcal{U}$ sets $r_1 := r_{\mathcal{S}}$, and computes the other $l - t - 1$ responses as specified in Step 2 of the protocol $(\mathcal{P}, \mathcal{V})$.

Clearly, the task performed by $\mathcal{S}$ is exactly an execution of the Schnorr proof of knowledge, in which it proves knowledge of $\log_{g_1} h_{\mathcal{S}}$ to $\mathcal{U}$, and the view of $\widetilde{\mathcal{V}}$ is the same as it would be in $(\overline{\mathcal{P}}, \widetilde{\mathcal{V}})$.

Case 2. F is an atomic formula consisting of zero or more "AND" connectives, one "NOT" connective, and no other connectives, in the form (3.4). As in Case 1, with the permutation $\pi(\cdot)$ having 1 as a fixed point, if x_1 does not appear in the formula to be demonstrated then the 1-st column in the matrix on the left-hand side of the system (3.4) contains all zeros.

To compute a in Step 1 of the showing protocol, $\mathcal{S}$ generates a random number $w_1 \in \mathbb{Z}_q$, computes $a_{\mathcal{S}} := g_1^{w_1}$, and sends $a_{\mathcal{S}}$ to $\mathcal{U}$. $\mathcal{U}$ generates $l - t$ random numbers, $w_0, w_2, \ldots, w_{l-t} \in \mathbb{Z}_q$, and computes

$$a := a_{\mathcal{S}}^{\delta} \, h^{-w_0} \prod_{i=2}^{l-t} g_{\pi(i)}^{w_i} \prod_{i=1}^{t} g_{\pi(l-t+i)}^{b_i w_0 - \sum_{j=2}^{l-t} \alpha_{ij} w_j} .$$

To compute the $l - t + 1$ responses in Step 2, $\mathcal{U}$ sends $\mathcal{V}$'s challenge c to $\mathcal{S}$. $\mathcal{S}$ computes $r_{\mathcal{S}} := c x_1 + w_1 \bmod q$, and sends $r_{\mathcal{S}}$ to $\mathcal{U}$. $\mathcal{U}$ computes $r_1 := r_{\mathcal{S}} \delta \bmod q$, and computes the other $l - t$ responses as specified in Step 2 of the protocol $(\mathcal{P}, \mathcal{V})$.

Again, the two claimed properties can easily be seen to hold.

Case 3. F is a formula connecting atomic subformulae by zero or more "OR" connectives and no other connectives, in the form (3.6). Recall from Section 3.5 that $\mathcal{P}$ simulates all but one of the subformula demonstrations, even if multiple subformulae hold true. The advantage of this is now clear: $\mathcal{U}$ needs the assistance of $\mathcal{S}$ only for the one subformulae demonstration that cannot be simulated, using the method of either Case 1 or Case 2.

Case 4. F is an arbitrary Boolean formula, in the form (3.7). Recall from Section 3.6 that $\mathcal{V}$'s challenge is the same for all j subformula demonstrations. The advantage of this is now clear: each of the j subformulae that must be demonstrated contains (at least) 1 subsubformula that holds true, yet $\mathcal{S}$ need only perform one execution of the Schnorr proof of knowledge to provide its assistance. Specifically, $\mathcal{U}$ can use $\mathcal{S}$'s response $r_\mathcal{S}$ for each of the j subformula demonstrations, using the method of either Case 1 or Case 2.

This completes the proof. $\qquad\qquad\qquad\qquad\qquad\qquad\qquad\qquad\qquad\qquad$ □

This construction works regardless of whether $\mathcal{V}$ is to receive a signed proof, a 4-move zero-knowledge proof, or otherwise.

Note that $\mathcal{U}$ can precompute all the required exponentiations, except for the operation of raising $a_\mathcal{S}$ to the power δ in Case 2 of the proof. In case $\mathcal{U}$ does not know the formula to be demonstrated until it communicates with $\mathcal{V}$, it does not help for $\mathcal{S}$ to provide its initial witness well before the start of the showing protocol execution. In many practical applications δ will be small, and the burden of raising $a_\mathcal{S}$ to the power δ is insignificant. In PKIs where speed is of utmost importance, $\mathcal{U}$ may prefer to avoid the exponentiation of $a_\mathcal{S}$ altogether by simply multiplying c by δ before passing it on to $\mathcal{S}$.[6] A drawback of the latter approach is that $\mathcal{V}$ cannot encode information into its challenge that is intended for $\mathcal{S}$, because $\mathcal{U}$ modifies it before passing it on. In Section 6.4 we will see why this may be undesirable.

The construction in Proposition 6.3.2 ensures not only that $\mathcal{S}$ need not provide its assistance for each (sub)subformula, but also lays the foundation for $\mathcal{U}$'s privacy. Note, for example, that $\mathcal{S}$ does not need to know h, l, the attributes $(x_2, \ldots, x_l)$, or the formula to be demonstrated. Section 6.4 will elaborate on this observation.

Security follows from the following result.

Proposition 6.3.3. *If the Schnorr proof of knowledge is witness-hiding, then $\widehat{\mathcal{U}}$ in the construction in Proposition 6.3.2 needs the assistance of $\overline{\mathcal{S}}$ in the t-th formula demonstration with respect to h, for any integer t.*

In other words, the only way to get around $\mathcal{S}$ is to physically break its tamper-resistance and extract x_1. The formal proof of this security result proceeds by generating $g_2, \ldots, g_l$ all as random powers of g_1. From a successful formula demonstration in which $\widehat{\mathcal{U}}$ does not use the assistance of $\overline{\mathcal{S}}$, a DL-representation of h with respect to $(g_1, \ldots, g_l)$ can be extracted. With overwhelming success probability this can be converted into $\overline{\mathcal{S}}$'s secret key x_1, resulting in a contradiction. (For signed proofs, we need to assume the random oracle model.)

In a practical implementation one might care to ensure that $g_1 \neq 1$, but from a theoretical viewpoint there is no need to exclude this possibility.

In case $\mathcal{U}$ is allowed to use the same h in arbitrarily many showing protocol executions, a construction for $\mathcal{S}$ that offers weaker security than Proposition 6.3.3

---

[6]Extra operations may be needed to make this work. Consider for example a formula connecting two atomic subformulae, both with a "NOT" connective, by an "AND" connective. With δ_1 denoting the δ for the first subformula and δ_2 that for the second, $\mathcal{U}$ computes γ such that $c\delta_1 + \gamma = c\delta_2$ and adjusts for γ when computing a and its responses for the first subformula.

clearly will not do. The property that the assistance of $\overline{S}$ is needed after arbitrarily many protocol executions is desirable, however, even in case of public keys for which $\overline{S}$ refuses to further assist $\mathcal{U}$ once it has assisted in a predetermined number of showing protocol executions. Namely, it allows S to use the same x_1 as its contribution to arbitrarily many different public keys, rather than having to use a new random x_1 for each. (As we will see in Section 6.4.3, this approach also improves privacy.) S's share x_1 can be regarded as its secret key, and h_S as its "public" key.

An even stronger security result can be proved by letting S perform an execution of Okamoto's extension of the Schnorr proof of knowledge [288, page 36], or more efficiently its optimization described in Section 2.4.3.

Proposition 6.3.4. *Let $l \geq 2$, and suppose that x_1 is generated at random from $\mathbb{Z}_q$, that x_2 is the outcome of a random coin flip, and that (x_1, x_2) is known to S but not to $\mathcal{U}$. Regardless of the distribution of $(x_3, \ldots, x_l)$, $<S, \mathcal{U}>$ can demonstrate to $\mathcal{V}$ any Boolean formula of the form (3.7) in which x_1 and x_2 do not appear, in such a manner that:*

- *The only task that S performs in each formula demonstration is one execution of the three-move proof of knowledge described in Section 2.4.3, in which it proves knowledge to $\mathcal{U}$ of a DL-representation of $g_1^{x_1} g_2^{x_2}$ with respect to (g_1, g_2).*

- *The view of $\widetilde{\mathcal{V}}$ when interacting with $<\overline{S}, \overline{\mathcal{U}}>$ is the same as it would be when interacting with $\overline{\mathcal{P}}$.*

The construction is readily apparent when studying the construction in the proof of Proposition 6.3.2. Because S's proof of knowledge is provably witness-hiding, Proposition 6.3.3 can be proved under the weaker assumption that the DL function used to implement the commitment to $(x_1, \ldots, x_l)$ is one-way. In a practical implementation one might care to ensure that $g_1, g_2 \neq 1$, but from a theoretical viewpoint there is no need to exclude this possibility.

In addition, it is possible to prove the following result.

Proposition 6.3.5. *If the DL function is one-way, and $\overline{S}$ performs no more than polylogarithmically many executions of its protocol with $\mathcal{U}$, then signed proofs of formula demonstrations with respect to h are unforgeable by $\widehat{\mathcal{U}}$ in the random oracle model, regardless of the distribution of $(x_3, \ldots, x_l)$.*

The same should be true for the construction of Proposition 6.3.2, but it is unclear how to prove this.

It is straightforward to combine our smartcard-enhanced showing protocols with any of the DLREP-based certificate issuing protocols described in Chapter 4. In case unlimited-show certificates are issued, S is not needed in the issuing protocol; the CA simply looks up (or reconstructs) the secret key of S, and encodes that into the certified key pair it issues. In the case of limited-show certificates, $\mathcal{U}$ in Step 2 of the issuing protocol must hash along its (master) initial witness (set) for the showing protocol, and so S must provide (each) a_S already at this stage. (Providing the initial witnesses in an early stage is desirable anyway, to enable U to precompute as many exponentiations as possible.) In addition, S must keep track of the number of times it has cooperated in demonstrating a formula with respect to a limited-show certificate, and refuse to cooperate more times than allowed. In practice, limiting the number of times a certificate can be shown is trivial: for each of its initial witnesses, S responds just once anyway.

Implementing our limited-show techniques in smartcards offers two security layers: showing a certificate more times than allowed is not possible without physically extracting the smartcard's secret key, and perpetrators (who manage to physically extract the secret keys from their smartcards and then commit fraud) can be traced. Thus, we get both the tamper-resistance protection and the software-only protection.

In the case of dynamic limited-show certificates (see Section 5.4.2), the correction factors can all be determined by U, as desired.

Any linear sharing method other than the methods in Propositions 6.3.2 and 6.3.4 can be used, with the obvious modifications. Different sharing methods may each have their own advantages, depending on other design aspects. For instance, when using DLREP-based scheme I or II, it may be preferable to let $(x_1, \ldots, x_{l-1})$ be known to U and let x_l be the sum of a secret key of S and the random blinding factor α_1 chosen by U in the issuing protocol; this enables the CA to encode $l - 1$ attributes into each certified key pair,[7] instead of only $l - 2$. Another advantage is that it is significantly easier to guarantee that a secret key of a certified key pair is generated secretly at random, and therefore that the device holder is the only one in possession of the secret key; it does not matter if another party can guess or determine the share of the secret key that is generated by one of the two devices, as long as the other device generates (part of) its share at random. Consequently, the legal status of digital signatures is easier to establish than in the software-only and smartcard-only paradigms.

In general, for any or all $i \in \{1, \ldots, l\}$, one can set $x_i = \alpha_i x_{iS} + \beta_i x_{iU} \bmod q$, for any $\alpha_i, \beta_i \in \mathbb{Z}_q$, where x_{iS} is S's share and x_{iU} that of U.

When combining our smartcard-enhanced showing protocols with a secret-key certificate issuing protocol, the delegation strategy is never an issue. The simple software-only measures described in Section 5.1.2, if necessary at all, suffice to ensure that $\widehat{U}$ cannot abuse delegation in order to circumvent the assistance of S in the showing protocol, even in those cases where delegation is not prevented but merely made harmless.

It is worth noting that $\overline{S}$ can provide its assistance in alternative manners that differ from a Schnorr proof of knowledge or the related proofs of knowledge described

---

[7]When a limited-show certificate is shown more times than allowed, this sharing method does not allow the CA to trace the perpetrator by computing the secret key of S. To achieve this property, one of $x_1, \ldots, x_{l-1}$ should be an identifier.

in Section 2.4.3. For instance, in the construction of Proposition 6.3.2 we may replace the verification relation of the Schnorr proof of knowledge, $g_1^{r_S} = h_S^c a_S$, by one that is closely related to that of the DSA signature scheme: $g_1^{r_S} = h_S^{\overline{a_S}} a_S^c$. S must then compute its response as $r_S := cw_1 + x_1 \overline{a_S} \bmod q$; it is easy to modify the actions of $\mathcal{U}$ correspondingly.

6.3.2   Technique based on the RSAREP function

For commitments based on the RSAREP function, the direct analogue of Proposition 6.3.1 applies. Specifically, if $(x_1, \ldots, x_{l+1})$ is shared between S and $\mathcal{U}$ in such a manner that $\widehat{\mathcal{U}}$ cannot compute with non-negligible success probability an RSA-representation of $h := \prod_{i=1}^{l} g_i^{x_i} x_{l+1}^v$ with respect to $(g_1, \ldots, g_l, v)$, then $\widehat{\mathcal{U}}$ cannot demonstrate any Boolean formula without the assistance of S. The technique of letting x_1 be a secret key of S and $g_1^{x_1}$ its public key is not recommended, though.[8] An efficient construction that achieves security for $\overline{S}$ is the following.

Proposition 6.3.6. *Suppose that x_{l+1} is generated at random from $\mathbb{Z}_n^*$, and is known to S but not to $\mathcal{U}$. Regardless of the distribution of $(x_1, \ldots, x_l)$, $<S, \mathcal{U}>$ can demonstrate to $\mathcal{V}$ any formula of the form (3.7), in such a manner that:*

- *The only task that S performs in each formula demonstration is one execution of the Guillou-Quisquater proof of knowledge, in which it proves knowledge of x_{l+1} to $\mathcal{U}$.*

- *The view of $\widetilde{\mathcal{V}}$ when interacting with $<\overline{S}, \overline{\mathcal{U}}>$ is the same as it would be when interacting with $\overline{\mathcal{P}}$.*

Proof. Let $h = h_S h_{\mathcal{U}}$, where $h_S = x_{l+1}^v$ and $h_{\mathcal{U}} = \prod_{i=1}^{l} g_i^{x_i}$. To show how the demonstration of a formula takes place, we consider four cases:

Case 1. F is an atomic formula consisting of zero or more "AND" connectives and no other connectives, in the form (3.3). To compute a in Step 1 of the showing protocol, S generates a random number $w_{l+1} \in \mathbb{Z}_n^*$, computes $a_S := w_{l+1}^v$, and sends a_S to $\mathcal{U}$. $\mathcal{U}$ generates $l - t$ random numbers, $w_1, \ldots, w_{l-t} \in \mathbb{Z}_v$, and computes

$$a := a_S \prod_{i=1}^{l-t} g_{\pi(i)}^{w_i} \prod_{i=1}^{t} g_{\pi(l-t+i)}^{-\sum_{j=1}^{l-t} \alpha_{ij} w_j}.$$

---

[8]The following proof of knowledge, proposed by Girault [185] (see also Poupard and Stern [310]), is conjectured to be witness-hiding: S sends an initial witness $g_1^{w_1}$ to $\mathcal{U}$, receives a challenge c, and sends the response $cx_1 + w_1$ (no modular reduction) to $\mathcal{U}$. Unfortunately, the response size in a practical implementation is much larger than $|v|$ bits.

To compute the $l - t + 1$ responses in Step 2, $\mathcal{U}$ sends $\mathcal{V}$'s challenge c to $\mathcal{S}$. $\mathcal{S}$ computes $r_{\mathcal{S}} := x_{l+1}^c w_{l+1}$, and sends $r_{\mathcal{S}}$ to $\mathcal{U}$. $\mathcal{U}$ sets

$$
r_{l+1} := r_{\mathcal{S}} \prod_{j=1}^{l-t} (g_{\pi(j)}) \prod_{i=1}^{t} g_{\pi(l-t+i)}^{-\alpha_{ij}})^{(cx_{\pi(j)}+w_j)\operatorname{div} v},
$$

and computes the other $l - t$ responses in the manner specified in Step 2 of the protocol $(\mathcal{P}, \mathcal{V})$.

The task performed by $\mathcal{S}$ is exactly an execution of the Guillou-Quisquater proof of knowledge, in which it proves knowledge of the v-th root of $h_{\mathcal{S}}$ to $\mathcal{U}$, and the view of $\widetilde{\mathcal{V}}$ is the same as it would be in $(\widetilde{\mathcal{P}}, \widetilde{\mathcal{V}})$.

Case 2. F is an atomic formula consisting of zero or more "AND" connectives, one "NOT" connective, and no other connectives, in the form (3.4). It is easy to see that $\mathcal{S}$ can provide its assistance in the same manner as in Case 1, and again the two claimed properties are readily seen to hold.

Case 3. As in Case 3 of the proof of Proposition 6.3.2.

Case 4. As in Case 4 of the proof of Proposition 6.3.2.

This completes the proof.   □

This construction works regardless of whether $\mathcal{V}$ is to receive a signed proof, a 4-move zero-knowledge proof, or otherwise.

Proposition 6.3.7. *If the Guillou-Quisquater proof of knowledge is witness-hiding, then $\widehat{\mathcal{U}}$ in the construction in Proposition 6.3.6 needs the assistance of $\overline{S}$ in the t-th formula demonstration with respect to h, for any integer t.*

Assuming that interactively issued Guillou-Quisquater signatures are unforgeable, one can also prove that if $\mathcal{S}$ follows the protocol, then signed proofs of formula demonstrations with respect to h are unforgeable by $\widehat{\mathcal{U}}$, regardless of the distribution of $(x_1, \ldots, x_l)$.

As with the DLREP-based variants, stronger provability can be achieved by letting $\mathcal{S}$ perform an execution of Okamoto's extension of the Guillou-Quisquater proof of knowledge [288, page 39], or more efficiently its optimization described in Section 2.4.4.

Proposition 6.3.8. *Let $l \geq 1$, and suppose that x_1 is the outcome of a random coin flip, that x_{l+1} is generated at random from $\mathbb{Z}_n^*$, and that (x_1, x_{l+1}) is known to $\mathcal{S}$ but not to $\mathcal{U}$. Regardless of the distribution of $(x_2, \ldots, x_l)$, $<\mathcal{S}, \mathcal{U}>$ can demonstrate to $\mathcal{V}$ any Boolean formula of the form (3.7) in which x_1 does not appear, in such a manner that:*

- *The only task that $\mathcal{S}$ performs in each formula demonstration is one execution of the three-move proof of knowledge described in Section 2.4.4, in which it proves knowledge to $\mathcal{U}$ of an RSA-representation of $g_1^{x_1} x_{l+1}^{v}$ with respect to (g_1, v).*

- *The view of $\tilde{\mathcal{V}}$ when interacting with $<\overline{\mathcal{S}}, \widehat{\mathcal{U}}>$ is the same as it would be when interacting with $\overline{\mathcal{P}}$.*

This time, Proposition 6.3.7 can be proved under the weaker assumption that the RSA function used to implement the commitment is one-way. In addition, if the RSA function is one-way and $\overline{\mathcal{S}}$ performs no more than polylogarithmically many executions of the protocol with $\mathcal{U}$, signed proofs of formula demonstrations with respect to h are unforgeable by $\widehat{\mathcal{U}}$ in the random oracle model, regardless of the distribution of $(x_2, \ldots, x_l)$.

Other ways to share $(x_1, \ldots, x_{l+1})$ can be used as well. In general, for any or all $i \in \{1, \ldots, l\}$, one can use the linear sharing $x_i = \alpha_i x_{i\mathcal{S}} + \beta_i x_{i\mathcal{S}} \bmod v$ and the multiplicative sharing $x_{l+1} = x_{\mathcal{S}}^{\alpha_{l+1}} x_{\mathcal{U}}^{\beta_{l+1}}$, for any α_i, β_i. A sharing method that fits well when combining the showing protocol with one of the RSA-based issuing protocols described in Chapter 4 is to let $(x_1, \ldots, x_l)$ be the attributes of $\mathcal{U}$, and let x_{l+1} be the product of the secret key of $\mathcal{S}$ and the blinding factor α_1 used by $\mathcal{U}$ in the certificate issuing protocol (x_1 may be either an identifier of $\mathcal{U}$ or a part of the secret key of $\mathcal{S}$). Indeed, if the construction of Proposition 6.3.6 is used in combination with an RSAREP-based issuing protocol, $\mathcal{U}$ for reason of privacy may not let $\mathcal{S}$ determine the blinding factor α_1.

The same considerations as described in Section 6.3.1 apply when combining the showing protocol techniques with one of the issuing protocols in Chapter 3. In particular, the delegation strategy is never an issue.

6.4 Privacy protection

In Section 6.1.1 we have seen that there are many ways in the smartcard-enhanced setting to get around the privacy protections of the showing protocol. The techniques that we will develop in this section build on top of those developed in the previous section and enable $\overline{\mathcal{U}}$ to prevent inflow, outflow, and even the development of common coin flips. They also ensure that the leakage through the halting, timing, and computation error channels is at most 1 bit in total; this is the best result achievable. Furthermore, the smartcard cannot learn any information about the formulae demonstrated, and cannot determine the number of encoded attributes or whether or not certificates are limited-show; all it can learn is (an upper bound on) the number of times its holder has engaged in a showing protocol execution.

All the privacy guarantees hold in the strongest possible sense, namely in the presence of conspiring $\mathcal{S}$, CA, and $\mathcal{V}$ that have unlimited computing resources and may establish secret information in an preparatory phase (e.g., a strategy for deviating from the protocol and keys for authenticating and encrypting covert messages). We also show how to tune our smartcard techniques to design systems for which one or more of the privacy protections cannot be achieved, while guaranteeing that $\mathcal{U}$ can verify and control any information exchanged by $\mathcal{S}$ and $\mathcal{V}$.

The security accomplishments of the previous section are fully preserved by the new techniques.

6.4.1   Inflow prevention

Inflow cannot occur in any of the certificate issuing protocols, since the smartcard does not receive any messages from the CA. In the smartcard-enhanced showing protocols in Section 6.3, the only possibility for inflow is $\mathcal{V}$'s challenge, c. If the demonstration is in the form of a zero-knowledge proof, the entire s-bit data channel (as well as part of $\mathcal{V}$'s commitment) can be used for inflow. Even in signed proofs, there may be ample opportunity for $\mathcal{V}$ to cause inflow. In this case, $\mathcal{V}$'s challenge is the result of the application of a sufficiently strong one-way hash function to certain data that may be at least somewhat under the control of $\mathcal{V}$, such as a nonce (e.g., a random number or an estimate of the time and date) or a random number γ as in Section 5.3. Any such data fields can be misused by $\mathcal{V}$ to encode a covert message, possibly encrypted under a key known to $\mathcal{S}$.

Proposition 6.4.1. *In the construction of Proposition 6.3.2, $\mathcal{U}$ can prevent inflow at the cost of essentially one additional exponentiation, which can be precomputed. $\mathcal{S}$ must now accept any challenge in $\mathbb{Z}_q$, but the tasks of $\mathcal{S}$ and $\mathcal{V}$ remain unchanged in all other respects.*

Proof. As in the proof of Proposition 6.3.2, we distinguish four cases:

Case 1. F is an atomic formula consisting of zero or more "AND" connectives and no other connectives, in the form (3.3). $\mathcal{U}$ proceeds as in Case 1 of the proof of Proposition 6.3.2, but when computing a from $a_\mathcal{S}$ it also multiplies in a factor $h_\mathcal{S}^\beta$, for a randomly chosen $\beta \in \mathbb{Z}_q$. Furthermore, instead of sending $\mathcal{V}$'s challenge c to $\mathcal{S}$, $\mathcal{U}$ sets $c_\mathcal{S} := c + \beta \bmod q$ and sends $c_\mathcal{S}$ to $\mathcal{S}$. No further changes are needed.

Case 2. F is an atomic formula consisting of zero or more "AND" connectives, one "NOT" connective, and no other connectives, in the form (3.4). $\mathcal{U}$ proceeds as in Case 2 of the proof of Proposition 6.3.2, but when computing a from $a_\mathcal{S}$ it also multiplies in a factor $h_\mathcal{S}^{\beta\delta}$, for a randomly chosen $\beta \in \mathbb{Z}_q$. Furthermore, instead of sending $\mathcal{V}$'s challenge c to $\mathcal{S}$, $\mathcal{U}$ sets $c_\mathcal{S} := c + \beta \bmod q$ and sends $c_\mathcal{S}$ to $\mathcal{S}$. No further changes are needed.

Case 3. F is a formula connecting atomic subformulae by zero or more "OR" connectives and no other connectives, in the form (3.6). $\mathcal{U}$ proceeds as in Case 3 of the proof of Proposition 6.3.2, applying the modification of either Case 1 or Case 2.

Case 4. F is an arbitrary Boolean formula, in the form (3.7). $\mathcal{U}$ proceeds as in Case 4 of the proof of Proposition 6.3.2, with the restriction that it uses the same random choice of β when forming a in each of the atomic subsubformulae for which a genuine proof is due. This ensures that the same blinded form of $\mathcal{V}$'s challenge works for all subsubformulae demonstrations for which $\mathcal{S}$'s assistance is needed.

Because β is chosen at random, there can be no inflow. □

This inflow prevention technique can also be applied to the construction in Proposition 6.3.4, and more generally to showing protocols based on any other kind of linear sharing discussed in Section 6.3. It can also readily be adapted to prevent inflow in any of the RSAREP-based smartcard-enhanced showing protocols in Section 6.3.2.

An even simpler technique to prevent inflow is to let $\mathcal{U}$ and $\mathcal{V}$ jointly develop $\mathcal{V}$'s challenge, in such a manner that it cannot contain covert message bits chosen by $\tilde{\mathcal{V}}$. This approach is not recommendable, though. It increases the number of message exchanges between $\mathcal{U}$ and $\mathcal{V}$, and makes it harder to encode meaningful data into $\mathcal{V}$'s challenge message (for the purpose of a signed proof). Also, the approach is not always practical. For example, in the technique described in Section 5.3, $\mathcal{V}$ must form a commitment γ; randomizing this requires the commitment function to be of a number-theoretic nature (e.g., a DLREP or RSAREP function), which excludes much faster alternatives. Another unique and important advantage of our inflow prevention technique is that it destroys other data leakage channels as a by-product, as we will see in Section 6.4.3.

6.4.2 Outflow prevention

Outflow cannot occur in any of the certificate issuing protocols, since the CA does not receive any messages from $\mathcal{S}$. In the showing protocols there is some opportunity for outflow, through the response(s) provided by $\mathcal{S}$. If $\mathcal{V}$ in the smartcard-enhanced showing protocols in Section 6.3 knows $\mathcal{S}$'s share of the representation of h, then $\mathcal{S}$ can encode its outflow message in the "random" number(s) that it uses to compute $a_\mathcal{S}$, possibly encrypted under a key of $\mathcal{V}$ or of the CA. For example, in the construction of Proposition 6.3.2 or 6.3.6, $\mathcal{U}$ demonstrates an atomic formula without "NOT" connectives by passing $\mathcal{S}$'s response $r_\mathcal{S}$ on to $\mathcal{V}$, enabling $\mathcal{V}$ to extract $\mathcal{S}$'s covert message by computing w_1. In practice, $\mathcal{V}$ can guess $\mathcal{S}$'s share with non-negligible success probability if it knows the list of all smartcard secret keys. It could even determine the correct secret key by verifying whether w_1 satisfies a redundancy pattern or the like.

This outflow method does not work if an atomic formula with a "NOT" connective is demonstrated, because $\mathcal{U}$ applies δ to $r_\mathcal{S}$ before passing it on. According to

Proposition 3.4.3, if x_l (or, in the RSAREP-based protocol, $\mathcal{U}$'s share of x_{l+1}) is a random number that does not occur in the formula, then the demonstration does not leak any information about δ. $\mathcal{S}$ can still cause outflow if δ has smaller entropy than a random number in $\mathbb{Z}_q$ or $\mathbb{Z}_v$; this will be the case in most practical applications. In fact, $\mathcal{S}$ can first leak δ (without knowing it), by generating $a_{\mathcal{S}}$ in a manner known to $\mathcal{V}$, and in subsequent demonstrations with the same h (if any) use the full response channel for outflow.

Also, if the formula that is demonstrated is of the form (3.7), then $\mathcal{V}$ may learn information about which of the atomic subsubformula are valid. For each of the atomic subsubformulae for which $\mathcal{U}$ requires $\mathcal{S}$'s assistance, $\mathcal{V}$ sees either $r_{\mathcal{S}}$ or $r_{\mathcal{S}}\delta_i$ for some δ_i, and can check for correlations. (See the construction of Proposition 6.3.2.)

Proposition 6.4.2. *Suppose that $\mathcal{U}$ generates x_l at random from $\mathbb{Z}_q$ and only demonstrates formulae in which x_l does not appear. In the construction of Proposition 6.3.2, $\mathcal{U}$ can prevent outflow at the cost of essentially one additional exponentiation, which can be precomputed. The tasks of $\mathcal{S}$ and $\mathcal{V}$ remain unchanged.*

Proof. As in the proof of Proposition 6.3.2, we distinguish four cases:

Case 1. F is an atomic formula consisting of zero or more "AND" connectives and no other connectives, in the form (3.3). $\mathcal{U}$ proceeds as in Case 1 of the proof of Proposition 6.3.2, but when computing a from $a_{\mathcal{S}}$ it also multiplies in a factor g_1^γ, for a randomly chosen $\gamma \in \mathbb{Z}_q$. Furthermore, instead of passing $\mathcal{S}$'s response $r_{\mathcal{S}}$ on to $\mathcal{V}$, it sets $r_1 := r_{\mathcal{S}} + \gamma \bmod q$. No further changes are needed.

Case 2. F is an atomic formula consisting of zero or more "AND" connectives, one "NOT" connective, and no other connectives, in the form (3.4). $\mathcal{U}$ proceeds as in Case 2 of the proof of Proposition 6.3.2, but when computing a from $a_{\mathcal{S}}$ it also multiplies in a factor g_1^γ, for a randomly chosen $\gamma \in \mathbb{Z}_q$. Furthermore, $\mathcal{U}$ computes $r_1 := r_{\mathcal{S}}\delta + \gamma \bmod q$. No further changes are needed.

Case 3. F is a formula connecting atomic subformulae by zero or more "OR" connectives and no other connectives, in the form (3.6). $\mathcal{U}$ proceeds as in Case 3 of the proof of Proposition 6.3.2, applying the modification of either Case 1 or Case 2.

Case 4. F is an arbitrary Boolean formula, in the form (3.7). $\mathcal{U}$ proceeds as in Case 4 of the proof of Proposition 6.3.2. (For each atomic subsubformula for which a genuine proof is due, $\mathcal{U}$ uses an independently generated γ.)

Because the γ's are chosen at random, there can be no outflow. $\qquad\square$

Because $\widetilde{\mathcal{S}}$ cannot cause outflow, accepting views of $\widetilde{\mathcal{V}}$ when interacting with $\overline{\mathcal{U}}$ are perfectly indistinguishable from those that result when interacting with $\overline{\mathcal{P}}$ in the showing protocols in Chapter 3. This immediately leads to the following results.

Corollary 6.4.3. *If $\mathcal{U}$ follows the construction described in the proof of Proposition 6.4.2, then Proposition 3.6.1(c) holds, regardless of the behavior of $\bar{S}$ and any joint initial set-up by $\bar{S}$ and $\tilde{V}$.*

Corollary 6.4.4. *If $\mathcal{U}$ follows the construction described in the proof of Proposition 6.4.2, then Proposition 3.6.2 and 3.6.3 both hold, regardless of the behavior of $\bar{S}$ and any joint initial set-up by $\bar{S}$ and $\tilde{V}$.*

In Section 6.3.1 we already saw that these security results are true assuming S follows the protocol but $\hat{\mathcal{U}}$ need not. In most applications both types of results are desirable: $\bar{S}$ should prevent $\hat{\mathcal{U}}$ and $\hat{V}$ from forging signed proofs and from making them appear to pertain to formulae that do not apply, while $\overline{\mathcal{U}}$ should prevent $\tilde{S}$ and $\tilde{V}$ from framing its holder by forming a signed proof that $\mathcal{U}$ did not originate.

The same outflow prevention technique can be applied to the construction in Proposition 6.3.4, and more generally to any other kind of linear sharing discussed in Section 6.3. In cases where $\bar{S}$ provides more than one response to $\mathcal{U}$, the latter must independently randomize each of these responses, and the corresponding adjustments must be made when forming a. It is also straightforward to apply the outflow prevention technique to any of the RSAREP-based smartcard-enhanced showing protocols discussed in Section 6.3.2.

Our outflow prevention technique actively prevents outflow by randomizing data on the flight. It is much more powerful than the approach of Chaum [103], which can only detect outflow after the fact with low probability. It is also highly preferable over Chaum's [97, 109] other outflow prevention technique (also applied by Cramer and Pedersen [122]), which in our situation would proceed by letting S and $\mathcal{U}$ form a_S in a mutually random manner by means of a coin flipping protocol. This would seriously degrade the communication and computation complexity, and would prevent the optimization that will be introduced in Section 6.5.1. Another important advantage of our outflow prevention technique is that other data leakage channels are destroyed as a by-product, as we will now show.

6.4.3   Prevention of other data leakage channels

Inflow and outflow prevention are orthogonal measures. $\mathcal{U}$ can prevent both inflow and outflow by randomizing V's challenge c as well as any responses provided by S, and multiplying the corresponding expressions into a when forming a_S. Assuming simultaneous repeated squaring, the computational cost for demonstrating an atomic formula is approximately one exponentiation that can be precomputed.

Our issuing and showing protocols in Chapters 3 and 4 by their very design greatly reduce the scope for leakage of covert messages: no interaction takes place between S and the CA, and the interaction between S and V is minimal. What's more, the application of our inflow and outflow prevention techniques is so powerful that any other data leakage channels in the issuing and showing protocols are destroyed as a by-product:

- The smartcard learns virtually nothing:

  - $\tilde{S}$ cannot learn $\mathcal{U}$'s attributes, nor how many are encoded by the CA, regardless of the behavior of $\tilde{V}$. $\tilde{S}$ cannot even learn the g_i's that it does not use itself, unless they are known in advance. (In Section 6.5.1 we will describe an optimization in which $\tilde{S}$ merely learns q and a secret seed value to generate pseudorandom numbers.)

  - When interacting with $\overline{\mathcal{U}}$, $\tilde{S}$ cannot learn any information about the formula that is demonstrated, regardless of the behavior of $\tilde{V}$. This holds even if $\mathcal{U}$ issues a signed proof and a unique description of the formula is hashed along when computing V's challenge. $\tilde{S}$ cannot even learn the message that it helps sign.

  - $\tilde{S}$ cannot learn whether it is assisting in showing a limited-show certificate or an unlimited-show certificate, regardless of the behavior of $\tilde{V}$, assuming S in both cases provides its initial witness in advance (e.g., during the corresponding issuing protocol). (Note, though, that $\mathcal{U}$ cannot show a limited-show certificate more times than allowed, because S uses a new random initial witness in each showing protocol execution.) Likewise, $\tilde{S}$ cannot decide whether multiple invocations of its assistance are for the purpose of showing the same certificate or different certificates.

  - $\tilde{S}$ cannot even learn any information on the number of certificates issued to $\mathcal{U}$, since $\mathcal{U}$ can query S even if it has not been issued any certificates. (This practice is not recommendable when limited-show certificates represent value, such as in an electronic cash system.)

  In other words, all that $\tilde{S}$ can learn about the actions of its holder is an upper bound on the number of showing protocol executions.

- The verifier learns virtually nothing either (beyond the status of the formulae demonstrated):

  - $\tilde{V}$ cannot decide from its accepting views in protocol executions whether or not $\mathcal{P}$ is assisted by a smartcard, regardless of the behavior of $\tilde{S}$. In PKIs in which certificate applicants may but need not hold a smartcard, this reduces the scope for discrimination and improves privacy.

  - The computation error channel is destroyed as a by-product of our outflow prevention technique: $\tilde{S}$ cannot leak more than 1 bit. Therefore, $\mathcal{U}$ may skip the verification of S's response(s), thereby circumventing the need for an exponentiation that cannot be precomputed. This holds even if S provides more than one response to $\mathcal{U}$'s challenge: the independent randomization applied by $\mathcal{U}$ prevents $\tilde{V}$ from learning any information about how many or which of $\mathcal{U}$'s responses were formed using an incorrect response supplied by $\tilde{S}$.

- Owing to the minimal interaction required in our smartcard-enhanced protocols, $\tilde{S}$ can leak at most 1 bit using the halting channel, assuming $\mathcal{U}$ does not engage in a showing protocol execution until after it has obtained a_S. This holds even if $\mathcal{U}$ interactively issues a signed proof or performs a 4-move zero-knowledge demonstration. No bits at all can be leaked when $\mathcal{U}$ non-interactively issues a signed proof to $\mathcal{V}$.

- To prevent the timing channel, $\mathcal{U}$ should time the delay between incoming and outgoing messages exchanged between the $\mathcal{S}$ and the other device. If the delay exceeds a reasonable time bound, $\mathcal{U}$ aborts the protocol execution; otherwise it first adds its own delay to ensure that the total delay time is approximately constant. What makes this approach truly practical for the DLREP-based protocols is that $\mathcal{S}$ and $\mathcal{V}$ need never perform any exponentiations that cannot be precomputed. (An upper bound on computation time will be much looser for time-consuming operations, and increases the delay that must be added.) As with the halting channel, the minimal interaction in our protocols ensures that at most 1 bit can leak.

It is easy to see that $\tilde{S}$ can leak at most 1 bit in total to $\tilde{V}$ via the halting channel, the computation error channel, and the timing channel. This is the best result that can be achieved, since $\mathcal{S}$ can always cause a protocol execution to abort by not providing its response(s) to $\mathcal{U}$. In practice the maximum leakage will be significantly less than 1 bit, since there will be other possible causes for incorrect responses to $\mathcal{V}$ or protocol abortion, such as incorrect behavior by $\mathcal{U}$ or a communication failure. In fact, any attempt by $\tilde{S}$ to leak bits through the halting channel or the computation error channel is futile, since it leaves $\tilde{V}$ unconvinced of the formula demonstrated.

Even common coin flips are prevented as a by-product. It is not hard to prove that if $\mathcal{U}$ follows the issuing and showing protocols, then the views of $\tilde{S}$ are statistically independent from the accepting views of the $\widetilde{CA}$ and $\tilde{V}$, regardless of the formulae demonstrated by $\overline{\mathcal{U}}$. Thus, physical access to the contents of a smartcard does not help the $\widetilde{CA}$ in cooperation with all verifiers to retroactively trace and link communications and transactions; all that can be learned is what certificate holders willingly disclose in executions of the showing protocol. More importantly, the card cannot leak information even if it could send out radio signals.

In general, however, it is impossible without breaking the tamper-resistance to verify that a smartcard does not have a sense of time, place, temperature, sound, or anything else that can be exploited by the CA once it gains physical access to the contents of the card. For instance, ultra-thin batteries that meet the required physical dimensions for smartcards are expected to become widely available within a few years. In light of this, a much more effective approach is for certificate holders to never return their smartcards to the CA (or anyone else) in the first place. This simple measure protects privacy in the strongest possible manner. In Section 6.5.1

we will show that our DLREP-based issuing and showing protocols can be efficiently implemented using low-cost smartcards without a cryptographic coprocessor. These cards might as well be destroyed, archived, or thrown away by their holders once their physical security has become outdated or their expiry date has been reached; there are no valid financial excuses for the CA to demand them returned.

An alternative is to enable cardholders to zeroize the contents of their smartcards before returning them. By feeding $\mathcal{S}$ a (pseudo)randomly generated file as large as $\mathcal{S}$'s memory, and requiring $\mathcal{S}$ to output the file, $\mathcal{U}$ can force $\mathcal{S}$ to overwrite its memory contents. $\mathcal{S}$ can be programmed to perform this action only if $\mathcal{U}$ also provides it with a MAC of the CA on a hash of the random file. Forensic experts may still be able to reconstruct the previous memory contents, though, and sting operations are not prevented (some cards may be given more memory than publicly specified).

We will now show that there are other persuasive reasons to prefer the model of not returning cards over the prevention of common coin flips.

6.4.4 Restricting the level of privacy protection

As we have seen in Section 6.2.2, $\mathcal{U}$'s ability to prevent $\widetilde{\mathcal{S}}$ and $\widetilde{\mathcal{V}}$ from developing common coin flips can be misused by an anonymous extortioner. When certificates represent significant value, it is in $\mathcal{U}$'s own interest that this level of privacy cannot be achieved. In case an extortioner strikes, this would enable $\mathcal{U}$ to find out how and where the extorted certificates have been misused, by comparing the common coin flips stored by the smartcard with the views of all the verifiers; in case the CA stores a copy of the relevant parts of all the showing protocol transcripts, this task is easy to accomplish with the cooperation of the CA. In an electronic coin system, for instance, this tracing ability strongly discourages the extortioner from making a large payment to his or her own account or to that of an accomplice; the extortioner will have little choice but to spend the money on goods or services that he or she can receive while remaining untraceable.

Even more effectively, by designing the showing protocol in such a manner that the verifier's challenge contains a verifier identifier that cannot be hidden from $\mathcal{S}$, the victim of an extortioner can determine in real time to which verifier(s) the extortioner is showing his or her certificates, since the identifiers must pass in unencrypted form through the user-controlled computer. This enables the victim to immediately notify the verifier that a fraud is going on, and so it will be very hard for the extortioner to profit from his or her crime. Verifier traceability by the certificate holder is desirable anyway, for many reasons: the certificate may need to obtain a digital receipt from the verifier in the showing protocol; the certificate holder may need the ability to complain about bad goods or services, or at least to warn others about the behavior of an unscrupulous service provider or to have an investigation instigated; and, absent verifier traceability it is impossible to recover (if needed) should the connection with the verifier become permanently lost during the showing protocol execution. It is important to note that in this approach only the originator of the showing protocol execution has the power to trace the verifier. To prevent smartcards from locking their holders out of legitimate transactions to designated verifiers, smartcards should learn only a salted hash or an encryption of the verifier's identity.

In high-risk PKIs, this approach may be exploited to give law enforcement the ability to trace the actions of a designated cardholder. Requirements should be in place to ensure that a court order or search warrant must be presented to the designated cardholder, so that the cardholder can challenge the investigation. Although a certificate holder can falsely claim that his or her smartcard has been lost, broken, or stolen, this does not invalidate the approach. To most honest certificate applicants, the inconvenience of having to obtain a new smartcard to retrieve new certificates is sufficient reason to refrain from false claims. Furthermore, the police can resort to traditional investigative techniques to locate a card claimed to have been lost, and to forensic methods to retrieve the memory contents of a smartcard that has been wrecked. Any audit logs by the user-controlled computer could be examined as well. Also, if the CA requires timely reporting of the loss or theft of smartcards, it would be suspect if an individual claims to have lost control over his or her smartcard right after a court order was presented.

It may be cumbersome for law enforcement to make a physical presence to gain access to the contents of a device. Moreover, physical access takes away the device holder's control over which parts of the transaction log are being inspected. It is possible to give authorized third parties the ability to remotely (over a network) query the contents of the smartcards of designated certificate holders. When presented with a digitally signed electronic search warrant (or court order) demanding that a part of the transaction log be disclosed (e.g., all transactions above a specified threshold, all the transactions to a designated organizations, or the ten most recent transactions), the user's computer checks the warrant's authenticity and contents, passes the query on to the smartcard, receives the requested information from the smartcard (authenticated using a MAC or a digital signature), checks the supplied data against its own copy of the transaction log, and passes it onward to the requesting party only if the verification holds.[9]

More generally, there may be a legitimate need for S to know information other than (just) the verifier's identity, to decide whether or not to assist $\mathcal{U}$ in performing the showing protocol execution. For instance, $\overline{S}$ may need to know (part of) the formula demonstrated, (part of) the message it is helping to sign, or the type of verifier to which a signed proof is to be issued. To accommodate these and other legitimate needs for restricting the level of privacy, we reject the goal of preventing common coin flips and instead open up (in a controlled manner) one communication channel from $\mathcal{V}$ to S: $\mathcal{V}$'s challenge message, c. To prevent $\widehat{\mathcal{U}}$ from altering c before passing it on to S, we have S form by itself the challenge message it will respond to, by

---

[9]MAC outflow can be prevented by using commitments, while randomization or deterministic signature generation suffice for digital signatures.

applying a sufficiently strong (publicly known) one-way hash function to the data provided by $\mathcal{U}$. For example, if $\mathcal{U}$ is to issue a signed proof to $\mathcal{V}$, the protocol $(\mathcal{S}, \mathcal{U})$ should be such that $\mathcal{S}$ computes c by applying $\mathcal{H}_i(\cdot)$ to data provided by $\mathcal{U}$. This forces $\mathcal{U}$ to provide (h, a, F, m) and any other data to be included in the hash.

To guarantee that $\mathcal{S}$ learns only the minimum information needed, we use *challenge semantics* based on hash structures. If, for example, $\mathcal{S}$ should be able to learn only the message m in a signed proof, $\mathcal{V}$'s challenge message could be set equal to $\mathcal{H}_i(\mathcal{F}_i(h, a, F), m)$, where $\mathcal{F}(\cdot)$ and $\mathcal{H}(\cdot)$ may be the same hash function. When $\mathcal{S}$ provides responses only to challenges c formed by itself by applying $\mathcal{H}_i(\cdot)$ to data provided by $\mathcal{U}$, the latter is forced to provide at least $\mathcal{F}_i(h, a, F)$ and m to $\mathcal{S}$. To improve privacy, $\mathcal{U}$ may hash along a random salt when applying $\mathcal{F}_i(\cdot)$. (Formally, $\mathcal{F}(\cdot)$ should be a commitment function that unconditionally hides the data; a DLREP function can be used.) More generally, c can be defined as an arbitrary structure of nested hashes of data fields, and the role of $\mathcal{S}$ in forming c can be arbitrarily defined as well. In case of a dispute, the hash structure can be opened selectively.

Note that $\widehat{\mathcal{U}}$ cannot block a message transfer from $\mathcal{V}$ to $\mathcal{S}$ without blocking the entire showing protocol execution. On the other hand, $\mathcal{U}$ can unconditionally prevent inflow and outflow, and can at all times see and control the common coin flips developed by $\mathcal{V}$ and $\mathcal{S}$.

Another benefit of rejecting the goal of preventing coin flips is related to attacks on $\mathcal{U}$. If $\mathcal{S}$ sees the message it is helping to sign and shows this on a display of its own, and waits for its holder to accord its next step through an on-board key pad, then a virus or a Trojan horse attack on $\mathcal{U}$ cannot trick $\mathcal{S}$ into signing a false message.

This technique of combining inflow and outflow protection with "controlled common coin flips" suffices to accommodate most legitimate needs to reduce the level of privacy attainable. It does not, however, enable the verifier in the showing protocol to distinguish whether or not the prover's demonstration is conducted using the assistance of a smartcard. This capability may be needed in case of high-risk limited-show certificates for which the techniques in Section 5.5 to trace and contain fraud offer inadequate security. One way to enable this capability is for the CA to encode into each certified key pair a "policy attribute" that indicates at least whether or not the verifier should resort to online certificate authorization. This policy attribute must always be disclosed when performing a demonstration. (Any other data that must always be disclosed, such as a certificate expiration date, can be encoded into the same attribute.)

6.5 Other techniques

In this section we describe how to implement our DLREP-based techniques using low-cost smartcards. We also design a protocol that enables certificate holders to return to the CA any retrieved certificates that have not yet been shown. Furthermore, we show how to discourage certificate holders from using their certificates to help remote parties gain access to services for which they do not hold the proper certificates themselves. Finally, we design secure bearer certificates with optimal privacy and address some loose ends.

6.5.1 Implementation in low-cost smartcards

The cheapest and most widely available smartcards contain a simple 8-bit microprocessor that can perform a DES operation in software in about 4 milliseconds. A single modular multiplication as needed in public-key cryptographic operations takes many minutes, and may not even fit in memory. (RAM is typically between 124 and 1024 bytes, EEPROM between 1 and 16 kilobytes, and ROM between 4 and 16 kilobytes.) Even can today's fastest coprocessor smartcards cannot compute more than 3 full RSA exponentiations per second, assuming a 1024-bit modulus and no use of the Chinese Remainder Theorem.[10]

Moreover, cryptographic coprocessors decrease reliability, are more vulnerable to timing attacks (see Lenoir [245]), take up precious space, and add about three to five dollars to the cost of each smartcard.

When using our DLREP-based techniques, two noteworthy optimizations are available:

- An elliptic curve implementation over a field of the form GF_{2^m}, with $m \approx 160$, guarantees that a conventional 8-bit smartcard microprocessor can rapidly perform a high-strength public-key exponentiation in G_q. For instance, the Schlumberger Multiflex smartcard used in the first smartcard-based pilot of SET [257] can compute an elliptic-curve DSA signature in exactly one second, using a 163-bit modulus; this chip contains an 8-bit Motorola chip with 240 bytes of RAM, 8 kilobytes of EEPROM, and 12 kilobytes of ROM. Since the Schnorr proof of knowledge requires virtually the same operations as the DSA scheme, the same performance in a low-cost smartcard can be achieved when using our techniques. For details on implementing elliptic curves in smartcards, see Certicom [85].

- The bulk of the workload of S can be shifted to the CA, by having the latter instead of the former provide a_S to U; this removes the need for S to perform any exponentiations. The CA can provide a_S during the execution of the issuing protocol in which it issues the certified key pair that uses a_S. Alternatively, the CA provides a great many a_S-values at once to U, possibly whenever the latter makes a request. The only remaining task for S in an execution of the showing protocol is to compute a linear relation over $\mathbb{Z}_q$ and perhaps a few

---

[10]In November 1999, Bull and other major hardware manufacturers demonstrated a smartcard that can perform the exponentiation in less than 350 milli-seconds. Their design features a RISC 32-bit processor, 64 kilobytes of EEPROM, 96 kilobytes of ROM, and 4 kilobytes of RAM.

hashes. Even the cheapest of 8-bit smartcards can compute dozens of such responses within a second. Note that this optimization does not require the use of elliptic curves.

To implement the latter optimization, the CA and S must share the list of random numbers that S will deploy. In practice these numbers may be generated in a pseudorandom fashion from a seed value that is known to both S and the CA, which the CA may form by diversifying a smartcard identifier using a master key. (The use of pseudorandom numbers is recommendable also to avoid physical attacks on noise generators.) The preferred method of generating pseudorandom numbers depends on certain characteristics of the certificates:

- In case certificates are shown in the order in which they are retrieved, S can regenerate in constant time and space its contributions to the secret keys of up to 2^t certified key pairs by storing merely a t-bit index for the pseudorandom number generator, and incrementing this upon each successful showing of a certificate. The DSS [277, Appendix 3] specifies two algorithms for generating pseudorandom numbers in $\mathbb{Z}_q$ for use with the DSA. Both algorithms feed a secret seed value and the previous pseudorandom number into a one-way function in order to derive the next pseudorandom number. Since $\mathcal{U}$ in a practical implementation need merely store some 40 bytes per certified key pair, regardless of the number of attributes encoded into it, the user's computer and the smartcard can retrieve and store a number of certified key pairs that is, for all practical purposes, virtually unlimited.

- In PKIs where the showing order of limited-show certificates may be unrelated to the certificate retrieval order, it is preferable to generate each new pseudorandom number by feeding the seed value and an increment of an index value to a sufficiently strong one-way hash function, to facilitate random addressing. S must keep track of all the indices for which it has already provided its assistance, because it may not respond to two different challenges using the same initial witness. The indices may be known to $\mathcal{U}$, and form a convenient manner for $\mathcal{U}$ to query S in the showing protocol: the CA in the issuing protocol can provide $\mathcal{U}$ with the indices used to generate the pseudorandom contributions of S, and when $\mathcal{U}$ needs to show a certificate it can send S the corresponding index in order to have S regenerate its random contribution to the secret key of the appropriate certified key pair.

Having the CA instead of S provide a_S to $\mathcal{U}$ also allows $\mathcal{U}$'s holder to leave S at a safe place during certificate retrieval, for improved protection against theft. Another advantage is that the same smartcard can be used for different PKIs, in fact even for applications not known at the time of card issuance. Hereto each CA should use the same q and preferably a different g_1, and the pseudorandom numbers of each smartcard should be generated by feeding an additional CA identifier into the pseudorandom generator.

Card performance can be pushed to the limit by either speeding up or circumventing the memory-intensive reduction modulo q that must be performed by $\mathcal{S}$. To achieve the former, one should use a modulus q of the form $2^t \pm B$, for small B. To circumvent the modular reduction altogether, a technique due to Shamir [347] can be applied. The idea is to replace the computation of $cx_1 + w_1 \bmod q$ by the computation of $cx_1 + w_1 + tq$, for t chosen at random from a suitable range; the result can be computed and output one byte after another by using a double convolution process.

6.5.2   Returning certificates

According to Proposition 6.3.1, the loss or theft of a smartcard prevents its holder from showing his or her certificates, in spite of any access control mechanism that may prevent others from operating the smartcard. In many PKIs it is desirable that any previously retrieved certificates that have not yet been shown can be returned to CA. The existence of a certificate return protocol would give the victims of lost, stolen, or crashed smartcards the opportunity to recover value that might be associated with their certificates. It also enables the CA to publish the certificates on an update of its CRL, and in this manner prevents attackers able to get around the smartcard access control mechanism from using the certified key pairs.

A return protocol may also be useful in the unlikely event that the cryptography is broken (see Section 5.5.5); since the CA can keep a positive list at certificate issuing time, even an adversary with unlimited computing power cannot return forged certificates. (In this particular case, it is recommended that each certificate applicant initially establish a secret key or a one-time pad with the CA, for the purpose of symmetric encryption and authentication of data sent in the return protocol.)

Furthermore, a return protocol is useful to resolve permanently lost connections between a certificate holder and a verifier; if the transcripts of all the showing protocol executions are deposited with the CA, fault tolerance can be implemented by returning the certificate to the CA so that the latter can find out whether the verifier has received the certificate.

Other uses of a certificate return protocol include: to exchange expired certificates for fresh ones; to cancel a transaction that has already been performed; and, to have recourse to the CA if a smartcard enters into suspension mode or produces an error.

Returning a certificate to the CA is easy, assuming certificate holders keep backup copies of their certified public keys (and, for secret-key certificates, their share of the corresponding secret keys). Backups can be stored conveniently on the user-controlled computer, on a floppy disc, in encrypted form in a cyberspace "strongbox," or in any other manner deemed secure by the certificate holder.

To perform the actual return of a certificate, $\mathcal{U}$ transmits the certified public key to the CA. In case of a secret-key certificate, $\mathcal{U}$ must also provide the CA with sufficient information to enable it to determine S's secret key, and must prove knowledge of its share of the secret key of the certified key pair. To return a certificate obtained using DLREP-based scheme I, for instance, U sends h', (c_0', r_0') to the CA and proves knowledge of a DL-representation of h'/h_S. In the proof of knowledge, U may selectively disclose properties about the encoded attributes, as in an execution of the showing protocol.

Note that this return protocol is software-only: it does not involve the cooperation of the smartcard. This is desirable not only to cope with loss, theft, and destruction of smartcards, but also for certificate holders who have never been issued a smartcard at all.

It is desirable, both for secret-key and for public-key certificates, that U always provide the CA with a signed proof on a message stating the reason it is returning a certificate. If the CA stores this signed message in a database, any disputes that may arise later on can be resolved.

In case U is to be reimbursed in some way or another, and executions of the showing protocol need not be authorized online, the CA may prefer to delay reimbursement until it is certain that the returned certificate has not been shown.

Care must be taken that a thief cannot return the certificate data stored on stolen backups for his or her own benefit. In an off-line electronic coin system, for instance, the CA should best redeem an account holder for a returned coin by crediting his or her account.

6.5.3 How to discourage remote lending

In Section 5.5.2 we presented software-only measures to discourage lending of certified key pairs. For stronger protection, certificate holders should be required to use smartcards with a biometric access control mechanism. In a face-to-face situation the verifier can visually inspect that the biometric data is properly entered. In general, a liveness detection mechanism is needed to prevent unauthorized cardholders from using biometric templates; a cardholder's fingerprints, for instance, may be all over his or her smartcard. (The same measure also protects against loss and theft.)

This leaves open the possibility of *remote lending*. Here, the holder of a certified key pair provides the "borrower" with the certified public key, and assists in the showing protocol execution by providing the required responses. The lender can provide his or her assistance over a radio link or a network such as the Internet. Remote lending is similar to the anonymous extortion attack described in Section 6.2.2, with the difference that the borrower voluntarily cooperates with the lender and may not be interested in hiding his or her identity and transaction details from the lender. (Remote lending differs also from the "mafia fraud" studied first by Desmedt [134]; in the latter, the prover is not aware that the protocol execution is being relayed.)

In communications and transactions that are not face-to-face, remote lending cannot be prevented, regardless of whether privacy-protecting certificates or fully traceable identity certificates are used. Indeed, the "lender" might as well perform the entire showing protocol execution and simply relay the provided service or goods to the "borrower." In many PKIs this is not considered a security problem, especially not if lending occurs only incidentally; it may even be a feature. In PKIs where large-scale lending is to be discouraged, the CA could issue limited-show certificates and establish one account per certificate applicant (see Section 5.2.1). Large-scale lenders will then be exposed because of their abnormal demand for certificates. Another measure is to charge a fee per certificate issued, so that a large-scale lender faces the problem of being compensated for the cost of his or her service without risking exposure.[11] A further measure to discourage large-scale lending is to program each smartcard in such a manner that it will only respond to a challenge when its biometric access control mechanism detects the live presence of the cardholder.

In face-to-face situations, additional measures are available. The CA could encode biometric characteristics and apply the measure described in Section 5.5.2. Even better, remote lending can be prevented altogether by having $\mathcal{V}$ bound its distance to the true certificate holder. The idea is for $\mathcal{S}$ and $\mathcal{V}$ in the showing protocol to rapidly exchange a series of random bits. Each bit of $\mathcal{S}$ is to be sent out immediately after receiving a bit from $\mathcal{V}$. To ensure that $\mathcal{S}$ cannot simply send out its i-th bit before receiving the i-th bit of $\mathcal{V}$, the i-th bit of $\mathcal{S}$ must depend on the i-th bit of $\mathcal{V}$. One way to accomplish this is to require $\mathcal{S}$ to send bits chosen in such a manner that the exclusive-or of these bits and those provided by $\mathcal{V}$ equals a previously established binary string. After the rapid bit exchange has taken place, $\mathcal{S}$'s binary string must be authenticated using the secret key of the certified key pair; one way to accomplish this is to hash along the binary string when forming $\mathcal{V}$'s challenge. $\mathcal{V}$ accepts if and only if the authentication is correct and its distance to the smartcard is sufficiently small. To compute an upper bound on the distance, $\mathcal{V}$ takes the maximum of the delay times between sending out its i-th bit and receiving the i-th bit of $\mathcal{S}$; this ensures that the cheating probability decreases exponentially fast in the number of bits exchanged. What makes this approach practical is that today's electronics can easily handle timings of a few nanoseconds, and light can travel only about 30cm during one nanosecond. Even the timing between two consecutive periods of a 50 MgHz clock allows light to travel only three meters and back. It is easy to integrate this *distance bounding technique* with the techniques described in Sections 6.3 and 6.4.

The smartcard techniques in this section may be used in addition to the software-only techniques in Section 5.5.2, rather than serving as a replacement.

6.5.4   Bearer certificates

As we have seen in Section 5.5.1, strong fraud prevention for software-only bearer certificates requires online clearing. The closest we can come to realizing the digital

---

[11] A business model relying on certificate prepayment has other advantages as well in many circumstances, and is naturally based on the issuance of limited-show certificates.

equivalent of paper-based bearer certificates is to implement digital certificates using smartcards, to ensure that each certificate can be at only one place at any moment in time.

Consider the following design of a digital bearer certificate system. The CA endows each smartcard with a unique card identifier and a secret key (possibly derived by diversifying the card identifier using a master secret key). Anyone can purchase one or more of these smartcards via a myriad of retail outlets, without needing to identify. Each smartcard can be used to open an anonymous account with the CA, by communicating with the CA in cyberspace. To enable the CA to associate the secret key of a smartcard with the account opened, the user's computer sends the card identifier to the CA, possibly together with a MAC of the smartcard on a challenge message of the CA. The CA issues only limited-show certificates, and encodes into each certified key pair the secret key of the applicant's smartcard. Retrieval and showing of digital certificates take place using the techniques described in Sections 6.3 and 6.4. The additional option available to smartcard holders is to sell, lend, or otherwise transfer their cards to others. For protection against theft, smartcards should have an access control mechanism (based on a PIN, a password, or a biometric) that can be changed only when authorized by the current holder. Verifiers may accept digital certificates without needing online authorization by the CA, but are required to deposit transcripts of their showing protocol executions. If a smartcard holder manages to physically extract the card's secret key and show certificates more times than allowed, the CA can compute the smartcard identifier, close the corresponding account, and blacklist the certificates using its CRL. This ensures that the perpetrator can continue only by physically compromising another smartcard.

This design offers adequate security assuming that the average cost of physically extracting the secret key from a smartcard exceeds the expected profit that can be made until the CRL update has been distributed and the account closed. At the same time, the privacy of users is maximally protected: their showing protocol executions are untraceable and unlinkable, and their certificate retrievals anonymous.

In PKIs with high-risk certificates, it is preferable that the perpetrators themselves can be traced, to stop them from opening new accounts and perhaps also to recover some of the losses. Hereto our smartcard techniques should be combined with the personalization techniques described in Section 5.5. This does not preclude the possibility of anonymous withdrawal of certificates, as we have seen.

6.5.5 Loose ends

To prevent organizations and other verifiers from discriminating against certificate holders who do not disclose their built-in identifier, the secret key of a smartcard should serve as the cardholder's identifier. The link between the cardholder's identity and the smartcard's identifier can be made either when the card is issued or when the account is opened. With this approach, the privacy interests of the cardholder and the security interests of the CA are perfectly aligned; identity bartering is out, because cardholders cannot disclose the identifiers that have been encoded into their certified key pairs.

In some situations it may be desirable that certificate holders can demonstrate not to be the originator of a transaction. The technique described in Section 5.5.1 to accomplish this is not in conflict with that of the previous paragraph. Namely, it is possible for $< \mathcal{S}, \mathcal{U} >$ to demonstrate that the secret key of $\mathcal{S}$ is not equal to the secret key of one or more perpetrator smartcards. Consider by way of example the setting of Proposition 6.3.2. With $h := \prod_{i=1}^{l} g_i^{x_i}$, the goal is for $\mathcal{U}$ (with the assistance of $\mathcal{S}$) to demonstrate that $x_1 \neq y \bmod q$, for some $y \in \mathbb{Z}_q$, without $\widehat{\mathcal{U}}$ learning the secret key x_1 of $\mathcal{S}$. Hereto $\mathcal{S}$ demonstrates to $\mathcal{U}$ that $x_1 \neq y \bmod q$ by means of our standard interactive showing protocol for atomic formulae with a "NOT" connective: $\mathcal{S}$ sends $a_{\mathcal{S}} := (g_1^y/h_{\mathcal{S}})^{w_1}$ to $\mathcal{U}$, receives $\mathcal{V}$'s challenge c from $\mathcal{U}$, and responds by sending $r := c\delta + w_1 \bmod q$, where $\delta := 1/(y - x_1) \bmod q$. It is not hard to see that $\mathcal{U}$ can perform its part of the protocol with respect to $\mathcal{V}$ if $\mathcal{U}$ would know $g_2^{w_1}, \ldots, g_l^{w_1}$. $\mathcal{U}$ would then form

$$
a := a_{\mathcal{S}}(g_1^y/h_{\mathcal{S}})^{\gamma_1} \prod_{i=2}^{l} \left((g_i^{w_1})^{w_i} g_i^{\gamma_i} \right)
$$

for random $w_2, \ldots, w_l \in \mathbb{Z}_q$ and random $\gamma_1, \ldots, \gamma_l \in \mathbb{Z}_q$, and compute $r_1 := r + \gamma_1 \bmod q$ and $r_i := rw_i + \gamma_i \bmod q$, for all $i \in \{2, \ldots, l\}$. (If desired, $\mathcal{U}$ can be allowed to blind c before passing it on, as detailed in Section 6.4.2.) Having $\mathcal{S}$ compute and provide $g_2^{w_1}, \ldots, g_l^{w_1}$ to $\mathcal{U}$ would result in serious overhead to $\mathcal{S}$, but as with the technique in Section 6.5.1 this burden can be moved to the CA. Alternatively, assuming that demonstrating a property of $\mathcal{S}$'s secret key is an exceptional task, $\mathcal{S}$ could store a precomputed tuple $(w_1, g_1^{w_1}, \ldots, g_l^{w_1})$ into its memory. Knowledge of $g_2^{w_1}, \ldots, g_l^{w_1}$ is believed to be of no help in attacking the protocol performed by $\mathcal{S}$; these numbers are essentially Diffie-Hellman keys.

The technique described in Section 5.5.3 can be applied straightforwardly to achieve non-repudiation. For example, I can be formed as the sum of the secret key of $\mathcal{S}$ and a random secret of $\mathcal{U}$. Alternatively, non-repudiation can be based on the tamper-resistance of the smartcard: if smartcards are tamper-evident, then a smartcard holder can prove his or her innocence by showing that the smartcard has not been tampered with in an attempt to physically extract the secret key.

6.6   Bibliographic notes

The smartcard techniques in Sections 6.3 and 6.4 originate from Brands [54]. The presentation fills in some details that were previously only hinted at, and the formal statements of security and their proofs appear here for the first time. Prior to Brands [54], Brands [46, 48] applied a special case of the smartcard techniques for the purpose of designing a secure off-line electronic coin system; coin payment requires the demonstration of the formula TRUE, and the static one-show blinding technique ensures that the bank can trace a doublespender who has defeated the tamper-resistance of his or her smartcard. In a variation [46, 58], the bank encodes an additional attribute into each coin to specify its denomination and expiry date.

The method in Section 6.5.1 for avoiding exponentiation by the smartcard is due to Brands [57]. Naccache, M'Raïhi, Vaudenay and Raphaeli [271, Section 6] proposed a similar method in a different context ("use-and-throw coupons" for smartcards).

The return protocol in Section 6.5.2 is similar to a protocol designed by Pfitzmann and Waidner [304] for the purpose of loss-tolerance in the electronic coin system of Brands [48]. New is the observation that certificate return is useful for many other purposes.

The distance bounding technique in Section 6.5.3 originates from Chaum [97], with improvements by Brands and Chaum [59].

Finally, the technique in Section 6.5.4 is based on Brands [54].

Epilogue: The Broader Perspective

An idealist believes the short run doesn't count. A cynic believes the long run doesn't matter. A realist believes that what is done or left undone in the short run determines the long run.

— Sydney J. Harris, quoted in *Reader's Digest*

In this epilogue we discuss a number of alternative approaches towards privacy, and show how they fail. On the basis of this analysis, we argue that privacy-enhancing technologies (such as those developed in this book) complemented by legislative measures provide the best way to protect privacy and guarantee security.

The limitations of privacy legislation

In many countries, particularly in Europe, the prevailing approach to protect privacy is privacy legislation. Legislation can discourage systematical abuse by the private sector, but is insufficient in all other cases:

- The key paradigm of legislation is to make undesired actions a crime and to prosecute them. This hardly deters criminals who commit their crimes using computers: in today's networked environment they can operate over large distances and remain virtually untraceable, making it difficult to enforce laws and to prosecute suspects.

- In an age where organizations can communicate and transact with individuals all over the world through telecommunication infrastructures, global harmonization of privacy laws is imperative. This, however, is a daunting task that may never be accomplished at all due to cultural differences.

- Attempts to stop organizations from using privacy-invading practices that are in conflict with privacy legislation can easily take many years. For example, in August 1998 the U.S. Federal Trade Commission finally succeeded in ordering Trans Union (one of the three largest U.S. credit bureaus) to stop distributing and selling target marketing lists based on consumer-credit data for unauthorized purposes; the original charge that Trans Union's sale of target marketing lists violated the Fair Credit Reporting Act dated back to 1992.

- Privacy laws put the burden upon individuals to protect their own data, but the complexity and diversity of privacy laws makes it almost impossible for individuals to be aware of their privacy rights. Privacy laws encompass international laws, constitutional laws, case law, and federal, state, and local legislation. According to StateNet, the number of privacy bills introduced in U.S. state legislatures exceeded 8500 in 1997 alone.

- The language of privacy legislation is necessarily broad, even when applicable only to a certain industry sector. This makes it difficult to interpret a piece of privacy legislation in the context of a given communication or transaction mechanism. Consequently, it is hard for data collectors and auditors alike to determine whether privacy legislation has been lived up to. To illustrate the point, the definition of personal data by the European Privacy Directive [157] considers anonymous and pseudonymous data to be different from personal data, but it is unclear where to draw the line. Reidenberg and Schwartz [318] study the degrees to which different E.U. countries and institutions view this data different from personal data, and conclude: "For on-line services, the determination of whether particular information relates to an 'identifiable person' is unlikely to be straightforward."

- New technologies develop much faster than law. With each new consumer technology it can take many years to understand its privacy implications and develop adequate new policies. Even seemingly simple issues, such as whether issuers of electronic cash fall within the definition of "financial institutions" of the U.S. Right to Financial Privacy Act of 1978, are hard to decide. As Oleinick [290, Chapter 7] points out, "What this policy lag means for our society is that the Judiciary is always struggling to extrapolate old laws to cover new technologies, that the Legislature is engaged in continual policy analysis of new technologies once the new technology has created a policy issue, and that the Executive is always struggling to mandate effective Federal policy to regulate agency usage of new technologies."

- Laws cannot protect against the theft or modification by hackers of personal data stored in computer databases, nor against misuse by employees and other individuals authorized to access databases. Netsolve Inc. analyzed over half a million security alarms from May to September of 1997, and found that "every one of its electronic commerce customers suffered at least one serious network attack per month. [...] The attacks stem from external sources seeking to gain root access to a site's network. Once they gain that access, they possibly could download customer lists, change files, access new product information, destroy data or transfer funds from the finance system." Insider abuse accounts for the majority of Internet security incidents reported to the CERT Coordination Center from 1989 to 1995; see Howard [213] for an analysis.

- Requirements to allow individuals to give notice, to request consent, and to correct inaccurate information in their files may be technically impractical for organizations, and may be difficult to carry out while at the same time adequately restricting employee access.

- New laws frequently exempt earlier provisions in law for the purpose of increasing the surveillance power of the government. For instance, the 1996 amendments to the U.S. Fair Credit Reporting Act of 1971 preempt provisions of stronger state credit reporting laws by permitting the subsidiaries of a parent company to share information without the consumer's permission or government regulation; see the Center for Public Integrity [83] for details. More generally, even in democratic societies there is the realistic threat that privacy laws will be amended, changed, exempted, overturned, or simply ignored.

Privacy legislation can actually contribute to degrading privacy. Where individuals at the time of data collection felt protected by privacy laws, they are likely to have been less inhibited in their behavior than they would have been otherwise. The harmful consequences of privacy intrusions in these cases may be more serious than had the individuals not been given the illusion of privacy in the first place. Furthermore, to check compliance with privacy legislation it is unavoidable that regular audits be performed on the databases of organizations; this increases the accessibility of personal data records, which broadens the scope for abuse. For instance, government agencies may abuse privacy laws to gain access to the databases of target organizations.

The ineffectiveness of self-regulation

The approach of privacy through self-regulation, defined by the Federation of European Direct Marketing [166] as regulation imposed by practitioners on practitioners, and heavily promoted by the United States, is even less effective. Marketers and other data miners have major commercial incentives to use personal data in any way they see fit. Large profits can be made by using and selling consumer profiles, and so any sane person would consider it a serious waste of resources to not put personal data that has already been collected to new business uses. Since organizations can rarely be held liable to compensate consumers for damages caused by the misuse of personal data, not in the least because individuals often have no clue as to the origin of privacy breaches, organizations are incited to stay on the edge of what would invoke immediate regulatory action.

Another problem is that self-regulation requires the participation of the entire industry, but this is an unrealistic goal: new companies may prefer not to comply, companies that agree to guidelines may in fact not comply with them, and there will always be short-term incentives to ignore voluntary privacy measures. As Canada's Task Force on Electronic Commerce [370] points out, this can "undermine fair competition in the marketplace, creating an unlevel playing field. It can also erode consumer confidence in an entire industry and create further confusion about rights and rules."

Also, self-regulation does nothing to protect against the abuse of private-sector and government databases by government officials and agencies. In fact, adopting privacy principles that explicitly state that law enforcement will not be given access to personal data are in violation of the law in most developed countries.

Most of today's self-regulation initiatives provide only the possibility of opt-out; they do not require explicit customer consent to use or distribute personal information. Many organizations are actively lobbying to prevent opt-in from happening. In discussing the amendments to the U.S. Fair Credit Reporting Act, the Acting Comptroller of the Currency [391] said: "I have even heard of people getting two separate notifications covering different types of information, requiring two separate letters to opt out. Such techniques may fall within the letter of the law, but they certainly fall short of its spirit." Furthermore, none of the industry self-regulation initiatives have an adequate enforcement mechanism, a method for consumers to access their own data, or a way of correcting errors that may have occurred in the transcription, transmission, or compilation of their personal information. Rotenberg [327] warns that self-regulation has "made it harder for us to focus on the larger questions of a coherent privacy policy. [. . .] Where once there was an understanding that individuals should have the right to get access to their own data, to inspect it, and to correct it, now those who favor self-regulation believe it is necessary only to provide access to a privacy policy."

Surveys consistently confirm the ineffectiveness of self-regulation. See, for instance, surveys conducted by or on behalf of the Center for Democracy and Technology [82], the Electronic Privacy Information Center [143, 144], the European Commission [315], the Federal Deposit Insurance Corporation [162], the Federal Trade Commission [165], and OMB Watch [291]. For other critiques, see the American Civil Liberties Union [10], Budnitz [65, 66], Clarke [118], Rotenberg [327, 328], and Varney [381].

Industry privacy violations confirm that self-regulation is just a smoke screen. Here is a small sample of recent privacy violations:

- In 1998, the U.S. Federal Trade Commission found that Web portal Geocities was selling demographic information collected from its millions of customers (provided when they signed up for free homepages) to advertisers, even though its online assurance pledged that it would not do so. Ironically, Geocities received a privacy label from TRUSTe (an organization that regulates Internet privacy policies for over 500 companies and gives out privacy seals to conforming Web sites) while it was being investigated by the Federal Trade Commission.

- In January 1999, the chief executive officer of Sun Microsystems (a prominent member organization of the U.S. Online Privacy Alliance) called consumer privacy a "red herring," and proclaimed "You have zero privacy anyway. Get over it."

- In March 1999, TRUSTe decided that Microsoft (one of TRUSTe's largest benefactors) would not be audited for its practice of embedding traceable serial numbers (covertly captured by Microsoft when customers registered their Windows 98 software) into all documents created with Word and Excel.

- One month later, the BBBOnLine Privacy Program (similar to that of TRUSTe) rewarded a privacy seal to Equifax (one of the three largest U.S. credit bureaus), which in the years before repeatedly breached basic privacy principles.

- In May 1999, the Federal Trade Commission settled with Liberty Financial Companies; the company's Young Investor Web site falsely represented that personal data collected from children in a survey would be maintained "totally anonymous," yet it stored all the data in an identifiable manner.

- In November 1999, DoubleClick, which serves over 1300 Web sites with target banner advertisements, acquired market researcher Abacus Direct, which collects data from 1100 merchandise catalog companies. DoubleClick's goal was to correlate the shopping and browsing habits of Internet users with their names and addresses, in spite of its Internet privacy policy that promised that all collected data would be anonymous.[12]

- Also in November 1999, it came to light that RealNetworks was surreptitiously gathering data about the listening activities of users of its music software, and that it recorded this data into a central database. TRUSTe did not revoke RealNetworks' privacy seal.

Since its inception in 1996, TRUSTe has investigated hundreds of privacy violations but has not revoked a single privacy seal.

The latest privacy contempt are infomediaries, a business model devised by Hagel and Singer [205]. Startups such as Enonymous, Lumeria, PopularDemand, PrivacyBank, Privada, PrivaSeek, InterOmni, and @YourCommand aim to become one-stop

---

[12]DoubleClick's stock took a huge hit after the news became public, and the Federal Trade Commission and several states started an investigation. Hereupon, DoubleClick announced to suspend its plans.

brokers of personal data by persuading individuals to funnel all their transactions through their company. The infomediary's sole goal is to earn revenue by selling the personal data of their customers to marketers. The business strategy to lure unwitting individuals into placing all their data and trust in them is to promise them a piece of the revenue and to post a privacy policy.

The fallacy of key escrow

Anyone who considers "key escrow" as a way of protecting privacy is, of course, in a state of sin. On a fundamental level, there can be no mistake about this. Westin's [387] widely accepted definition of privacy (see Section 1.2.1) clearly requires that individuals themselves are in control over their own information. Key escrow (also known under such names as "key recovery," "revocable privacy," "controlled anonymity," or "trustee-based tracing") takes away this control completely, and therefore offers zero privacy. Splitting the ability to recover the secrets of an individual among multiple key escrow authorities (using secret-sharing) does not change this fact, not even if there would be a gazillion authorities that would pledge to notify individuals before reconstructing their secrets.

On a more practical level, all key escrow systems have the following dangers in common:

- As the NSA [279] (of all parties) warned, law enforcement agents and officials operating key escrow centers could well pose the greatest threat to a key escrow encryption system. Clearly, the same objection holds for any other kind of key escrow system. Abelson, Anderson, Bellovin, Benaloh, Blaze, Diffie, Gilmore, Neumann, Rivest, Schiller, and Schneier [2] note that insider abuse "can even become institutionalized within a rogue company or government."

- On a related note, judicial knowledge and consent may easily be circumvented. Epstein [154] warns that any key escrow system "cuts out the notice and knock provisions that must be satisfied before a warrant could be executed. It vests vast powers in third-party agents who have neither the incentive nor knowledge to contest any government intrusion. It presupposes uniform good faith by public officials and overlooks the major costs of even a tiny number of official misdeeds or mistakes." Also, it will be difficult for courts to enforce the time-limits of a warrant.

- The key escrow authorities become a highly visible target to criminals who seek to trace or decrypt the communications and transactions of certain targets. They may be able to obtain the key shares of their interest through bribery, hacking, or extortion.

In the words of Rivest, in his letter of June 1997 to the senators of the Senate Commerce and Judiciary Committees, "Putting key recovery into cryptography is like

soaking your flame-retardant materials in gasoline – you risk a catastrophic failure of the exact sort you were trying to prevent."
Other general objections to key escrow include the following:

- As Directorate-General XIII of the European Commission [137] points out, "if citizens and companies have to fear that their communication and transactions are monitored with the help of key access or similar schemes unduly enlarging the general surveillance possibility of government agencies, they may prefer remaining in the anonymous off-line world and electronic commerce will just not happen."

- Once a key escrow system is in place, the case for weakening the rules under which escrow access may be gained will gradually be weakened. Already, the FBI and law enforcement agencies in other democratic countries are seeking to gain access to personal data records without needing a court order or a search warrant.

- Key escrow systems may not be legitimate. The Office of Technology Assessment, in its 1985 evaluation [284] of the FBI's National Crime Information Center, pointed out that "first amendment rights could be violated to the extent a national computer-based surveillance system was used to monitor the lawful and peaceful activities or associations of citizens or if it were to have the effect of discouraging such activities or associations. Fourth amendment rights could be violated if the surveillance amounted to an unreasonable search and seizure of personal information. And, [...] fifth amendment rights to due process could be violated if such surveillance was conducted without first establishing probable cause or reasonable suspicion and without serving advance notice on the subject individual." Key escrow systems reverse the presumption that individuals are free until they pose a threat of material harm, and are likely to violate all three amendments on the same grounds. See also Sullivan [366].

In recent years, cryptographers have worked fiercely to replace privacy-protecting systems by key escrow systems:

- The first area that fell victim is electronic voting. Following several proposals that guaranteed unconditional privacy, Cohen and Fischer [119] and Benaloh and Yung [26] introduced key escrow electronic voting. Virtually all electronic voting schemes proposed since then are key escrow systems; for recent achievements, see Cramer, Franklin, Schoenmakers, and Yung [124] and Cramer, Gennaro, and Schoenmakers [125].

  Surprisingly, the transition from privacy-protecting electronic voting schemes to key escrow voting schemes has gone by almost unnoticed and unchallenged. This is because key escrow electronic voting was not proposed to enable law enforcement to trace votes, but as a way to achieve the property of "universal verifiability;" the terminology "key escrow" never entered the electronic voting vocabulary. It is not clear, though, that universal verifiability is such an important property that it is worthwhile to sacrifice privacy, nor has it been proved that privacy and universal verifiability cannot be achieved at the same time.

Another issue worth mentioning in this context is that the key escrow voting schemes that achieve information-theoretical "untraceability" (with respect to other parties than the key escrow authorities) require the voter to encrypt each of his or her votes for each of the key escrow authorities. The more efficient schemes achieve only computational untraceability: anyone who can feasibly solve (an instance of) the underlying hard problem can trace all votes without the involvement of the key escrow authorities. For a discussion of the drawbacks of computational privacy, see Section 1.3.5.

• The approach of key escrow is most widely associated with public key encryption. See Denning and Branstad [132] for a taxonomy of key escrow encryption systems, and Denning [131] for descriptions of 33 proposed key escrow encryption products and proposals. (Many others have been proposed since the latter reference.)

The security benefit pursued in this case is the ability to wiretap the conversations of criminals in (near) real time. Numerous publications and testimonies, though, convincingly argue that key escrow encryption will cause much more harm than good. See, for instance, Abelson et al. [2], Bowden and Akdeniz [43], Epstein [154], Froomkin [176], Nathan Associates [274], the NSA [279], Shearer and Gutmann [349], the U.S. National Research Council [278], Walsh [386], and a 1998 background report [15] for the Danish Ministry of Research and Information Technology.

• The most recent area that has fallen victim is electronic cash. Starting with Chaum [105], a floodgate of papers on key escrow electronic cash opened: Brickell, Gemmell, and Kravitz [62], Stadler, Piveteau, and Camenisch [360], Camenisch, Maurer, and Stadler [70, 71], Fujisaki and Okamoto [178], Jakobsson and Yung [220, 221, 222], Davida, Frankel, Tsiounis, and Yung [128], Radu, Govaerts, and Vandewalle [317], Frankel, Tsiounis, and Yung [173, 374], Nakayama, Moribatake, Abe, and Fujisaki [272], and many others.

Here, the primary excuse to squander privacy has been to combat money laundering. However, money laundering concerns can be addressed effectively without giving up privacy by (prudently) applying one or more of the following measures: placing limits on amounts; ensuring payee traceability (by the payer only); limiting off-line transferability; limiting the issuance of electronic cash to regulated institutions; disallowing anonymous accounts; issuing only personalized paying devices; identifying payers in high-value transactions; and, checking the identity of parties who convert other forms of money into electronic cash.

Other excuses for key escrow have been to deal with theft or extortion of the bank's secret key, and to deal with attackers with "infinite" computing power. In Section 5.5.5, however, we have seen that these are not valid excuses either to destroy privacy. Also, in Section 6.4.4 we have shown how to combat extortion of the certified key pairs of certificate holders.[13]

Furthermore, the proposed key escrow electronic cash systems that circumvent involvement of the key escrow authorities in the withdrawal protocol achieve only computational "untraceability" (with respect to other parties than the key escrow authorities).[14]

Much of the key escrow work sports exaggerated and even downright ignorant statements about how privacy will hurt individuals, organizations, and societies at large. Some comfort may be derived from the observation that most authors of key escrow papers in all likelihood had little more on their minds than the urge to publish yet another paper. Waving the key escrow magic wand is the quickest way to success whenever more honorable approaches to improve a line of research are unsuccessful. By radically changing the model to key escrow, the researcher all of a sudden finds him or herself in the luxurious position of being able to claim and glorify new security benefits and features. At the same time, the key escrow smoke screen enables the researcher to downplay the annihilation of privacy by claiming that the new system provides "balanced" privacy; many authors do not even shy away from claiming that their key escrow systems "preserve" or even "improve" privacy.

This down-to-earth explanation of why key escrow approach has been running rampant does not make the trend any less disquieting or harmful, though. If nothing else, the key escrow work has resulted in greatly eroded levels of awareness among fresh researchers of the meaning and importance of privacy.

Some proponents of the key escrow approach argue that the assumption of an anonymous channel (over which to send blind signatures, say) is essentially as strong as the assumption that the key escrow authorities will not pool together their key shares, "because" anonymous channels also rely on some kind of threshold assumption. (Indeed, the electronic voting schemes of Chaum [94] and Bos [42, Chapter 3] rely on a "mix" network.) This argument does not hold water, though. In the physical world, covert mass surveillance of identified individuals is completely infeasible;

---

[13]In another proposal by Pfitzmann and Sadeghi [302], each user plays the role of the key escrow authorities by him or herself. The drawback of this proposal is that payments are only computationally untraceable. On the upside, the proposal works also in software-only settings. The same technique can be used to protect against extortion of certified key pairs in our software-only setting.

[14]Another drawback is that virtually all the proposed key escrow cash systems require payments to be online to guarantee prior restraint of double-spending or do not address any of the privacy issues associated with smartcards (see Chapter 6). The only exception is a system proposed by Camenisch, Maurer, and Stadler [71], which hereto uses techniques developed in this book.

an anonymous channel may be as easy as dropping a letter in a mailbox or walking to a nearby office. In cyberspace, alternative means are available, as we have seen in Section 1.2.2. The trend of wireless connection through handhelds could make it even easier to escape identification. Even if senders over the Internet use methods that enable others to trace their actions without their assistance, it may be very hard, costly, or time-consuming to examine and link the records of Internet access providers and other organizations. The parties that need to be approached to enable tracing may differ in each circumstance, may be in different jurisdictions, may not keep any records at all, and may have no intention of breaching the privacy vows they made to their customers. At the very least, automated key recovery and routine tracing are not an option.

More importantly, and this is the crucial difference with key escrow, users are free to choose for themselves which mechanism and which (and how many) parties they will use for each communication or transaction. With key escrow, in contrast, all system participants are forced to deliver the ability to instantly recover all their secrets to a single set of authorities that they cannot choose freely, and that are under a legal obligation to keep records and cooperate when subpoenaed or presented with a court order or a warrant.

Privacy is protected only if each individual is able at all times to control and determine for him or herself which parties, if any, are capable of recovering a secret. If a user decides to give up some of that control, that is his or her choice, but it should not be hardwired into the design of the system.

The benefits of privacy-enhancing technologies

Oleinick [290, Chapter 4] rightfully notes that "The transfer of control over personal information that occurs in a disclosure of personal information is a transfer of power." Privacy protection requires that each individual has the power to decide how his or her personal data is collected and used, how it is modified, and to what extent it can be linked; only in this way can individuals remain in control over their personal data. The techniques developed in this book demonstrate that these goals can be achieved through the use of privacy-enhancing technologies that are entirely feasible and secure.

When designing abuse protection techniques, it is of fundamental importance that any user secret can be computed only with the consent of that user (unless perhaps if he or she commits a crime). The security techniques described in this book, notably in Section 5.5 and in Section 6.4.4, all meet this objective. In particular, in Section 5.5.1 we have described techniques for *self-revocable* unlinkability and untraceability: certificate holders can prove to have been the originator of a showing protocol execution, can provide evidence to have been the originator of multiple transactions without disclosing their identity, and can prove that they were not involved in certain transactions.

Organizations often claim that restrictions to the flow of personally identifiable information hinder their ability to use up-to-date personal information for the purpose of reducing identity fraud. Privacy-enhanced PKIs overcome this objection, and in fact offer a myriad of benefits to organizations:

- The need to consult Certificate Revocation Lists or online certificate validation services is minimized.

- CAs and other central parties cannot learn data about the customers of certificate verifiers, and so they cannot compete unfairly. (Organizations typically pay, through discounts or otherwise, to learn the identity and other personal data of customers.)

- The scope for identity fraud and other abuses is minimized.

- Industry-wide adoption of privacy-enhanced PKIs fosters fair competition with respect to the collection and use of personal data. (Organizations can only learn and link data with the consent of the certificate holders to whom the data pertains.)

- The need to protect online databases against intrusions by hackers and insiders is minimized.

- Guaranteed privacy protection makes consumers feel much more comfortable to engage in electronic transactions. Likewise, privacy cultivates goodwill, which is a distinct competitive advantage.

- The trend is for regulations to require mechanisms for assuring adherence of privacy standards. This will significantly raise compliance costs to industry. (See, for example, the Masons Study [256] on compliance with the European Privacy Directive.) The use of privacy-enhanced PKIs enables individuals to reveal only the minimum information needed to complete a transaction, and thus minimizes the burden on industry to demonstrate adherence to privacy standards.

- More generally, privacy-enhanced PKIs are the cheapest and most effective way to comply with as many of the privacy principles of codes of conduct and privacy legislation as possible, since their restrictions and requirements do not apply to anonymous information. In a 1998 report [133], the U.S. Department of Commerce set out the following nine specific characteristics of effective self-regulation for privacy online: awareness, choice, data security, data integrity, consumer access, accountability, verification, consumer recourse, and consequences. Our techniques enable one to implement the first seven of these in the strongest possible sense. They also facilitate automated dispute resolution (non-repudiation), which greatly helps to realize the privacy characteristics of consumer recourse and consequences.

- The scope for law enforcement intrusions on the data records of organizations is minimized; there will be little to infer.

- Transaction finality is improved.

- The scope for discrimination is greatly reduced.

Adoption of the techniques in this book could also stimulate the public acceptance of smartcards, because smartcards cannot be misused for the purpose of surveillance. Our techniques are desirable even from an economic viewpoint, because they can be implemented using low-cost smartcards without cryptographic coprocessors. Furthermore, tamper-resistant devices for certificate holders are unavoidable if digital signatures are to have a firm legal grounding.

What needs to be done

It is time to stop tolerating (let alone promoting) seal programs, infomediaries, key escrow systems, and other misleading practices towards privacy. Schemes in which users do not have control over their own personal data offer zero privacy. No smoke and mirrors can change this fact.

While privacy-enhancing PKIs minimize the need for legislative intervention, they cannot remove the need for privacy legislation altogether. Privacy legislation is needed to set the general boundaries of what kinds of personal data may be bartered for what purposes,[15] what attribute types may be encoded, under what circumstances (if any) a verifier may refuse access to the holder of a valid certificate, on what grounds (if any) a CA may refuse certificate requests or applicants, and so on. Legislation may also be needed to mandate organizations to delete personal data that has been voluntarily disclosed to them as soon as it has fulfilled the purpose to which the individual consented.[16] Furthermore, legislation is needed to provide a right to judicial remedies, and to enable prosecution of fraudulent behavior (means of redress). Privacy-enhanced PKIs should be the norm, with the kinds of linking and tracing information that may be bartered (and other issues that technology cannot resolve) defined by (preferably overarching) privacy legislation. See the American Civil Liberties Union [10], Clarke [118], and Marx [255, Table II] for discussions of

---

[15] As we have seen in Section 6.5.5, smartcards can prevent identity bartering, but this is not sufficient.

[16] A precedent for such legislation has been set in 1997 by the Privacy Commissioner of Sweden, who instructed American Airlines operating in Europe to delete all health and medical details on Swedish passengers after each flight unless explicit consent could be obtained; both the District Court and the Court of Appeal have rejected actions by American Airlines.

the kinds of privacy provisions that are desirable. One tantalizing idea that has been put forward is to give individuals property rights over their personal information. Several influential organizations have in recent years made the case for building privacy into electronic communication and transaction mechanisms. For example:

- In 1995, the NII Task Force [313] stated that "Privacy should not be addressed as a mere afterthought, once personal information has been acquired. Rather, information users should explicitly consider the impact on privacy in the very process of designing information systems and in deciding whether to acquire or use personal information in the first place."

- In 1996, the Working party on Illegal and Harmful Content on the Internet in its report [155] for the Council of Europe stated: "Anonymous use of the Internet takes a number of forms: anonymous browsing, anonymous publishing of content on the World Wide Web, anonymous e-mail messages and anonymous posting of messages to newsgroups. In accordance with the principle of freedom of expression and the right to privacy, use of anonymity is legal. [...] A user should not be required to justify anonymous use."

- Also in 1996, the International Working Group on Data Protection in Telecommunications [217] stated its conviction that "it is necessary to develop technical means to improve the users privacy on the Net. [...] In general users should have the opportunity to access the Internet without having to reveal their identity where personal data are not needed to provide a certain service. [...] Anonymity is an essential additional asset for privacy protection on the Internet. Restrictions on the principle of anonymity should be strictly limited to what is necessary in a democratic society without questioning the principle as such."

- In 1997, an advisory committee of the European Commission to the European Parliament [156] recommended that "Technological developments and take-up promotion projects in European Union R&D programmes should concentrate on providing a wide range of interoperable, compatible electronic commerce building-blocks. [...] They should favour technologies which minimise the need for personal data and thus enhance the protection of the right to privacy of consumers (privacy enhancing technologies)."

- Also in 1997, the Working Party of the European Union [373] declared that "where the user can choose to remain anonymous off-line, that choice should also be available on-line. [...] The ability to choose to remain anonymous is essential if individuals are to preserve the same protection for their privacy on-line as they currently enjoy off-line. [...] The principle that the collection of identifiable personal data should be limited to the minimum necessary must be recognized in the evolving national and international laws dealing with the

Internet. It should also be embodied in codes of conduct, guidelines and other 'soft law' instruments that are developed. Where appropriate this principle should specify that individual users be given the choice to remain anonymous."

- In October 1997, Directorate-General XIII of the European Commission [137] warned that privacy safeguards are needed because otherwise "digital signatures could be abused as an efficient instrument for tracing individual on-line consumption patterns and communication or for intercepting, recording or misusing documents or messages."

- In 1998, the Group of Experts on Information Security and Privacy [198], in their background report for an OECD Ministerial Conference, noted: "Privacy enhancing technologies should not be seen as primarily novel technical developments or as additions to existing systems. Rather, they should be seen as a matter of design philosophy: one that encourages (in appropriate circumstances) the removal of identifiers linked to personal data thereby anonymising the data."

- A 1998 draft paper [375] by the U.S. government states: "If electronic commerce is to realize its enormous potential consumers must be confident that their personal information is protected against misuse. Electronic commerce in the next century will thrive only to the extent that individuals' privacy is protected. [...] Technology will offer solutions to many privacy concerns in the online environment, and will serve as an important tool to protect privacy."

- Also in 1998, the Steering Committee of the Federal Public Key Infrastructure [163] warned that "for many applications, identity-based authentication is not only unnecessary, it may be inappropriate. Agencies will need to consider carefully which applications require user authentication (e.g., to protect private information). In many instances, such as downloading forms, anonymous transactions are appropriate."

- In October 1998, the governments of the member countries of the OECD [199] declared that "they will take the necessary steps, within the framework of their respective laws and practices, to ensure that the OECD Privacy Guidelines are effectively implemented in relation to global networks, and in particular [...] encourage the use of privacy-enhancing technologies."

Nevertheless, countries have yet to establish a climate that allows privacy-enhancing technologies to flourish. Without efforts to fund and promote the development and adoption of privacy-enhancing technologies, and without the enactment of laws that forbid the use of privacy-invading technologies in communication and transaction applications in which there is no strict need to establish identity, the above statements are nothing more than hollow phrases.

Unfortunately, the benefits of protecting privacy by means of technological measures are not widely acknowledged. Several countries have drafted, or are in the process of drafting, legislation that requires public keys to be bound to true names or traceable pseudonyms. As Baker and Yeo [17] point out, "The effect of these provisions will be to make it more difficult, if not impossible, to establish the legal validity of non-identity certificates and to enforce transactions that are authenticated by non-identity certificates."

The widespread adoption of automated transaction systems that lack any provisions to protect privacy is a very dangerous trend. As Swire [367] points out, "The systems in place in one period can have a powerful effect on what systems will develop in subsequent periods. [...] Once the costs of the database and infrastructure are already incurred for initial purposes, then additional uses may be cost-justified that would not otherwise have been." Holmes [212] notes that "the danger to democratic countries is not that they will openly embrace totalitarianism. It is [...] that they will unwittingly, almost imperceptibly, and with the best of intentions, allow themselves to drift so far in that direction that the final step will then be but a small one." Chaum [104] observes that the current situation "does not want to go halfway in between. It really has a natural tendency to flip into one of two extreme positions." For a compelling case of how only architectures of freedom can prevent tyrannies, see Rummel [331].

Today, the foundations for the communication and transaction technologies of this century are being laid. Digital certificates will be hardwired into all operating systems, network protocols, Web browsers, chipcards, application programs, and so on. To avert the doom scenario of a global village founded wholly on inescapable identification technologies, it is imperative that we rethink our preconceived ideas about security and identity—and build in privacy before the point of no return has been reached.

References

[1] M. Abadi, E. Allender, A. Broder, J. Feigenbaum, and L. Hemachandra. On generating solved instances of computational problems. In S. Goldwasser, editor, *Advances in Cryptology–CRYPTO '88*, volume 403 of *Lecture Notes in Computer Science*, pages 297–310. Springer-Verlag, 1988.

[2] Hal Abelson, Ross Anderson, Steven M. Bellovin, Josh Benaloh, Matt Blaze, Whitfield Diffie, John Gilmore, Peter G. Neumann, Ronald L. Rivest, Jeffery I. Schiller, and Bruce Schneier. The risks of key recovery, key escrow, and trusted third party encryption. *World Wide Web Journal*, 2(3):241–257, 1997. Also in: Report in Centre for Democracy and Technology Policy Post, Vol. 3, no. 6, May 21, 1997. A revised edition appeared June 1998.

[3] Accredited Standards Committee X9. American National Standard X9.59-199x: Electronic Commerce for the Financial Services Industry: Account-Based Secure Payment Objects. Working Draft # 17, January 1999.

[4] C. Adams and S. Farrell. Internet X.509 public key infrastructure certificate management protocols. Internet Draft of the PKIX Working Group, May 1998.

[5] Carlisle Adams and Robert Zuccherato. A general, flexible approach to certificate revocation. Entrust white paper, June 1998.

[6] G.B. Agnew, R.C. Mullin, and S.A. Vanstone. An implementation of elliptic curve cryptosystems over $F_{2^{155}}$. *IEEE Journal on Selected Areas in Communications*, 11(5):804–813, June 1993.

[7] William Aiello, Sachin Lodha, and Rafail Ostrovsky. Fast digital identity revocation. In Hugo Krawczyk, editor, *Advances in Cryptology–CRYPTO '98*, Lecture Notes in Computer Science, pages 137–152. Springer-Verlag, 1998.

[8] American Bankers Association. X9.45-199x: Enhanced management controls using digital signatures and attribute certificates. Working draft, June 1997.

[9] American Bar Association. Digital signature guidelines; legal infrastructure for certification authorities and secure electronic commerce, August 1996. ISBN 1-57073-250-7.

[10] American Civil Liberties Union. Elements of effective self regulation for the protection of privacy and questions related to online privacy. Letter to Ms. Jane Coffin, Office of International Affairs, National Telecommunications and Information Administration, July 1998.

[11] American National Standards Institute. American National Standards Committee X.9.55-1995: Public key cryptography for the financial services industry, 1995.

[12] Ross Anderson and Markus Kuhn. Tamper resistance - a cautionary note. In *Second USENIX Workshop on Electronic Commerce*, pages 1–11, Oakland, California, November 1996. USENIX Association. ISBN 1-880446-83-9.

[13] Ross Anderson and Markus Kuhn. Low cost attacks on tamper resistant devices. In *Security Protocols, 5th International Workshop, Paris, France*, volume 1361 of *Lecture Notes in Computer Science*, pages 125–136. Springer-Verlag, April 1997.

[14] Ross Anderson and Serge Vaudenay. Minding your p's and q's. In Kwangjo Kim and Tsutomu Matsumoto, editors, *Advances in Cryptology–ASIACRYPT '96*, volume 1163 of *Lecture Notes in Computer Science*, pages 26–35. Springer-Verlag, 1996.

[15] Arthur Andersen Computer Risk Management. Report on companies' use of encryption & evaluations re. monitorable encryption systems. Background report for the Danish Ministry of Research and Information Technology, February 1998.

[16] Eric Bach. How to generate factored random numbers. *SIAM J. Computing*, 17(2):179–193, April 1988.

[17] Stewart Baker and Matthew Yeo. Survey of international electronic and digital signature initiatives. Steptoe & Johnson LLP, Internet Law and Policy Forum, version of April 14, 1999.

[18] Stewart A. Baker. Don't worry be happy – why Clipper is good for you. Wired 2.06, 1996.

[19] James Bamford. *The Puzzle Palace: A Report on America's Most Secret Agency*. Houghton Mifflin, Boston, 1982.

[20] Banksys / Groupement des Cartes Bancaires. Interoperable C-SET: Protocol specification. Deliverable: D 6.1, Issue 2, Version 0, November 1997.

[21] Mihir Bellare, Juan A. Garay, and Tal Rabin. Fast batch verification for modular exponentiation and digital signatures, June 1998. Extended abstract in: Advances in Cryptology – Proceedings of Eurocrypt 98, Lecture Notes in Computer Science Vol. 1403, K. Nyberg ed., Springer-Verlag, 1998.

[22] Mihir Bellare and Oded Goldreich. On defining proofs of knowledge. In Ernest F. Brickell, editor, *Advances in Cryptology–CRYPTO '92*, volume 740 of *Lecture Notes in Computer Science*, pages 390–420. Springer-Verlag, 1992.

[23] Mihir Bellare, Oded Goldreich, and Shafi Goldwasser. Incremental cryptography: The case of hashing and signing. In Yvo G. Desmedt, editor, *Advances in Cryptology–CRYPTO '94*, volume 839 of *Lecture Notes in Computer Science*, pages 216–233. Springer-Verlag, 1994.

[24] Mihir Bellare, Markus Jakobsson, and Moti Yung. Round-optimal zero-knowledge arguments based on any one-way function. In Walter Fumy, editor, *Advances in Cryptology–EUROCRYPT '97*, volume 1233 of *Lecture Notes in Computer Science*, pages 280–305. Springer-Verlag, 1997.

[25] J. Benaloh and J. Leichter. Generalized secret sharing and monotone functions. In S. Goldwasser, editor, *Advances in Cryptology–CRYPTO '88*, volume 403 of *Lecture Notes in Computer Science*, pages 27–35. Springer-Verlag, 1988.

[26] J. Benaloh and M. Yung. Distributing the power of a government to enhance the privacy of voters. In *Proceedings of the 5th Symposium on Principles of Distributed Computing*, pages 52–62, New York, August 1986. ACM.

[27] Shimshon Berkovits, Santosh Chokhani, Judith A. Furlong, Jisoo A. Geiter, and Jonathan C. Guild. Public Key Infrastructure study. Final Report for the National Institute of Standards and Technology. Task performed by The MITRE Corporation, McLean, Virginia, April 1994.

[28] Ingrid Biehl, Bernd Meyer, and Christoph Thiel. Cryptographic protocols based on real-quadratic a-fields. In Kwangjo Kim and Tsutomu Matsumoto, editors, *Advances in Cryptology–ASIACRYPT '96*, volume 1163 of *Lecture Notes in Computer Science*, pages 15–25. Springer-Verlag, 1996.

[29] Eli Biham and Adi Shamir. The next stage of differential fault analysis: How to break completely unknown cryptosystems. Distributed on October 30th, 1996.

[30] Eli Biham and Adi Shamir. Differential fault analysis of secret key cryptosystems. In Burton S. Kaliski Jr., editor, *Advances in Cryptology–CRYPTO '97*, volume 1294 of *Lecture Notes in Computer Science*, pages 513–525. Springer-Verlag, 1997.

[31] David Birch. Exploiting Privacy Enhancing Technologies. Proceedings of UK Data Protection '99 IIR, London, July 1999. Draft of 5/7/99.

[32] M. Blaze, J. Feigenbaum, J. Ioannidis, and A. Keromytis. The role of trust management in distributed system security. In J. Vitek and C. Jensen, editors, *Secure Internet Programming: Security Issues for Distributed and Mobile Objects*, volume 1603 of *Lecture Notes in Computer Science*, pages 185–210. Springer, 1999.

[33] Matt Blaze, Joan Feigenbaum, and Jack Lacy. Decentralized trust management. In *Proceedings of the 17th Symposium on Security and Privacy*, pages 164–173, Los Alamitos, 1996. IEEE Computer Society Press.

[34] Daniel Bleichenbacher. Generating ElGamal signatures without knowing the secret key. In Ueli Maurer, editor, *Advances in Cryptology–EUROCRYPT '96*, volume 1070 of *Lecture Notes in Computer Science*, pages 10–18. Springer-Verlag, 1996.

[35] Daniel Bleichenbacher, Eran Gabber, Phil Gibbons, and Yossi Matias. On personalized yet anonymous interaction. Manuscript 1997.

[36] D. Boneh and G. Durfee. Cryptanalysis of RSA with private key d less than $n^{0.292}$. In *Advances in Cryptology–EUROCRYPT '99*, volume 1592 of *Lecture Notes in Computer Science*, pages 1–11. Springer-Verlag, 1999.

[37] Dan Boneh. Twenty years of attacks on the RSA cryptosystem. *Notices of the American Mathematical Society*, 46(2):203–213, 1999.

[38] Dan Boneh, Richard A. DeMillo, and Richard J. Lipton. On the importance of checking cryptographic protocols for faults. In Walter Fumy, editor, *Advances in Cryptology–EUROCRYPT '97*, volume 1233 of *Lecture Notes in Computer Science*, pages 37–51. Springer-Verlag, 1997.

[39] Dan Boneh and Matthew Franklin. Efficient generation of shared RSA keys. In Burton S. Kaliski Jr., editor, *Advances in Cryptology–CRYPTO '97*, volume 1294 of *Lecture Notes in Computer Science*, pages 425–439. Springer-Verlag, 1997.

[40] Dan Boneh and Ramarathnam Venkatesan. Breaking RSA may be easier than factoring. In Kaisa Nyberg, editor, *Advances in Cryptology–EUROCRYPT '98*, volume 1233 of *Lecture Notes in Computer Science*, pages 59–71. Springer-Verlag, 1998.

[41] J.N.E. Bos and D. Chaum. SmartCash: a practical electronic payment system. Technical Report CS-R9035, Centrum voor Wiskunde en Infomatica, August 1990.

[42] Jurjen N.E. Bos. *Practical Privacy*. PhD thesis, Centrum voor Wiskunde en Informatica, March 1992. In: Verification of RSA Computations on a Small Computer, pages 103–116.

[43] Caspar Bowden and Yaman Akdeniz. Cryptography and democracy: Dilemmas of freedom. *Liberating Cyberspace: Civil Liberties, Human Rights, and the Internet*, pages 81–125, 1999.

[44] Joan Boyar, S.A. Kurtz, and M.W. Krentel. A discrete logarithm implementation of perfect zero-knowledge blobs. *Journal of Cryptology*, 2(2):63–76, 1990.

[45] Stefan Brands. Cryptographic methods for demonstrating satisfiable formulas from propositional logic. Patent PCT/NL96/00413. Filed November 1995.

[46] Stefan Brands. An efficient off-line electronic cash system based on the representation problem. Technical Report CS-R9323, Centrum voor Wiskunde en Informatica, April 1993.

[47] Stefan Brands. Off-line cash transfer by smart cards. Technical Report CS-R9455, Centrum voor Wiskunde en Informatica, September 1994. Also in: Proceedings of the First Smart Card Research and Advanced Application Conference (October 1994), France, pages 101–117.

[48] Stefan Brands. Untraceable off-line cash in wallet with observers. In Douglas R. Stinson, editor, *Advances in Cryptology–CRYPTO '93*, volume 911, pages 302–318. Springer-Verlag, 1994.

[49] Stefan Brands. Off-line electronic cash based on secret-key certificates. In R. Baeza-Yates, E. Goles, and P.V. Goblete, editors, *Proceedings of the Second International Symposium of Latin American Theoretical Informatics*, volume 911, pages 131–166. Springer-Verlag, 1995.

[50] Stefan Brands. Restrictive blind issuing of secret-key certificates in parallel mode. Technical Report CS-R9523, Centrum voor Wiskunde en Informatica, March 1995.

[51] Stefan Brands. Restrictive blinding of secret-key certificates. In Louis C. Guillou and Jean-Jacques Quisquater, editors, *Advances in Cryptology–EUROCRYPT '95*, volume 921 of *Lecture Notes in Computer Science*, pages 231–247. Springer-Verlag, 1995.

[52] Stefan Brands. Secret-key certificates. Technical Report CS-R9510, Centrum voor Wiskunde en Informatica, February 1995.

[53] Stefan Brands. Secret-key certificates (continued). Technical Report CS-R9555, Centrum voor Wiskunde en Informatica, June 1995.

[54] Stefan Brands. Privacy-protected transfer of electronic information. U.S. Patent ser. no. 5,604,805, February 1997. Filed August 1993.

[55] Stefan Brands. Rapid demonstration of linear relations connected by Boolean operators. In Walter Fumy, editor, *Advances in Cryptology–EUROCRYPT '97*, volume 1233 of *Lecture Notes in Computer Science*, pages 318–333. Springer-Verlag, 1997.

[56] Stefan Brands. Secret-key certificates. U.S. Patent ser. no. 5,606,617, February 1997. Filed October 1994.

[57] Stefan Brands. Secure cryptographic methods for electronic transfer of information. U.S. Patent ser. no. 5,668,878, September 1997. Filed August 1995.

[58] Stefan Brands. Electronic cash. In Mikhail J. Atallah, editor, *Algorithms and Theory of Computation Handbook*, chapter 44. CRC Press LLC, November 1998. ISBN 0-8493-2649-4.

[59] Stefan Brands and David Chaum. Distance-bounding protocols. In Tor Helleseth, editor, *Advances in Cryptology–EUROCRYPT '93*, volume 765 of *Lecture Notes in Computer Science*, pages 344–359. Springer-Verlag, 1994.

[60] G. Brassard, D. Chaum, and C. Crépeau. Minimum disclosure proofs of knowledge. *Journal of Computer and System Sciences*, 37(2):156–189, 1988.

[61] D.M. Bressoud. *Factorization and Primality Testing*. Springer-Verlag, New York, 1989.

[62] Ernest Brickell, Peter Gemmell, and David Kravitz. Trustee-based tracing extensions to anonymous cash and the making of anonymous change. In *Proceedings of the 6th Annual Symposium on Discrete Algorithms*, pages 457–466, 1995.

[63] Ernest F. Brickell, David Chaum, Ivan B. Damgård, and Jeroen van de Graaf. Gradual and verifiable release of a secret. In Carl Pomerance, editor, *Advances in Cryptology–CRYPTO '87*, volume 293 of *Lecture Notes in Computer Science*, pages 156–166. Springer-Verlag, 1988.

[64] Murray J. Brown. Secure wireless messaging: A new approach to digital certificates. Wireless Magazine, October 1998.

[65] Mark E. Budnitz. Industry self-regulation of internet privacy: The sound of one hand clapping. Computers, Freedom & Privacy 1999, April 6–8, Washington DC.

[66] Mark E. Budnitz. Privacy protection for consumer transactions in electronic commerce: Why self-regulation is inadequate. 49 S. Caro. L. Rev. 847, 1998.

[67] Mike Burmester. A remark on the efficiency of identification schemes. In I.B. Damgård, editor, *Advances in Cryptology–EUROCRYPT '90*, volume 473 of *Lecture Notes in Computer Science*, pages 493–495. Springer-Verlag, 1991.

[68] W. E. Burr. Public key infrastructure (PKI) technical specifications: Part A - technical concept of operations. Working draft TWG-98-59, September 1998.

[69] J. Callas, L. Donnerhacke, H. Finney, and R. Thayer. OpenPGP message format. Network Working Group, Request for Comments no. 2440, November 1998.

[70] Jan Camenisch. *Group Signature Schemes and Payment Systems Based on the Discrete Logarithm Problem*. PhD thesis, ETH, 1998. Reprinted as Vol. 2 in ETH Series in Information Security and Cryptography, edited by Ueli Maurer, Hartung-Gorre Verlag, Konstanz, ISBN 3-89649-286-1.

[71] Jan Camenisch, Ueli Maurer, and Markus Stadler. Digital payment systems with passive anonymity-revoking trustees. *Journal of Computer Security*, 5(1), 1997. Abridged version in: Computer Security – ESORICS 96, Vol. 1146, pages 33–43, Springer-Verlag.

[72] Jan Camenisch, Jean-Marc Piveteau, and Markus Stadler. Blind signatures based on the discrete logarithm problem. In Alfredo De Santis, editor, *Advances in Cryptology–EUROCRYPT '94*, volume 950 of *Lecture Notes in Computer Science*, pages 428–432. Springer-Verlag, 1995.

[73] Jan Camenisch and Markus Stadler. Efficient group signature schemes for large groups. In Burton S. Kaliski Jr., editor, *Advances in Cryptology–CRYPTO '97*, volume 1294 of *Lecture Notes in Computer Science*, pages 410–424. Springer-Verlag, 1997.

[74] Jan Camenisch and Markus Stadler. Proof systems for general statements about discrete logarithms. Technical Report TR 260, Institute for Theoretical Computer Science, ETH Zürich, March 1997.

[75] Duncan Campbell. Interception capabilities 2000. Report to the Director General for Research of the European Parliament (Scientific and Technical Options Assessment programme office) on the development of surveillance technology and risk of abuse of economic information, April 1999.

[76] Ran Canetti, Oded Goldreich, and Shai Halevi. The random oracle methodology, revisited. In *Proc. 30th ACM Symp. on Theory of Computing*. ACM Press, 1998.

[77] Stefania Cavallar, Bruce Dodson, Arjen K. Lenstra, Walter Lioen, Peter L. Montgomery, Brian Murphy, Herman te Riele, Karen Aardal, Jeff Gilchrist,

Gérard Guillerm, Paul Leyland, Joël Marchand, Francois Morain, Alec Muffett, Chris Putnam, Craig Putnam, and Paul Zimmermann. Factorization of a 512-bit RSA modulus. To appear in: Proceedings of Eurocrypt 2000.

[78] Ann Cavoukian. Identity theft: Who's using your name? Information and Privacy Commissioner of Ontario, Canada, June 1997.

[79] Ann Cavoukian, Catherine Johnston, and David Duncan. Smart, optical and other advanced cards: How to do a privacy assessment. Joint report of the Information and Privacy Commissioner of Ontario and the Advanced Card Technology Association of Canada, 1996.

[80] CCITT. Recommendation X.500: The directory–overview of concepts, models and services, 1988.

[81] CCITT. Recommendation X.501: The directory–models, 1988.

[82] Center for Democracy and Technology. Policy vs. practice; a progress report on federal government privacy notice on the world wide web, April 1999.

[83] Center for Public Integrity. Nothing sacred: The politics of privacy, July 1998. ISBN: 1882583-12-4.

[84] M. Cerecedo, T. Matsumoto, and H. Imai. Efficient and secure multiparty generation of digital signatures based on discrete logarithms. *IEICE Trans. Fundamentals E76-A(4)*, pages 532–545, April 1993.

[85] Certicom. The elliptic curve cryptosystem for smart cards. Whitepaper no. 7, May 1998.

[86] B. Chalks. Privacy enhancement for Internet electronic mail – part IV: Key certification and related services. RFC 1424-C, February 1993.

[87] D. Chaum. Showing credentials without identification: Transferring signatures between unconditionally unlinkable pseudonyms. In J. Seberry and J. Pieprzyk, editors, *Advances in Cryptology–AUSCRYPT '90*, volume 453 of *Lecture Notes in Computer Science*, pages 246–264. Springer-Verlag, 1990.

[88] D. Chaum. Achieving electronic privacy. *Scientific American*, 267(2):96–101, August 1992.

[89] D. Chaum, C. Crepeau, and I. Damgård. Multi-party unconditionally secure protocols. In *Proc. 20th ACM Symp. on Theory of Computing*, pages 11–19, Chicago, 1988. ACM Press.

[90] D. Chaum, A. Fiat, and M. Naor. Untraceable electronic cash. In S. Goldwasser, editor, *Advances in Cryptology–CRYPTO '88*, volume 403 of *Lecture Notes in Computer Science*, pages 319–327. Springer-Verlag, 1988.

[91] David Chaum. Blind signatures for untraceable payments. In R.L. Rivest, A. Sherman, and D. Chaum, editors, *Advances in Cryptology–CRYPTO '82*, pages 199–203. Plenum Press, 1983.

[92] David Chaum. Blind signature system. In D. Chaum, editor, *Advances in Cryptology–CRYPTO '83*, page 153, New York, 1984. Plenum Press.

[93] David Chaum. Security without identification: Transaction systems to make Big Brother obsolete. *Communications of the ACM*, 28(10):1030–1044, October 1985.

[94] David Chaum. Blind signature systems. U.S. Patent ser. no. 4,759,063, July 1988. Filed August 1983.

[95] David Chaum. Blind unanticipated signature systems. U.S. Patent ser. no. 4,759,064, July 1988. Filed October 1985.

[96] David Chaum. Privacy protected payments: Unconditional payer and/or payee untraceability. In D. Chaum and I. Schaumüller-Bichl, editors, *SMART CARD 2000*, pages 69–93. Elsevier Science Publishers B.V. (North-Holland), 1989.

[97] David Chaum. Card-computer moderated systems. U.S. Patent ser. no. 4,926,480, May 1990. Filed May 1988.

[98] David Chaum. One-show blind signature systems. U.S. Patent ser. no. 4,987,593, January 1991. Filed April 1990. Continuation of abandoned application Ser. No. 07/168,802, filed March 1988.

[99] David Chaum. Selected-exponent signature systems. U.S. Patent ser. no. 4,996,711, February 1991. Filed June 1989.

[100] David Chaum. Unpredictable blind signature systems. U.S. Patent ser. no. 4,991,210, February 1991. Filed May 1989.

[101] David Chaum. Zero-knowledge undeniable signatures. In I.B. Damgård, editor, *Advances in Cryptology–EUROCRYPT '90*, volume 473 of *Lecture Notes in Computer Science*, pages 458–464. Springer-Verlag, 1991.

[102] David Chaum. Designated-confirmer signature systems. U.S. Patent ser. no. 5,373,558, December 1994. Filed May 1993.

[103] David Chaum. Optionally moderated transaction systems. U.S. Patent ser. no. 5,276,736, January 1994. Filed July 1992.

[104] David Chaum. David Chaum on electronic commerce: How much do you trust Big Brother? *IEEE Internet Computing*, pages 8–16, November 1997.

[105] David Chaum. Limited-traceability systems. U.S. Patent ser. no. 5,712,913, January 1998. Filed February 1994.

[106] David Chaum, Ivan B. Damgård, and Jeroen van de Graaf. Multiparty computations ensuring privacy of each party's input and correctness of the result. In Carl Pomerance, editor, *Advances in Cryptology–CRYPTO '87*, volume 293 of *Lecture Notes in Computer Science*, pages 87–119. Springer-Verlag, 1988.

[107] David Chaum and Jan-Hendrik Evertse. A secure and privacy-protecting protocol for transmitting personal information between organizations. In A.M. Odlyzko, editor, *Advances in Cryptology–CRYPTO '86*, volume 263 of *Lecture Notes in Computer Science*, pages 118–168. Springer-Verlag, 1987.

[108] David Chaum, Jan-Hendrik Evertse, and Jeroen van de Graaf. An improved protocol for demonstrating possession of a discrete logarithm and some generalizations. In D. Chaum and W.L. Price, editors, *Advances in Cryptology–EUROCRYPT '87*, volume 304 of *Lecture Notes in Computer Science*, pages 127–141. Springer-Verlag, 1987.

[109] David Chaum and Torben Pryds Pedersen. Wallet databases with observers. In Ernest F. Brickell, editor, *Advances in Cryptology–CRYPTO '92*, volume 740 of *Lecture Notes in Computer Science*, pages 89–105. Springer-Verlag, 1992.

[110] David Chaum and Hans van Antwerpen. Undeniable signatures. In G. Brassard, editor, *Advances in Cryptology–CRYPTO '89*, volume 435 of *Lecture Notes in Computer Science*, pages 212–216, 1990.

[111] David Chaum, Eugène van Heijst, and Birgit Pfitzmann. Cryptographically strong undeniable signatures, unconditionally secure for the signer. Technical report, University of Karlsruhe, February 1991. Interner Bericht 1/91.

[112] David Chaum, Eugène van Heijst, and Birgit Pfitzmann. Cryptographically strong undeniable signatures, unconditionally secure for the signer. In J. Feigenbaum, editor, *Advances in Cryptology–CRYPTO '91*, volume 576 of *Lecture Notes in Computer Science*, pages 470–484. Springer-Verlag, 1992.

[113] Lidong Chen. Access with pseudonyms. In Ed Dawson and Jovan Golic, editors, *Cryptography: Policy and Algorithms*, number 1029 in Lecture Notes in Computer Science, pages 232–243. Springer-Verlag, 1995.

[114] S. Chokhani and W. Ford. Internet public key infrastructure certificate policy and certification practices framework. Internet Draft of the PKIX Working Group, work in progress, September 1997.

[115] Yang-hua Chu, Philip DesAutels, Brian LaMacchia, and Peter Lipp. PICS signed labels (DSig) 1.0 specification. W3C Recommendation, May 1998.

[116] Yang-hua Chu, J. Feigenbaum, B. LaMacchia, P. Resnick, and M. Strauss. REFEREE: Trust management for Web applications. *World Wide Web Journal*, 2:127–139, 1997.

[117] Roger Clarke. Chip-based ID: Promise and peril. Invited Address to a Workshop on 'Identity cards, with or without microprocessors: Efficiency versus confidentiality', at the International Conference on Privacy, Montreal, 23-26 September 1997.

[118] Roger Clarke. Internet privacy concerns confirm the case for intervention. *Communications of the ACM*, 42(2), February 1999. Version of 14 October 1998.

[119] J. Cohen and M. Fischer. A robust and verifiable cryptographically secure election scheme. In *Proceedings of 26th Symposium on Foundations of Computer Science*, pages 372–382, New York, October 1985. IEEE Computer Society.

[120] Chris Connolly. Smart cards: Big Brother's little helpers. Technical Report 66, Privacy Committee of New South Wales, August 1995. Also in: First Australian Computer Money Day, Newcastle, March 28, 1996.

[121] M.J. Coster. Some algorithms on addition chains and their complexity. Technical Report CS-R9024, Centrum voor Wiskunde en Informatica, June 1990.

[122] R.J.F. Cramer and T.P. Pedersen. Improved privacy in wallets with observers. In Tor Helleseth, editor, *Advances in Cryptology–EUROCRYPT '93*, volume 765 of *Lecture Notes in Computer Science*, pages 329–343. Springer-Verlag, 1994.

[123] Ronald Cramer, Ivan Damgård, and Berry Schoenmakers. Proofs of partial knowledge and simplified design of witness hiding protocols. In Yvo G. Desmedt, editor, *Advances in Cryptology–CRYPTO '94*, volume 839 of *Lecture Notes in Computer Science*, pages 174–187. Springer-Verlag, 1994.

[124] Ronald Cramer, Matthew Franklin, Berry Schoenmakers, and Moti Yung. Multi-authority secret-ballot elections with linear work. In Ueli Maurer, editor, *Advances in Cryptology–EUROCRYPT '96*, volume 1070 of *Lecture Notes in Computer Science*, pages 72–83. Springer-Verlag, 1996.

[125] Ronald Cramer, Rosario Gennaro, and Berry Schoenmakers. A secure and optimally efficient multi-authority election scheme. In Walter Fumy, editor, *Advances in Cryptology–EUROCRYPT '97*, volume 1233 of *Lecture Notes in Computer Science*, pages 103–118. Springer-Verlag, 1997. Also in: European Transactions on Telecommunications, Vol. 8, No. 5., September/OCtober 1997, pages 481-490.

[126] I.B. Damgård. Payment systems and credential mechanisms with provable security against abuse by individuals. In S. Goldwasser, editor, *Advances in Cryptology–CRYPTO '88*, volume 403 of *Lecture Notes in Computer Science*, pages 328–335. Springer-Verlag, 1988.

[127] Ivan Bjerre Damgård. Practical and provably secure release of a secret. In Tor Helleseth, editor, *Advances in Cryptology–EUROCRYPT '93*, volume 765 of *Lecture Notes in Computer Science*, pages 200–217. Springer-Verlag, 1994.

[128] George Davida, Yair Frankel, Yiannis Tsiounis, and Moti Yung. Anonymity control in e-cash systems. In Rafael Hirschfeld, editor, *Financial Cryptography '97*, volume 1318. Springer-Verlag, February 1997.

[129] Simon Davies. Europe plans huge spy web. Telegraph Online, January 7, 1999.

[130] Simon Davies. Europe to U.S.: No privacy, no trade. *Wired magazine*, May 1998.

[131] Dorothy E. Denning. Descriptions of key escrow systems. Companion document to [132]. Version of February 26, 1997.

[132] Dorothy E. Denning and Dennis K. Branstad. A taxonomy for key recovery encryption systems. Version of May 11, 1997. Revision of "A Taxonomy of Key Escrow Encryption," Communications of the ACM, Vol. 39, No. 3, March 1996, pages 34–40.

[133] Department of Commerce of the National Telecommunications and Information Administration. Elements of effective self regulation for protection of privacy. *Federal Register*, 63(108):30729–30732, June 1998. Draft discussion paper.

[134] Yvo Desmedt. Major security problems with the "unforgeable" (Feige)-Fiat-Shamir proofs of identity and how to overcome them. In *SecuriCom '88, SEDEP Paris*, pages 15–17, 1988.

[135] Yvo Desmedt, Claude Goutier, and Samy Bengio. Special uses and abuses of the Fiat-Shamir passport protocol. In Carl Pomerance, editor, *Advances in Cryptology–CRYPTO '87*, volume 293 of *Lecture Notes in Computer Science*, pages 16–20. Springer-Verlag, 1988.

[136] W. Diffie and M. Hellman. New directions in cryptography. *IEEE Transactions on Information Theory*, IT-11(6):644–654, November 1976.

[137] Directorate-General XIII of the European Commission. Ensuring security and trust in electronic communication; towards a European framework for digital signatures and encryption. Communication to the European Parliament,

the Council, the Economic and Social Committee and the Committee of the Regions. COM (97) 503, October 1997.

[138] DoD Public Key Infrastructure Program Management Office. Public Key Infrastructure roadmap for the Department of Defense. Version 3.0, October 1999.

[139] DoD Public Key Infrastructure Program Management Office. X.509 Certificate Policy for the Department of Defense. Version 5.0, December 1999.

[140] S. Dusse, P. Hoffman, B. Ramsdell, and J. Weinstein. S/MIME version 2 certificate handling. Network Working Group, Request for Comments no. 2312, March 1998.

[141] S. Dusse, P. Hoffman, R. Ramsdell, L. Lundblade, and L. Repka. S/MIME version 2 message specification. Network Working Group, Request for Comments no. 2311, March 1998.

[142] Cynthia Dwork, Jeffrey Lotspiech, and Moni Naor. Digital signets: Self-enforcing protection of digital information. In *Proc. 28th ACM Symp. on Theory of Computing*. ACM Press, 1996.

[143] Electronic Privacy Information Center. Surfer beware: Personal privacy and the Internet, June 1997.

[144] Electronic Privacy Information Center. Surfer beware II: Notice is not enough, June 1998.

[145] Electronic Surveillance Task Force. Communications privacy in the digital age. Interim Report of the Digital Privacy and Security Working Group, June 1997.

[146] Taher ElGamal. A public key cryptosystem and a signature scheme based on discrete logarithms. *IEEE Transactions on Information Theory*, IT-31:469–472, July 1985.

[147] Carl Ellison. Establishing identity without certification authorities. 6th USENIX Security Symposium, San Jose, July 1996.

[148] Carl Ellison and Bruce Schneier. Ten risks of PKI: What you're not being told about Public Key Infrastructure. *Computer Security Journal*, 16(1), 2000.

[149] Carl M. Ellison. What do you need to know about the person with whom you are doing business? Written testimony before the House of Science and Technology Subcommittee Hearing on "Signatures in a Digital Age", October 1997.

[150] Carl M. Ellison. SPKI requirements. Internet draft, October 1998.

[151] Carl M. Ellison, Bill Frantz, Butler Lampson, Ron Rivest, Brian M. Thomas, and Tatu Ylonen. SPKI certificate theory. Internet draft, work in progress, November 1998.

[152] Carl M. Ellison, Bill Frantz, Butler Lampson, Ron Rivest, Brian M. Thomas, and Tatu Ylonen. Simple Public Key Certificate. Internet draft, work in progress, 1998.

[153] EPIC and Privacy International. Privacy and human rights: An international survey of privacy laws and practice. Released by Global Internet Liberty Campaign. Primary authors: David Banisar and Simon Davies, October 1998.

[154] Richard A. Epstein. Testimony before the Senate Judiciary Subcommittee on the Constitution, Federalism and Property Rights. Hearings on "Privacy in the Digital Age: Encryption and Mandatory Access", March 1998.

[155] European Commission. Report of the Working Party on Illegal and Harmful Content on the Internet, November 1996.

[156] European Commission. A European initiative in electronic commerce. Communication to the European Parliament, the Council, the Economic and Social Committee and the Committee of the Regions, April 1997. COM(97) 157.

[157] European Parliament. Directive 95/46/EC of 24 October 1995 on the protection of individuals with regard to the processing of personal data and on the free movement of such data. *Official Journal of the European Communities*, pages 31–45, November 1995.

[158] Carol H. Fancher. Smart cards: As potential applications grow, computers in the wallet are making unobtrusive inroads. *Scientific American*, pages 40–45, August 1996.

[159] Federal Bureau of Investigation. The Digital Telephony and Privacy Improvement Act, March 1994.

[160] Federal Bureau of Investigation. The Digital Telephony and Privacy Improvement Act (update), June 1994.

[161] Federal Card Services Task Force. Federal smart card implementation plan; "the future is in the cards". Electronic Processes Initiatives Committee, January 1998.

[162] Federal Deposit Insurance Corporation. Online privacy of consumer personal information, August 1998.

[163] Federal Public Key Infrastructure Steering Committee. Access with trust. Government Information Technology Services Board, Office of Management and Budget, September 1998.

[164] Federal Trade Commission. Consumer Identity Fraud meeting. Official Transcript Proceedings before the Federal Trade Commission, August 1996. Washington, D.C.

[165] Federal Trade Commission. Privacy online: A report to Congress, June 1998.

[166] Federation of European Direct Marketing. Codes of practice, direct marketing and on-line services, November 1997.

[167] Jalal Feghhi, Peter Williams, and Jalil Feghhi. *Digital Certificates : Applied Internet Security*. Addison-Wesley, October 1998. ISBN 0201309807.

[168] Uriel Feige, Amos Fiat, and Adi Shamir. Zero knowledge proofs of identity. *Journal of Cryptology*, 1(2):77–94, 1988.

[169] Uriel Feige and Adi Shamir. Witness indistinguishable and witness hiding protocols. In *Proc. 22nd ACM Symp. on Theory of Computing*, pages 416–426, May 1990.

[170] Uriel Feige and Adi Shamir. Zero-knowledge proofs of knowledge in two rounds. In G. Brassard, editor, *Advances in Cryptology–CRYPTO '89*, volume 435 of *Lecture Notes in Computer Science*, pages 526–544. Springer-Verlag, 1990.

[171] Amos Fiat and Adi Shamir. How to prove yourself: Practical solutions to identification and signature problems. In A.M. Odlyzko, editor, *Advances in Cryptology–CRYPTO '86*, volume 263 of *Lecture Notes in Computer Science*, pages 186–194. Springer-Verlag, 1987.

[172] Warwick Ford and Michael Baum. *Secure Electronic Commerce : Building the Infrastructure for Digital Signatures and Encryption*. Prentice Hall, April 1997. ISBN: 0134763424.

[173] Yair Frankel, Yiannis Tsiounis, and Moti Yung. "Indirect discourse proofs": Achieving efficient fair off-line e-cash. In Kwangjo Kim and Tsutomu Matsumoto, editors, *Advances in Cryptology–ASIACRYPT '96*, volume 1163 of *Lecture Notes in Computer Science*, pages 286–300. Springer-Verlag, 1996.

[174] Alan O. Freier, Philip Karlton, and Paul C. Kocher. The SSL protocol, version 3.0. Internet draft, Netscape Communications, November 1996.

[175] Richard L. Fricker. The INSLAW octopus, March 1993.

[176] A. Michael Froomkin. It came from Planet Clipper: The battle over cryptographic key "escrow". Page 15 of the 1996 Law of Cyberspace issue of the University of Chicago Legal Forum.

[177] A. Michael Froomkin. The essential role of trusted third parties in electronic commerce. *Oregon Law Review*, 75(1):49–115, 1996.

[178] E. Fujisaki and Tatsuaki Okamoto. Practical escrow cash system. In *Proceedings of the 1996 Cambridge Workshop on Security Protocols*, pages 33–48. Springer-Verlag, June 1996.

[179] Eiichiro Fujisaki and Tatsuaki Okamoto. Statistical zero knowledge protocols to prove modular polynomial relations. In Burton S. Kaliski Jr., editor, *Advances in Cryptology–CRYPTO '97*, volume 1294 of *Lecture Notes in Computer Science*, pages 16–30. Springer-Verlag, 1997.

[180] Simson Garfinkel. The downside of digital IDs. Hotwired, October 9, 1996.

[181] Simson L. Garfinkel. 2048: Privacy, identity, and society in the next century. Unpublished book, 1997.

[182] Dan Geer. Risk management is where the money is. *Forum on Risks to the Public in Computers and Related Systems, ACM Committee on Computers and Public Policy*, 20(6), November 1998.

[183] General Accounting Office. Identity fraud: Information on prevalence, cost, and Internet impact is limited. Briefing Report, May 1998. GAO/GGD-98-100BR.

[184] Rosario Gennaro, Stanislaw Jarecki, Hugo Krawczyk, and Tal Rabin. Robust threshold DSS signatures. In N. Koblitz, editor, *Advances in Cryptology–CRYPTO '96*, volume 1109 of *Lecture Notes in Computer Science*, pages 354–371. Springer-Verlag, 1996.

[185] Marc Girault. Self-certified public keys. In D.W. Davies, editor, *Advances in Cryptology–EUROCRYPT '91*, volume 547 of *Lecture Notes in Computer Science*, pages 490–497. Springer-Verlag, 1992.

[186] Beth Givens. Identity theft – how it happens, its impact on victims, and legislative solutions. Presentation of the Privacy Rights Clearinghouse, May 1997.

[187] Brian Gladman, Carl Ellison, and Nicholas Bohm. Digital signatures, certificates & electronic commerce. Version 1.1, June 1999.

[188] Global Network Navigator. The seduction of Crypto AG: How the NSA held the keys to a top-selling encryption machine, 1997.

[189] Ian Goldberg and Adam Shostack. Freedom network 1.0 architecture. Zero-Knowledge Systems, Inc. white paper, November 1999.

[190] Ian Goldberg, David Wagner, and Eric A. Brewer. Privacy-enhancing technologies for the Internet. In *COMPCON '97*. IEEE, February 1997.

[191] Oded Goldreich, Silvio Micali, and Avi Wigderson. Proofs that yield nothing but their validity or all languages in NP have zero-knowledge proof systems. *Journal of the ACM*, 38(1):691–729, 1991.

[192] Oded Goldreich, Birgit Pfitzmann, and Ronald L. Rivest. Self-delegation with controlled propagation - or - what if you lose your laptop. In Hugo Krawczyk, editor, *Advances in Cryptology–CRYPTO '98*, Lecture Notes in Computer Science, pages 153–168. Springer-Verlag, 1998.

[193] Shafi Goldwasser, Silvio Micali, and Charles Rackoff. The knowledge complexity of interactive proof systems. *SIAM Journal on Computing*, 18(1):186–208, February 1989.

[194] Shafi Goldwasser, Silvio Micali, and Ronald L. Rivest. A digital signature scheme secure against adaptive chosen-message attacks. *SIAM Journal on Computing*, 17(2):281–308, April 1988.

[195] David Goodman and Colin Robbins. Understanding LDAP & X.500. Distributed by the European Electronic Messaging Association, Version 2.0, August 1997.

[196] Daniel M. Gordon. A survey of fast exponentiation methods. *Journal of Algorithms*, 27:129–146, April 1998.

[197] J. Orlin Grabbe. The White House "Big Brother" data base & how Jackson Stephens precipitated a banking crisis, 1997.

[198] Group of Experts on Information Security and Privacy. Draft background report for the ministerial declaration in the protection of privacy on global networks. Background report for the OECD Ministerial Conference on 7-9 October 1998 in Ottawa, Canada, September 1998.

[199] Group of Experts on Information Security and Privacy. Draft ministerial declaration on the protection of privacy on global networks. Scheduled for transmission to the OECD Ministerial Conference of 7–9 October 1998 in Ottawa, Canada, September 1998.

[200] Richard A. Guida. Truth about PKI isn't always common knowledge. GCN Spotlight, May 3, 1999.

[201] Louis C. Guillou and Jean-Jacques Quisquater. A practical zero-knowledge protocol fitted to security microprocessors minimizing both transmission and memory. In C.G. Günther, editor, *Advances in Cryptology–EUROCRYPT '88*, volume 330 of *Lecture Notes in Computer Science*, pages 123–128. Springer-Verlag, 1988.

[202] Louis Claude Guillou and Jean-Jacques Quisquater. A "paradoxical" identity-based signature scheme resulting from zero-knowledge. In S. Goldwasser, editor, *Advances in Cryptology–CRYPTO '88*, volume 403 of *Lecture Notes in Computer Science*, pages 216–231. Springer-Verlag, 1988.

[203] C. Gülcü and G. Tsudik. Mixing email with Babel. Symposium on Network and Distributed System Security, San Diego, February 1996.

[204] Peter Gutmann. How to recover private keys for Microsoft Internet Explorer, Internet Information Server, Outlook Express, and many others - or - where do your encryption keys want to go today?, 1997.

[205] John Hagel and Mark Singer. *Net Worth: Shaping Markets When Customers Make the Rules*. Harvard Business Press, 1999.

[206] Nicky Hager. Exposing the global surveillance system. *CovertAction Quarterly*, pages 11–17, 1996.

[207] Nicky Hager. *Secret Power - New Zealand's Role in the International Spy Network*. Craig Potton Publishing, Nelson, New Zealand, 1996.

[208] J. Håstad, A.W. Schrift, and A. Shamir. The discrete logarithm modulo a composite hides $O(n)$ bits. *JCSS*, 47(3):376–404, 1993.

[209] Pat Hensley, Max Metral, Upendra Shardanand, Donna Converse, and Mike Myers. Proposal for an Open Profiling Standard. Submitted to W3C, June 1997.

[210] I.N. Herstein. *Topics in Algebra*. John Wiley & Sons, New York, 2 edition, 1975. ISBN 0-471-02371-X.

[211] Austin Hill and Gus Hosein. The privacy risks of public key infrastructures. Presented at the 21st Data Protection Commissioner's Conference in Hong Kong, September 13, 1999.

[212] Robert Holmes. Privacy: Philosophical foundations and moral dilemmas. In *Proceedings of the 16th International Conference on Data Protection–Facing Dilemmas*, September 1994.

[213] John D. Howard. *An Analysis Of Security Incidents On The Internet, 1989 – 1995*. PhD thesis, Carnegie Mellon University, April 1997.

[214] P. J. Hustinx. Platform for Privacy Preferences (P3P) and the Open Profiling Standard (OPS). Adopted by the Data Protection Working Party of the European Union on 16 June, 1998.

[215] Computer Security Institute. 1998 computer crime and security survey. Conducted by CSI with the participation of the San Francisco office of the FBI's International Computer Crime Squad, March 1998.

[216] International Telecommunication Union. ITU-T recommendation X.509, information technology – open systems interconnection – the directory: Authentication framework, June 1997.

[217] International Working Group on Data Protection in Telecommunications. Data protection and privacy on the Internet – report and guidance. Adopted at the 20th Meeting in Berlin ("Budapest - Berlin Memorandum"), November 1996.

[218] ITU & ISO/IEC. Working document on amendments for certificate extensions, January 1998. Collaborative meeting on the Directory, Phoenix Arizona.

[219] Markus Jakobsson, Kazue Sako, and Russell Impagliazzo. Designated verifier proofs and their applications. In Ueli Maurer, editor, *Advances in Cryptology–EUROCRYPT '96*, volume 1070 of *Lecture Notes in Computer Science*, pages 143–154. Springer-Verlag, 1996.

[220] Markus Jakobsson and Moti Yung. Revokable and versatile electronic money. In *Third ACM Conference on Computer and Communications Security*, pages 76–87. ACM Press, 1996.

[221] Markus Jakobsson and Moti Yung. Applying anti-trust policies to increase trust in a versatile e-money system. Financial Cryptography '97, February 1997.

[222] Markus Jakobsson and Moti Yung. Distributed "magic ink" signatures. In Walter Fumy, editor, *Advances in Cryptology–EUROCRYPT '97*, volume 1233 of *Lecture Notes in Computer Science*, pages 450–464. Springer-Verlag, 1997.

[223] Don Johnson and Alfred Menezes. The Elliptic Curve Digital Signature Algorithm (ECDSA). Technical Report CORR 99-34, University of Waterloo, Canada, Dept. of C&O, August 1999.

[224] Ari Juels, Michael Luby, and Rafail Ostrovsky. Security of blind digital signatures. In Burton S. Kaliski Jr., editor, *Advances in Cryptology–CRYPTO '97*, volume 1294 of *Lecture Notes in Computer Science*, pages 150–164. Springer-Verlag, 1997.

[225] Burt Kaliski and Matt Robshaw. The secure use of RSA. *CryptoBytes*, 2(3), 1995.

[226] C. Kaufman. DASS - distributed authentication security service. Network Working Group, Request for Comments no. 1507, September 1993.

[227] Jane Kaufman Winn. Couriers without luggage: Negotiable instruments and digital signatures. *South Carolina Law Review*, 49(4), 1998.

[228] Jane Kaufman Winn and Carl Ellison. Regulating the use of electronic authentication procedures by US consumers in the global electronic marketplace. Comment P994312 to the Federal Trade Commission, March 1999.

[229] John Kelsey, Bruce Schneier, and David Wagner. Protocol interactions and the chosen protocol attack. Security Protocols Workshop, Cambridge, 1997.

[230] S. Kent. Privacy enhancement for Internet electronic mail – part II: Certificate-based key management. RFC 1422, February 1993.

[231] Anthony L. Kimery. Big Brother wants to look into your bank account. Wired Magazine, December 1993.

[232] Donald E. Knuth. *Seminumerical Algorithms*, volume 2 of *The Art of Computer Programming*, pages 441–462. Addison-Wesley Publishing Company, 2 edition, 1981. ISBN 0-201-03822-6.

[233] N. Koblitz. A family of Jacobians suitable for discrete log cryptosystems. In S. Goldwasser, editor, *Advances in Cryptology–CRYPTO '88*, volume 403 of *Lecture Notes in Computer Science*, pages 94–99. Springer-Verlag, 1988.

[234] Neil Koblitz. Elliptic curve implementation of zero-knowledge blobs. *Journal of Cryptology*, 4(3):207–213, 1991.

[235] Paul Kocher. Quick introduction to Certificate Revocation Trees (CRTs). ValiCert whitepaper, 1997.

[236] Paul C. Kocher. Timing attacks on implementations of Diffie-Hellman, RSA, DSS and other systems. In N. Koblitz, editor, *Advances in Cryptology–CRYPTO '96*, volume 1109 of *Lecture Notes in Computer Science*, pages 104–113. Springer-Verlag, 1996.

[237] Paul C. Kocher, Joshua Jaffe, and Benjamin Jun. Differential Power Analysis. In Michael Wiener, editor, *Advances in Cryptology–CRYPTO '99*, volume 1666 of *Lecture Notes in Computer Science*, pages 388–397. Springer-Verlag, 1999.

[238] Loren M. Kohnfelder. Towards a practical public-key cryptosystem. Master's thesis, MIT Laboratory for Computer Science, May 1978.

[239] Oliver Kömmerling and Markus G. Kuhn. Design principles for tamper-resistant smartcard processors. In *Proceedings of the USENIX Workshop on Smartcard Technology (Smartcard '99)*, pages 9–20. USENIX Association, May 1999. ISBN 1-880446-34-0.

[240] David W. Kravitz, Peter S. Gemmell, and Ernest F. Brickell. Off-line compatible electronic cash method and system. U.S. Patent ser. no. 5,832,089, November 1998. Filed June 1995.

[241] Hugo Krawczyk and Tal Rabin. Chameleon hashing and signatures, September 1997.

[242] Markus Kuhn. Sicherheitsanalyse eines Mikroprozessors mit Busverschlüsselung. Master's thesis, Friedrich-Alexander-Universität Erlangen-Nürnberg, July 1996.

[243] Art Kunkin. The Octopus Conspiracy: Has the U.S. been spying on your bank accounts? World Wide Free Press, 1996.

[244] L. Lamport. Constructing digital signatures from a one-way function. Technical Report CSL–98, SRI International, October 1979.

[245] Peter Lenoir. Timing attack on classical RSA using Montgomery multiplications. Rump session of CRYPTO '97, August 1997.

[246] Arjen K. Lenstra and Adi Shamir. Analysis and optimization of the TWINKLE factoring device. To appear in: Proceedings of Eurocrypt 2000.

[247] Arjen K. Lenstra and Eric R. Verheul. Selecting cryptographic key sizes. Proceedings of the 2000 International Workshop on Practice and Theory in Public Key Cryptography (PKC2000), Melbourne, Australia, January 2000. An earlier version appeared in: PricewaterhouseCoopers Cryptographic Centre of Excellence (CCE) Quarterly Journal, autumn '99 issue.

[248] Garby Leon. Inslaw, the continuing caper, 1996.

[249] Lawrence Lessig and Paul Resnick. The constitutionality of mandated access control: A model. Circulating Draft 4, April 14, 1999. Earlier version in: Proceedings of the Telecommunications Policy Research Conference (1998).

[250] R. Levien and A. Aiken. Attack resistant trust metrics for public key certification. In *Proceedings of the 7th USENIX Security Symposium*. USENIX Press, January 1998.

[251] Jamie Lewis. Public Key Infrastructure architecture. The Burton Group, Network Strategy Report, July 1997.

[252] Chae Hoon Lim and Pil Joong Lee. A key recovery attack on discrete log-based schemes using a prime order subgroup. In Burton S. Kaliski Jr., editor, *Advances in Cryptology–CRYPTO '97*, volume 1294 of *Lecture Notes in Computer Science*, pages 249–263. Springer-Verlag, 1997.

[253] Anna Lysyanskaya, Ronald Rivest, Amit Sahai, and Stefan Wolf. Pseudonym systems. To appear in: Proceedings of SAC 99, 1999.

[254] Wayne Madsen. Crypto AG: The NSA's Trojan Whore? CovertAction Quarterly, Winter 1998, no. 63.

[255] Gary T. Marx. Privacy and technology. Revision of paper in The World and I, September 1990 and Telektronik January 1996.

[256] Masons Sollicitors and Privy Council Agents. Handbook on cost effective compliance with Directive 95/46/EC, 1998.

[257] MasterCard & Visa. SET secure electronic transaction specification, version 1.0. Book 1: Business Description, Book 2: Programmer's Guide, Book 3: Formal Protocol Definition, May 1997.

[258] Ueli M. Maurer and Stefan Wolf. Diffie-Hellman oracles. In N. Koblitz, editor, *Advances in Cryptology–CRYPTO '96*, volume 1109 of *Lecture Notes in Computer Science*, pages 268–282. Springer-Verlag, 1996.

[259] Kevin S. McCurley. The discrete logarithm problem. In *Proc. of Symposia in Applied Mathematics: Cryptography and Computational Number Theory*, volume 42, pages 49–74. American Mathematical Society, August 1990.

[260] P. D. McDaniel and S. Jamin. Windowed certificate revocation. Technical Report Technical Report CSE-TR-413-99, Dept. of Electrical Engineering and Computer Science, University of Michigan, November 1999. Also in: Proceedings of IEEE Infocom 2000. IEEE, March 2000. Tel Aviv, Israel.

[261] P. D. McDaniel and A. Rubin. A response to 'can we eliminate certificate revocation lists?'. Technical Report Technical Report 99.8.1, AT&T Research Labs, 1999. Also in: Financial Cryptography 2000, February 2000, Anguilla.

[262] Niall McKay. Europe is listening. Wired News, December 2, 1998.

[263] A.J. Menezes. *Elliptic Curve Public Key Cryptosystems*. Kluwer Academic Publishers, New York, 1993.

[264] Alfred Menezes. Elliptic curve cryptosystems. *RSA Laboratories*, 1(2), 1995. CryptoBytes.

[265] Alfred Menezes, Scott Vanstone, and Tatsuaki Okamoto. Reducing elliptic curve logarithms to logarithms in a finite field. In *Proc. 23rd ACM Symp. on Theory of Computing*, pages 80–89, New Orleans, 1991. ACM Press.

[266] Alfred J. Menezes, Paul C. van Oorschot, and Scott A. Vanstone. *Handbook of Applied Cryptography*. CRC Press, New York, 1997.

[267] Ralph C. Merkle. A digital signature based on a conventional encryption function. In Carl Pomerance, editor, *Advances in Cryptology–CRYPTO '87*, volume 293 of *Lecture Notes in Computer Science*, pages 369–378. Springer-Verlag, 1988.

[268] Silvio Micali. Efficient certificate revocation. Technical Report TM-542, Laboratory of Computer Science, Massachusetts Institute of Technology, November 1995.

[269] Silvio Micali and Leonid Reyzin. Signing with partially adversarial hashing. MIT Laboratory for Computer Science, Februari 27, 1998.

[270] M. Myers, R. Ankney, A. Malpani, S. Galperin, and C. Adams. Internet public key infrastructure Online Certificate Status Protocol – OCSP. IETF Draft, August 1998.

[271] David Naccache, David M'Raïhi, Serge Vaudenay, and Dan Raphaeli. Can D.S.A. be improved? – complexity trade-offs with the digital signature standard. In Alfredo De Santis, editor, *Advances in Cryptology–EUROCRYPT '94*, volume 950 of *Lecture Notes in Computer Science*, pages 77–85. Springer-Verlag, 1995.

[272] Yasushi Nakayama, Hidemi Moribatake, Masayuki Abe, and Eichiro Fujisaki. An electronic money scheme; a proposal for a new electronic money scheme which is both secure and convenient. IMES Discussion paper series, Bank of Japan, June 1997. Discussion Paper No. 97-E-4.

[273] Moni Naor and Kobbi Nissim. Certificate revocation and certificate update. Technical report, Weizmann Institute of Science, January 1999. Preliminary version in: Proceedings of the 7th USENIX Security Symposium, 1998.

[274] Nathan Associates Inc. The cost of government-driven key escrow encryption, June 1998. Prepared by the Family, Industry, and Community Economics group, and commissioned by the Business Software Alliance.

[275] National Institute of Standards and Technology. FIPS PUB 140-2: Security requirements for cryptographic modules. Federal Information Processing Standard Publication, U.S. Department of Commerce, January 11, 1994. (Supersedes FIPS PUB 140-1 of January 1994).

[276] National Institute of Standards and Technology. Secure hash standard (SHA), April 1995. Federal Information Processing Standards Publication, FIPS PUB 180-1.

[277] National Institute of Standards and Technology. Digital signature standard (DSS). Federal Information Processing Standards Publication, FIPS PUB 186-1, December 1998.

[278] National Research Council. Cryptography's role in securing the information society. Prepublication copy, May 1996. Kenneth Dam and Herbert Lin, Editors.

[279] National Security Agency. Threat and vulnerability model for key recovery. Unofficial NSA document, February 18, X3, 1998.

[280] L. O'Connor. An analysis of exponentiation based on formal languages. In Jacques Stern, editor, *Advances in Cryptology–EUROCRYPT '99*, Lecture Notes in Computer Science. Springer, 1999.

[281] A. M. Odlyzko. Discrete logarithms in finite fields and their cryptographic significance. In T. Beth, N. Cot, and I. Ingemarsson, editors, *Advances in Cryptology–EUROCRYPT '84*, volume 209 of *Lecture Notes in Computer Science*, pages 224–314. Springer-Verlag, 1985.

[282] Andrew Odlyzko. Discrete logarithms: The past and the future. Version of July 18, 1999. To appear in: Designs, Codes, and Cryptography (1999).

[283] Andrew M. Odlyzko. The future of integer factorization. Technical Report 2, RSA Laboratories, July 1995.

[284] Office of Technology Assessment. Federal government information technology: Electronic surveillance and civil liberties. U.S. Congress, Office of Technology Assessment, OTA-CIT-293, Washington, DC: U.S. Government Printing Office, October 1985.

[285] Office of Technology Assessment. Electronic record systems and individual privacy, June 1986. OTA-CIT-296 (Washington, DC: U.S. Government Printing Office).

[286] Office of Technology Assessment. Electronic surveillance in a digital age, July 1995. OTA-BP-ITC-149 (Washington, DC: U.S. Government Printing Office).

[287] Office of the Privacy Commissioner of Canada. Privacy framework for smart card applications, July 1996.

[288] Tatsuaki Okamoto. Provably secure and practical identification schemes and corresponding signature schemes. In Ernest F. Brickell, editor, *Advances in Cryptology–CRYPTO '92*, volume 740 of *Lecture Notes in Computer Science*, pages 31–53. Springer-Verlag, 1992.

[289] Tatsuaki Okamoto and Kazuo Ohta. Divertible zero knowledge interactive proofs and commutative random self-reducibility. In J.-J. Quisquater and J. Vandewalle, editors, *Advances in Cryptology–EUROCRYPT '89*, volume 434 of *Lecture Notes in Computer Science*, pages 134–149. Springer-Verlag, 1989.

[290] Lewis Willian Oleinick. *Computerized Governmental Database Systems containing Personal Information and the Right to Privacy*. PhD thesis, University of Texas at Austin, December 1993.

[291] OMB Watch. A delicate balance: The privacy and access practices of federal government World Wide Web sites, June 1998. ISBN: 1882583-12-4.

[292] Paul Van Oorschot, Warwick Ford, Stephen Hillier, and Josanne Otway. Method for efficient management of Certificate Revocation Lists (CRLs) and update information. U.S. Patent ser. no. 5,699,431, December 1997. Filed November 1995.

[293] OpenCard Consortium. OpenCard framework general information web document. IBM Germany, October 1998. Second Edition.

[294] Organisation for Economic Co-operation and Development. Recommendation of the Council concerning guidelines governing the protection of privacy and transborder flows of personal information, September 1980.

[295] Organisation for Economic Co-operation and Development. Cryptography policy guidelines, March 1997.

[296] Organisation for Economic Co-operation and Development. Inventory of approaches to authentication and certification in a global networked society. Document of the Working Party on Information Security and Privacy, October 1999.

[297] PC/SC Workgroup. Interoperability specification for ICCs and personal computer systems, part 1–8. Revision 1.0, December 1997.

[298] Torben Pryds Pedersen. *Distributed Provers and Verifiable Secret Sharing Based on the Discrete Logarithm Problem*. PhD thesis, Aarhus University, March 1992. DAIMI PB–388.

[299] Torben Pryds Pedersen. Non-interactive and information-theoretic secure verifiable secret sharing. In J. Feigenbaum, editor, *Advances in Cryptology– CRYPTO '91*, volume 576 of *Lecture Notes in Computer Science*, pages 129–140. Springer-Verlag, 1992.

[300] Radia J. Perlman and Charles Kaufman. Method of issuance and revocation of certificates of authenticity used in public key networks and other systems. U.S. Patent ser. no. 5,261,002, November 1993. Filed March 1992.

[301] Birgit Pfitzmann. *Fail-Stop Signature Schemes*. PhD thesis, Institut für Informatik, Universität Hildesheim, May 1994.

[302] Birgit Pfitzmann and Ahmad-Reza Sadeghi. Self-escrowed cash against user blackmailing. 4th International Conference on Financial Cryptography (FC '00), to be published by Springer-Verlag, February 2000. An earlier German version appeared in: Verlässliche IT-Systeme, GI-Fachtagung VIS '99.

[303] Birgit Pfitzmann and Michael Waidner. How to break and repair a "provably secure" untraceable payment system. In J. Feigenbaum, editor, *Advances in Cryptology–CRYPTO '91*, volume 576 of *Lecture Notes in Computer Science*, pages 338–350. Springer-Verlag, 1992.

[304] Birgit Pfitzmann and Michael Waidner. Strong loss tolerance of electronic coin systems. *ACM Transactions on Computer Systems*, 15(2):194–213, May 1997. Extended version appeared as: Hildesheimer Informatik-Berichte 15/95, University of Hildesheim, June 1995.

[305] David Pointcheval. *Les Preuves de Connaissance et leurs Preuves de Sécurité*. PhD thesis, University of Caen, December 1996.

[306] David Pointcheval and Jacques Stern. Provably secure blind signature schemes. In Kwangjo Kim and Tsutomu Matsumoto, editors, *Advances in Cryptology–ASIACRYPT '96*, volume 1163 of *Lecture Notes in Computer Science*, pages 252–265. Springer-Verlag, 1996.

[307] David Pointcheval and Jacques Stern. Security proofs for signature schemes. In Ueli Maurer, editor, *Advances in Cryptology–EUROCRYPT '96*, volume 1070 of *Lecture Notes in Computer Science*, pages 387–398. Springer-Verlag, 1996.

[308] Patrick S. Poole. Echelon: America's spy in the sky. Fourth installment in the Free Congress Foundation/Center for Technology Policy's The Privacy Papers series, October 1998.

[309] Guillaume Poupard and Jacques Stern. Generation of shared RSA keys by two parties. In *Advances in Cryptology–ASIACRYPT '91*, volume 1514 of *Lecture Notes in Computer Science*, pages 11–24. Springer-Verlag, 1998.

[310] Guillaume Poupard and Jacques Stern. Security analysis of a practical "on the fly" authentication and signature generation. In Kaisa Nyberg, editor, *Advances in Cryptology–EUROCRYPT '98*, volume 1403 of *Lecture Notes in Computer Science*, pages 422–436. Springer-Verlag, 1998.

[311] Privacy Commissioner of the Commonwealth of Australia. Smart cards: Implications for privacy. Information Paper No. 4, December 1995.

[312] Privacy International. Identity Cards: Frequently asked questions, August 1996.

[313] Privacy Working Group. Privacy and the National Information Infrastructure: Principles for providing and using personal information, June 1995. Publication of the Information Policy Committee of the Information Infrastructure Task Force.

[314] Public Interest Research Group. Mistakes do happen: Credit report errors mean consumers lose, March 1998.

[315] Charles D. Raab, Colin J. Bennett, Robert M. Gellman, and Nigel Waters. Application of a methodology designed to assess the adequacy of the level of protection of individuals with regard to processing personal data: test of the method of several categories of transfer - final report. Study carried out for the European Commission. Tender No. XV/97/18/D, September 1998.

[316] Cristian Radu, Rene Govaerts, and Joos Vandewalle. A restrictive blind signature scheme with applications to electronic cash. In P. Horster, editor, *Proceedings of the IFIP TC6/TC11 international conference on communications and multimedia security II*, pages 196–207. Chapman and Hall, 1996.

[317] Cristian Radu, Rene Govaerts, and Joos Vandewalle. Efficient electronic cash with restricted privacy. In Rafael Hirschfeld, editor, *Financial Cryptography '97*, volume 1318. Springer-Verlag, February 1997.

[318] Joel R. Reidenberg and Paul M. Schwartz. Data protection law and on-line services: Regulatory responses. Study prepared as part of the project "Vie privée et sociétée de l information: Etude sur les problèmes posés par les nouveaux services en ligne en matière de protection des données et de la vie privée," commissioned by Directorate General XV of the Commission of the European Communities, December 1998.

[319] Lawrence A. Reinert and Stephen C. Luther. Tokeneer; user authentication techniques using public key certificates. Part 1: Certificate options. National Security Agency, Central Security Service, R22 INFOSEC Engineering, December 1997.

[320] Lawrence A. Reinert and Stephen C. Luther. Tokeneer; authentication protocol for smartcards. National Security Agency, Central Security Service, R22 INFOSEC Engineering, January 1998.

[321] M. Reiter and S. Stubblebine. Toward acceptable metrics of authentication. In *Proceedings of the 1997 IEEE Symposium on Security and Privacy*, pages 10–20, Oakland, CA, May 1997. IEEE.

[322] Michael K. Reiter and Aviel D. Rubin. Crowds: Anonymity for Web transactions. ACM Transactions on Information and System Security, April 1998. Also as: DIMACS 95-15, June 1997, AT&T Labs–Research, Murray Hill, New Jersey.

[323] Ronald L. Rivest. Can we eliminate certificate revocation lists? In Rafael Hirschfeld, editor, *Financial Cryptography '98*, volume 1465, February 1998.

[324] Ronald L. Rivest and Butler Lampson. SDSI - a Simple Distributed Security Infrastructure. Working document defining SDSI version 1.1., October 1996.

[325] Ronald L. Rivest, A. Shamir, and L. Adleman. A method for obtaining digital signatures and public-key cryptosystems. *Communications of the ACM*, 21(2):120–126, February 1978.

[326] Ronald L. Rivest and Robert D. Silverman. Are "strong" primes needed for RSA? Submitted draft, November 1998.

[327] Marc Rotenberg. Communications privacy. Prepared Statement Before the Subcommittee on Courts and Intellectual Property of the House Committee on the Judiciary, United States of House of Representatives, Washington, D.C., March 26, 1998.

[328] Marc Rotenberg. On the European Union Data Directive and Privacy. Testimony and Statement for the Record Before the Committee on International Relations, U.S. House of Representatives, May 7, 1998.

[329] Marc Rotenberg, editor. *The Privacy Law Sourcebook: United States Law, International Law, and Recent Developments*. Electronic Privacy Information Center, 1998.

[330] RSA Laboratories. PKCS #6: Extended-certificate syntax standard. Version 1.5, November 1993.

[331] R. J. Rummel. *Death by Government: Genocide and Mass Murder in the Twentieth Century*. Transaction Publishers, New Jersey, 1994. ISBN: 1560009276.

[332] Dick Russell. Spook wars in cyberspace–is the FBI railroading Charles Hayes?, June 1997.

[333] Tomas Sander and Amnon Ta-Shma. Flow control: A new approach for anonymity control in electronic cash systems. In *Financial Cryptography '99*. Springer-Verlag, February 1999.

[334] Alfredo De Santis, Giovanni De Crescenzo, Giuseppe Persiano, and Moti Yung. On monotone formula closure of SZK. In *Proc. 35th IEEE Symp. on Foundations of Comp. Science*, pages 454–465, Santa Fe, 1994.

[335] T. Satoh and K. Arako. Fermat quotients and the polynomial time discrete log algorithm for anomalous elliptic curves. Preprint, 1997.

[336] Bruce Schneier and Adam Shostack. Breaking up is hard to do: Modeling security threats for smart cards. First USENIX Symposium on Smart Cards, USENIX Press, 1999.

[337] Claus P. Schnorr. Efficient signature generation by smart cards. *Journal of Cryptology*, 4:161–174, 1991.

[338] Claus P. Schnorr. Security of 2^t-root identification and signatures. In N. Koblitz, editor, *Advances in Cryptology–CRYPTO '96*, volume 1109 of *Lecture Notes in Computer Science*, pages 143–156. Springer-Verlag, 1996.

[339] Claus P. Schnorr and Markus Jakobsson. Security of discrete log cryptosystems in the random oracle + generic model. Presented at the Conference on The Mathematics of Public-Key Cryptography, The Fields Institute, Toronto, Canada, June 1999.

[340] Berry Schoenmakers. Efficient proofs of Or. Unpublished manuscript, September 1993.

[341] Berry Schoenmakers. An efficient electronic payment system withstanding parallel attacks. Technical Report CS-R9522, Centrum voor Wiskunde en Informatica, March 1995.

[342] Berry Schoenmakers. Sharp interval proofs and other predicates. Submitted for publication, February 1997.

[343] Ari Schwartz. Smart cards at the crossroads: Authenticator or privacy invader? *At Home With Consumers*, 19(3), December 1998.

[344] Scientific and Technological Options Assessment. An appraisal of technologies of political control. STOA Interim Study (PE 166.499), September 1998.

[345] Adi Shamir. Factoring large numbers with the TWINKLE device. EURO-CRYPT '99 rump session talk. Extended abstract distributed on May 5, 1999.

[346] Adi Shamir. Identity-based cryptosystems and signature schemes. In G.R. Blakley and D.C. Chaum, editors, *Advances in Cryptology–CRYPTO '84*, volume 196 of *Lecture Notes in Computer Science*, pages 47–53. Springer-Verlag, 1985.

[347] Adi Shamir. Memory efficient variants of public-key schemes for smart card applications. In Alfredo De Santis, editor, *Advances in Cryptology–EUROCRYPT '94*, volume 950 of *Lecture Notes in Computer Science*, pages 445–449. Springer-Verlag, 1995.

[348] Adi Shamir and Nicko van Someren. Playing hide and seek with stored keys. In *Financial Cryptography '99*. Springer-Verlag, February 1999.

[349] Jenny Shearer and Peter Gutmann. Government, cryptography, and the right to privacy. *Journal of Universal Computer Science*, 2(3), March 1996.

[350] Peter W. Shor. Algorithms for quantum computation: Discrete logarithms and factoring. In *Proc. 26th ACM Symp. on Theory of Computing*, pages 124–134, Santa Fe, 1994. IEEE.

[351] Victor Shoup. On the security of a practical identification scheme. In Ueli Maurer, editor, *Advances in Cryptology–EUROCRYPT '96*, volume 1070 of *Lecture Notes in Computer Science*, pages 344–353. Springer-Verlag, 1996.

[352] Victor Shoup. Lower bounds for discrete logarithms and related problems. In Walter Fumy, editor, *Advances in Cryptology–EUROCRYPT '97*, volume 1233 of *Lecture Notes in Computer Science*, pages 256–266. Springer-Verlag, 1997.

[353] Robert D. Silverman. A cost-based security analysis of symmetric and asymmetric key lengths. *News and Advice Bulletin*, (13), April 2000.

[354] Gustavus J. Simmons. The Prisoners' Problem and the subliminal channel. In D. Chaum, editor, *Advances in Cryptology–CRYPTO '83*, pages 51–67. Plenum Press, 1984.

[355] Gustavus J. Simmons. The subliminal channel and digital signature. In T. Beth, N. Cot, and I. Ingemarsson, editors, *Advances in Cryptology–EUROCRYPT '84*, volume 209 of *Lecture Notes in Computer Science*, pages 364–378. Springer-Verlag, 1985.

[356] Solveig Singleton. Privacy as censorship – a skeptical view of proposals to regulate privacy in the private sector. *Cato Policy Analysis*, January 1998.

[357] Nigel Smart. The discrete logarithm problem on elliptic curves of trace one. Internal Note at Hewlett-Packard Laboratories, 1997.

[358] Smart Card Forum. Consumer privacy and smart cards - a challenge and an opportunity. Prepared by the Legal & Public Policy Committee, 1997.

[359] South African Law Commission. Review of security legislation; the Interception and Monitoring Prohibition Act (ACT no. 127 of 1992). Discussion Paper 78, Project 105, November 1998. ISBN 0-621-28847-0.

[360] Markus Stadler, Jean-Marc Piveteau, and Jan Camenisch. Fair blind signatures. In Louis C. Guillou and Jean-Jacques Quisquater, editors, *Advances in Cryptology–EUROCRYPT '95*, volume 921 of *Lecture Notes in Computer Science*, pages 209–219. Springer-Verlag, 1995.

[361] Standards Australia. Strategies for the implementation of a Public Key Authentication Framework (PKAF) in Australia. PKAF Report, Miscellaneous Publication SAA MP75-1996, October 1996.

[362] Statewatch. European Union & FBI launch global surveillance system. Report, January 1997.

[363] Marc Strassman and Robert D. Atkinson. Jump-starting the digital economy (with department of motor vehicles-issued digital certificates). Policy Briefing of the Democratic Leadership Council & The Progressive Policy Institute, June 1999.

[364] Res Strehle. *Verschlüsselt - Der Fall Hans Beühler*. Werd Verlag, Zürich, 1994. U.S. Library of Congress #: DS318.84.B84S77 1994.

[365] S. Stubblebine. Recent-secure authentication: Enforcing revocation in distributed systems. In *Proceedings of the 1995 IEEE Symposium on Research in Security and Privacy*, pages 224–234, May 1995.

[366] Kathleen M. Sullivan. Testimony on behalf of Americans for Computer Privacy before the Senate Judiciary Subcommittee on the Constitution, Federalism and Property Rights. Hearings on "Privacy in the Digital Age: Encryption and Mandatory Access", March 1998.

[367] Peter P. Swire. Financial privacy and the theory of high-tech government surveillance. Draft of September 24, 1998.

[368] Paul Syverson, D. Goldschlag, and M. Reed. Anynonymous connections and onion routing. In *Symposium on Security and Privacy*. IEEE, 1997.

[369] Kazuo Takaragi, Kunihiko Miyazaki, and Masashi Takahashi. A threshold digital signature issuing scheme without secret communication. Presented at the November 1998 meeting of the IEEE P1363 Working Group, November 1998.

[370] Task Force on Electronic Commerce. The protection of personal information – building Canada s information economy and society. Industry Canada/Justice Canada, January 1998.

[371] The Baltimore Sun. NSA's crypto sting. Issue of December 10, 1995.

[372] The Washington Weekly. NSA, CIA, and U.S. NAVY all use PROMIS software. Published in the March 31, 1997 issue.

[373] The Working Party on the Protection of Individuals with regard to the processing of personal data. Recommendation 3/97; anonymity on the Internet. Discussion paper adopted by the Working Party on 3 December '1997 at the 8th meeting.

[374] Yiannis S. Tsiounis. *Efficient Electronic Cash: New Notions and Techniques*. PhD thesis, Northeastern University, June 1997.

[375] United States Government. Privacy and electronic commerce. Draft, June 1998.

[376] U.S. Federal Reserve. Order approving notices to engage in nonbanking activities. Press release, November 10, 1999.

[377] U.S. General Services Administration. Access Certificates for Electronic Services (ACES). Draft Request for Proposals, Solicitation Number TIBA98003, Office of Governmentwide Policy, Federal Technology Service, March 1998.

[378] U.S. General Services Administration and Federal Telecommunications Service and Office of Information Security. Access Certificates for Electronic Services (ACES). Request For Proposals, January 1999.

[379] Wim van Eck. Electromagnetic radiation from video display units: An eavesdropping risk? *Computers & Security*, 4, 1985.

[380] E. van Heijst and T.P. Pedersen. How to make efficient fail-stop signatures. In R.A. Rueppel, editor, *Advances in Cryptology–EUROCRYPT '92*, volume 658 of *Lecture Notes in Computer Science*, pages 366–377. Springer-Verlag, 1993.

[381] Christine Varney. You call this self-regulation? Wired News, June 9, 1998.

[382] Eric R. Verheul and Marc P. Hoyle. Tricking the Chaum-Pedersen protocol. Submitted for publication, August 1997.

[383] J. von zur Gathen and M. Nöcker. Exponentiation in finite fields: Theory and practice. *Proc. AAECC-12*, pages 88–113, 1997. To appear in: Springer LNCS.

[384] S. S. Wagstaff Jr. Greatest of the least primes in arithmetic progression having a given modulus. *Mathematics of Computation*, 33(147):1073–1080, July 1979.

[385] M. Wahl. A summary of the X.500(96) user schema for use with LDAPv3. Network Working Group, Request for Comments no. 2256, December 1997.

[386] Gerard Walsh. Review of policy relating to encryption technologies. Publication suppressed by the Australian Attorney-General's Department in February 1997, censored version released to the Electronic Frontier Association under the Freedom of Information Act, June 1997.

[387] Alan Westin. *Privacy and Freedom*. New York: Atheneum, 1967.

[388] A. Wheeler and L. Wheeler. Internet Public Key Infrastructure: PKI Account Authority Digital Signature Infrastructure, November 1998.

[389] Michael J. Wiener. Cryptanalysis of short RSA secret exponents. *IEEE Transactions on Information Theory*, 36:553–558, 1990.

[390] Michael J. Wiener. Performance comparison of public-key cryptosystems. *CryptoBytes*, 4(1):1–5, 1998.

[391] Julie L. Williams. Remarks before the Banking Roundtable Lawyers Council, on the treatment of confidential customer information and privacy issues, Washington, D.C., May 8, 1998.

[392] Norman A. Willox. Identity theft: Authentication as a solution. National Fraud Center, Inc., March 2000.

[393] World Wide Web Consortium. Platform for Privacy Preferences (P3P) Syntax Specification. Second public W3C Working Draft, edited by M. Marchiori and D. Jaye, July 1998.

[394] Tom Wright. Smart cards. Publication of the Information and Privacy Commissioner of Ontario, April 1993.

[395] Eric C. Zimits and Christopher Montano. Public Key Infrastructure: Unlocking the Internet's economic potential. *IStory*, 3(2), April 1998. The Hambrecht and Quist Internet Research Group.

[396] Phil R. Zimmerman. *The Official PGP User's Guide*. MIT Press, Boston, 1995.

Index

Curriculum Vitae

Stefan Brands was born in Utrecht, the Netherlands. He completed his undergraduate studies in Mathematics at the University of Utrecht in August of 1991, and was affiliated from February 1992 until February 1996 with the Center for Mathematics and Computer Science (CWI) in Amsterdam. The electronic cash system he published in April 1993 (and improved and extended later on) forms the basis of a full-fledged system implemented and tested by CAFE, an ESPRIT project with 13 academic and commercial member organizations from seven European countries.

In 1995 and 1996 Stefan was invited to present his work at various research institutes abroad, including ETH (Zürich), MIT (Boston), ENS (Paris), AT&T (New Jersey), IBM (Zürich), Johann Wolfgang Goethe–University (Frankfurt am Main), University of San Diego (UCSD), and University of Hildesheim. He also served on the program committees of Eurocrypt '96, CARDIS 1996, the second USENIX Workshop on Electronic Commerce, and Eurocrypt '99.

Stefan is the holder of eight international patents on electronic cash and digital certificates.

In January 1997 he joined DigiCash in Amsterdam as a senior cryptographer and its Distinguished Scientist, as part of a licensing arrangement aimed at implementing and commercializing his electronic cash techniques. He resigned a year before DigiCash went bankrupt, leaving the company in June 1998.

Following this, Stefan completed his dissertation and worked on an upcoming book on electronic money. His doctorate was awarded on October 4, 1999, by Eindhoven University of Technology. The Thesis Reading Committee consisted of Professors Ron Rivest, Claus Schnorr, and Adi Shamir.

In February 2000, Stefan made an exclusive licensing arrangement with Zero-Knowledge Systems, Inc., and joined the company as a senior cryptographer and its Distinguished Scientist. He currently lives and works in Montreal and can be reached at brands@zeroknowledge.com or through his personal homepage www.xs4all.nl/~brands.